WEB-BASED and TRADITIONAL OUTSOURCING

Infosys® Press

In an initiative to promote authorship across the globe, Infosys Press and CRC Press have entered into a collaboration to develop titles on leading edge topics in IT.

Infosys Press seeks to develop and publish a series of pragmatic books on software engineering and information technologies, both current and emerging. Leveraging Infosys' extensive global experience helping clients to implement those technologies successfully, each book contains critical lessons learned and shows how to apply them in a real-world, enterprise setting. This open-ended and broad-ranging series aims to brings readers practical insight, specific guidance, and unique, informative examples not readily available elsewhere.

PUBLISHED IN THE SERIES

.NET 4 for Enterprise Architects and Developers
Sudhanshu Hate and Suchi Paharia

Process-Centric Architecture for Enterprise Software Systems
Parameswaran Seshan

Process-Driven SOA: Patterns for Aligning Business and IT
Carsten Hentrich and Uwe Zdun

Web-Based and Traditional Outsourcing
Vivek Sharma and Varun Sharma

IN PREPARATION FOR THE SERIES

Scrum Software Development
Jagdish Bhandarkar and J. Srinivas

Software Vulnerabilities Exposed
Sanjay Rawat, Ashutosh Saxena, and Ponnapalli K. B. Hari Gopal

WEB-BASED and TRADITIONAL OUTSOURCING

Vivek Sharma
Varun Sharma

CRC Press
Taylor & Francis Group
Boca Raton London New York

CRC Press is an imprint of the
Taylor & Francis Group, an **Informa** business
AN AUERBACH BOOK

CRC Press
Taylor & Francis Group
6000 Broken Sound Parkway NW, Suite 300
Boca Raton, FL 33487-2742

Printed in the United States of America on acid-free paper
Version Date: 20111117

International Standard Book Number: 978-1-4398-1055-2 (Hardback)

Library of Congress Cataloging-in-Publication Data

Sharma, Vivek.
    Web-based and traditional outsourcing / Vivek Sharma and Varun Sharma.
        p. cm. -- (Infosys press)
    Includes bibliographical references and index.
    ISBN 978-1-4398-1055-2 (hardback : acid free paper)
    1. Contracting out. 2. Information technology--Economic aspects. 3. Electronic data processing departments--Contracting out. 4. Technological innovations--Economic aspects. 5. Intranets (Computer networks) I. Sharma, Varun. II. Title.

HD2365.S53 2012
658.4'05802854678--dc22   2010035450

Visit the Taylor & Francis Web site at
http://www.taylorandfrancis.com

and the CRC Press Web site at
http://www.crcpress.com

The essence of life—in two words —knowledge and action.

Contents

SECTION II WEB-BASED OUTSOURCING

SECTION III SLOWDOWN AND OUTSOURCING

SECTION IV OUTSOURCING—MISCELLANEOUS CONCERNS AND THE FUTURE

Foreword

With hardly any foreign exchange reserves in 1990, India's government was forced to change economic policies, and thus the economic liberalization opened up gates for new industries. Over the last 15 years, on the strength of rupee depreciation and cost arbitrage, India has grown into an economic powerhouse with one of the highest GDP growths for emerging economies. Coupled with an abundant English-speaking talent pool essential for the information technology (IT) and information technology enabled services (ITES) industry, India is one of the destinations for most IT companies to set up operations. India was earlier viewed as a cost arbitrage opportunity, but today it is a strategic IT destination. Some of the institutions like the Indian Institute of Technology (IIT), the Indian Institute of Management (IIM), and the Indian School of Business (ISB) are ranked among the top engineering and management institutions in the world. Each year, world-class companies come to these campuses to pick up talent for their global operations. Every large product company like Microsoft, Oracle, Intel, SAP, etc., has a large R&D hub out of India which works on cutting edge technologies by leveraging the talent pool available in the country.

The Indian IT industry has grown by leaps and bounds with the economic liberalization. In the 1990s most of the U.S. companies were looking at reducing their IT labor cost (including work for Y2K), and Indian IT vendors were mainly working on maintenance and smaller enhancements of existing projects. Hence, the Indian IT industry was mostly viewed as a cost arbitrage for U.S. companies in those days. Using Y2K as an entry point, many Indian IT vendors made entries into IT services, and over a period of time Western businesses developed greater confidence regarding IT outsourcing to the Indian providers. Some Indian IT vendors redefined the outsourcing landscape as they successfully competed with the IBMs and Accentures of the world. Indian service providers used the different time zones (especially between the United States and India) for strategic advantage by offering business continuity over these zones. The trend moved toward outsourcing of larger projects to Indian vendors, and the India IT industry steadily expanded on its competencies and now includes both niche players offering specific services and generic companies offering end-to-end services. With hardly any Indian vendor having revenues of $10 million in the early 1990s, today at least a few of the them have more than a billion dollars of profit. Accentures and IBMs also have large setups in India. In the consolidation phase of the IT industry today, Indian vendors are taking the lead and expanding their reach by acquiring niche consulting players to increase their competencies.

Western companies are increasingly looking at Indian IT vendors as strategic partners in order to focus on core competencies and gain competitive advantage. Vendors are expected to not only define the technology landscape but also take complete end-to-end responsibility for IT infrastructure and bring a strategic business advantage. Indian industry has a robust outsourcing business with the United States, and in the last few years they have also expanded their footprint in Europe and other parts of the world. Being aware of the best practices, Indian vendors are now able to set up global centers of excellence in related business verticals and efficiently make use of cross-domain knowledge.

The Internet was officially launched in 1989 and the World Wide Web in 1993. It was cited as the biggest business opportunity ever, and the industry was flooded with enormous unviable business models. The venture capitalists (VCs) thought of it as excellent opportunities, and funds were pumped into businesses without evaluating their viability. Huge funds poured into unviable businesses finally resulted in a big Internet bubble burst in the early part of this century. Most unviable business models perished with this bubble, but some companies (like Google) not only came out with innovative models but also changed the business landscape entirely by using the Web. They completely redefined how business could run on the Internet, and coupled with the huge technological advancement in communication technologies, the world has grown flat with the emergence of the Internet. Communication between different parts of the globe has improved drastically, and you can access any machine in any place in the world from any other place in the world. Technology has become cheaper with open source code communities, and virtually everything is available free with the open source. With technology innovations like cloud computing, entry barriers to start IT operations have come down drastically, and business on the Web has become a norm. With technology moving toward 3G, 4G, and wi-max, there is an abundance of network bandwidth and the cost of communication has been tremendously reduced. Thus the Web is the main channel of business today. It has already emerged as an excellent base for large-scale, business-critical applications.

The authors of this book have been part of this vibrant industry for the last 20 years. They have seen the various changes in the IT landscape in India during the last two decades, including the Internet bubble in the early part of this century and the meltdown of the financial markets with the collapse of Lehman Brothers in 2008. They completely understand the IT landscape and have produced this book, which highlights how outsourcing will be done in the future. It covers not only the strategic aspects of outsourcing but also the practical challenges in the deployment. They have drawn examples in the book based on their experience.

This book also targets people who want to do business on the Web and would like to outsource work to a vendor, discussing the different aspects of choosing the right vendor, starting from vendor selection, pricing models, what to outsource and what not to, challenges in outsourcing to Indian vendors, and Web-based outsourcing models. The material is well organized and comprehensive, and I am sure these experiences will be found useful by most readers.

I have known Vivek Sharma for more than 14 years, and he has always been known to us as "Swamiji." We joined Infosys within a span of few months and were part of the same group for 13 years. Over this period, we have worked together on multiple outsourcing projects from customers located worldwide for resolving critical issues. Swamiji is one of the best technology consultants. He carries great respect among customers and peers alike, and his advice was an authority of sorts on the subject. He believes in his intuition, and it never fails him.

C. S. Prasad Subramanian
Technology and Management Consultant
IncValue Advisors Pvt. Ltd.
Bangalore, India

Preface

Outsourcing and Wealth Creation

Competition and wealth creation have assumed new dimensions with the outsourcing phenomenon. Process reengineering and innovation have been at the core of business process outsourcing. The concept may seem new, about two decades old, but actually it is one of the oldest in mankind's history. Major breakthroughs have occurred in the field, starting right from the outsourcing decision and strategy making, up to implementation and business evolution. Speed of execution and increased focus, along with quality enhancement and revenue augmentation, are some of its hallmarks. Managers feeling the heat of global economic uncertainty relentlessly try to figure out optimal management strategies, models, and tactics leading to higher levels of success.

This book elucidates various outsourcing aspects and tackles nagging questions:

- Should outsourcing be considered at all or not? If so, what functions are potential candidates?
- What factors contribute to outsourcing success, and why do some companies flounder?
- What do successful companies that solve customer problems do differently?
- How can the Web be tapped to open a whole new world of outsourcing online?
- During economic slowdown, what outsourcing business strategies need to be applied?

The current business culture demands focus on delivery under pressure within stringent timelines and with limited resource, in a fast-changing world with so many optional choices available to customers. There is a continuous emphasis to do more with less.

Offering counsel on whether or not a function should be in house or contracted/outsourced and further how it should be properly evaluated is considered a complex and debatable topic, and often there seem to be too many variables that favor one over the other. This book provides deep insight into such aspects of the outsourcing industry, which is under great flux. Lowering costs, enhancing quality, and development of life cycle have been at the core of the information technology–information technology enabled service (IT–ITES) space. Outsourcing is now considered a strategic tool in the arsenal with businesses reaping its benefits in a fiercely competitive global business environment.

Outsourcing is here to stay, and companies cannot afford to ignore it, for it touches umpteen aspects of everyday life. Costly infrastructures could be associated with outsourced functions, and that cannot be reasonably underwritten by most organizations. Basic rules of thumb with exceptions exist when deciding between an insourced and an outsourced model. Business approaches need to undergo suitable necessary and sometimes radical changes in an economic climate.

Before one outsources, it is important to answer some questions:

- What is the strategic gain?
- To maximize quality, and cost advantage, which functions should be outsourced, and how does one effectively exchange knowledge?
- What risks need to be tackled when shifting business operations offshore, and what change management issues need to be addressed?
- To evaluate and choose offshore vendors, what evaluation criteria should clients use, what talents and skills will the employees need, what primary location selection criteria are needed, and what is the best location for your infrastructure needs?

This book is concerned with various outsourcing facets and provides current exhaustive business-relevant material about the industry. Managing outsourced projects involves continuous people–technology dynamics along with cross-cultural and geographic challenges. The authors have elucidated in the book that the greatest business enablers are the concept, people, and technology. Emerging trends and practices in the outsourcing industry have been dealt with, including practical ideas to facilitate success in outsourcing initiatives.

Structure and Content of This Book

Outsourcing has become a mainstream business with a bright future, although during recessionary periods the line between opportunity and risk is often blurred. There is greater emphasis on faster turnaround as outsourcing pushes the world beyond information economy toward knowledge economy. Quick sharing of knowledge through technology aids in value enhancement and cost reduction. Emergence of more geographical outsourcing destinations globally and service provider performance benchmarking tools have enhanced outsourcing attractiveness.

Clients can streamline business operations and incorporate greater flexibility by accessing professional, experienced, and high-quality service. Less capital expenditure, greater focus on core competencies, and fewer management hiccups are some outsourcing benefits along with increased control, saving on investing in latest technology, and sharing of business risks. Firms are spared the nightmare of hiring and retaining employees regularly, installing and upgrading equipment, and finding solutions to inherent process-related problems.

The initial chapters of the book provide an overview dealing with the factors favoring outsourcing, basic rudiments, if an organization should consider outsourcing at all or not, the nature and types of projects, processes, and functions that are potential candidates for outsourcing, best practices, various categories of vendors, and optimal operations execution which have greatly boosted this megatrend.

The Internet with its tremendous opportunities and potential for leveraging outsourcing online is introduced. Supported by many examples and criteria for success, this subject has been largely untouched in the past. Additionally mostly unexplored, innovative business models and concepts which allow entrepreneurs to make significant gains are put forth. These new ideas can mostly be deployed with relatively small investments. E-commerce to transport content and electronic payment systems are also discussed.

Chapters on outsourcing during recession and economic slowdown discuss strategies, approaches to be used during times of slashed IT budgets, dwindling orders, contract renegotiations, layoffs, depression, and fatigue; how organizations reposition to sustain business value; examples from outsourcing organizations that successfully managed slowdown; and entrepreneurial advice from leading business figures on mitigation methods.

The final chapters provide insight into intellectual property rights, data security, and the future of outsourcing. The future will be driven by value and competing ideas, and not so much on competing organizational sizes. The future outsourcing trends shall provide valuable insights to organizations, leaders, readers, and others.

GENERAL
OUTSOURCING

Chapter 1

Outsourcing Rudiments

Old ways give way to the new.

Brief Background

As barriers crumbled in the passage of time.

Contracting is one of the oldest and most common practices of work. Even in ancient times, trade existed between countries, providing access to goods and services not available in the home countries. In the early years, when the word outsourcing actually came about, people would vend things to a third party. This is contracting in its basic form. Thus there would be value addition, with the consumers getting products and services they needed, and the suppliers getting money or some acceptable mode of exchange in return.

As a concept it is prevalent in all aspects of our lives—domestic and professional. Some visible examples are "security services," "housekeeping," "pantry," "laundry service," and "car driver." In domestic lives, household chores are done by "domestic aids." Thus persons or institutions, not household members, execute activities requested by the household for a fee. Some may not be so visible, but are nonetheless important.

In the business context, outsourcing is all-pervasive. In the outsourcing world people learn about products differently (e.g., a virtual marketplace through electronic publishing and various other customer interface channels), buy them differently using electronic cash and secure payments systems, and have them delivered differently. There may also be a difference in how they allocate their loyalty. In this business jungle, the outsourcing organization has to adapt rapidly to a world where the traditional concepts no longer hold, where "quality" has a new meaning, where "content" is not equated to product, and where "distribution" does not necessarily mean physical transportation. Brand equity can rapidly evaporate in this new environment, forcing firms to develop new ways of doing business and leveraging from the same.

Suitable business strategy and design drivers evolve through the ability to make quick changes based on the nature and magnitude of the outsourcing business. The ability and flexibility to quickly change and reposition is needed to survive in the world of outsourcing. Supporting automation, infrastructure, resources, etc., are basic logistics needed for this.

Competition is no longer between outsourcing companies but between ideas, concepts, products, services, speed and ease of transaction initiation, execution, delivery, and closure.

Outsourcing organizations and vendors in order to remain business leaders will not just add value, they will invent and furthermore create value. The world as it exists today is replete with many examples of organizations, ideas, and products which have successfully created need and value through innovation. In the world of business outsourcing versus other traditional business industries, business setup is much quicker.

An advisable strategy is quick setup and execution, evaluating results, and rapidly making suitable changes (big or small) or exiting altogether. The cycle is quickly repeated for other ideas and products till desirable results are achieved. Thus not too much time and effort should be invested in very long-term strategy planning.

Should the outsourcing organization maintain strategic status quo and seek manageable challenges by tweaking the existing product set, or radically change the strategy to possibly induce a state of chaos, risk, and uncertainty? While such models may not be needed in a stable environment, they are relevant in the current age of volatility, especially in the very fast-changing world of the Web. This was aptly referred to as a force of "creative destruction" by Joseph Schumpeter (http://en.wikipedia.org/wiki/Joseph_Schumpeter), a professor of economics at Harvard. By destruction he meant doing away with the inertia and replacing old ways with new ones. Inability to throw away a time-tested, used, and currently successful business strategy may lead to failure over a long term. Thus organizations may need to improve on, change, and even do away with older strategies, approaches, and resources over time. This foresight to cannibalize has inherent risks and needs suitable lead times for executing and reaping benefits from introducing change. A common concern with manufacturing organizations may be that selling directly to customers may destroy the existing balance between mechanisms, structures, distribution, relationships, etc. For Internet-based businesses, the Web automatically induces deployment of the end-to-end business or transaction cycle, in its respective context, thus the need to have a focus toward innovation and research and development, whatever be the nature of the outsourcing business.

The Goals of the Game

Adding value up and down the life cycle chain.

Businesses have some basic goals, despite changes taking place: stay competitive, improve productivity through innovation, deliver quality, minimize transaction time. For firms plotting their course in the turbulent waters of outsourcing, these goals are the guiding buoys.

Altogether different management strategies are required in collaborative or committed relationships in an interconnected world. They call for relationships based on data access across the end-to-end process life cycle by all interacting players, employing openness and mutual collaboration instead of an adversarial relationship in the outsourcing business. The same is true for organizations in this highly competitive business world of outsourcing. Relationship forms another component of the strategy. A great relationship between the buyer and the vendor can be immensely helpful. The compatibility and coordination of the vendor can prove to be very useful.

Leveraging outsourcing to rewrite the rules of the game is a highlight. Such ventures aid in creating and distributing wealth and have long-term impact on the economy, environment, and social fabric of the society at large of various nations. It is the firm conviction of optimists that, even during the worst financial periods, opportunities exist in outsourcing that are just waiting to be tapped.

Market-driven outsourcing business is governed by a few principles. Customer orientation is the first. This is achieved through customization specific to the customer's needs, products, and services. Mass customization (not customization for the masses) must always remain a focus point of delivery. The outsourcing business must strive through such mass customization to meet the personalized needs of the end consumers/customers. Cross-functional coordination between teams across the organization to achieve seamless delivery is the second. Advertising, marketing, and business spread make up the third.

Market conditions are driving convergence. High performance and increasingly low-cost technologies (like high computing power, storage and display devices, communication systems, and operating systems) are driving vendors to deliver ever improving products and services at consistently faster speeds, with higher quality and at continuously lower costs. The outsourcing customer organizations accordingly demand customized products and services in this age and era of fierce competition.

Integrate, Integrate, and Still Integrate

Integrating the various pieces into a cohesive whole.

Such end-to-end life cycle integration requires overhaul of major processes, approaches, resources, and systems for seamless flow and integration with the parts of the outsourcing business life cycle. A virtually interconnected organization built on a networked foundation of enabling resources, processes, and people will automatically push and drive various interacting players, suppliers, etc., to become networked or fail and exit the relationship. Enormous information technology investments have been made by outsourcing players to automate key processes, some of which are purchasing, invoicing, and other business functions. Information technology is becoming an appealing investment for many businesses as the prices for computer hardware and network equipment continue to fall, and information technology can especially be used for high-impact applications such as linking their distributed operations. However, it would be akin to driving with blinders on, if investment is made without a clear need, idea, approach, and game plan for Web-based outsourcing. The full potential of Web-based outsourcing cannot be delivered by any one single technology. Integrated architecture, the likes of which has never been seen before, is required. We are beginning to see sophisticated applications being developed in the virtual world as Web-based outsourcing matures ever so rapidly. Constraints of availability of skilled local resources, learnability, and deadlines are being constantly shrunk in the fast-changing virtual world of outsourcing business.

Usually the greater the distance between the countries of the buyer and the supplier, the greater is the number of intermediaries. Not so in the case of outsourcing. The various players that comprise a global outsourcing business usually consist of basically the outsourcing organization, the vendor provider, and suitable enabling infrastructure. The outsourcing organization and the vendor provider are usually located in different geographic areas.

Any strategy has timelines and schedules attached to it. Speed is the essence. The colossal advancement in science and technology has increased the speed tremendously. Present-day computers can perform millions of computations in seconds. People's traveling time across geographies has shrunk from months and days to a couple of hours. Speed and success go hand in hand. The endeavor of the vendor is to continuously strive to reduce the timeframe/schedule set by the buyer and deliver the services in time. Of course, this may involve effort and innovation, but it not only benefits the buyer but also helps in placing the vendor head and shoulders above other suppliers, thus becoming the supplier of choice for many buyers. Outsourcing deliverables can now be executed by vendor organizations who can complete it much faster than the outsourcing organization through optimal usage of skilled people, large experience pools, resources, and technological means.

Another important component upon which any strategy hinges is "subject matter expertise." Here managerial skills may prove very vital. Improper management can give rise to exceeded budgets. A well-informed and knowledgeable manager can greatly reduce the budget for a project. On the other hand, lack of information and knowledge can lead to inflated budgets, and even after investing more money, it may not guarantee success. Usually if one party is knowledgeable, it can judge fairly how knowledgeable the other party is. In a global contracting/outsourcing assignment, knowledge of the market conditions becomes all the more imperative, especially if one is conducting business with the supplier in that country for the first time. If the buyer has not done its spadework well, then frequent travels over long distances to resolve issues will prove to be very expensive, yet may not give the desired results. Thus information is power, and knowledge a greater power. Knowledge is a byproduct of information and data. Data exists in large volumes, of which most may be useless and incoherent. Information results from the filtering of large volumes of data, and when information is further refined, it gives rise to knowledge which is the summation. *Thus outsourcing business is essentially a knowledge industry.*

Although geographic barriers have gotten blurred with the advent of the Internet, language/culture issues along with the government policies need to be considered. The government and industry should lend constant support to local entrepreneurs so that there is more social justice.

Outsourcing Basics

The rules and limits of each game, select wisely
based on your playing potential.

Traditional entrepreneurship is conditioned by three types of cultural and business environments according to Tugrul Atamer (2007), dean of the faculty and deputy managing director at EMLYON Business School in France. These three environments are referred to as "ethos":

The free market system or ethos: The market creates and distributes wealth, known as the Anglo-Saxon model.

The cooperative system or ethos: Though the market is the primary wealth creator, the state plays an important role in its redistribution. European countries including France are examples.

The parallel system or ethos: Creation of wealth and social justice is done locally, and neither the state nor the market plays a significant role. Emerging countries, the famous BRIC (Brazil, Russia, India, and China) are examples of this ethos. Outsourcing industries prosper best in this environment. Big Indian outsourcing players like Infosys, HCL, Wipro, etc., are some examples, providing employment to millions.

Outsourcing—An organization (buyer) purchases goods or services from another organization (vendor or supplier), and the buyer "owns" and controls (not always) the process. In other words, the buyer tells the supplier exactly what it wants and how it wants the supplier to deliver the product or perform those services. The supplier cannot vary from the buyer's instructions in any way, and the buyer can replace the supplier with relative ease by terminating the contract.

As organizations continued to look for more innovative ways to improve efficiency and cut costs to survive the fast-paced marketplace, outsourcing took off with two broad approaches, which still continue to be popular: (1) *centralizing non-core processes in-house as shared service functions to derive the benefits of centralization through a suitable wholly owned subsidiary or in-house process*; (2) *to identify an acceptable external third-party service provider or supplier to bring in value-added services.* Markets favor either of the two depending on various factors like nature of business, organizational competence, organizational strategy, etc. With an increase in supplier market competition, the product or service is not seen as strategically critical, and environmental uncertainty makes internal investment risky, thereby making outsourcing more attractive.

Contracting or outsourcing grows in good times because companies want to focus on growth and in bad times because companies want to cut costs. Contracting enhances productivity and cost reduction and is a unique win–win situation wherein the supplier adds strategic value to the project and aids in shareholder value increment, thus making the difference between leaders and followers. Contracting involves transfer of some projects or processes to the contractor. The outsourcing company may retain "what" aspects of the projects like results collection, monitoring, strategic decision taking, direction setting, etc., but hands over the "how" aspect of the process to the supplier like governance, execution, technology setup, etc. The decision rights may be totally retained by the buyer or totally passed over to the supplier so that there is a greater shared responsibility between the two organizations.

Outsourcing involves many perspectives, some of which are

1. *Differentiating value and need* to outsource certain business aspects
2. Alignment of corporate strategy with the supplier strategy
3. Establishment of clear timelines and mechanisms
4. Identification of proficient, prolific suppliers

The suppliers aim to

1. Create *business value* and bring in suitable *transformation*
2. Provide first-rate quality
3. Produce at a cost that is lower than what it costs the buyer to do it in-house
4. Accomplish tasks faster than it could be done by the buyer in-house

Businesses contract/outsource almost any project if it costs less to perform the activity outside the organization than inside. It is not from the benevolence of the butcher, the brewer, or the baker that we expect our dinner but from their regard to their own interest. It is this self-interest which leads to innovation, wealth creation, and the tendency to focus on what one can do best.

Insourcing versus Outsourcing

The two sides of a coin.

Both insourcing and outsourcing (the paths in Figure 1.1) have some advantages and disadvantages which should be borne in mind while making a decision regarding them. *For an organization owning proprietary designs or processes, insourcing is advisable because a high degree of control over operations is needed.* Also, for a company enjoying business volume necessary to achieve economies of scale, insourcing can lower manufacturing costs (e.g., Merck products are sold exclusively by its workforce, unlike many smaller pharmaceutical firms). *Finally, core competencies are developed during insourcing.* Identifying and building core competencies like organizational strength or abilities developed over long periods, which customers find valuable and competitors find difficult or even impossible to copy, are a major part of business strategy development effort. Prime candidates for insourcing are products or processes that could also evolve into core competencies. *Insourcing*

Figure 1.1 The outsourcing paths.

is preferred when environmental uncertainty is low, reducing the risk of investing in capacity, when supplier market is not well developed, and when the product and service being considered are not directly related to the buying firm's core competencies. Insourcing disadvantages may consist of risks that decrease the firm's strategic flexibility. Insourcing risk was glaringly evident in the semiconductor industry wherein associated manufacturing technologies had extremely short life cycles, some of just six months, after which they were expected to be superseded by newer technologies. Thus risk of investing in process technologies which became outdated very fast was continuously faced by the semiconductor manufacturers, and to justify growth under such risky conditions, investing for higher capacities was linked to the feasibility study of quick paybacks.

Deploying in-house scarce resources to upgrade their processes versus outsourcing, if suppliers can provide the product or service more effectively than the company itself, is a key consideration. The financial viability of the firm can be put to the test, even risk, as its ability to invest in other projects also gets restricted, in trying to catch up with technologically advanced suppliers, which can prove to be an expensive proposition. In outsourcing, a firm's flexibility and access to the state-of-the-art products and processes increase. Also, changing supply-chain partners is easier than changing internal processes as markets or technologies change. Outsourcing improves a firm's cash flow in addition to increasing the firm's strategic flexibility and access to new technologies, with less up-front investment for resources needed to provide a product or service. Dell, which sells computers, supported $3 billion in annual revenues with only $60 million of fixed assets by using contract manufacturers. Thus the benefits can be obviously significant. Risks and disadvantages of outsourcing can come from suppliers misstating their capabilities. Their performance may not meet the buyer's expectations; the process and technology may not match to deliver the requirements. Consider the case of Apple Computers, which accumulated a backlog of more than $1 billion when demand for new line Macintosh computers increased dramatically in the 1990s. Timely delivery of critical parts including modems and custom chips could not be obtained, because many of them had been custom designed and outsourced from a single supplier. Many customers who did not want to wait for new products became alienated because Apple was unable to deliver in time. Another issue with outsourcing is that buying firms need to use suitable mechanisms to ensure sustained quality, availability, confidentiality, and performance of outsourced goods or services. Key skills and technologies that are a part of their core competencies may be lost at worst. Many companies manage these challenges by closely overseeing key design, operations, and supply-chain activities. They also solicit constant feedback from customers and react suitably by changing their products and services.

Thus, in a nutshell, insourcing advantages consist of economies of scale and/or scope, ability to oversee the entire process, and a high degree of control. The disadvantages are that it requires sufficient and sustained investment, and potential suppliers may offer superior products and services. Thus strategic flexibility may be reduced. On the other hand, outsourcing merits consist of low investment risk, improved cash flow, access to state-of-the-art products and services, and high strategic flexibility. Demerits are loss of control over substantial processes and core technologies, possibility of choosing a bad supplier, and "hollowing out" of the corporation, in exceptional cases.

Offshoring versus Outsourcing

The choices we consciously make, in life, big and small.

It is important to differentiate between offshoring and outsourcing. *Off-shored processes may be handed off to third-party vendors or remain in house, while outsourced processes are necessarily handed over to third-party vendors.* All offshoring does not necessarily involve outsourcing. The advantage of lower cost labor in another country is made use of by both.

Business Process Outsourcing (BPO)

A means, an end, and the path walked in between.

Business process outsourcing (BPO) involves migration of services to an external service provider. It includes call centers, back office services, transaction processing across various industries like manufacturing, finance, accounting, human resources, IT, etc. Supplier vendors use best practices and technology-driven applications to deliver quality service and products.

Types of Outsourcing

The options and their relative needs and deeds.

Outsourcing can be of different types depending upon the geographical distance between the buyer outsourcing organization and the supplier vendor.

Onshore Outsourcing

If the supplier is in the same country as the buyer but outside the company of the buyer, then it is an onshore type of outsourcing. Since the country is the same, there are likely hardly any language-related issues, and even if languages spoken are different, it will be easier to find translators/representatives to bridge the communication gap. The government policies will be almost uniform throughout the country, and travel time and distances between the buyer's and seller's locations will not be much.

Nearshore Outsourcing

If the supplier is located in a neighboring country (usually on the same continent), then it is a nearshore type of contracting/outsourcing. It provides the benefits of the same time zone and a possibly low-cost alternative to domestic sourcing. Additionally there are similarities in language and culture, and the travel time and distances not being much. U.S. and European businesses could see Latin America emerging as a nearshoring location due to its Spanish language capability. Another example is if the buyer is located in the United Kingdom and the seller is located in Germany or France.

Offshore Outsourcing

If a supplier is located in a foreign country which is far away from the country in which the buyer is located (usually a different continent), then it is an offshore type of outsourcing. The distance being great, factors like long travel times and respective government policies are matters of significance. In this case low labor rates may be of immense benefit to the company. So the decision for offshore outsourcing needs careful deliberation to reap a rich harvest. Outsourcing is not the panacea for all business problems. Offshoring from the United States to India is the most prevalent example. Global footprint expansion and opening of delivery centers by Indian firms in China, Philippines, Cairo, etc., are also similar examples.

Outsourcing Decision and Its Consequences

"Selection and maintenance of aim," an old war saying.

Managers should clearly understand the issues and the differences pertaining to outsourcing within a country and outside a country. Only then can a decision be made which is mutually beneficial both to the buyer and the seller. Lack of knowledge regarding the intricacies of outsourcing can prove expensive and in some cases can cause irretrievable loss. *It could cause a loss of name, reputation, waste of time, and effort apart from huge revenue losses.* The decision to outsource is driven by many reasons, among which could be reduced cycle times in which technology plays an important role, gaining from the core competencies and the best practices of the supplier, reduction in cost, improvement in quality, and lesser risk. Outsourcing provides the buyer with more time and enables it to focus better on its in-house key core activities and processes. These subjects are discussed in the following chapters of this book.

Growth of Outsourcing Worldwide

"Be the change you wish to see in the world."—*Gandhi*

Companies from around the globe arrive in the Asia Pacific region with great expectations because opportunities are abundant and businesses envision tantalizing growth scenarios. In this region all things seem possible, but at the same time many matters may not be clear and simple about how to realize those possibilities. Every business that ventures here must be flexible and willing to adapt. Many companies see value in working with established outsourcing partners in this dazzling but complicated market. Outsourcing has enabled clients to save up to 50% on operational costs of finance and recover 1% of audited expenditure. Managers are grasping the offshore outsourcing megatrend—strategies, implications, high-growth application areas, and related issues. *U.S. and European companies have widely outsourced offshore, with larger Fortune 1000 firms outsourcing to markets like Ireland, Singapore, Russia, Malaysia, South Africa, Hungary, Thailand, Vietnam, Philippines, China, and India. Offshore outsourcing now has many synonyms like value sourcing, global sourcing, global resourcing, global delivery capability, blended outsourcing, and alternative staffing with companies calling it by different terms.*

As the vistas expand to include a myriad set of services.

Chapter 2

Outsourcing Benefits

Like a wave cascading out into the masses.

Immense strides in science and technology have given an impetus to outsourcing in a big way. Outsourcing can have a great positive impact on the lives of many if deployed appropriately, by improving people's careers and lifestyles. Contingencies for rapid business growth and business slowdowns need to be considered. Business transformation metrics and standards need to be constantly evolving. The challenges may consist of cultural hurdles, technical barriers and financial issues but the benefits can far surpass the obstacles.

The Strategic Call

Harkening to the call, so individual.

The companies that kept a tight business focus, even if it meant shedding profitable operations, were the winners in return on invested capital. *In the Asia Pacific environment, the do what you do best lesson may be particularly fitting.* A business can do what it does best and compete more aggressively in the market, unfettered by the responsibility for back office services.

Firms thus focus on their "in-house" core business activities by outsourcing. This helps to take the load off the organization, allowing it to spend more time on its in-house core processes, business needs, and strategic business areas. The senior management is freed to do the creative thinking, once the less high-value work is outsourced. There is an increase in focus as outsourcing is a means of managing burden. Real growth in outsourcing business has been fostered with the rise of the virtual organization, a business that focuses on its core activities and lets others deal with the rest, in this age of fast changing economic conditions. Companies that focus on operating the core business prosper best in a stalled economy, according to a 2008 study by Accenture of 850 largest companies in the United States following various global recessions.

The Various Approaches

The synergies of disparate entities.

Outsourcing in its present-day form has its roots spread across joint ventures, subcontracting, and business partnerships. In a highly competitive environment and as the products become more and more complex, organizations find it more prudent to subcontract certain components. This mutual interdependence of manufacturers/buyers and subcontractors/suppliers increases sustained performance and innovation and gives rise to quality improvement and reduced costs. *Note*: No two outsourcing arrangements are the same; therefore an approach has to be tailored to accommodate the business objectives, timelines, and budgetary needs of clients.

Subject Matter Expertise

*Those men and means that burn the paths
in their wake, for others to follow.*

The access to new technologies with proven expertise, reduction in costs/time incurred in recruiting and training staff, economies of scale, and higher efficiencies through the implementation of best practices have made outsourcing an attractive option. The proven expertise of the service provider effectively manages the analytical and transactional activities. Risks are mitigated, and business continuity is enhanced, resulting in such saving opportunities. By turning to a niche provider and taking advantage of lower wage ranges in outsourced regions (e.g., India), service costs are substantially reduced.

The causes for outsourcing may include lack of local talent, lower working wages offshore, a jump start to attain presence, and benefiting from the best practices. Such enabling vendors have large expanses of knowledge gained from many previous outsourcing engagements. *Sharing of knowledge, and doing things cheaper, faster, and better are thus known advantages.*

Technology's Transformation Touch

In times of massive changes, do we currently exist?

Vendors transform traditional business models and achieve measurable results meeting customer service and quality standards. A diversified suite of proven applications coupled with proven expertise enables vendors to deliver tailored solutions, freeing the client to focus on the essential aspects of business while harvesting the customer and asset value of outsourced blocks. By turning static operations into dynamic ones, companies are realizing greater financial flexibility.

Contracting or outsourcing has the impetus, with the widespread prevalence of enabling technological means. *Some of the enabling technologies which have immensely increased the scope of contracting/outsourcing are business-to-employee (B2E), e-business, business intelligence, enterprise applications, infrastructure management, web technology, embedded product engineering, telecommunication, and internetworking.* Today's technologies—*mobile technologies, Internet, pervasive computing,* etc.—are geared to reduce transaction costs. Benefit can be accrued from the extensive use of automation and infrastructure tools used by the vendor. Communication is a great enabler, with location being of secondary importance in a well-connected enterprise with the consolidation of server hardware and software applications and database accomplished via outsourcing. There is global access to IT skills and expertise.

The Cost Factor

The numbers game, always a significant bearing.

Outsourcing is being increasingly done by businesses for creating strategic value through process improvements quickly and cost effectively. This is a win–win approach because the outsourcing organization pays less and the vendor makes more simply through currency conversion from a strong into a weaker currency. Lower labor rates in other countries can contribute immensely to cost saving. Apart from reduction in transaction costs, outsourcing is being used as a tool for achieving a wide range of strategic business goals.

Considering an example of "procurement outsourcing," organizations are able to reduce transaction costs by up to 50% in a few years. Correspondingly, cycle times are reduced by up to 30%, and material cost lowered by about 10% over a period of time. Administrative costs are reduced by 30% to 50%. Quality improvements of about 10% and reduction in turnaround time by 40% to 50% are seen after sufficient maturity has been achieved.

Holistic Offerings

The wave effect of forces in motion.

Analysts are of the view that contracting/outsourcing will be strengthened and future business opportunities will be created due to key trends like rapidly increasing consolidation and maturity of the industry and further fueled by a large number of mergers and acquisitions. Traditional IT companies have entered the arena of contracting/outsourcing, and this has escalated maturity. *The synergies between the information technology enabled service/business process outsourcing (ITES/BPO) operations and IT services are leveraged, and the customers are provided with a complete umbrella of end-to-end service offerings.* Customers are offered advantages such as low risks, scalability, and economical pricing due to the increase in multivendor and build–operate–transfer (BOT) contracts. High-end services such as equity research and analysis, insurance, and technology support and development are being offered by many contracting/outsourcing vendors in order to help them move up the value chain. Because clients have to be offered increasing benefits in terms of scalability, delivery, capability, track record, customer referrals, etc., there has been a trend for the outsourcing segment getting concentrated more around the large players. Nevertheless, the enormous outsourcing business has given growing companies critical mass to compete with multinationals such as EDS, Computer Science Corporation (CSC), and Accenture, thereby increasing the confidence of clients to trust them with larger contracts. Indian ITES/BPO vendors are further setting up facilities in low-cost ITES/BPO destinations such as China and the Philippines in order to expand the spectrum of their offerings and to tap these markets. Thus there has been an expansion of the services footprint.

Speed of the Game

This benchmark that keeps shifting upward, in all fields.

Outsourcing models enable clients to rapidly launch new products, capitalize on additional distribution channels, or segment specific markets. Predictable and accurate data results are delivered through automatic programs and stringent auditing techniques. Accountability and continuous improvement over time is ensured by business-based metrics and service level standards.

The Engagement Players

Regional flavor, global distribution.

Outsourcing involves a large pool of expert suppliers who can provide better services at lower rates. Since there is no dearth of competent suppliers it is advisable to outsource if it provides tangible and intangible benefits, such as lower labor wages and high focus the supplier brings to the service being delivered. If the company were to perform those services in house it would prove to be more expensive, of lower quality, and the cycle time would usually be much more. In the bargain the buyer gets ample time to focus on its core competencies. A project may be broken into individual components, and each component could be further outsourced to a separate supplier, depending on vendor expertise. Once a need is identified by the outsourcing organization, it can work with the provider to implement it. Geographical boundaries have become irrelevant, given the advances in communications, dedicated networks, the Internet, etc. Thus vendors are commonly located in different countries.

Resources Optimization

Changing the rules of the game and the players therewith.

Outsourcing enables optimization and management of the process. Thus client resources are not needed for supplier follow-ups and tracking. This results in greater visibility through normalizing and rationalization of data. To help shore up bottom lines, competitive companies today are reducing costs incurred on non-core and nonstrategic activities through outsourcing. Through effective and efficient sourcing methods, costs are reduced. As an example favoring outsourcing the procurement processes, the procurement department usually can spend more than 50% of its time in managing transaction-intensive processes like procure-to-pay process, managing various subactivities like expediting, order processing, escalations, tracking, and analytics. Thus a large number of costly people and resources are tied down, which results in higher-cost transactions, longer lead times, and higher error rates. Outsourcing as a solution creates strategic value and process improvement, savings of transaction costs, improvements in lead times, higher customer satisfaction, continuous service level agreement (SLA) improvement, and improved utilization of resources. Innovative and automation technologies used by vendors help counter challenges like higher demand variability, better and newer products, time-to-market pressure, and distribution visibility. In addition, the client is freed from the high volume of nonstrategic, noncore activities, inefficient processing, and the need for information capture and tracking. The supplier uses best practices and technology enhancements to increase visibility, the number of transactions, and cost reduction.

For a client, gaining experience can be time consuming, but the experienced outsource vendors can optimize processes because they understand how to integrate people, process, and technology to deliver results that provide real business value. Predictable outcomes, business discipline, and transparency improve process effectiveness. There is customer segmentation and insight along with access to global best practices. The need to attract, develop, and retain noncore employees is greatly alleviated because there is access to expertise from the vendor. The effectiveness of the enterprise improves as a result of customer retention, satisfaction, and profitability, thus increasing management focus and the possibilities of taking advantage of new business opportunities and changes.

Around-the-Clock Operations

The business never sleeps.

Vendors can operate around the clock, if required. Vendors' workers and resources can operate across various shifts on a 24-hour clock. The same set of resources are used by the workers in different shifts. These include infrastructure (seating, etc.), logistics, resources, technical applications, systems, etc.

Western countries, if outsourcing to Asian vendors, can leverage from the time zone difference between the countries. The outsourcing organizations can raise issues/project work needing execution toward the "end" of their working day and retire for the day. It receives immediate action by the vendor. The initiator gets an update when returning to work the next day.

Demand Spikes

Rising to meet those unforeseen spikes, a winner's approach.

The objective of some other organizations resorting to conventional outsourcing is not strictly to reduce costs but to handle the volumes and capacity fluctuations. There is an improved ability to handle capacity fluctuations using the less expensive resources and labor of the supplier vendor. By allowing an agile response to changing conditions, outsourcing supports this by eliminating the need to hire and manage new people during growth or do the opposite in a downturn. Outsourcing can be scaled to go any way, depending on the direction the business takes. Thus, forecasting the trends of the future is important so that any slowdown can be properly tackled.

Hiring Consultants for Setup

Giving birth, usually a significant task.

In order to expedite the course of starting up work on an outsourced process in a distant location, some organizations commission consulting firms to build, staff, and launch a new center. The center is established by the consultants and transitioned to the new management (e.g., Indian) when it is complete with the metrics, tools, and service level agreements to manage performance.

Geography Is History

Communicating through the void.

Outsourcing is driving business closer to the ideal—"What the customer wants, when and where it is wanted, and at the lowest possible cost." Geographic and location dependencies of the various players (the outsourcing organization, the providers, the place of deployment, etc.) are greatly alleviated and becoming meaningless.

The Quality Imperative

If not you, somebody else will.

High-quality deliverables are sustainably delivered due to usage of best practices, continuous benchmarking against the best in class, and large reserves of experiential knowledge, not to mention it being a key need for survival. Enabling technology and set standards add to the quality equation. Vendors continuously try to push the limits of quality in the rapidly changing world. It is no wonder that such vendors are often referred to as "value adding partners" by the outsourcing organizations.

Reuse of Projects, Resources, Experiences, Learning

Emulation, one of the basics of the human learning process.

Outsourcing organizations, instead of trying to "reinvent the wheel," can pick up and reuse similar projects which have already been done previously by individuals/vendors elsewhere in geographically dispersed locations. The same may be customized with required changes to meet the desired ends. This enables the organization to achieve completion in a very reduced time frame. *Reuse of tools, applications, knowledge, and experience is a critical defining advantage of the outsourcing game.*

Higher Control and De-Risking

*Contracts and trust, which define how much control
you are willing to relinquish.*

The credibility of a company's disclosure can rise after outsourcing with a quality provider. A healthy separation is created between the managers and accountants by the third-party service provider, and by using a standardized approach across multiple geographies and business units, outsourcing offers a built-in control factor, because processes must be transparent. Flexibility is the key to operating in the Asia Pacific region, with economic performance uneven from country to country. Financial risk is reduced by the contractual and financial commitments. Operational risks are also addressed by outsourcing. In case of a disaster in one region of Asia, the outsourcer can operate from another location in Asia or elsewhere in the world, thereby reducing service risk, financial risk, and business-continuity risk.

The Many, Many Benefits

Benefit, a relativistic perception, differing from person to person.

Companies find that working with an outsourcing partner already on the scene can help them navigate the landscape and focus competitive drive, irrespective of whether the companies are starting up or increasing their local presence. Benefits come in multiple layers with outsourcing (Figure 2.1). Productivity advancement and reduced costs occur. The vendor brings in advanced analytics, identifying patterns and compliance with contracts to improve business. Apart from the increase in revenue, the critical high value gain of outsourcing may be one without a number, with the organization having more time for decision support and strategic areas of planning and financial analysis. The financial people not only look back at historical numbers but also productively forward at where the business needs to go. Access to world-class expertise is an absolute must for any company determined to succeed in the Asia Pacific region with talent sometimes at a premium. Costly in-house expatriate resources are used by many companies although outsourcing can be a reliable, cost-effective, and talent-assured alternative. Without having to add or grow talent in house, with outsourcing companies have immediate and direct

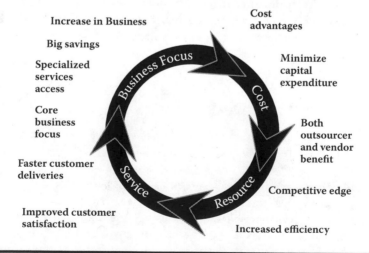

Figure 2.1 Benefits at a glance.

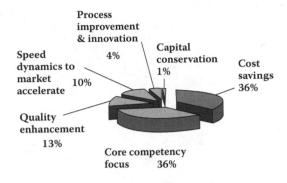

Figure 2.2 The relative weights of the outsourcing benefits.

access to skilled talent. The other factor is the expected benefits like speed, savings, cost reduction, and focus on core processes. Outsourcing models ensure a smooth transition to world-class operations whether you are launching a new product, revitalizing closed block portfolios, or growing through acquisition. It raises the shareholder value of all players. Figure 2.2 shows "relative weights" of the various advantages.

Challenges

Immense strides in science and technology have given an impetus to outsourcing in a big way. Contracting/outsourcing has enabled companies to focus on core competencies and reduce costs. For IT outsourcing, some important factors that need to be considered include the political viability. IT contracting can have a great impact on the lives of people. It can alter the lifestyle of people. Therefore an in-depth evaluation is a must. The hurdles and barriers cannot be overlooked. *These may consist of cultural hurdles, technical barriers, cost, and contract-related problems.*

Contingencies for rapid business growth and for business slowdowns need to be built in. Business transformation terms need to be developed such as service level agreements, financial details, and appropriate length of the contracting agreement. A capable vendor will not only meet the service level requirements but will also try to surpass and improve upon the schedule and time cycles. With suitable data, such vendors are able to predict periodic demand highs and lows.

The value to him, her, them, and all around.

Chapter 3

To Outsource or Not?

*Playing the game for some, playing to win for some,
and the majority who fail to play.*

To Be or Not to Be

Organizations looking to outsource their business should deliberate, holistically break down, and prioritize into multiple categories the organization's activities and functions. The following list may thereafter be used to consider which functions/activities qualify or not for outsourcing (see Figure 3.1).

A. Such functions that should always remain with the firm and never be outsourced.
B. Such functions that are fit for immediate outsourcing. Though they may be vital for the firm, the firm does not has (nor wishes to have) expertise to operate these functions.
C. Peripheral activities in which the firm does not have much expertise, and which are not critical. More outsourcing is required in this case. There is a high probability that a large chunk of such may already been subcontracted.
D. Last on the list of outsourcing: for historical reasons the firm may have developed competence in less business-critical areas. Such should be outsourced once good vendors are available.

Another report predicted that outsourcing expertise will emerge as a definitive area of competitive differentiation for IT service providers targeting industry-specific

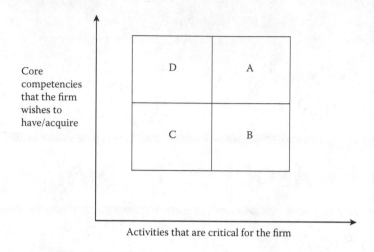

Activities that are critical for the firm

Figure 3.1 Identifying which organizational activities to outsource.

business processes, and business process expertise will define future success, particularly since technical skills and competitive prices are not in scarce supply and cannot serve as competitive differentiators. One of the outsourcing industry's leading research analysts firms, Forrester Research, observed in a research report that outsourcing is the beginning of the *process-focused IT era*, and process expertise and IT capabilities are the most important factors in evaluating business process outsourcing (BPO) companies.

It is on the seminal contributions of R. H. Coase (1937) and Oliver Williamson (1975) that the current approach toward an outsourcing strategy rests. Regardless of the installed capacity, the approach argues that a potential user will outsource if the price offered by the vendor is lower than the incremental (avoidable) cost of providing the function in house. In other words, market transactions replace internal processing where the cost of locating outsource suppliers, the cost of negotiating outsource contracts, and the costs under the contract fall below the resource allocation (overhead) of internal processing.

As a well-known matter, firms in more stable industries usually outsource less than high-tech companies facing short product life cycles and uncertain market conditions. Hence the decision to outsource or insource is influenced by the following factors:

- High environmental uncertainty favors insourcing, while low environmental uncertainty favors outsourcing.
- Low competition in the supplier market favors insourcing, while high competition favors outsourcing.
- If the need and ability to monitor supplier's performance is high, then insourcing is favored; otherwise outsourcing is advisable.

■ Insourcing is favored if the relationship of the product/service to the buying firm's core competencies is high, and outsourcing is resorted to if the relationship of the product/service to the buying firm's core competencies is low.

Realities and Myths

As best practices permeate to become prevalent norms.

Primary issues that clients should think about when relocating services offshore are the expertise in handling remote locations, cost of labor, telecom bandwidth, caliber and skill of the labor force, language skills, political stability, infrastructure, enforceability of intellectual property rights and business contracts, and general maturity of the business environment. Then, there are additional assumptions—some true and some not so true—that power the megatrend of offshoring.

Myth and Reality—Survival and competition is one assumption. You will not survive if you do not outsource. If General Electric, IBM, or ADP achieves 20% lower cost advantage over their competitors due to offshore outsourcing, it puts tremendous pressure on the competitors to either follow suit or prepare to exit that business. Either you cut costs or shut the company down. *The stark reality, however, is that not all companies have the leadership and capability to extract advantage from globalization.*

Myth and Reality—The second assumption pertains to lower costs. By taking advantage of the low-cost labor offshore, companies can substantially reduce their technology budgets and operating costs and realize vast savings. *But reality is that final costs are not all that low, and higher cost savings take time, usually running into a number of years, even when offshoring is done right.* Employees are sent abroad by companies to set up operations, and the on-site compensation of these employees usually runs high. Frequent travel adds to the price. Some offshore employees may be brought to the United States for several months for extensive training in language and culture. Labor costs also follow an ever-escalating path in popular outsourcing destinations like India.

Myth and Reality—The third assumption pertains to quality and best practices. Offshoring is about higher quality and not just about costs. By immediately leapfrogging from where they are today, companies can become best practice organizations that have superior capabilities and processes. The fact is companies may be dissatisfied with the quality of service that they receive. *Therefore, to assume that the process quality will be the same or better than before it was offshored comes with its challenges.*

Myth and Reality—The fourth assumption is regarding unresponsive IT departments. Since we had some dramatic shifts in processes and people due to outsourcing, our IT department is unable to adjust. *But the fact is that often such outsourced projects and processes are not simple but very complicated.* The line of business may not understand the complexity, so it is wrongly assumed that the IT department is unresponsive.

Myth and Reality—The fifth assumption pertains to internal IT. Our cost structure is too high to be competitive, and we are not getting all things done that we would like to get done in IT. Since IT projects are complex and costly, the reality is that offshore staff resources are occasionally used by organizations to supplement their internal IT to meet internal projects. *Projects always cost more and take longer than you expect is an old adage, and offshoring is no different.* So the best case is that these assumptions hold, and the worst case is that they do not.

To look behind the obvious and ask what the underlying logic, rationale, or assumptions are, is the job of every manager.

Strategy and Considerations

Selling time through value.

The global economy calls for intense creativity and innovation, and outsourcing meets these objectives. *So companies concentrate on their in-house core activities and on what they can do best and contract/outsource the rest.* The suppliers may be experts in these activities and may have large experiential and R&D knowledge, thereby inducing creativity and innovation.

The decision to contract an activity or integrate it vertically is a strategic one and often has far-reaching consequences. So one should first estimate how critical the activity is which is being contracted. Critical is the extent of damage resulting from failure to meet the requirements of the activity. If it is a highly critical activity and the damage caused would be enormous, then it would be best to perform the activity in house rather than outsourcing it. *Never outsource an activity if the resulting damage is irretrievable or colossal.* Perform the activity in house with proper management, so a proper control mechanism is maintained and risk is greatly mitigated. Apart from criticality, the next factor to be considered before outsourcing an activity is cost. According to Oliver Williamson, production costs are analogous to the cost of building an "ideal machine." In the economic sector this would be a perfectly efficient market, a market in which complete information is available to all parties, with perfect competition in place. There is no resistance or friction, and the situation is ideal. In an ideal situation the transaction costs are zero. If there is greater benefit in performing a function in house than in contracting it, then the function should be vertically integrated, and the function should be performed in house. However, if the benefits in the form of reduced costs, greater speed and quality, and little risk tilt in favor of the vendor, then the activity should be contracted. There are running costs known as transaction costs over and above the production costs that need to be considered before making any outsourcing decision. Transaction costs are zero in an ideal situation, but in a practical business environment transaction costs are incurred.

The frequency with which an activity is performed should be considered. If an activity is performed very rarely, then it may not be advisable to perform it in house.

Most companies do not set up their own management consultancy departments, because the services of a management consultant department are infrequently used. Setting up one's own consultancy department would neither be cost effective, nor will it be able to deliver expected quality unless the company offers services to other businesses also. But again it would have to compete with other consultants who are specialists in their fields. It would be more prudent for the company to concentrate on its core functions. The next factor that needs to be considered is uncertainty. By uncertainty is meant the extent of difficulty with which one can foresee the eventualities that might occur during the course of the transaction. The greater the length of time of business transactions, the greater the uncertainty factor, and the shorter the time span for a transaction, lesser the uncertainty. *Uncertainty is inbuilt in time.* Failures and problems occur because it may not be possible to foresee and predict all the uncertainties over a period of time. So risk is greatly reduced if the length of time is less. Lack of information, information asymmetry, and opportunism also cause uncertainty. The third factor that needs to be pondered over is specificity. If a transaction is highly specific, then transaction costs are likely to be lower in house; for example, a blast furnace is highly specific to a steel plant. On the other hand, nonspecific assets can be outsourced.

Many institutions are indeed looking to transform their business process in order to increase competitiveness and win the battle for customers. Much process reengineering, interestingly, in the past was carried out on a piecemeal basis, leading to isolated efficiency improvements. The single biggest pressure facing various industries, including banks, comes from the overwhelming pressure to reengineer their business processes. To reduce costs is a natural, key driver.

Strategy—Differs from Market to Market, Industry to Industry

Of moves and countermoves.

Better technology and usage of best practices can cut costs immensely, reduce labor costs, and increase revenue. *Contracting/outsourcing has moved from a niche technology management tool to a mainstream strategic weapon for many firms, although its rate and scope may vary from market to market.* The financial service organizations have embraced contracting/outsourcing much differently than the government agencies, and moreover the nature of contracting can vary within a given industry itself. Vendors must invest in key resources and determine the proper market entry strategies. When outsourcing services, the vertical market and the vendors should also be aware of larger business, regulatory, and competitive issues, with a view to increase business activity.

Managers should be well versed with the differences between outsourcing within a country and outside a country, which among other things may include differences in language, thereby requiring a representative, a translator, or a third party to address the issue. Distance between two countries makes traveling time consuming and expensive, and there could be different time zones with as much as 12 to 14 hours difference. Terms pertaining to business may be defined differently in different countries, and certain terms could have many definitions. Therefore, clarity regarding business terms being used in a particular country is necessary. It is advisable for the buyer to be familiar with the local customs in the supplier's country. The economic, social, and political environment, along with the strength of unionization, should be properly considered. Political instability, social unrest, or economic recession can prove very expensive and irrevocable to the buyer. In global contracting/outsourcing, it is possible that the number of intermediaries may increase. The policies and the laws of the government along with the customs regarding labor and environment protection should be given a thought. Sometimes government laws and the social customs actually prevalent could be at variance and therefore may require some thinking before a decision for or against contracting/outsourcing is made. Different standards and safety requirements may be required of suppliers in various regions. Tariffs and exchange-rate fluctuations of currencies are other factors. Identification of an expert supplier may take more time and be more difficult if the supplier is located in a different country because of language-related issues, distance, and little knowledge about business in that country. Therefore local representation may be needed to ensure success of the outsourcing assignment. Most problems between buyer and supplier will have to be resolved over the phone, teleconference, voice/data mechanism, e-mail, chat, and other Internet-related methods. Because of distance between the two countries, frequent in-person meetings may not be possible or advisable.

The decision to outsource is an important and a strategic one, and some factors need to be taken into consideration, such as communication problems and language barriers. The buyer may not have knowledge of the native language of the supplier, and this may give rise to certain issues. Although the representatives and the translators of both the buyer and the seller can resolve the issue to a great extent, gaps in communication could still take place, which can in some cases prove costly if one is not careful. It is common knowledge that, apart from the language, the dialect also undergoes a change over short distances. This factor should not be overlooked. Even when two people are equally conversant in a particular language, misunderstanding or poorly comprehending the other party's point of view can take place. This may happen despite the fact that both belong to the same country or city and speak the same language and are equally fluent. Thus the language aspect is a very important one and should be given due consideration. Another aspect is the operating condition and the working hours prevalent in a country, which may include long lunch breaks and frequent tea breaks when all work comes to a total standstill. This could prove costly and should be properly looked into; otherwise it may give rise to missed schedules, and timelines will not be met, thereby damaging the company and its reputation. In any outsourcing assignment another aspect could be the need to appoint two auditors, so that there is greater transparency and clarity.

For an outsourcing relationship to be successful:

A. Work out a strategy and identify suppliers who can deliver the goods. The aim is to find the best suppliers. Suppliers with recognized certifications would be preferable. Searching over the Internet and e-mails could aid in making the right choice.
B. The relationship between the buyer and the seller should be constantly evaluated and monitored so that success is achieved. Reviews and inspections boost their relationship, enabling suppliers in improving the service being offered and instilling confidence in the client as valuable data may be at stake. The client should ensure whether proper protection mechanisms are in place or need to be upgraded.

Strategy—Is Outsourcing Part of the Solution or Not?

Lack of initiation, not cost, is the most common human failing.

It is important to focus on building the right business case before entering into outsourcing. The business outcomes that one wants to achieve should be properly thought over in selecting the right vendor that will provide one the right task force. The business goals should be defined because planning is critical. The priorities should be confirmed with key business stakeholders like the CFO, CEO, and business division leaders. The business results should be measurable. Make sure there is a communication plan to key stakeholders, and summarize current costs and service levels. One possibly can never overcommunicate. The task force may consist of two to three key IT management and two to three key business unit leaders. The applications to be outsourced should be identified. One should not go by or accept estimates. Make sure the baseline is by application portfolio area. Time estimates should be allocated to the right areas such as maintenance, support, enhancement, and development. Effort estimates may sometimes erroneously misallocate development work to the support bucket. *Wrong outsourcing estimates can lead to cost overruns of 20% to 25%.*

Carrying out less efficient processes internally has become a bit more difficult, considering the recent economic downturn and uncertainty. Globalization has given rise to increased competitive pressure, reduced product development cycle, and reduced product life cycle, thereby prompting organizations to keep and focus on specialized core activities which provide competitive advantage and contract/outsource the others. *According to C. K. Prahalad's core competency theory, organizations should concentrate on their critical advantages and get out of everything else, which implies that a function unique to a company or related to its strategic direction should not be outsourced or contracted.* In other words, activities core to an organization and which differentiate it in the marketplace should not be contracted, and

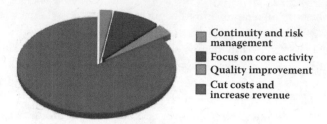

Figure 3.2 Reasons for outsourcing.

this may include a late-stage research and development, because R&D is a critical factor in business development. On the other hand, noncore functions are contracted. These functions may include IT, thus improving focus and services, and cutting costs. Fierce competition has heaped tremendous pressure on managers to improve both the bottom line and the top line. Contracting/outsourcing is the solution to achieve these objectives thus revitalizing organizations and making them more competitive.

The most important factors in favor of contracting and outsourcing (see Figure 3.2) are

A. Cost reduction
B. Improving company's focus on core activities

According to one view, all deals are either win–win or lose–lose, and there are no win–lose or lose–win relationships because, if it is a bad deal for one party, it is going to end up being a bad deal for everybody. It will affect service, if the provider is losing money.

Suppose a process has been identified for improvement and the client is wondering whether outsourcing should be a part of the solution or not. In that case he or she needs to gauge if the opportunities outweigh the risks or not. *The checklist of the client, in order to make the outsourcing decision, should consist of factors such as competency, confidentiality, control, cost, and competitiveness.* The outsourcing partner's competency in dealing with the business process and your internal and external customers should be assessed. Another important aspect to be considered is that, in case the outsourcing decision is taken, the client will lose a core competency in house that has been developed at considerable cost to the organization. Noncore competencies like administration efforts can be transferred to the outsourcing provider. Since customer records need to handed over in an outsourcing arrangement, maybe even customer contact, the quality of technical safeguards as well as legal guarantees need due consideration. How and when the client's process is run should be well under control. There should be a balance, because too little control is dangerous and too much control may mean that the client is doing the job its outsourcing partner is being paid to do. The backup and contingency plans should be at least as good as the client's internal arrangements. The negotiating power gets reduced along with the ability to move quickly if things go wrong, if the client gets locked into a supplier.

In outsourcing arrangements, calculating the value for money can be difficult. With elapsed time or in particular circumstances, you need to ensure charges can be unbundled and will not escalate. Through outsourcing, cost benefits can be most easily achieved when the provider can share high fixed costs of processing, probably as a result of technology investment among a number of users, but it should be checked that competitive pricing is not going to be delivered at the expense of competency requirements. The competitiveness of the operations improves if the outsourcing is successful. By delivering a new feature or service for which the investment cannot be justified in house, an outsourcing arrangement makes an additional contribution to competitiveness.

For more than a decade now, Accenture has been a global outsourcing leader with clients spread across six continents. Apart from professional and global expertise, much of the value to the clients comes from an early knowledge of the trends that are driving business decisions. The momentum of outsourcing is driven by results already delivered to clients and proven by hard numbers. Executives see a broader range of benefits to be gained from working with an outside partner, and it can have a significant impact on the bottom line apart from the cost reduction. Management is free to concentrate on critical in-house core business issues after outsourcing. Substantial gains can be produced for the company, with operational savings of 30% to 50% in a few years. Apart from reduced operational cost, outsourcing also aids in cost avoidance. Back office costs often escalate faster than revenue, as a company grows either organically or through acquisition. By keeping these costs down, outsourcing avoids that and also contributes to the reduction of working capital. Benefits can be accrued by efficient management of working capital and by leveraging best practices in forecasting. Outsourcing is viewed by many executives as a way to help the company leverage its management talent and focus on the core business.

To meet individual needs, outsourcing solutions can be tailored depending upon the complexity of the outsourced process. Companies have turned to outsourcing for virtually everything, as they are eager to focus on things they do best. For survival, it is necessary that the cost base be reduced and core competencies be focused on. To meet business needs, institutions are considering capabilities required in vendors for the purpose. Some of the key trends include an increase in virtualization, a shift from product-centric to customer-centric strategies, cost cutting measures with an increase in focus, and the emergence of application integration as a strategic differentiator. Outsourcing offers tremendous benefits, given the increasing competitive marketplace, with cost reduction, access to business best practices and expertise, performance enhancement, and focus on core business being some of them.

Costs Evaluation

The knowledge economy.

The cost issues associated with insourcing versus outsourcing should be understood. Both good judgment and application of sound quantitative techniques are necessary to determine the actual cost of a product or service. Direct and indirect costs must be considered by managers in making such decisions. *In the case of insourcing, some of the direct costs may consist of labor costs and variable overheads, and indirect costs may consist of building lease, utilities, equipment depreciation, fixed overhead, maintenance costs, and supervision/administration support. In the case of outsourcing, direct cost may consist of price (from invoice), and indirect costs may comprise monitoring, purchasing, receiving, and quality control.* Those costs that are tied directly to the production of the product or service are called direct costs, such as labor costs and variable overhead. Those costs which not tied directly to the production of the product or service are called indirect costs. Examples of indirect costs are staff salaries, depreciation of equipment, building lease, etc. Indirect costs represent the cost of doing business. Managers must assign indirect costs to individual units of production to understand the true cost of insourcing or outsourcing.

The task may not be as easy as it may sound. It is usually easier to determine outsourcing costs than insourcing costs. On the supplier's invoice the indirect costs are included in the direct purchase price in the case of outsourcing. In the outsourcing decision the only additional costs that need to be considered are the administrative costs associated with managing the buyer–supplier relationship (purchasing and quality control). The task of estimating the true cost becomes more difficult in the case of insourcing because the bulk of costs may fall into the indirect category. The time frame of the sourcing decision must be considered by managers in determining the total costs. Perhaps only direct costs and some portion of indirect costs should be applied if an insourcing arrangement is expected to be of relatively short duration, as it might be for a product with a limited life cycle. Instead of risking a significant decline in business, firms are better off recovering their direct costs and some portion of their indirect costs. All relevant costs, including indirect costs that might be reasonably incurred in the long run, should be considered if managers expect an insourcing arrangement to become part of outgoing operations. In the long run the firm must recover all its costs or go out of business.

Managers should be well informed to take full advantage of contracting/outsourcing. Suppose a country has lower wage rates but poor work force quality and efficiency; then outsourcing may not be the correct decision. Senior management discussions and brainstorming are imperative before deciding. Overall cost should be properly calculated, which includes purchase cost along with the transaction cost.

Pre-Outsourcing Evaluation

Of deciding matters that meet the eye and some that don't.

Before one offshores it is important to answer some questions. To obtain maximum efficiency which projects/processes should be moved offshore, and how does one effectively exchange knowledge from/to the offshore center? Throughout the transition how does one maintain business continuity, and what are the tax and legal requirements? When shifting business operations offshore what risks need to be mitigated, and what change management issues need to be addressed? To evaluate and choose offshore providers what evaluation criteria should your company use, what talents and skills will the employees need, what primary location selection criteria are needed, and what is the best location for your infrastructure needs? To win stakeholder commitment and approval, does one have a compelling business case for offshoring? Which business processes are candidates for offshoring, and what change management issues need to be addressed?

How to decide which business process to offshore is an interesting management question. Without being closely tied to other pieces of the value chain, is it possible to perform certain parts of the business process remotely with just a computer? Are the business processes mature and standardized? Is offshoring possible taking into consideration the regulatory constraints, are specialized skills required and available in the remote location, and is there sufficient scale? The process is a candidate if the answers to the questions are yes. Even if some operations are kept onshore for redundancy, the savings can be enormous. *Outsourcing is not a panacea for every business, although it has its strengths.* Identification and management of important risks, the readiness of the company for disruption, the stability of the processes, the magnitude of the opportunity, and the identification of processes that are candidates for outsourcing need to be considered by the company.

Before considering outsourcing, it is wise to predetermine a good clear process to ensure quality and prevent confusion later on. Offshoring/outsourcing cannot be disregarded as a part of the overall strategy of companies currently not engaged in it. Companies need to be very careful about picking the right delivery model when they evaluate offshoring, because there will be certain project failure if the wrong delivery model is chosen. *Vendors of U.S.-based customers use a blended model distributing the workforce into on-site teams, off-site centers within the United States, and offshore teams located in countries such as China, Russia, and India, with flexible delivery alternatives.* For mission-critical projects in particular, many companies require the presence of project teams at their premises. To meet the customer requirements and specifications, the customer's team and the project team collaborate in developing requirements and goals. Being physically close to the customer is a key factor in successfully meeting customers' needs, and therefore off-site centers are located in the same country as the customer. By establishing off-site centers in major markets, vendors have expanded and improved the offshore model. These off-site centers allow close interaction with the customer and quick reaction to a service request, being in the same geographic location and time zone as the customer. Workforce may be quickly moved back and forth between the on-site team and the off-site team, on a need basis. To compete more effectively with local service providers, vendors recruit locally hired managers, marketers, and possible technical associates in off-site centers. In order to determine the scope and requirements of a particular project in the case of offshore centers, companies typically assign teams to visit a customer's premises. To facilitate direct liaisons with the customer, some members of the initial team remain on-site while others return offshore to establish and supervise a larger project team to implement the project. *Depending on the nature and complexity of the project, typically 20% of a project team will be on-site and 80% at off-site and offshore locations.*

Business process offshoring has been executed by the financial services industry, and operations depend primarily on data, which is becoming expensive to process in the United States. Therefore operating offshore is particularly attractive to companies in the financial services industry. Savings of 10% to 20% in a few years of the overall overhead costs can be achieved, if processing is offshored. In order to reduce costs, this trend will probably repeat with other financial institutions. In India the salaries for business graduates are sometimes as little as 10% of those in New York and London. Functions including application processing, direct sales, and credit scoring, approval, and verification are being offshored by businesses because the mortgage loan processing business is a data-intensive operation. Also other functions like insurance tax and escrow processing, early collections calling, and many of the customer service call center functions are outsourced along with at least a part of loan service setup, post-closing documentation, manual payoff processing, account balancing, printing statements, and refinancing. Offshoring of mortgage processing, insurance claims management, and credit card processing is also taking place.

Example—Outsourcing and Banks

Banks want to develop customer-centric product ranges that cut across traditional boundaries. In order to improve brand value, banks aim at improving customer service and reassess the fundamental structures of the business and the way it relates to suppliers, partners, and even competitors. Lower cost is achieved by banks that succeed in remodeling their operations in this way, along with improved customer service. *There has been little cross-fertilization of ideas between banking and other sectors of economy, and this needs to change for the banking industry.* Banks have over the years tended to develop along the lines of a series of vertically integrated silos. Extensive duplication and redundancy have occurred as a result across both business and geographies.

To support a range of banking operations, banking organizations are increasingly relying on services provided by other entities. Outsourcing of data processing and noncore transaction activities to affiliated institutions or third-party organizations would improve efficiency, reduce related personnel costs, improve services, and use expertise not available internally. An institution may be exposed to additional risks, at the same time, due to reduced operational control over outsourced activities. Procedures have been established by the federal banking agencies to examine and evaluate the adequacy of institutions' control over service providers. The U.S. Federal Reserve has put forth expectations regarding the risks involved in outsourcing of critical information and transaction processing activities by banking organizations. Under its supervisory letter, such critical transactions include the initiation, processing, and settlement of payments and financial transactions, customer account creation and maintenance, lending, deposit taking, fiduciary, or trading activities.

Example—BPO Operations—Business and Technology Convergence

E-business applications, enterprise resource planning (ERP) software like SAP, Peoplesoft, and portal services are being used by BPO service providers. If used as competitive tools in their day-to-day activities, companies and consumers are discovering that global networking and other technological innovations are powerful assets, which can be used for a wide spectrum of activities ranging from entertaining and educating users to building business and serving customers on the Internet. BPO organizations need to take up such activities since increased demands for the efficient collection, dissemination, and processing of information are evident because of various economic factors, global competition and other market forces, and consumer demand for high service and improved quality. Companies are being forced by these demands to integrate previously isolated islands of automation into coherent tools. Consumers and business professionals are not interested in technology per se but in solutions to their problems. *Business and technological issues are becoming increasingly inseparable.* There must also be some understanding of the underlying technology to truly understand available solutions and to choose the correct strategy for a given environment and application. The implication of technology trends should also be understood because they will affect the management qualifications or skills that will be needed, the character of jobs that will be created, and the type of high-tech training or credentials needed in the coming years.

Example—IT Staff in an Accounting Firm—To Outsource or Not

A staffing paradox for IT personnel has been identified while providing IT consulting services to non-IT businesses like an accounting firm. While providing IT consulting services to accounting firms, it would seem that an extremely technical IT person would be best suited in order to meet the technological requirements of an accounting firm with complete reliance on network systems, but in reality the opposite is true for most accounting firms. Actually a sound infrastructure and not a highly technical person is needed. Technology infrastructure plays a major role in the stability and effectiveness of the accounting firm regardless of the size of the firm. Most of the staff of the accounting firm is responsible for preparing taxes, conducting tax research, preparing financial statements, tracking time, all of which is done using technology platforms; therefore if the network is down for any length of time, the staff might as well go home. This can become a critical issue for billable personnel and meeting deadlines. IT personnel and certified public accountants (CPAs) also share no great chemistry because of very different core professions. Hence outsourcing such IT staff is obvious.

Outsourcing—Not a Final Solution in Itself

Outsourcing is a simpler route to reliable processing leading to economies of scale. However, by no means is outsourcing an end in itself. Outsourcing can be valuable as one of the building blocks of specific and strategic solutions for the improvement of key business processes rather than as a total solution in itself. Technical flexibility and scalability, as well as the core competency and the reliability of the outsourcing partner, are the characteristics of a successful outsourcing component. Many risks are involved to achieve short-term cost cutting exercises at one end of the scale or overambitious multiprocess schemes at the other. Some of the potential pitfalls of outsourcing can be identified by rigorous evaluation of proposed solutions. For processes optimization, outsourcing can be a valuable and rewarding tool, and the benefits can go well beyond those welcome bottom line cost savings, to deliver the best in class, creative business solutions that represent real value to the organization and its customers.

For a significant new project, some additional support may be required, but an increase in headcount may be out of the question. By outsourcing management and reporting, tedious manual administration can be saved and staff time freed up. An outsourcing solution that is tailored, flexible, and provides additional competencies or infrastructure to the user can yield quite a few benefits.

Examples—In back office web-enabled solution, database management, calculations, and reporting can be handled by trained staff, while corporate staff can maintain information pertaining to participant details, margins, and charges online. The interaction between the outsourcing partners is made seamless by web technology, allowing full control over the process and the final result, thereby getting an improved and streamlined process.

Global cash management by a bank is a secure anywhere-to-anywhere payment process, and it cannot be replicated by individual corporations. All of a

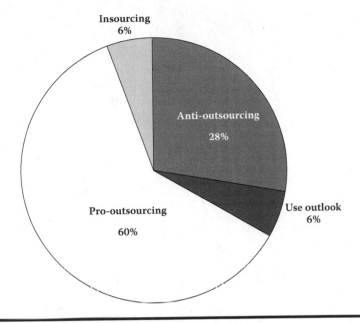

Figure 3.3   From a survey—for and against outsourcing.

company's payment needs to go through one central access point, one interface; then one file format can be delivered according to specific instructions, with the flexibility of host-to-host, or via computer, or web-enabled electronic banking services.

Reasons for Not Outsourcing—Companies may choose not to outsource for some of the following reasons:

1. Nature of business being such as not needing outsourcing
2. Lack of expertise with the vendor and no business advantage garnered
3. In-house performance and cost structure better versus when outsourced
4. Insufficient coordination, monitoring, and control
5. Ownership, security issues, and higher risks

Simple rules of game play, a formula for big wins.

As machines learn to leapfrog time, humans may become the disposables.

Chapter 4

What to Outsource?

Of archives that echo the passage of time.

Outsourcing Scope

Of extensible scope, upstream, downstream, and across.

The outsourcing range is expanding, with more and more functions coming within its ambit. It is estimated that more than one-third of new IT development of major U.S. companies is being done in other countries. *Finance, general accounting, accounts receivable, accounts payable, payroll, employee benefits, administration, recruiting, training, IT, and business process outsourcing (BPO) are some of the long list of functions that are outsourced.* Both strategic and back office operations are contracted/outsourced. While network infrastructure and telecom issues are being addressed by local players at such outsourcing destinations, local infrastructure such as roads, bridges, airports, and urban transportation which need governments action are often bottlenecks. To be an attractive outsourcing destination, these issues need to be tackled. Depending on the scope and risk of outsourced function, this may necessitate backup arrangements with other U.S. or foreign service providers in other geographic areas.

From global IT giants such as Unisys, IBM, and Syan down to smaller niche operations like Singapore-based call centers, outsourcer outsourcing insight and suppliers of outsourcing services vary dramatically. Different approaches taken in outsourcing are reflected in the supplier market. Outsourcing organizations need to strategically decide whether to use primarily one supplier vendor or identify each element that should be outsourced and then pick the respective (multiple) best of breed suppliers available. As financial institutions also seek more cost-effective

41

software development options, offshore outsourcing has gained tremendous importance. In this market, India has proved to be highly successful (e.g., Citibank has for many years operated its offshore software arm from India).

What to Outsource?

The many colors in a business mix.

Broadly, three types of projects/processes may be outsourced by organizations:

A. **Such core projects/processes that give the company strategic advantage when using outsourcing**. Niche suppliers with vast reserves of experience and knowledge may lead to reengineering of the project, thus creating a life of its own with greater revenue capability. Outsourcing may reengineer the entire way the project is done. Organizations no longer give on contract or outsource only noncore processes, but also essential ones like sales, customer care, help desk, or manufacturing, which are critical activities where goof-ups can prove expensive. Such is the case with intellect and creativity such as advertisement, public relations, research and development, and software development. These are extremely creative processes and call for tremendous reserves of knowledge and intellectual capabilities. Hence sufficient case-to-case basis study should be done in such cases. In various cases it may *not* be advisable to contract/outsource the core projects/processes. Investing in them is more prudent.

B. **Critical, noncore projects that are important but not competitive differentiators for the company**. As strategic thinkers and dealmakers, lateral leaders must have skills as well as the ability to anticipate resistance to change and to surmount it constructively. Companies outsource to get the costs down, but may sometimes miss giving due consideration to the process, and that is really where you get the breakthrough. That is where you get the leverage of somebody else's investment and creativity.

C. **Noncore, noncritical, repetitive processes that are required to make the business, systems, and environment work**. The company can retain control or transfer full or partial control to the vendor contractor. The buyer instructs the supplier on certain aspects of the project, and it is for the supplier to accomplish the results.

Activities to Outsource?

As means mutate to achieve the same end.

To improve focus, streamline operations, and eliminate inefficiencies, many companies have turned to outsourcing back office functions. Walmart is a prime example of successful outsourcing of IT and operations. Walmart focuses on customer service while its key suppliers manage goods on the shelves. Similarly, financial accounting and general ledger processes, data center operations, and tax reporting processes are outsourced by British Petroleum to service providers. Some of the advantages of outsourcing consist of transferring noncore activities to third parties to improve focus on core business, gain access to world-class expertise, mitigate risk, reduce cost, align with the current accounting standard, improve control, and gain access to better technology. In the mid-1980s, functions such as human resources/payroll, transaction processing, and routinized customer service turned to BPO services. There was quick growth in each of these BPO services, because smart application of technology and deep understanding of best practice operating processes created real operating and financial value for their clients.

Ravi Aron and Jitender Singh wrote in a paper, "IT outsourcing began with the outsourcing of data centers and data processing. . . . The most recent wave of outsourcing, one that is beginning to impact the nature of the modern firm itself, is the outsourcing of tasks that were once thought to lie at the core of the firm— the business processes." On a similar note Keith Zimmerman, managing director and chief strategy officer of Cambridge Integrated Services Group, said, "There are many companies, especially in the United States, that are coming to the conclusion that if you can't be a world-class provider of service, then the best option is to partner with someone who can provide that level of service." Cambridge Integrated Services Group is a subsidiary of Aon Corporation that provides claims processing and risk management outsourcing services. *Because technology and training are not a core competency, companies need to align with established leaders.* For claims processing, risk managers who self-insure have long turned to third-party administrators.

When an economy is booming, management is more concerned with growth than expense control. Risk managers in a recovering economy need partners that can handle routine transaction processing efficiently, as well as manage and reduce claim-related losses, because profits are down and worker's compensation health care costs are on the rise. Keith Zimmerman says, "As corporations have improved their own productivity, they look to service providers to demonstrate and deliver these improvements." Aron says, "As corporations standardized on a few enterprise-wide platforms, and with the availability of software tools that made it easy to port large data sets between dispersed information systems, the flow of data and information between geographically dispersed locations became a viable and nearly costless option." By the convergence on corporate computing platforms and advances in communications technology, information technology and business process outsourcing have leapfrogged forward. Managers have increasingly turned to outsourcing, aided with this technology to respond to the relentless pressures of global competition. From data transformation (e.g., data entry through customer interface services like customer support call centers) to problem resolution functions, where the outsourced worker decides whether or not a course of action is in consonance with the client's policies, outsourcing thus has moved up the knowledge continuum. Accounts payable functions and insurance claims processing are included in it. Over the past several decades, the claims management business model has changed very little, according to Zimmerman, and there remains a heavy reliance on the paper process.

As a result of interviews of numerous CFOs, a golden rule about outsourcing emerged: Any F&A (finance and accounting) decisions involving interpretation, policy setting, or commercial judgment are retained inside. Anything else is a potential outsourcing candidate. In other words, finance processes where defined inputs have a defined outcome are good candidates for outsourcing. The less appropriate ones are the processes requiring a significant degree of interpretation, analysis, or creative insight. In order to measure service and quality, the commercial relationship between an outsource provider and its client requires a degree of predictability over outcomes.

Depending on each client's organizational structure, culture, and the maturity of their operating model, outsourcing relationships vary in their defined objectives. To transform discrete areas such as accounts receivable or payroll at a lower cost, some companies look for a process specialist while other companies look for transformational capability at the organization-wide level. It is important to start with a baseline and a benchmark of current competencies in each process area. To provide objective and realistic views of what can be achieved, extensive benchmarking material is available from external specialists and advisors. From skill and ease of implementation to scale and complexity, CFOs consider a range before deciding which activities to outsource. Clear outsourcing candidates are the routine tasks associated with transaction processing along with the more technically demanding finance and accounting activities associated with general ledger maintenance, consolidation and statutory accounting, and management report preparation and interpretation, thereby allowing more time to focus on analysis, decision making, and influencing business organization. Commercial analysis and decision support are less commonly outsourced. It is important to minimize any breaks in the process, after identifying a process for outsourcing. Around each end-to-end process, clear performance measures should be established. For processes, vision should be developed for the future, taking advantage of what best practice research, benchmarking, studies, new technology, shared services, and outsourcing have to offer. Identification of core processes is important along with the processes that will provide competitive advantage. The client should be aware of the strengths and weaknesses of the provider along with the processes in which the provider can provide competitive advantage, economies of scale, and risk mitigation. In process scoping, one should go end to end, avoiding the creation of unnatural breaks in the process, and including significant organizational change, if necessary. The organization should be redefined for a new role after retaining the strategic, policy-setting, and commercial activities. To achieve high performance, the decision of what to outsource and what to insource (i.e., scoping) is fundamental. To maximize benefits, infuse new sills, build core competencies, and streamline business processes, senior executives should make the appropriate decision on what to outsource. It should be ensured that whatever solution is selected, whether in house or outsourcing, it should integrate with the existing systems, as well as with new technologies that are emerging.

BPO—What to Outsource?

The differing relative values of diverse flows.

Telemarketing and call centers have been set up by a host of international companies to outsource customer support and telemarketing services in an efficient manner at very low costs. Services offered by the supplier help in turning potential candidates into clients and these clients/customers into advocates. To build an enduring bond, focus is required that provides the value addition to maintain and grow client base. The staff of Indian suppliers are comfortable with English and are computer literate, with effective presentation and communication skills. State-of-art technology in BPOs consists of sophisticated integrated voice response system, automatic call distribution, and database server. Via an optic fiber link, direct links are provided by an earth station to a satellite that in turn connects to a foreign country. India has sufficient infrastructure, technology, resources, and people required to handle large-scale outsourcing needs. *A host of services are provided by Indian vendors/call centers including sales lead generation; direct-response television; management of customer services for banks, software development, and credit card sales; telecom services; self-augmentation services; continuity sales calls; knowledge management solutions; surveys and market research; message delivery; prevention calls; third-party verification; fraud detection; technical product support; cleaning and updating of database; record verification; outsourced technical help desk; and welcome and thank you calls apart from telemarketing products.*

A vertical market consists of an industry or a group of industries which market similar products and services using similar methods (e.g., transportation, banking, real estate, and insurance). Thus vertical marketing is one of the very important media by which service providers/suppliers can maintain the critical market share. The financial sector is one of the most technically savvy and aware industries, and in this age of fierce competition, the Internet is changing the dynamics by providing access to news information and real-time financial information to companies as well as customers.

Example—Outsourcing by Banks

Banks, a crucial component of the larger financial ecosystem.

Substantial changes occurred in the business environment in the last decade and a half. *To competitors, deregulation opened the most profitable segments to retail financial services while IT innovations extended production options to offer cost reductions to both new and existing banks.* Integration solutions were challenged by technology that gave existing and new competitors a new range of strategies based on sourcing and outsourcing, which redefined supply chains in respect to client capture, distribution, or asset securitization. In bank markets, there are theoretical issues and empirical work regarding outsourcing of IT-based business processes like transactions processing, information storage retrieval, and analysis. Innovation in banking was due to improved IT/informantion system (IS) capabilities, many of them developed outside the banking system. There have been attempts by many banks to use new technology to control the costs of processing transactions. Competition in bank markets is growing, and outsourcing of IT-based banking processes is increasing.

There has been a major influence on the growth of bank markets due to outsourcing capabilities and outsourcing decisions which have altered their strategic position. It is no wonder that banks are big outsourcing players.

When outsourcing is a part of a tailored solution to an underlying need, it is flexible enough to meet the requirement for close interaction, and where the outsourcing partner has particular competencies from which the corporation can benefit, then outsourcing can deliver value. Outsourcing is one tool of the trade, rather than an end in itself, and can lead to process optimization. Tangible value to the business is delivered through process optimization.

Example—Public Relations (PR) Function Outsourcing

To be or not to be: consider well.

Advantages of "in" sourced public relations (PR)—The advantages of an insourced public relations (PR) function result in personnel who are more knowledgeable about the value of PR. *Insourced PR is advisable where the nature of operations is business to business and not business to customer.* The number, size, and scope of the insourced analysts is usually limited. Confidentiality is maintained about the products and services and solutions of the organization. Financially the organization may be large.

Criteria for "out" sourcing PR—It is advantageous to outsource the PR function when the size and scope of the number of such analysts is considerable and the senior management views PR as another communication tactic in the overall marketing mix. *Outsourced PR is adviseble when the products, services, and solutions of the organization's business are commodity-like in nature; the market of the organization is business to customer in nature, not business to business; and the market is general rather than specific.* The financial and human resources available within the organization are limited, and knowledge about the value of PR is lacking within the organization.

Proper evaluation is critical for long-term success regardless of whether the PR function is to be insourced or outsourced. For success the desired outcomes should be stated in the official agreements. Compatibility must exist between the two parties, and the outcomes should be realistic, specific, and quantifiable. Examples may vary, such as, there is a x% increase in the customer acceptance of the products, services, and/or solutions of the organization; the brand awareness of the organization increases by x%; there is an increase in the number of products, services, and solution reviews of the organization by x%; the favorable products, services, and solutions reviews should be x in number; the key public perceives the organization as x, with the organization's objectives being consistent; the coverage of the organization by analysts increases by x%; the media favorability rating of the organization increases by x%; and the peers recognize the organization in a certain way.

Advantages of PR—The PR can only be a valuable resource when the organization's overall objectives are known and the PR's goals, strategies, and tactics fully support them regardless of whether it is insourced, outsourced, or hybrid. To attract new customers and build loyalty and retention and enhanced convenience, relationship-based products can package financial and nonfinancial services with value-added programs.

Example—End Customer Management through Customer Relationship Management (CRM) Solutions

"The customer is God."—*Gandhi*

Businesses are facing a constantly changing environment requiring an immediate and proactive adaptability in operations, customer relationship management, and back office processes, and the advent of the Internet and latest technologies have accentuated it. Customers are demanding fast and highly personalized services due to diminishing product and service offerings differentiation. An increasing gap is being seen between the business needs and the technology solutions available in the market because of the prevalence of standalone systems and the inability to integrate such systems. The interoperability issues are addressed by outsourcing, and suppliers/BPO companies integrate the disparate systems and provide centralized technology management and support, so that the expected return on investment (ROI) is realized on technology investments. To take care of issues like customer retention, account management, campaign management, and call center interactions, the implementation of customer relationship management (CRM) solutions is helpful and aids in devising strategies for increasing productivity, revenue, and customer satisfaction.

Customers now have more options to choose from—both products/services and suppliers—and therefore new ways have to be found and constant innovation is necessary to attract new customers. Organizations have to manage their businesses and seamlessly integrate the front end business processes with those that run at the back end, in the face of ever-increasing competition and challenges. The changing role that information technology is increasingly assuming in the world of business and the global economy at large is illustrated by business solutions such as CRM. Views will soon be adopted by society that will perceive technology as a merging of products and services that seamlessly enable new approaches to business activities and redefine how people work and interact with each other. E-business, supply-chain management, enterprise relationship management, and customer relationship management are some of the excellent examples of this trend.

Example—Corporate Receivables Outsourcing to Banks

Extending the financial chain, front and aft.

Approximately 20% of all business-to-business payments are outsourced by corporate customers to a bank for receivables management. The intense pressures to reduce costs and facilitate straight-through processing to enable improved cash flow, streamlined information capture, easier regulatory compliance, and enhanced corporate responsiveness and client service are the driving forces behind this initiative. Cost savings of 20% to 50% can be achieved by strategic outsourcing of receivables management, and depending on the industry the returns can be impressive. Substantial costs associated with reconciling lockbox transactions are reined in by outsourcing receivables services, because invoice processing costs if carried out internally within the organization have risen by about 35% to 40% in the last couple of years. Bank lockbox providers offer receivables services like automated capture of receivables and customer information such as invoice data, demographic information on remittance coupons, or requests for more information. Receivables solutions are provided by more banks now, especially designed for the unique needs of specific vertical markets. The list is topped by health claims, and capturing of data at a much more detailed level at the lockbox not only gives health care firms better insight into their receivables but also streamlines reconciliation, billing, and patient care. Regardless of whether the lockbox provider was the original recipient of electronic payment, the paper-based and electronic payment streams are consolidated. Receivables solutions now play a larger role in lockbox processing portfolios offered by major cash management banks.

Receivables services provide increased control and visibility, and this is one of the biggest benefits of corporate billers. *A corporate biller can do data mining, drill down into the information, access more meaningful reports, and electronically monitor what is going on with its financial supply chain and even with its partners and clients.* Expanded receivables capabilities give banks an opportunity to grow fee income from an otherwise mature product line. It becomes more difficult for the client to change the lockbox provider as an electronic tether is created between the bank and its customers. Bank lockbox is kept vital and viable by receivables functions. At most companies, with accounts receivable being the largest current asset on the balance sheet, according to the Institute of Management and Administration, it is no surprise that corporate billers are paying close attention. Financial executives get a clear picture of the financial life cycle and an overview of receivables regardless of department, location, or payment type.

Aided by such advances in technology, strategically minded banks are finding new ways to help boost their customer's bottom line and add value to their lockbox processing services. Banking managers are being motivated by this to outsource receivables. Greatly expanded receivables services from cash management are the result. Increasing cash flow and strengthening the bottom line is as good as it gets, as return on investment goes, particularly when it is the corporate finance department that spearheaded the initiative. Many of these corporations are finding out that their bank lockbox provider is rolling out receivables services, providing a single source for outsourced financial supply chain management. Many of these receivables solutions enable information capture and management, which lightens the load of meeting onerous financial reporting regulations. Some market penetration is enjoyed by outsourced receivables and it is not new.

Much needed help is provided by the information capture and delivery capabilities that are built into the next generation lockbox processing systems. Automation of receivables matching is carried out by integrating them with accounting applications. This accelerates processing remote check capture and/ or electronic conversion of payments received outside of a lockbox or the normal receivables process. For handling industry-specific receivables, customized business rules exist such as the processing of explanation of benefits (EOB) in the health care profession.

For tracking deposits from multiple departments, reconcilement, electronic bill presentment and payment (e-bills), order processing, and collection, the images are made more usable by using color scanning of checks and documents. Such images more closely replicate the original paper-based receivables. To eliminate the so-called information float, the delay in accessing data, companies can outsource services whether it is for data capture, payables, electronic payments, or other accounts receivable (A/R) functions. Real-time information can be received by companies from invoices that can be integrated into their enterprise resource planning (ERP) and customer relationship management (CRM) systems or fed into industry-specific solutions that apply logic on how receivables should be handled. Companies can use receivables data to learn more about their customers, to improve cash forecasting, or negotiate better contract terms. The digital mailroom where incoming mail, including receivables, is digitally scanned and routed electronically is regarded as strategically important by 64% of multinational companies according to a survey. There are less quantifiable benefits, such as senior management spending less time chasing payment exceptions. On nearly every department of a corporation, the A/R exceptions have a negative effect. These exceptions can adversely affect operations, suppliers, inventory turns, trade credit, borrowing costs, and day's sales outstanding, with resolutions taking up to four months. The receivables solutions offered by banks provide information capture that can help speed the resolution of exceptions and plug the resource drain they cause.

Example—BPO Outsourcing of Sales Tax Compliance

Those must-do bits that would be best done by someone else.

In a challenging and an ever-changing environment, today's businesses operate with pressures of staff turnover, merger and acquisition activity, new markets and jurisdictions, cost cutting, and Sarbanes–Oxley compliance. Disruptions like these put strain on mandatory tax compliance processes that require quick reaction, continuous investment, and ongoing maintenance. For most finance and tax executives, sales tax compliance is a distraction. It is a natural candidate for outsourcing, given the pass-through nature of these taxes and the fact that the compliance function is largely backward versus forward looking. Rather than administrative compliance process, given a choice, the CFO or VP of tax would typically focus their personnel on tax planning, audit management, tax matrix management, and other forward-looking functions. *Sales and transaction tax personnel, all too often, spend a disproportionate share of their time focused on the administrative compliance process and on work that is inherently not value creating.* A company can focus on broader business issues, and by engaging a sales tax compliance service provider, an outside industry expert attends to operational and administrative details.

It should be evaluated how sales and tax compliance pays and the extent to which it either creates or reduces value. The single most compelling reason, for many businesses, for engaging a tax compliance service is that operational and administrative issues are siphoning off huge amounts of resources and management attention. Sales and use tax compliance is a recurring, data-intensive and highly administrative function. A consistent application of resources that has both sales and use tax domain expertise and substantial administrative capacity is required by the process. By outsourcing the back office administrative function of sales tax compliance, many financial and tax executives are refocusing and redeploying their valuable tax personnel. The nature of the work performed in their departments comes to focus when finance and tax executives survey their operations and consider how their resources are allocated and deployed.

Companies are subject to a very large array of sales and tax rules and regulations from many individual jurisdictions. Focus on the company's strategic intent is distracted as a result of managing day-to-day issues resulting from compliance, and managers quickly lose sight of the big picture, often to the detriment of other more important tax finance functions. A company's highly skilled tax personnel should be focused on the areas of the tax process where they add the most value and strip out the most risk. Tax determination and matrix management are key areas on the front end, where tax professionals should focus their time to ensure the correct tax is calculated and collected. Tax professionals on the back end should spend their time ensuring that the reconciliation process is complete, analyzing their taxes to search for tax minimization or tax savings opportunities, and responding to audits.

Example—BPO—Outsourcing Support Operations

The ability to respond, day or night.

The importance of customer support is increasing in today's business environment. Other than price and quality, customers have several options to choose from, and the support and treatment received from a company is a key factor which attracts new customers to it and retains the loyalty of the existing ones. One aspect of customer support is catering to general customer complaints and questions, but what about the technical problems of the product or service? To deliver high value to customers, it requires a dedicated and experienced team which will work around the clock as support. Such teams need to be officially given their due recognition. Outsourcing support work enables the outsourcer to focus on core processes without sacrificing customer support, by letting a professional and dedicated team devote their energy and expertise to providing support services. This not only gives a boost to the customer satisfaction rate, but also proves financially profitable to the company. With its renowned progress in the field of information technology and being one of the most popular outsourcing destinations in the world, it makes sense to outsource business processes to India. High-quality support to customers at optimal costs is provided by the Indian service providers. *With advanced technologies for knowledge management and automated support, the solutions integrate 24/7 "personalized" support services.* The support agents are customer friendly, motivated, skilled in communication and etiquette, certified, experts in multiple technologies, and experienced to provide solutions. Outsourcing support services result in domain knowledge and shorter lead times, customer satisfaction, learnability, operational efficiencies, lower risk, and cost savings. It results in improved operational efficiencies and customer satisfaction as the service providers' expertise spans across products in the desktop, Internet, server, and networking domains.

Example—Banking Operations Outsourcing

The financial nerve center of the institution.

In the case of banking partners, consider those processes that financial officers are routinely encouraged to outsource, such as accounts payable/receivable, reconciliation processing, or liquidity management. Banks must always remain in overall control. They are actively involved in arranging funds for payment runs, providing data for transaction matching, dealing with exceptions and queries, or managing account structures, intercompany loan rules, etc. Real value is delivered, with the close working between the financial corporation and the processing partner making use of a robust solution.

Among finance professionals, it is not surprising that outsourcing is a topic of fierce debate. Many financial institutions hesitate to outsource. The reason is that an important aspect of a bank's role is the control of processes (e.g., financial collections), which directly affect the financial health of the organization. The first response to the outsourcing proposition is the fear of losing control to a third party. Banks are justifiably cautious because of the hype that presents outsourcing as a ready-to-go panacea for every area. Another reason is that, as of now, there is little appetite for large-scale, complex projects of the sort that promise high rewards but might prove hard to measure and which could take years to achieve. In the current climate, projects with clear and near payback are more likely to get approved. Outsourcing may sometimes occur only for the relatively easy parts of a process life cycle. On 70% of a given process run, it may be possible to get efficiencies of scale, but if that leaves a costly and difficult manual job to do on the remaining 30%, then the final value achieved by such an outsourcing exercise can be minimal.

Example—Tax Process Outsourcing

Helping stay in line with the law.

Consider a noncore function like tax, in which the provider is seen as an integral part of the tax function, acting as the buyer's tax eyes and ears on a day-to-day basis in much the same way as the in-house function would have previously operated, thus forming a strategic alliance. The vast resources available with the provider leverage the value of the outsourced process and benefit the buyer.

Miscellaneous Examples

Options, almost as many as can be imagined.

It may be advantageous to outsource in areas like disaster prevention and recovery, network and infrastructure monitoring, backup system architecture and policies, Spam control, wide-area networking, service pack upgrades, level 2 network support (backup to internal IT staff), remote-access solutions, IT staff monitoring,

Internet security (firewalls, security audits, penetration testing, monitoring), group-ware (exchange/group wise) upgrades, conversion, and migrations, server operating system migrations, and strategic technology planning.

Some additional miscellaneous examples of projects which are outsourced by companies:

A. Projects associated with suppliers (e.g., supply chain management)
B. Projects/processes associated with customers (e.g., sales, marketing, and customer support)
C. Productions projects (e.g., R&D and contract manufacturing)
D. Support projects (e.g., finance and human relations)

As trends rise and perish in the sands of time.

Chapter 5

Outsourcing to India

Brand, so important yet so much less understood.

Asian Economy

As the globe shrinks into a virtual multidimensional village.

Asia Pacific is clearly the region on the financial rise. Over the last several years, the region has been riding economic peaks and valleys, with some national economies prospering while others struggled, and the dominant players one year were not necessarily so the next. Everywhere around the globe uncertainty rules along with complexity. The success of any company requires skillful operation and close attention as in a multicountry, multilanguage, multicurrency, and multitax environment. It is an evolving experience to learn to grow profitably. *The Asia Pacific region, with about 60% of the world's population, is the area where countries currently enjoy some of the fastest economic growth in the world.* The gross domestic product in China alone rose 10% over the last decade, and South Korea's gross domestic product was up 6% compared with 3% in the United States. Boundless opportunities are offered by markets in Asia Pacific, and companies from every industry are in energetic pursuit. It is not hard to figure the reasons behind the outsourcing trend, for cost cutting and core business focus are at the top of companies' agendas. Advanced process, economies of scale, leading-edge technology, and expertise come with outsourcing, and companies become free to focus aggressively on their core business.

Brief History of Outsourcing in India

The distances physical, virtual, and those in the mind.

During the early years of outsourcing in India, between 1996 and 2000, the driving factors were pioneers and size. High-quality infrastructure supporting large operations were built, and operational cultures previously seen only in Western shared service centers were developed. Precedent was set for working in shifts for both men and women, and it was demonstrated by the pioneers that the major stakeholders and regulators in the United States and the United Kingdom would not prevent work from being outsourced. British Airways, American Express (AMEX), and General Electric (GE) formed this list of pioneers.

The second outsourcing phase in India, between 2000 and 2002, was characterized by strategy factors and increasing adopters. New operations were started by companies as part of strategic initiatives.

Example—The global insurance companies became interested in building offshore processing units in India and hoped to position themselves in the domestic market, because the Indian government was looking at opening the Indian insurance market to partial foreign competition. At this stage though the supply market was still considered immature, yet risk profiles improved dramatically, and the advantage of size was demonstrated by the early risk takers. Perceived risks were dealt with such as managing of media in home market, moving of highly skilled work offshore, and the complex issue of how to apply the European Data Protection Act. Credibility of business model was reinforced. AXA, Ford, HSBC, and Citibank are some of the companies that entered the market during this phase.

The third phase of outsourcing in India was between 2003 and 2008, and the driving factors were competition and bandwagon. Many obstacles were overcome, and it was shown that public relations risks of moving jobs offshore are manageable. U.K. and U.S. financial service regulators issued guidelines for outsourcing, supplier selection, and data protection. There was fear of rising labor costs because of the relatively high number of English-speaking graduates and the focus of the Indian government on education as a way to increase the Indian middle class size. Competitive disadvantage was realized by companies who did not outsource. The number and quality of credible suppliers have increased dramatically, with a large percentage of players in the financial services sector, and the risks are manageable. Increasing liberalization of the Indian telecommunications industry has led to a decline in data communication costs.

Third-party service providers, multinational corporations (MNCs), and the outsourcing vendors have been expanding their capacities with captive units which account for 65% to 70% of their total capacity.

Where to Outsource? SWOT Analysis of Outsourcing to India

Strengths, as per SWOT (strengths, weaknesses, opportunities, and threats) analysis of the Indian information technology enabled service (ITES) sector, consist of around-the-clock advantage for Western companies, due to the huge highly skilled workforce, fluency in English, cheaper costs, efficient services with low response time, dedicated workforce aiming at making a long-term career in outsourcing, lower attrition rates compared to the West, and compatible time zone difference with the West. Wage differences of up to 70% to 80% compared to Western counterparts exist according to the National Association of Software and Service Companies (NASSCOM).

Weaknesses of the Indian ITES sector, according to SWOT analysis, consist of higher costs of network infrastructure and telecom compared to the United States, a somewhat rising attrition rate with IT/ITES workers jumping jobs or quitting to pursue higher education, and a tendency of not pursuing ITES as a long-term profession.

Opportunities, as per SWOT analysis, consist of India being branded as a high-quality, low-cost IT/ITES destination. To assuage issues and concerns of Western governments, IT/ITES companies should work closely with them and with associations like NASSCOM to portray India as the most favored destination globally.

Threats, according to SWOT analysis, include China, Philippines, and South Africa, among other IT/ITES destinations, which could have an edge on the cost factor. Also, anti-outsourcing legislation exists in New Jersey, with more U.S. states such as Connecticut, Missouri, and Wisconsin planning legislation against outsourcing. There have been some minor protests against outsourcing of work to Indian business process outsourcing (BPO) companies by British Telecom workers.

Benefits of Outsourcing to India

As players differentiate on positioning, value, cost, and time.

To stay ahead Indian companies are ensuring stable quality systems, and continuous technology improvements, and are rapidly scaling up to match or surpass international quality standards. High quality and cost signify outsourcing to India now. An entirely different trend now prevails in the Indian BPO, which previously relied primarily on its cost effectiveness to attract customers. The new buzzword is quality and is dominating business processes and services like never before. Specialized quality departments responsible for ensuring accurate, reliable services to customers are a part of 90% of the ITES–BPO companies. Standards of quality that are at par with, if not superior to, their counterparts abroad are ensured by Indian call centers.

According to NASSCOM, an India-based ITES–BPO center in the banking and financial service sector usually performs better than a U.K.- or U.S.-based facility on significant factors such as the number of correct transactions/total number of transactions per hour and the average speed of answer. There is more sensitivity to incorporate internationally accepted standards of quality control in ITES/BPO industries. More than half of Indian companies have implemented varied levels of ISO (the International Organization of Standardization, which conceives sets of quality management standards) such as ISO 9002, ISO 9001, ISO 9001:9002, and ISO 9001:2001, according to a NASSCOM survey. At least 45% of Indian service providers have certifications like Six Sigma (a disciplined, statistical quality control method that measures the number of defects compared to the opportunities to make defects) and CMMI (Capability Maturity Model Integration—which is a process improvement method that provides a set of best practices that address productivity, performance, costs, and customer satisfaction), according to the survey. Quality standards are being upgraded by many organizations from ISO 9000 to the new ISO 9000:2000 and from the Capability Maturity Model (CMM) framework to the new CMMI framework.

The Benefits, at a Glance

- India has a pool of talent and has the second largest English-speaking population with computer knowledge in the world after the United States.
- The technology in India is state of the art.
- The policies of the government of India are favorable.
- IT industry is on the front foot and growing at a steady pace, and contracting or outsourcing form an important part of the ITES industry.
- Outsourcing to India improves competitiveness and flexibility.
- Outsourcing to India improves customer satisfaction and access to relevant skills and expertise.
- Outsourcing to India improves credibility and image, increases the operational efficiency, and serves large markets.
- Outsourcing to India improves process performance and monitors organizational activities better.
- High responsibility taking by efficient Indian vendors exists.
- Contracts can be enforced in letter and spirit in India.
- Outsourcing to India reaps significant reduction in costs over an optimal operational period.
- Demand spikes are manageable when outsourcing to enabled Indian vendors who can predict periodic fluctuations.
- Indian vendors can be changed, if needed.
- Outsourcing buyer can retain full or part control, or vest control with the Indian vendor, as the case may demand.

- Outsourcing to India can take off with little or no change in organizational culture.
- The India advantage provides superior market leverage.
- Outsourcing to India allows high control over outcomes consistently.
- Geographically siloing is enabled whereby different suppliers may be located in different locations.
- Capabilities of outsourcing organization are enhanced due to expert, versatile, and flexible pool of Indian suppliers.
- Sufficient measures for mitigation of risk exist with Indian vendors.
- Outsourcing organizations reap proficient managerial and technical skills, when outsourcing to India.
- Time zone advantage—India time being 12 hours ahead of U.S. leads to significant operational benefits.
- India ranks high in areas such as qualification, capabilities, quality of work, linguistic capabilities, and work ethics and is thus ahead of competitors such as Singapore, Hong Kong, China, Philippines, Mexico, Ireland, Australia, and Holland.

India—Preferred BPO Destination

Established Indian suppliers handle services proficiently because they are equipped with sufficient field experience and resources needed to manage a range of services. Indian call centers serve as full-time departments regardless of BPO products or services. *Calls are taken around the clock, even during peak call overflow times with add-on services like payment/credit card processing, order fulfillment, and a wide range of voice mail options.* Web support is provided wherein customer support representatives respond to customer issues raised over the Internet. Smaller businesses that are not large enough for a 24-hour BPO help desk are also outsourced. For example, survey calls are taken by professional customer support representatives, achieving high survey response and completion rates. Activities like registrations, membership, and subscription renewals are handled seamlessly along with screening of applicants or callers and making or changing appointments, etc.

Top Outsourcing Cities in India

Cities that become centers of a specialized craft, prevalent en masse.

In 2008, six Indian cities made it to the list of the "top outsourcing destinations." In spite of the financial turmoil, India remains a preferred outsourcing destination. *Six out of the top eight "global outsourcing cities" are from India—Bangalore, Chennai, Delhi (National Capital Region), Hyderabad, Mumbai, and Pune (Chennai,*

Hyderabad, and Pune being new entrants), according to a Cyber Media's global services study and Tholons advisory. The other two cities are Dublin (Ireland) and Makati City (the Philippines). Additionally, from 3 in 2007, India's representation in the top 50 "emerging" global outsourcing cities has increased to 4 in 2008. The latest addition to the list is Jaipur, while the other three cities in the list include Kolkata, Chandigarh, and Coimbatore. The maximum number, 19 out of the top 50 cities, are located in Asia, and 13 in Central and Eastern Europe. Apart from tier-1 Asian cities, outsourcing centers are being set up in many tier-2 and tier-3 cities. Tradeoffs between cost benefits and complexity of services offered by cities exist. For instance, Ho Chi Minh City and Delhi NCR provide high-end, complex functions, but at a cost that is not necessarily low. Avinash Vashishtha, CEO, of Tholons says, "Clients' focus on identifying outsourcing locations has driven the emergence of 'centers of excellence.' Rise of Manila, National Capital Region—an agglomeration of 16 adjacent cities—is an example. Though less than 1/13th of India's population, its BPO revenues are already half as large as India's BPO revenues."

Indian Vendors' Growth Challenges

Managing to grow and growing to manage.

Indian vendors are using several methods like tie-ups with existing players, acquisitions, investing in research and development, and leveraging industry best practices in order to expand and move up the value chain. In the highly competitive market, profits are shrinking, and players are looking for newer revenue sources and opportunities to keep cash flowing in. Service level agreements have become more stringent, and sales cycles are stretching far in international deals. *Because many clients prefer size, it is therefore critical for vendors to be able to scale up quickly.* Large vendors command a premium price in the market, along with economies of scale which help margins. There is a significant impact on profitability if the vendor has the ability to improve the shift factor. Macroeconomic risks like currency fluctuations and business-specific risks like increase in performance metrics should be covered. Lengthening of sales cycle and backlash in some foreign countries has made this more relevant. Growth aspirations and workforce attrition are issues that need to be addressed. Stress caused by odd hours at jobs causes attrition, thereby increasing recruitment and training costs. A clear career progression path and a comprehensive human resource policy need to be spelled out by service providers, so that the workforce sees a long-term career in the field. Incentives for work done should be made more attractive by including cash for performance, gift vouchers, cash for working on national holidays and festivals, along with schemes and awards to confer recognition. Another issue is of plummeting revenues, with many banks struggling to secure revenue growth in the face of a weak economic scenario and intensifying competition.

Dispersing location risk is one reason why Indian companies are spreading geographically, and non-English operations is another. In the event of disruption in India, BPO clients increasingly insist on disaster recovery backups or mirror sites from which operations can continue uninterrupted. Tie-ups for disaster management are needed even for those who do not have their own centers in other places. It provides backup and comfort level to existing and potential customers.

Example—GE

In the offshore outsourcing arena, GE is a pioneer. A new rule that governed GE's offshore actions was introduced in the early 1990s by Jack Welch, the former CEO of GE. It is called the 70:70:70 rule. Welch mandated that 70% of GE's work would be outsourced, and this was informed to the GE employees by an e-mail. Out of this, 70% of the work would be completed from offshore development centers, and out of this about 70% would be sent to India, resulting in about 30% of GE's work being outsourced to India.

Thirty different business units in the United States have delivered more than 450 processes by GE Capital International Services (GECIS), which employs more than 12,000 people. Sites in India where it operates include Gurgaon, Hyderabad, Bangalore, and Jaipur.

The example of GECIS changed the mindset of companies which used to think that foreign work lacked quality and was hard to supervise. Offshoring can save companies up to 50% in operational expenses compared to a U.S. call center, so low cost is the most obvious benefit of offshoring. Besides cost, there is more to why call centers are being set up in other countries such as India. Complementary time zones, low employee turnover, and an educated English-speaking labor pool all make offshoring attractive. The geographical location of India lends itself to a 24/7 operation, and India is the home to the largest educated English-speaking population in the world. About a 12-hour time zone difference exists between the United States and India. A highly motivated workforce is another positive feature of India, whereas the U.S. call centers often experience low morale and a very high turnover, approximately 40% to 70% annually. It becomes difficult to maintain quality service at low cost, considering the time and costs associated with training new agents. Indian call centers have an average turnover rate of approximately 5%.

The back office operations for GE capital's businesses, GE Capital International Services (GECIS), which was set up in 1997, include service offerings like enterprise resource planning (ERP), oracle database consulting, IT help desks, knowledge services, software solutions, analytics, data mining and modeling, e-learning, customer contact centers, and remote network monitoring.

Example—Awards to Indian BPOs

An award—the feeling lingers for life.

The Indiatimes' Company of the Year Award for 2008 was won by Infosys BPO, while its head, Amitabh Chaudhary, was awarded as the CEO of the Year for elevating the company to new heights. Mr. Chaudhary said, "Getting the award brings a sense of personal achievement, but its my entire team I attribute this success to. Infosys BPO has become much more globally present company in every sphere of world in the last three years. But we are looking at scaling up global workforce, becoming a trusted transformation player, and offering more platforms (not just FTE based) over the next three years."

India's largest BPO, Genpact, bagged the most admired company to work for award.

At the Indiatimes BPO Industry Awards 2008, organized in the capital Delhi, the Professional Excellence Award for 2008 went to Mumbai-based BPO Firstsource process excellence executive vice president (EVP) Chandeep Singh. According to a company peer, Chandeep Singh has been instrumental in transforming the quality process. "We now try to make operations people talk about quality. We are training them in process excellence to drive up the bottom line and sales. We have deputed a black belt at each of our seven overseas buyout locations acquired in the last seven years," Mr. Singh adds.

Meanwhile S. V. Ramanna, chief technology officer (CTO) at Genpact, bagged the Operational Excellence and Quality Award. Only companies with goal fulfillment capabilities and improved performance track records qualify for the operational excellence and quality award. HCL BPO got the Indiatimes BPO technology award.

There were many competitors for the 2008 BPO Innovator of the Year Award, such as Citigroup Global Services, which was bought by TCS recently for $505 million, and Firstsource, the Mumbai-based BPO which has operations across the United States, United Kingdom, Argentina, and the Philippines. But the award went to Adventity, a knowledge process outsourcing (KPO) company specializing in transaction processing services across the hospitality, banking, and airline industries.

Of the CEOs, Suhale Kapoor, executive vice president and cofounder of Absolute Data is an exception. He was ecstatic after Absolute Data bagged the 2008 Indiatimes BPO Award for Emerging Company of the Year. The company is headquartered in California and provides consulting-oriented advanced analytics and market research services to organizations globally. The KPO has an India delivery center in New Delhi. Says Suhale Kapoor, "We are delighted to receive the award. In the long run, both BPO and KPO services will remain in vogue. But we decided to venture into KPO services like market research analytics as they are difficult to replicate. Moreover it is much more rewarding. An analytical process like market research can fetch anywhere between $20 to $50 per hour billing rate compared to $10 per hour for typical voice-based BPO services. Year on year we have been growing at 135% despite slowdown."

Potential Countries for Outsourcing

As external players try to jump onto the speeding bandwagon.

Philippines, Canada, Ireland, Brazil, Mexico, China, and South Africa are some of the potential countries for setting up BPO centers. With the aim of tapping non-English–speaking markets, players are also setting up shops abroad, although currently English-speaking areas account for 90% of the industry's export revenue. A Spanish-language call center was set up in Tijuana in Mexico by Bangalore-based Msource, because Spanish-speaking skills are 35% to 40% cheaper there than in the United States. Local players of other countries are entering into a tie-up with companies who do not have their centers located abroad. To gain advantages of cheaper resources and language proficiency, operations are set up in one country to provide services to another country. For smooth operations and coverage, the company wanting to start its operations in a third country has to consider operational aspects and strategic factors.

In the Philippines attrition is low, and the country is suitable for voice work because U.S. market understanding exists. However, the talent pool is small, and it is more expensive than India for outsourcing. Canada, Australia, Ireland, and South Africa understand the U.S. market, have high-end skills and their time zone is similar to Europe. This translates into about 25% cost savings and is suitable for niche work. The disadvantages are a shortage of skills and high costs. China is a low-cost destination, but does not have the required English capability. Russia and Ukraine have technology skills but poor infrastructure and have corruption and language problems. The Czech Republic and Hungary have European language skills but small talent pools with high costs. Mexico is about 30% cheaper than the United States and has Spanish skills but is suitable only for low-end jobs. The Philippines has an excellent telecom infrastructure, and cost savings are 30% to 50% compared to U.S. operations, but wages are nearly 12% more than in India. The Philippines' attrition rate is low, labor costs are high, and population is less. There are plenty of accountants trained in U.S. accounting in the Philippines. Nearly all facilities have fewer than 1,000 people, because ramping up is a problem, but the country is considered one of the top destinations for information and communication technology (ICT) services. Accounting, contact center services, human resource administration, claims administration, and logistics are some of the noncore yet critical backroom operations that are outsourced to Philippines because the pool of superior talent and excellent telecommunication infrastructure facilitate outsourcing of such services.

India versus Other Outsourcing Destinations

Of bridging the geographical divide.

India is one of the most favored destinations for contracting/outsourcing projects and services, with the country poised to become a price setter globally. Policies and government investments are favorable, providing impetus to the outsourcing process, and according to NASSCOM almost every Fortune 100 company wants to outsource its IT services to India, with more than half of Fortune 500 companies having already done it. A key advantage with India is that, for more than 60 years now, it has remained a stable and a secular democracy without major social, economic, and political upheavals. World-class institutions and infrastructure make India comparable with any developed country in the world. There has been reduction of red tape and simplification of rules to promote business. There has been quantum improvement in technical, telecommunication, and technological infrastructure, and India's GDP has grown at an average rate of 5% to 7% in the last ten years, making it one of the better economic performers in the world. Inflation is under control, and purchasing power parity is relatively high, being the fourth largest in the world. Considerable resources are devoted to technical and scientific research, with India having a very vast telecom network. One of the greatest contributing factors that has enabled India to continuously succeed first in IT and then in ITES services is the large and trained pool of English-speaking people. There are large number of schools, colleges, universities, and institutions where the medium of instruction is English. Graduates and postgraduates complete their entire education being instructed in English, though there could be slight variations in accent, pronunciation, and spellings, which can be remedied through training. Also there is no dearth of qualified technical personnel with commendable skills, apart from the cost advantage gained from outsourcing to India. Multiple back office functions in India are carried out by a leading international airline company, and it is said to be saving about US $30 million per year in staff costs over and above the productivity levels. Payable and reconciliation services are provided by AMEX's center in India to its businesses globally.

The geographical location of India, among other factors, has also favored outsourcing, because companies can provide around-the-clock services to their customers because India is about 12 hours ahead of U.S. time. India has turned out to be a top choice for outsourcing for companies wishing to contract/outsource globally, according to a Golobal Institute McKinsey analysis. Among others the reasons for this include the affordable salary scales, huge pool of technically talented personnel, knowledge and quality aspects, and command over English as a language both written and spoken. Government policies have been favorable, with excellent infrastructure, political and economic stability, bandwidth and electricity availability, and the difference in time zones. Red tape and bureaucratic bottlenecks have been overcome by the government to promote outsourcing, state-of-the-art technology is available, and the country has made giant strides in technical advancement. The ability to adapt fast to changes has been proved by the IT industry, and there has been a great boost in the telecom sector with the entry of private players, thereby leading to improvement in quality and significant reduction in telecom costs. *The Indian government has offered tax incentives and tax-free zones to IT/ITES services suppliers.* Profits derived from export/transmission of software outside India or provision of technical services outside India in connection with development/ production of computer software are exempt from tax up to a specified limit according to the provisions of section 80HHE of the Indian Income Tax Act, 1961. Central and many state governments have worked at an excellent pace to ensure that various hurdles are eradicated and rules simplified to promote outsourcing.

Outsourcing, including software development, maintenance, drug recovery process services, integrated circuit design, and BPO are India's outsourcing strengths. Particularly regarding BPO services, English is a strong point because it is a primary language in India. Due to availability of a skilled workforce, communications infrastructure, and business-friendly environment, many U.S. companies have established operations in Gurgaon, Delhi, Noida, and Bangalore in India. For business, Bangalore has become an expensive place, along with employee mobility issues. Compared to other Indian cities, office lease, office and communications infrastructure, and personnel costs are higher in Bangalore, whereas Pune, Chennai, and Hyderabad have lower costs, less mobile workforce, and less employee competition, thus prompting U.S. companies to increasingly consider establishing operations there.

Canada and Ireland are similar to the United States in terms of language, people, and culture and hence preferred outsourcing destinations too. Economic and political risks are low, and infrastructure is good, but the labor force of Ireland is expensive and small. Compared to India, salaries in Canada are higher, but the salaries and real estate prices in Canada are lower than those in the United States. Cost savings of U.S. firms outsourcing to Canada is about 25% over a period of time, as against getting it done within the United States. For smaller operations needing 200 to 300 people Canadian towns are well suited and are a viable option for businesses which require geographical proximity to the United States. The employee retention rate is superior in Canada.

Time zones of Mexico and Brazil are similar to the United States, in addition to geographical proximity. The countries, however, suffer from skills deficiency and lack English language proficiency, although labor costs are low. Operations like document management requiring U.S. proximity are done in Brazil or Mexico. Compared to Mexico, Brazil's strengths include huge investments in IT and telecom and a large, low-cost labor pool, whereas Spanish language skills is Mexico's forte. By outsourcing to Mexico, U.S. organizations save 25% to 40% costs, and to serve Spanish-speaking customers, AOL–Time Warner opened a branch there in

2002. Mexico is preferred for low-cost jobs requiring a low skill set like data entry because it lacks technical and mathematical skills.

Companies with high-volume work and transaction-based business processing are attracted to China. Its greatest strength is low-cost labor. Japanese and Asian language capabilities are provided by China, and Microsoft and HSBC have BPO centers there. English language is being pushed by the country in a big way in both schools and colleges.

Robust English-based education system, strong labor pool, and time zone compatible with Europe are some of the advantages that are causing South Africa to emerge as a hot BPO destination. As compared to Europe, costs in South Africa are about 25% lower, and Computer Science Corporation has set up a facility there, though skills are not easily available.

The world, a local village, abuzz.

Chapter 6

Vendor Selection

Some battles are fought over the airwaves.

Vendor Classifications

By day, by night, awake to the competing might.

Vendors' suppliers are commonly classified into the following three groups:

A. **Transaction suppliers**—*They handle a single process, can be paid per transaction, and may be used for small, simple projects, or business transactions.* Such vendors can carry out simple transactions, but complex projects are beyond their ability.

B. **Niche suppliers**—*They handle several projects/processes and can be paid on the basis of outcomes.* Niche suppliers are able to provide specific services. They have the expertise and the experience to meet the requirements of the buyer. Capability to understand issues pertaining to the project and training mechanisms exist to meet the service levels.

C. **Comprehensive suppliers**—They handle whole transactional, administrative, and technological aspects of projects and processes, increasing effectiveness by introducing best practices, technology enablers, and a skilled workforce. These suppliers are experts in their respective fields. *Customization and innovation are their hallmark.* They can comprehend buyer's requirements and predict performance and results based on previous experience. They constantly update technology so that the best can be delivered. A thorough review and analysis of performance on a regular basis is done, so that the performance goals that have been set are met. Benchmarks exist, and there is a continuous endeavor to achieve excellence. Buyers would not want to forego such suppliers who constantly strive to outperform.

The decision to outsource is of strategic importance, and an outsourcing organization with no experience entering into a new contract should first establish pilots. Signing a large-scale contract without prior experience can prove very costly, leading to an inflated budget, missed schedules, and in some cases irretrievable damage, bringing a bad name to the company. With the establishment of pilots, risk is greatly mitigated, and as experience is gained, the schedule can be accelerated. With experience comes speed, a byproduct of which is a reduced timeline.

There is no "one size fits all" approach to any contracting/outsourcing assignment. Nevertheless there are certain requisites for success, and consistency is one of them. There should be consistency between the agenda of the outsourcing buyer and the vendor supplier, and consistency should exist between the promises of the vendor and his ability to deliver. Competency is the next requisite, and the vendor should possess the skills succeed. Continuity, which is the next requisite, means that proper mechanisms should exist to ensure continuity in achieving desired results. Contract, the fourth requisite, should be resilient enough to deal with future changes and requirements.

Speed, often a byproduct of competence.

Vendor Identification, Evaluation, Competency, Selection, and Management

The various pieces that make up the offering mix.

The outsourcing phenomenon has stretched to previously untouched areas of business, and the rise of the outsourcing consultant has begun to help outsourcing buyers not only to make the decision but also to facilitate the choice of their provider with the appearance of a considerable number of new providers of outsourcing services. A skillful consultant helps in optimal identification and avoiding potential pitfalls.

For information/request for proposal, a draft should be made building selection criteria, prioritizing items, and defining critical functionality. For vendor selection, the client should narrow down to track records that match its criteria. Outsourcing should be segmented based on the business results desired, technology, and whether the applications are static or undergoing enhancements. *The Capability Maturity Model (CMM) of the vendor should be looked into carefully.* One's applications may not derive the quality and cost benefits CMM provides just because the provider is CMM level 5 assessed. Time and effort are needed. Within a specified period, the provider should have the ability to get one's application support to an appropriate level. All business users who will be impacted by change receive suitable communication.

How one wants to manage the provider should be clearly articulated along with the manner of handling problems and discrepancies. The least possible service the vendor can provide should be measured by referencing one's baseline. What constitutes a change should be spelled out, and who has the rights to intellectual property, code, and documentation should also be specified. Make sure you get a fixed-price contract if CMM is important to you. For your applications, without a fixed-price contract you can expect to receive few or no cost reductions or quality improvements over time.

The process of outsourcing may involve certain steps with respect to the supplier. After management has made a decision to outsource, the first step would be to identify a suitable set of vendors/suppliers. It is not just identifying a supplier but identifying the best supplier. The next step that goes hand in hand with supplier identification is supplier assessment. The supplier's experience, compatibility, focus, and skills are some of the factors that need to be kept in mind during evaluation. The staff involved in evaluation also need to be knowledgeable so that a proper assessment can be made. If trained staff does not exist on the payroll of the company, then professional service may be solicited so that proper assessment is made. Proper evaluation is of great importance, and it should not be underestimated. After completing this step the next logical step is the selection of the supplier. Once the supplier has been selected and the contract awarded, then steps in supplier management. There should be seamless exchange of information between the two parties. A mechanism of feedback and monitoring should exist. Regular analysis of the work on the project should be done so that schedules and timelines are met. The buyer should gain from the best practices of the supplier. The lessons learned should be documented. Along with maintaining a good relationship with the global supplier, it is necessary to have the same with intermediaries. If the contract proves mutually beneficial to both the buyer and the supplier, then it is their desire to have long-term relationships. If a supplier has bagged a contract from a buyer, it will strive to maintain the relationship so that any further contracts may also be awarded. Similarly, if the supplier turns out to be a supplier of choice by doing excellent work, then the buyer will desire to have a long-term relationship with the supplier and give more contracting assignments. Nevertheless, the strategy along with the length of the contract should clearly specify the conditions under which the relationship with the suppliers and the intermediaries will be severed or terminated. Although considerable time and effort go into supplier assessment, at times mistakes may occur in vendor selection. The supplier may not be able to meet the requirements, or there may be missed schedules, which may lead to inflated budgets. All this may deem it prudent to terminate the services of the supplier so that losses can be curtailed. Even if the supplier is very competent, some situations like political instability or acts of God (eg., earthquakes, hurricanes, etc.), may warrant that the contract be severed or redeployed elsewhere. Therefore any global contracting/outsourcing assignment should not be awarded in a hurry, and only after profound deliberation and consultation should the step be taken. Professional or third-party services should be solicited to arrive at a proper decision. Adequate time spent in selecting the right supplier for contracting saves time later and earns revenue for the company.

Before resorting to outsourcing, it is important to look into the nature of the service itself to determine if it is easy to outsource. With the limitation of interacting only over telephone and e-mail, it should be possible to conceptualize, define, and execute the service. In order to implement the service, people with specific skills and knowledge should be required. The skills required to implement the service should be possessed by the provider in the region in which the service is being outsourced. It should be possible to easily monitor the results of the service, and such service should be difficult to automate and manual human effort. The outsourcer should assess if the outsourcing vendor can meet these operations through the life cycle of the project.

In outsourcing, choosing the right partner is the foundation for success. Precise deliverables, specific metrics, and proven methodologies are some of the factors underlying its success, and this is a partnership for performance. The way we do it, apart from what we do, are some of the aspects on which the outsourcing partnership rests. Collaboration with clients and innovation in achieving goals contribute to outsourcing success. Data and analysis should be applied around basic processes to continually improve the client's business, making use of best practice technologies and innovating in every possible way. The quality of the relationship contributes to every successful outsourcing partnership as well. The ability to adapt to the client's needs through collaborative partnership should exist. An innovative cosourcing partnership is adopted by Thomas Cook and Accenture to transform and deliver high performance. At a significantly reduced risk, the multipurpose cosourcing approach delivers benefits and value fast. Credentials can be offered on the foundation of innovation and collaboration. Performance should be guaranteed by agreements, with metrics in place to help ensure that we deliver. From transaction processing to financial management and decision support, outsourcing capabilities should be offered to meet the full range of an organization's needs to ensure success. Services should be provided with the motive of reducing procurement costs, improving your working capital position, and enhancing cash management. To support executive decision making requires state-of-the-art performance and reporting. To have ongoing access to the latest financial applications and technologies, standard-setting architecture and applications must exist.

Some of the risks that could arise as a result of outsourcing to offshore locations are data insecurity, poor infrastructure, regional and political instability, and sufficient Western culture exposure, to name a few. Moreover, whenever a company sends its customer data to a third-party service provider, there is always a risk of the data being misused. All these concerns need to be addressed once the decision to outsource is taken and vendor selection phase has begun. India has been building and promoting its technology sector since the 1980s, and it is safe to travel and live across India. But enormous infrastructural improvements have been made by India and its cities like Gurgaon, Bangalore, Mumbai, and Hyderabad to become offshoring hubs.

Before outsourcing the competency and compatibility of the supplier should be properly evaluated. The capability of the supplier to execute the contract should be thoroughly judged. *The precontract phase should not be neglected but given proper consideration.* The precontract phase may include comprehending the client's requirements and assessing the capabilities to meet them, and this may involve exchanges of information between the buyer and the supplier.

Companies considering business process outsourcing should develop a sourcing strategy before drafting a request for proposal and evaluating vendors, according to Gartner, Inc. Metrics on the cost and efficiency of the current service delivery should be included in the strategy and clear goals to achieve through outsourcing. Firms in outsourcing need managers with capacities for lateral leadership—the ability to negotiate results "outward" across boundaries rather than issue orders "downward" through a hierarchy, according to Michael Useem.

As opportunities for using outsourcing in customer relationships expand, their potential value increases, but capturing that value becomes more challenging. No longer does the conventional wisdom about when and how to outsource apply, and the successful firms craft and manage their relationships in a way that fits their unique needs and circumstances. These firms first select a capable provider, and the type of relationship needed to accomplish the objectives is formed. Selecting the wrong provider can spell disaster. *By picking a provider based on low cost alone, success may not be achieved.* Objectives can be achieved more effectively by choosing a provider that meets the unique needs of the organization. The relationship should be carefully managed once an appropriate provider is selected. In contractual relationships, most firms already have well-established methods of working with service providers. How deep the relationship between the partners should be needs to be decided by the organization. Firms know how to set and assess minimum service levels and negotiate fee for service contracts. Additional management techniques can be used to substantially improve performance levels, such as inducing a competitive spirit among providers by pitting them against other providers or an organization's own internal center group. The director of a reputable firm said that, by outsourcing work to two separate providers and maintaining one center in house, the providers are kept sharp, and this way the service levels do not go down.

Competition among suppliers can cause the purchase price to plummet, and in order to bag the contract some suppliers may offer very competitive rates. Also strategies should be evolved to improve the quality benchmark. Choosing a skilled and experienced supplier leads to cycle time improvement. Attention should be paid to the kind of technology being used by the supplier, which can prove decisive. Use of outdated technology or technical snags can prove costly to both the parties.

When considering a service provider for selection for critical information or transaction processing functions, an institution should perform sufficient due diligence to satisfy itself of the service provider's competence technologically and stability financially and operationally to provide the expected service and meet any related commitments. The institution and the service provider should have a written contract which clearly specifies, at a level of detail commensurate with the scope and the risks of outsourced activity, all relevant terms and conditions, responsibilities, and liabilities of both parties. The institution should assess the terms and conditions to ensure that they are appropriate to the particular service being provided and result in an acceptable level of risk to the institution. The institution's legal counsel should review the contracts for outsourcing of critical functions. Internal control policies and procedures should be implemented by the service provider, including data security and contingency capabilities and other operational controls analogous to those that the institution would utilize if the activity were performed internally.

Vendor Competency Evaluation

The spirit and deed to reach out to the like-minded.

Some organizations are able to meet their requirements successfully by outsourcing a small part of the company's entire operation to one or more niche providers. Niche providers can be a viable choice, because outsourced processes can be performed quite independently by different organizations as long as an integrated system and applications are used. *It is difficult, if not impossible, for a niche provider to transform an entire life cycle's functions, if that is on the agenda.* All or most of the functions of AT&T and the U.S. Post Office have been outsourced to a solutions integrator. There is more dependence on the provider and more risk involved if the provider underperforms. By starting small, clients can mitigate the risk of outsourcing to a solutions integrator, and as trust builds and the client–vendor relationship matures, they can shift additional projects and processes to the provider. For example, organizations can start by outsourcing inbound calls only, and over time they can successfully add outbound sales calls, analytics, customer segmentation, and eventually parts of marketing program management.

Any contract/outsourcing assignment involves coordination, compatibility, capability, shared vision, and leadership. An effective mechanism of feedback and communication should be prevalent. A responsible person should be appointed to allay any doubts and apprehensions. Continuous innovation by the vendor will greatly enhance the quality and speed of the project, reduce costs, and generate more revenue. Innovation gives a vendor a competitive advantage and makes it the supplier of choice. Innovation gives rise to knowledge which can be applied to various fields and can be used to fulfill different requirements. One should first know where one stands and then should be able to identify the areas that need improvement. A measurement mechanism should be in place, so that one can gauge exactly where one stands and then locate the areas that need more attention. Continuous improvement should be the philosophy, even if one is head and shoulders above others. Improvements should be client centric and achieve buyer orientation.

Competent suppliers ensure that the cost and quality criteria are met if not exceeded and client data is protected.

In any global outsourcing assignment vendor selection forms a very important part. Adequate time and effort should be devoted to it so that it proves to be mutually beneficial. The request for proposal (RFP) process may employ several selection criteria, which among others may include the skills of the vendor. The consistency between the promises and the capability of the vendor to deliver the services should be assessed. In this regard those assessing the skills of the supplier should be knowledgeable and skilled. The quality and reliability of service offered by the vendor needs to be evaluated. The financial standing and the business presence of the vendor should be considered. A vendor with a sound financial stability and vast business presence can be banked upon more than one who is a new market player and may not be financially very sound. A solid financial standing enables the supplier to withstand the vicissitudes and slowdowns in business. They can cope with work, even during periods of recession. Lack of funds can, on the other hand, bring work to a standstill. The buyer should assess the global capabilities of the vendor in the area of the outsourcing contract. The kind of culture that exists in the supplier's organization, whether formal or informal, hierarchical or flat, etc., should be considered to assess compatibility. In case the contract is outsourced to the vendor, what will be the value added? This questions needs to be answered after thorough deliberation. The technology being used by the vendor, the technical skills of the staff, and the backup depth should be evaluated. The most important resource of an organization is its manpower, and the quality of manpower with the vendor determines the success of a contracting/outsourcing assignment. The price being offered by the vendor and the cost savings/revenue generation are important factors in the assessment of the vendor. Cost saving should not be the only factor on which a contract should be outsourced to a vendor, but it is a very vital factor when considering the decision to outsource. The reputation of the vendor, track record, industry-specific experience, and references need to be considered. The flexibility of the vendor, its capability to change in a changing marketplace, the ability to handle the impact on cost and service due to change in the marketplace, and other related consequences should be evaluated. Extensive deliberation should go into the vendor selection process, with various aspects being considered. *The outsourcing solution should be such so that it is always mutually beneficial and furthers a "win–win" relationship between the buyer and the seller.* Deciding whether to outsource or not and what to outsource is an important strategic decision which can have far-reaching ramifications. The decision should not be rushed into, and adequate time should be devoted for extensive analysis and documentation. Extensive documentation gets rid of ambiguity and misconceptions, whereas lack of it will cause serious misunderstandings in the relationship.

Many activities regarding the global outsourcing contract should be carried out concurrently rather than sequentially. Trying to perform activities individually and sequentially can prove too expensive and time consuming. The buyer should be able to thoroughly ascertain the difference if any between the offerings made by the vendor and its actual ability to deliver. That will give an insight into the real value added. This is crucial for vendor selection. The offering of the vendor should be broken down into individual components, and then an assessment should be made of the value that will be added if the contract is awarded to the vendor. Breaking the offering down into individual components makes it easier and provides exactness and greater accuracy in determining the value added. Savings can be made as a result of improvements in management and financial engineering.

How people and businesses deal in information and entertainment products and services, how work is created, owned, distributed, reproduced, displayed, performed, licensed, managed, presented, organized, sold, accessed, used, and stored is dramatically changing.

There are some skills that a supplier being awarded a contract should have, like team work with seamless coordination. The team members should be highly motivated and be capable of delivering the goods. They should possess explicit knowledge of the product/service with excellent verbal and written communication. They should have the knowledge of a foreign language if needed and should be process oriented. They should have quality systems knowledge, with regular reviews so that quality standards are met and continuously improved upon. Continuous improvement in quality and innovation are strongly linked with each other and can prove extremely beneficial. Innovation can impact various aspects of the project like life time, cycle time, cost reduction, and revenue generation, to mention a few. Risk is mitigated, thus instilling greater confidence in both the buyer and the supplier. The supplier should have knowledge about technical aspects, value analysis, and the market. Lack of knowledge about security-related issues of the market and its trends can give rise to serious miscalculations.

A competent supplier has an efficient measurement and control mechanism, and there is an ongoing review of progress periodically.

From territory to territory, the development of technology capabilities by providers has kept pace with the needs, and many providers, not just content with data extraction tools, have also developed some very comprehensive solutions and approaches to outsourcing. When outsourcing, the provider's expertise to deliver after a smooth transition to the new business model should be considered. At every step of the transaction process, value should be demonstrated by a provider with a proven track record. Existing procedures should be improved upon, with the ability to scale and to anticipate changing demands and new marketing campaigns to ensure peaks and valleys in demand are met. The provider should be on a sound financial footing and have strong cash flow and transparent financial systems to handle changes in the business cycle. An experienced vendor ensures that the key activities are performed efficiently to customer satisfaction. It may be challenging to provide a better product or service at lower costs; therefore consistent innovation and process reengineering should be a part of the vendor's strategy. The key to improving performance and delivering results across business operations is the integration of the right people, processes, and technology. Capable and experienced people combined with proven processes and contemporary technological solutions can work wonders for the client. By outsourcing, firms stand to benefit in more ways than one. Some of these may include an increase in productivity and accuracy, improved customer satisfaction levels, faster entry into new/emerging markets, increased automation, improved service levels and performance metrics, process innovation and access to new technology, and reduced administrative and regulatory compliance costs. Management can devote time to the most complex decision making as the provider delivers value by employing modern process management and workflow technologies to automate the entire functioning. Better management decisions can be made regarding future resource needs, and costly capital investments can be avoided in unproductive areas.

Specialized skills in a variety of products and deep business process knowledge improve revenue flow and customer satisfaction. Experienced professionals implement the best solution for the outsourced model, product needs, and budgets. An experienced vendor enables the client to achieve measurable business results by regular meetings to build trust, exceeding service level requirements, delivering projects on time and on budget, and offering creative and innovative solutions to challenging problems. Through the use of technology, vendors help clients to achieve strategic and operational results, and experienced professionals ensure that service levels are maintained. Specific business challenges can be addressed by working collaboratively with clients to develop innovative technology strategies and solutions. Combining the newest technology with capability can achieve startling results, and vendors distinguish themselves through their time-tested ability to plan, build, and operate highly reliable efficient and secure business solutions. With outsourcing making forays into newer areas, the outsourcing agreements which were once focused primarily on controlling cost are now leveraged by companies looking to gain operational flexibility and responsiveness as well. Providers help clients leverage outsourcing strategically to achieve high performance through decreased costs and improved quality of service. Proven approaches and technology enablers provide significant business performance improvements.

BPO-Specific Vendor Competency

Through varying strokes, delivering value, far reaching.

Adequate training is imparted to the supplier staff to handle the outsourced work proficiently. However, at times, some new accents and terms peculiar to a particular foreign country may be difficult to understand, and these problems can be overcome through training, close coordination, and interaction between the various parties. The competency of the service provider in analyzing the usage of an application can take care of troubleshooting services. The user can be instructed on how to use an application in training services to resolve a customer's service request. Advisory services give related functional, technical, and operational advice. Suitable monitoring and escalation mechanisms exist to provide value-added service. Support is delivered through channels like telephone, chat, remote diagnostic and collaborative browsing tools, self-help resources, and e-mail.

One of outsourcing industry's leading research analysts firms, Forrester Research, observed in a research report that outsourcing is the beginning of the process-focused IT era, and process expertise and IT capabilities are the most important factors in evaluating BPO companies. The analysts of Gartner in another report predicted that outsourcing expertise will emerge as a definitive area of competitive differentiation for IT service providers targeting industry-specific business processes, and business process expertise will define future success, particularly since technical skills and competitive prices are not in scarce supply and cannot serve as competitive differentiators.

Role of Technology in Vendor Selection

As languages natural, artificial, high, and low
merge across people and devices.

Technology plays an important role, especially in IT-related contracts, and the quality and availability of technology determine the level of service in terms of security and reliability. The execution of any project provides experience, information, and knowledge. *The synthesis, analysis, and refinement of knowledge gives rise to innovation and furtherance of higher objectives.* Thus best practices evolve and give impetus to performance. It is the pool of knowledge that enables organizations to outperform.

Information technology and voice data communication have revolutionized and accentuated the activity manyfold, whereby suppliers in different countries perform jobs on a contractual basis, meeting and even surpassing the service levels laid down in the contract in terms of efficiency, quality, speed, and cost. Information technology, voice/data communication, and the Internet have immensely reduced both the internal and the external transaction costs, so organizations grow large at a much faster rate. A low cost structure rather than the size of the organization gives the competitive advantage.

Example—A BPO provider should be equipped with shared resource service enabling framework. The framework includes various aspects of network management like virtual private network (VPN), private branch exchange (PBX), voice telephony over asynchronous transfer mode (VToA), voice over frame relay (VoFR), voice over Internet protocol (VoIP), and public switched telephone network

(PSTN). A customer interaction center incorporated by a BPO service provider should be able to deal with various facets of service management like business process management systems, e-mail/chat/voice interaction services, web servers, and media servers; service providers deliver services like BPO, e-customer relationship management (eCRM), proactive service delivery, and managed network services.

The Geographical Bearings of Buyers and Vendors and Some Generalizations

The bearings, some real and some imaginary, so commonly prevalent.

Findings suggest that people in different countries have different mindsets in general. For example, it is found that countries like Brazil and Mexico score high in terms of "*personal relationships*" but low in terms of "*focus of problems.*" Countries like Canada and Singapore score high in terms of both "personal relationships " and "focus on problems," whereas countries like Germany, United Kingdom, and United States are rated low for "personal relationships" and high in terms of "focus on problems." These observations are mere generalizations, with a view to aid the buyer and the supplier in a global contracting/outsourcing assignment. Nevertheless, keeping these observations in mind, firms can chalk out their business plans.

Vendor's Past Performance History Check

*People and organizations usually follow
the course commonly traversed before.*

Check if the provider is informal in its work approach, with no procedures being followed even if they exist. Check if senior management is sensitive to issue escalation and reacts quickly toward crisis resolution. Check for past missed schedules and inflated/exceeded budgets. Check for the existence or the lack of mechanisms for exchange of information, feedback, responsibility taking, and efficient execution. It is not prudent to conduct business with such providers even if the transaction costs and rates seem much lower. Business with such vendors will eventually result in exceeded timelines and cost overruns.

Vendor Selection Checklist

Of scaling the attention charts exponentially.

To determine the best candidate for outsourcing, the business process should be closely assessed so as to drive quality, cost, and service improvements. The offshore checklist should be properly followed when pondering offshoring options. The checklist may consist of questions about the execution capabilities of the provider along with an integrated methodology to guide the client. To deliver the solution, does the client have the right industry and domain skills? The total cost will increase if the provider does not have the required skills, and the client may end up providing these capabilities to the provider. To deliver the goods, does the provider have process and change management skills? Whether a fixed price contract is more appropriate than a time and materials (T&M) contract should be reviewed. The applications should be segmented based on user requirements, and then matched with the skills and strengths of the offshore provider. To hold the provider accountable, the measurable business results should be defined. Alignment of the provider's business and legal standards with company's practice and expectations is a must. To ensure that the working relationship succeeds, agreements that hold the provider to another country's legal and business standards should be scrutinized with care. The companies should build an oversight organization to manage the process, to ensure the outsourcing engagement's success, but this is bound to add money to the mix. This will lead to an additional expenditure of about 5% to 16% of overall engagement costs. This is because the oversight staff earns higher salaries. The overall engagement is served by managers as business liaisons to the offshore provider and as quality assurance officers. To source and contract personnel and manage the project from the client side, in addition, someone has to be in charge. To generate a new business niche, the facet of outsourcing is lucrative. The cost of reducing offshore staff must also be considered while moving specific functions and departments offshore to save money and labor. Layoffs also account for significant costs, and the cost of severance and job search for its displaced workers must be factored by companies. When you replace in-house staff with an offshore provider, your intellectual property goes out of the door, too. Time is needed to adjust to the changed landscape with offshore outsourcing. The company's ability to adhere to certain standards of customer service and regulatory compliance may be hindered because outsourcing can have enormous impact on a multitude of supporting systems. As a result of compensating people with higher salaries—key IT management staff to oversee transition—other hidden costs may be generated. The wave of the future for IT is offshore outsourcing. It can result in tremendous savings and add significant business value if done right.

Chapter 7

Contracts—Types, Pricing Models, and Issues

Of identifying that self-actualizing proposition.

Contract Types—Three Major Legal Structures

Of searching deep, that universe, within.

For establishing offshoring operations, generally three legal structures or approaches exist: (1) offshoring to a third party for services; (2) offshoring to a subsidiary after establishing it in the required country where services need to be performed; and (3) "build–operate–transfer" (BOT) model (i.e., offshoring services to a third party with an option to suitably acquire the service operations later on). They are discussed in detail, one by one in the following sections.

(1) Third-Party Outsourcing

The foreign company contracts with a third party to provide services in the "contract with a third party for services" structure. To perform the services the third party, which is an independent contractor, uses its own infrastructure and employees. Rather than prematurely creating a subsidiary, one should start with this structure in outsourcing. The track record of the service provider is one of the major considerations under this structure. Otherwise, the chances are that, more often than not,

79

the offshore outsourcing projects will fail. In terms of financial stability, employee mobility, intellectual property protection, and performance on projects, due diligence must be done on potential service providers. The financial status should be evaluated and the service provider's financial condition assessed, along with the possible risk that business operations may cease. In terms of performance, find out if the service provider has performed on similar projects and has any specialty or niche that is hard to find. The quality of work, protection of intellectual property, and employee mobility issues should be ascertained through customer references. To measure the performance of the service provider, what metrics will be used? In terms of the number of employees, what is the size of the company, because it may not have mature processes if the strength is less than 200. Existence of quality process certifications such as SEI CMM certification for software (level 3 or better) with the service providers is an important aspect. For protecting the intellectual property (IP) of its customers, the service provider should have sufficient processes, procedures, and controls in place. Similarly for handling confidential information, the service provider needs to have sufficient procedures and technical resources like firewalls, physical or electronic security, etc. In this evaluation the foreign company's CIO or equivalent should be involved.

Each employee and contractor of the vendor need to assign all intellectual property (IP) rights to the employing vendor and enter into confidentiality obligations at par with those between the vendor and its outsourcing organization (e.g., the U.S. company). Without written consent of the outsourcing organization (i.e., the U.S. company), the third party should not subcontract or otherwise use any nonemployee service providers to provide the services. Under the laws of the country where the services will be performed, the assignment of intellectual property rights should address "moral rights" ownership. If the third-party intellectual property rights are breached, the service provider should agree to indemnify the outsourcing organization (the U.S. company) as a liability for infringement of third-party intellectual rights. *The outsourcing organization (say the U.S. company) should have suitable agreements with the vendor, preferably for "unlimited" indemnity right for copyright and trade secret claims. The vendor conversely should try to push for a cap on the amount of indemnity.* Except as required to perform the services, the service provider must not disclose any confidential information of the U.S. company or use any confidential information. Following the end of the agreement, the service provider may try to limit the period of the confidentiality obligation. *For at least three years, the obligation should continue and for a period of at least one year, the service provider should agree that it will not seek to take away or interfere with any customer of the U.S. company or solicit or hire its employees or contractors.* Without the prior written consent of the U.S. company, the service provider should be prohibited from assigning its obligations under the agreement, and any attempt to do so should be void. Under the agreement, the service provider should be responsible for all taxes due on payments. As long as there is no license involved, there should not be any local country withholding taxes on a service transaction. Based on the U.S. governing law, the U.S. company will want the parties to agree to settle any dispute in a U.S. jurisdiction (state), and the governing law should expressly exclude the application of conflicts of law principles. Regardless of what the agreement provides, the intellectual property laws of the jurisdiction where the work is performed will apply. In the country where the work will be done, the U.S. company must understand the "work for hire," moral rights, assignment of ownership, and other statutory framework applicable to intellectual property. Including any currency exchange and export control restrictions and agreement registration requirements, both parties should agree to comply with all applicable laws and regulations.

For voice-based and related service delivery, English language is the commonly used standard. The service provider needs to have sufficient demonstrated capability and track record regarding it. Are subcontractors or only employees used by the service provider? In terms of location and infrastructure, are adequate facilities like phone service, communication bandwidth, etc., available on the location where work will be performed? What is the workforce mobility rate, and does the location have a qualified labor pool? The "contract with a third party for services" structure is the fastest to implement, because the third party usually has preexisting personnel and infrastructure which can be quickly engaged. The legal formalities of a subsidiary or the building of local infrastructure do not have to be done by the foreign company in this case. One should consider the startup cost. Of the three major legal structures, this structure may appear to be most costly, but the costs of establishing and operating a subsidiary are often underestimated. Smaller suppliers may provide better performance reliability, and a larger service provider with substantial revenues and well-established reputation may be more expensive. On the flexibility front, this structure provides a way to quickly ramp up or ramp down without the need to keep on "bench," but the factor of risk exists. Because the services will be performed by an independent third party, the foreign company will have less control than in the subsidiary structure. If an acquirer targets the foreign company for acquisition, the degree of control may be a considered for valuation.

Employees performing service would be employed directly by the subsidiary, under the subsidiary structure, and therefore the foreign company will have more ability to oversee the performance of services. The foreign company has less ability to measure performance in real time and quickly take corrective actions, less control to implement its own policies to protect intellectual property and confidential information, and the inability to closely monitor employees in the case of third-party provider structure.

The service provider's track record for protecting intellectual property is very important, because the foreign company will have less control over intellectual property protection procedures. Along with the adequacy of enforceability mechanisms, it is important to understand the country's legal framework for intellectual property protection, such as moral rights and ownership assignment requirements. If the service provider uses contractors who are not employees to perform services, then intellectual property risks increase. Under the country's intellectual property legal framework, ownership of work performed by contractors may be more difficult to obtain. By core development of intellectual property done on site (e.g., in the United States) and dividing other noncore tasks to different service providers, intellectual property risks in software development projects can be partly mitigated. For such integration of work from multiple service providers, the on-site customer organization may need to deploy additional internal resources and cost. Performance of the service provider on similar projects can reveal the financial condition, and the track record of the provider and business risk can be evaluated.

(2) Parent–Subsidiary Relationship

The second legal structure is "establish a subsidiary and then contract for services with the subsidiary." As the company matures and gains experience with outsourcing under the third-party service provider approach, this structure makes the most business sense. An offshore subsidiary that is wholly owned or controlled by the customer organization (e.g., the U.S. company) is most advisable for such projects involving sensitive data. Such a subsidiary is usually a separate legal entity in the country in which it is incorporated. Thus a subsidiary setup has advantages of better control over day-to-day operations of the offshore services, but in turn needs more time and resources to be devoted by the monitoring primary customer organization. That the subsidiary will perform without oversight should not be assumed by the U.S. company. The employees providing the services and implementing procedures for handling of intellectual property and confidential information are more under the control of the U.S. company. The management team of the subsidiary is primarily responsible for due diligence of the structure. The required skill sets for the services and the availability of reliable employee pool are necessary. While considering the subsidiary location, one should consider the ability of implementing the necessary technical network and other security. To run the day-to-day operations, the subsidiary will have suitable local management offshore. A preexisting relationship with the local management is an important practical consideration, because this adds a sense of comfort within the primary organization. Thus the local manager needs to be selected with diligence, allowing only required functions of authority. Such local management should have regular status reporting and approval taking from the primary organization. The decision of where to locate the subsidiary may be partly driven by the place of residence of this key person. Country and geographic locations within a country greatly influence the time and cost involved in the incorporation process. In countries outside the United States, more governmental approvals are needed for the incorporation process, and the process of winding down a company is more difficult and time consuming. It should not be assumed by the U.S. company that effective management will occur without careful oversight, and therefore it should make use of its greater ability to manage the subsidiary in this structure. There should be regular and effective communication by the U.S. company management with the subsidiary management, and visits should be made to subsidiary operations on a regular basis. The U.S. company is able to monitor the performance of the subsidiary to a greater degree and ensure alignment of performance objectives with it. The value of the U.S. company may increase in an acquisition by virtue of having a subsidiary with more control rather than a third-party service provider relationship. For handling sensitive data and intellectual property, the U.S. company will have greater flexibility to implement procedures. Even if subcontractors are used by the subsidiary, the primary organization still has greater control. A disadvantage of the subsidiary structure is that it takes the longest time to implement. To establish the subsidiary, the amount of time necessary to complete the administrative and legal formalities varies by country and by region within each country. To have a true cost comparison with the third-party service provider structure, both the startup and the recurring costs need to be carefully calculated. Startup costs may be involved in terms of fulfilling the administrative formalities and completing the legal requirements in establishing the subsidiary. Costs are incurred in building out the subsidiary infrastructure and locating office space. For small subsidiary operations, it may not be easy to achieve recurring cost savings, because it will not enjoy the benefits of economy of scale that a large service provider enjoys. A bench of people, who may be needed on projects from time to time rather than on a daily basis, may have to be maintained by the subsidiary at additional cost and risk. Significant time and resources of the U.S. company are required for the management of the subsidiary. In order to ensure that the subsidiary performs as per expectations, the management of the U.S. company will have to devote substantial time for oversight of the subsidiary. It should not be assumed by the parent company's management that basic physical and technical security or intellectual property protection safeguards will automatically be implemented because it is a subsidiary.

To ensure timely delivery of products and services, the customer organization will need to supervise performance closely. In the case of a subsidiary setup, the customer (e.g., the U.S. company) has greater ability to monitor and manage employees of the subsidiary. Measurement metrics of non–software-development services also need to be in place. The vendor may be processing sensitive information such as medical records, tax returns, etc., for the customer (e.g., the U.S. company), which may be providing related sensitive information. In such cases of outsourcing to external vendors, the risk of data breach or theft is much higher because the customer (e.g., the U.S. company) has far less ability to monitor and control processes and resources for handling of confidential information. By retaining sensitive data within the organization's own servers and providing limited access to the external vendor, the risks are somewhat minimized though not completely eliminated.

In an outsourcing scenario, a relationship between the parent and subsidiary should be "arm's length" for tax purposes. Provisions that would normally be found in agreements between two unaffiliated parties should be included in the agreement between the parent and the subsidiary. In the agreement with the subsidiary, many of the provisions described under the third-party service provider structure are also included. Of course, there are some provisions in the agreement with a subsidiary that are in addition to or different from the provisions of the agreement with a third party. In the case of a subsidiary structure, the transfer pricing among the companies may be scrutinized by the U.S. Internal Revenue Service and the local income tax authorities. The U.S. company agrees to pay a service fee to the subsidiary equal to the subsidiary's costs and expenses plus a profit, such as 10%, according to the agreement, which will usually include a cost-plus provision. On a monthly basis or some other short time period, the subsidiary should provide a detailed report of the subsidiary's costs and expenses incurred in performing the services. As directed by the U.S. company, the subsidiary will agree to provide services. Instead of being a detailed "statement of work" or project oriented, the agreement is usually a more general services one. All the information provided by the U.S. company must be kept confidential because the subsidiary is a separate entity. This includes any intellectual property and business information, and the subsidiary should agree to use this information only for the purpose of providing services, and the obligation must also be implemented with the subsidiary employees. The parent corporation, by virtue of owning the subsidiary organization, does not automatically own its intellectual property. All intellectual property which may be created by the subsidiary needs to be manually assigned to the parent U.S. company or its designee. If there are favorable tax consequences for holding the intellectual property at the subsidiary level, or if the U.S. company has an offshore intellectual property holding corporation for tax purposes, then exceptions could arise, and the obligation must be implemented with the subsidiary employees. In the build–operate–transfer structure agreement, provisions described in the third-party service provider structure are applicable, with the addition of provisions covering the option to buy and transfer the operation. The option process and pricing and transition process are the additional agreement provisions. To minimize operational disruption, the transition should be carefully covered. Suitable agreements need to be inked with the subsidiary for obtaining ownership of results of outsourcing services. The outsourcing company may not own the results of the work done by the subsidiary. The subsidiary needs to be positioned as an independent contractor providing service and not an "employee" that explicitly transfers intellectual property ownership to the outsourcing organization. The ownership assignment requirements in China, India, and the United States for both employee and independent contractor relationships may vary. Intellectual property assignment requirements of China and the United States are similar, but differ from those of India. The contractor needs to have suitable agreements with its employees and subcontractors, and this should be ensured in the outsourcing arrangement.

In India, the subsidiary will most likely have a services fulfillment function because India, in contrast to China, is not considered a major market. Indian subsidiaries providing backend fulfillment services for their parent U.S. firm are usually not considered a "permanent establishment" of the parent. However, work defines if the Indian subsidiary qualifies as a permanent one or not. On behalf of the parent, if the Indian subsidiary has the authority to execute contracts, secure orders, or deliver goods, then it constitutes a permanent establishment.

Captive Centers

Captive centers or shared service centers are set up by the company itself as offshore operations to handle back office work. To conduct customer support for their global business and do their back office processing, companies like GE, American Express, and Dell have set up captive centers in India. Third-party service providers such as EXL Services Pvt. Ltd. and Daksh form the second category of vendors in the contracting/outsourcing industry. The third kind of players are the software companies that have entered the ITES/BPO arena. This is a comparatively recent trend. Acquisitions and fully owned subsidiaries such as Infosys BPO and Wipro BPO (Spectramind) have been established, thereby leveraging the brand name as well as their contacts for the outsourcing business. End-to-end services—from customer service, to back office services, to system integration, to software development—are offered by the companies to the client. In addition, consulting companies like Accenture and big industrial houses/banks like ICICI are making forays in this industry.

(3) Build–Operate–Transfer (BOT) Model

In an outsourcing arrangement, one should carefully chose the local head (managing director), because he or she will be responsible for running the daily operations of the subsidiary and may bind the subsidiary with third parties. The BOT structure is a hybrid of "contract with third party for services" structure and "establishing a subsidiary and then contracting for services with the subsidiary" structure. Service is provided to the U.S. company by a third-party service provider, an independent contractor who establishes a team. On the floor of the service provider's facility or in a separate facility, the team may be segregated, but the team is usually dedicated to the primary organization (e.g., the U.S. company). There may be restricted access to the floor or floors on which the team works for security in operations. In order to reduce overhead costs, some persons on the dedicated team, such as management level, accounting, and other administrative-type employees, may not be solely dedicated to the team. The agreement in addition has an option built by which the U.S. company can elect to purchase the business unit represented by the dedicated team. *The structure is basically the same as the third-party service provider structure prior to the transfer and is a subsidiary structure following the transfer option exercise.* There can be a complicated transition process, and therefore this structure is not often used, and the option price will usually be a multiple of months of service fees for the team plus the cost for the infrastructure. Because the primary outsourcing organization (e.g., the U.S. company) uses the services of dedicated subsidiary teams as a third-party service provider, the price factor will decline over time. When the primary organization also has the right to hire employees for the third-party service provider, then it is a subset of the build–operate–transfer (BOT) structure. The price is usually based on the length of time the third-party service provider has provided services to the outsourcing organization (the U.S. company) and is often a multiple of months of service fee for the employee. With the added element of transition phase, the due diligence investigation on the possible service provider is generally the same as under the third-party service provider structure. One should review the track record of the provider in other transitions. Because the third party usually has preexisting personnel and infrastructure which can be quickly engaged, the initial service phase can be quickly implemented. The critical issues in such agreements are negotiation of the transfer price and specification of the transfer process. During the third-party service provider phase, the more dedicated and segregated the service provider's team will be, the higher will be the cost. At the outset of the agreement, the customer may need to pay certain start-up costs. As compared to non-BOT arrangement, there can be additional oversight costs. With the addition of transition risk, the risks are the same as in the third-party service provider structure. In order to avoid business disruption, the transition needs to be carefully planned and executed. At the time of entering into the BOT agreement, the subsequent transition needs should be sufficiently clear. Related issues could be employees' movement to the primary organization from the service provider, retirement benefits prior to transfer, compensation benefits to employees for employee stock ownership plan (ESOP), and miscellaneous incentives of the service provider. Is it really possible to transfer the infrastructure, and are the processes portable and self contained, are some of the questions that need to be answered. Based on whether the transaction is for the development of software or design of an integrated circuit, preclinical trial animal testing, or some form of business processing such as insurance claim processing or tax return preparation, the agreement provisions will differ. In all these services, intellectual property will be involved. One needs to protect technical support scripts, protocols for preclinical animal testing, and other intellectual property. A detailed physical and technical security safeguard provision in the agreement should not be overlooked. This is very important, because the service provider will have access to sensitive personal and business information, and therefore the U.S. company should address these safeguards in every agreement. When there are multiple transactions between parties, a master agreement is often used. When a multiple-project relationship is contemplated, a master agreement may be entered into between the primary outsourcing organization (e.g., a U.S. company) and the vendor. The master agreement contains suitable details of each child project to be performed for the customer. The exhibit is the "statement of work exhibit." The type of services being produced will be responsible in deciding many of the provisions of the agreement. A detailed description of the services to be performed, including detailed specifications of the work product, deliverables, delivery schedule, and milestones for completing the work product, should be included in the statement of work exhibit. In addition, the exhibit should also consist of the schedule of project meetings, reports to be provided by the service provider, and pricing. In the case of software development, integrated circuit design services, and other situations where work product will be delivered, a statement of work will be used. Following delivery of work product, the U.S. company should have a specified acceptance period, to evaluate quality and require the service provider to make additional modifications to the work product if it does not conform to the specifications. A performance warranty needs to be given to the U.S. company, stating that the work product is free from defect for a period following acceptance. A warranty that the work product will not infringe the intellectual property rights of third parties needs to be given by the service provider. Seeking to reduce the specified time period limit for performance warranty and limiting the amount of potential liability under the warranties will be the endeavor of the service provider. In the type of service where no work product will be delivered, such as tax return preparation or financial services, service level performance requirements will be tailored. For software or other development projects, pricing models may be fixed-price projects, time and material (T&M) on unit basis, or production such as per tax return. Including all intellectual property developed or created by the service provider, the ownership of all work products should be assigned to the U.S. company or whomever it designates. The U.S. company should obtain a worldwide fully paid perpetual license to any intellectual property rights of the service provider that the U.S. company needs to conduct its business, if the service provider seeks to retain ownership of any preexisting "base software" or "core IP."

Pricing Models

Rules that define men and those that rewrite them.

To ensure that companies achieve real business value, measurable business results are replacing metrics such as service levels. The benefits of defining measurable business results up front are high, although defining measurable business results is not easy. As long as both risk and reward are tied to the objective, the provider will be motivated to achieve the result. The provider who is aligned to the business goals can hire the best people who can bring the greatest level of industry knowledge and business processes, as well as creativity and innovation.

The task of creating a pricing model begins once the decision to engage an offshore model is made. Offshore outsourcing contracts, as mentioned, can be of five types—fixed pricing, transactional pricing, activity-based pricing, cost-plus pricing and gain-sharing (risk–reward). To ensure that the ultimate outsourcing contract meets ones needs, managers should examine the pros and cons of each pricing model. If you feel that the proposed billing terms do not satisfy your needs, do not hesitate to have a friendly discussion with your vendor, and do not sign a contract that makes you uncomfortable. The advantages and disadvantages of each pricing model should be carefully assessed. A high proportion of services are provided on a fixed-price basis rather than on a time and material basis by some companies, especially in the case of software development projects. Revenues are conditional upon predetermined performance levels in certain fixed-price service level agreement (SLA) contracts, and if the performance is unsatisfactory, it could lead to lower revenue than anticipated. Failures in meeting the contractual obligations or failing to make correct estimate of the resources and time required for the project would impact profitability of the offshore vendor. Fixed-price project models have low tolerance toward incorrect estimation of various project nuances, deliverables, etc. Budgeting and pricing may be somewhat easier for projects where the number of atomic transactions is fixed. To guarantee that the fixed costs are covered and risk minimized, offshore vendors may feel the need to overestimate their unit prices. To the offshore vendors, fixed pricing may prove detrimental, while it can be of advantage for the U.S. companies, because wages in India are increasing at a faster rate than in the United States, which could result in increased costs for software professionals, particularly project managers and other mid-level professionals.

Equitable pricing is only a part of the contract, with each outsourcing contract being unique. In combination with other performance incentives, the resulting pricing structure may use one or more of these pricing models. It is not advisable to use the contract negotiation process only to slash prices, and more often than not companies that win these pricing victories end up losing some productivity and quality in the process.

It is hard to change midstride once a certain path is chosen, and therefore companies need to spend a lot of time thinking about the offshore delivery model. Vendors manage the execution of the project once the project priorities are established by the customer.

Fixed-Price Model

It is seen that the company contracting for services is always at inherent conflict with the IT services provider. How the client pays for services is the root cause of conflict—whether it is a time and material (T&M) or fixed price. Risk is the issue, and one side tries to push most of the risk to the other. For major Indian offshore providers and integrators, the vast majority of revenue is derived from T&M contracts. The risk shifts to the client on whom any project overrun costs fall; therefore companies prefer T&M contracts. The onus is on the service provider in the case of the fixed-price delivery model to get the right requirements, manage scope, estimate, and manage the project. Thus the clients are insulated from risks that erode savings. The service provider becomes a better partner in the case of the fixed-price model, because it is in the provider's best interest to get the project done and done right. The methodology and the experience of the provider are critical. Providers that not only offer fixed-price contracts, but also attach results fees are preferred.

Transactional Pricing Model

Transactional pricing, the traditional unit pricing, is the most popular pricing structure in business process outsourcing. The client companies agree to pay off-shore outsourcing vendors a flat fee per unit of work in the transactional pricing model, and the unit of work may be defined as a customer complaint, mortgage loan application, or a claims case handled. The advantages of this model consist of clearly defined terms with little room for misinterpretation, designing and implementing the pricing structure is easy, and pricing is easy to understand and easy to budget, especially when predictable volumes are involved. The disadvantage may be that, in order to minimize their risk and guarantee they will recover their fixed costs, offshore vendors may feel the need to overestimate their unit prices.

Activity-Based Pricing Model

In another type of model known as activity-based pricing, to cover the offshore outsourcing vendor's fixed costs, including leases, computer equipment, telecommunications connectivity, and management, the client agrees to pay a flat fee. To cover variable costs such as hiring costs, transportation, equipment maintenance, operations, and project execution, they also commit to a variable fee. This type of pricing is particularly popular with offshore development center (ODC) or build–operate–transfer models. Some of the advantages of this type of pricing are that the expenses incurred and the services rendered are reflected more accurately. To protect themselves from losses related to fixed costs, offshore vendors do not have to build fat into their unit prices, and because the invoices are highly detailed, the contracts allow companies to track logistics costs more accurately. The disadvantages are that, in the case of many unknowns in a new relationship, activity-based pricing is difficult to structure because it is complex to develop, and without a well-defined gain-sharing program included in the contract, there are no inherent financial incentives for the offshore vendor to pursue continuous improvement.

Cost-Plus Pricing Model

If the nature of the contractual assignment is changing, then cost-plus pricing is particularly effective. Organizations undergoing some transition that makes requirements volatile such as launching a new marketing campaign or starting new operations are some of the examples to which this cost structure can be applied. Captive centers and build–operate–transfer models often use a cost-plus pricing model. Some of the advantages of this pricing structure are that, in the case of unpredictable volumes/business levels, the offshore vendor is protected from losses, and the pricing model protects shippers from protective overestimating that may occur in transactional pricing. To keep cost under control, service providers are guaranteed a profit and procedures are put in place. The demerits of this model are that it could encourage an offshore vendor to generate costs, because each cost carries a specified profit margin because cost-plus is not a viable long-term pricing model. What constitutes a cost may give rise to disagreement, and because the only constant is the markup, budgeting is more difficult for the shipper.

If one wants to use an interim contractual measure, then cost-plus pricing, also known as open book, is most often used. Fee for the cost of services plus a mutually agreed upon markup or profit margin form a part of the pricing structure.

Gain-Sharing Model

Another pricing type is the gain-sharing model. *This form of incentive for continuous improvement is advisable regardless of the pricing structure, and in new relationships where the learning curve is highest, gain sharing works the best.* It is built on a benchmarking foundation, and key performance indicators (KPIs) or areas where improvement is needed are identified by benchmarking, and improvements and exceptional performance are rewarded.

It is advantageous because the vendor benefits if the client benefits, and so the offshore vendors work harder to create value as financial incentives are involved. The disadvantage is that there is a lot of emphasis on value measurement because companies have to develop metrics to carefully monitor value being created.

In the outsourcing contracting process, the following areas should be included: risk assessment, service provider selection, access of information, audit, contingency plans, international considerations, oversight and compliance, foreign banking organizations, and examination implementation. In case of risk management, before entering into an outsourcing arrangement, the institution should assess the key risks that may arise and options for controlling these risks. While assessing risk, some of the factors that should be considered include the criticality of the function to the institution, the nature of activities to be performed by the service provider, including handling funds or implementing credit decisions, the availability of particular risks, and the cost and time required to switch service providers should problems arise.

Contract Drawing

Of markets and practices evolving through time.

The agreements between the outsourcer and the vendor should be realistic; otherwise they will fail to meet expectations, and areas of dispute will surround quality and timing. It is advisable to first outsource a sample process so that both buyers and providers understand the new ball game where the adoption of scoping, pricing, and contracting methodologies are a prerequisite to success. As compared, the traditional relationship enjoyed between business and professional services firms is different in many ways. In an outsourcing arrangement, there should be adequate preagreed service levels, and the tight management of these service levels along with the incorporation of emerging trends in the outsourcing industry. There is an increasing need for the providers to demonstrate what they have added and increasing use of arrangements like gain sharing.

There has been a shift toward strategic alliance in some outsourcing relationships, with key performance indicators surrounding timing and delivery being increasingly adopted. The need for integrated planning has arisen with international cost reduction initiatives and globalization of trading activities fueled by the e-commerce revolution. Sophisticated technologies enable access to critical information, which is indispensable for directors with international responsibilities, who are being increasingly subject to performance metrics. For efficient delivery of a service, the underlying technology for it is absolutely necessary, and access to information from all jurisdictions is critical for the organization. The provider should invest in the most contemporary technology solutions to deliver proficient service and meet the tight budgetary constraints of the buyer. Adequate payback on the provider's investments may require that the outsourcing contract is for three or four years.

To keep pace with the changing business and legislative environment and the advent of increasingly sophisticated bridging software and data warehousing techniques, contracts are becoming more flexible and are being constantly reengineered. The different pieces of the process jigsaw are being brought together by the automation of data capture routines and the access to colossal information coupled with the strides in technology.

Suppliers of intermediate goods are also essentially outsourcing vendors. Raw data or access to it and service parameters are provided by the client, and the vendor resells the data processed to contract specifications back to the client. Unless the parties can devise efficient contracts offering adequate incentives to support the release of resources, outsourcing is a zero sum game between the parties, assuming equal power of negotiation. However advantageous it is in principle, incompatibility regarding incentives can be a source of failure for outsourcing contracts.

In any outsourcing contract, the issues to be resolved comprise the uniqueness of the investment to be made (asset specificity), the arrangements to resolve problems not covered by the formal agreement (settling disputes), and the frequency of the transaction according to Williamson (1975). The arguments of Williamson (1975) are supported by evidence presented by Lacity and Hirschheim (1993), Datamonitor (1994), Mcfarland and Noland (1995), Alexander-Young (1996), O'Heney (1996), and Lacity et al. (1996). It is increasingly becoming necessary for providers to forge close working relationships with systems development and implementation teams and data management consultants, as well as risk management colleagues as the emphasis on data processing becomes more and more sophisticated. For value-added service, clients should be provided with visibility by the provider possessing rigorous knowledge transfer protocols and internal controls to guarantee quality, reliability, and data security.

Contractual Issues

The pros and cons of the relationship.

The precontract phase consists of the following phases:

A. Establishing an unambiguous and a clear contract between the buyer and the supplier
B. Managing the ever-shortening service life cycles without compromising on quality which should meet the required service level

The contract execution phase may consist of the following issues:

A. Improving service in relation to quality
B. Proper exchange of information between the buyer and the supplier and compliance with service levels
C. Managing security and technological changes that take place during the life of the project

The postcontract phase provides a vast reservoir of contractual experience. It provides a profound insight into the various issues connected with the project. The postcontract phase may consist of the following issues:

A. Management practices between the buyer and the supplier
B. Factors most conducive to the continuity of contract or the reasons for the occurrence of contract termination: capability, compatibility, and proper coordination between the organization and the supplier, enabling uninterrupted continuity of operations

To be able to execute a contracted project properly, the supplier should first understand the requirements of the organization properly. We are presently living in the information/knowledge age, and continuous augmentation of knowledge is a prerequisite for executing a project well in a fiercely competitive global environment. Outsourcing is a knowledge-based industry in which the knowledge possessed by personnel is the key determining factor for service capability and quality. Thus the effective coordination of people, technology, resources, and techniques is of paramount importance for the seamless execution of the project.

A group at Gartner, Inc. recommends that before outsourcing employers should do reference checks and site visits to their providers' facilities, call centers, etc., paying close attention to the quality of staff that will be assigned to their account and insist that individuals who are mission critical remain with them. Service level agreements (if applicable) should be included in all contracts, spelling out the parties' obligations and expectations in detail, from estimated workloads to performance measures such as the provider's speed in answering phone calls. Due diligence should also be provided by external service providers to ensure that they have properly scoped and priced their proposal. Analysts at Gartner say providers and prospective clients should discuss and share their experiences and do due diligence before the deal is signed to ensure the service level agreements are realistic. In the hope that discrepancies will mean more revenue for them after the contract is signed, service providers may often keep quiet about the discrepancies they uncover. Such approaches often lead to the enterprise's trust in the external service provider being damaged, and the relationship suffers if the enterprise feels that the external service provider knows certain things and does not disclose.

In an outsourcing arrangement providers can be quite unhappy at times. A provider who took over insurance claim processing for a client found an unexpectedly high workload on one business line because the error rate of the client's agents was more than three times the projections. It is recommended that companies build flexibility into their contracts and review service level agreements every two years, because business process outsourcing is relatively new.

Contractual Risks

Those who take to wings must know how to ride the winds.

In some outsourcing arrangements direct financial risks to the serviced institution are involved. A service provider has the ability to process transactions that result in extensions of credit for some transaction processing activities on behalf of the serviced institution. Collection or disbursement of funds may be done by a service provider, exposing the institution to liquidity and credit risks should the service provider fail to perform as expected. *The Federal Reserve expects that institutions should ensure that controls over outsourced information and transaction processing activities are equivalent to those that would be implemented if the activity were conducted internally.* The board of directors and the senior management of institutions should understand the key risks associated with the use of service providers for its crucial operations, commensurate with the scope and risks of the outsourced activity and its importance to the institution's business. An appropriate oversight program should be in place to monitor each service provider's control, condition, and performance.

The parties will usually look toward a long-term contract, to justify the level of investment by both the customer and the supplier. The technology and customer needs, however, are likely to be continually changing and developing over the contract term, in most businesses. To cope with this, any contract has to be dynamic and flexible enough. It is essential to have a robust change control mechanism, which should include procedures for proposing and accepting changes and their impact on pricing, service levels, etc. It is important that the customer reserves the right to make unilateral changes in certain circumstances, particularly in business-critical areas although usually the change control procedure requires the agreement of both parties. There may be additional tax considerations; in particular offshore taxation liability and VAT implications need to be considered. The local tax laws should be investigated thoroughly by local tax specialists, because some countries like India also have favorable tax laws which could benefit outsourcing companies. It is important to specify as an express provision within the contract when entering into an international arrangement, which country's law applies and also where the disputes can be heard (jurisdiction). There may be circumstances where proceedings would be best brought locally; therefore agreements should advisably be subject to the jurisdiction of both the English courts and the courts in the offshore territory. Local laws and practices of the country where the service provider is located may be sufficient to handle any judicial issues.

Collaborations—Joint Ventures

"Union is strength," as the saying goes.

Altogether different management strategies are required in collaborative or committed relationships. They call for relationships based on trust, openness, and mutual collaboration instead of an adverse client–vendor relationship. Therefore organizations will want to establish joint outcome–based business goals they can work on accomplishing together. To seal a close relationship some firms even choose to take equity positions in their provider or establish a joint venture.

Example—To establish a greater degree of both commitment and control, when British bank Bradford and Bingley decided to outsource most of its back office customer service and financial processes, it chose to form a joint venture with its provider.

Contract Termination

In moments, often, the damage may be minimized.

It is important that the management of the contract over its life has an eye on the exit scenario. One should ask oneself several important questions which are the key to getting the right exit provisions in the contract. *Upon material breach that is not cured within a specified period, one may want to terminate the agreement, because most outsourcing agreements permit termination "for cause."* Otherwise, termination is permitted "for convenience," that is, without a cause but for a substantial price, and the price is referred to as a "termination for convenience fee." When the service provider is meeting its contractual obligations but failing in some larger way, what is the right to terminate without paying a termination for convenience fee? For example, the service provider may be unable to keep pace with its own or customer's market or a *force majeure* event may have adversely impacted the service provider or bankruptcy or failing to meet financial covenants may cause it to go out of business. You can include provisions in the contract that give you the exit rights you need after considering all the instances where you may want to terminate. You cannot expect to find the termination provisions in a service provider's contract or even in most customer-friendly form contracts, and so the termination provisions require thought. Considerable cost, risk, and disruption are involved in transitioning away from a service provider, and because outsourcing is a dependent relationship, you should also decide what termination rights you intend to give to the service provider. *The service provider's right to terminate is sharply restricted by smart customers.* Only upon a sustained failure to pay undisputed amounts might the service provider have the right to terminate. A contingency plan needs to be in place in case the vendor fails to deliver. This could happen despite the best intentions on the part of the vendor and the outsourcing organization.

Exit provisions are among the most valuable contractual protections when you are an outsourcing customer. After termination of an outsourcing relationship, the provisions are vital for allowing your business to continue and provide leverage for renegotiations. *Detailed contractual provisions are more essential than ever, because any outsourcing arrangement is fraught with challenges, and these are magnified in the termination scenario.* The customer may have to deliver the services from onshore again at the end of the contract or may have to transition the services to another offshore supplier. The contract should possibly incentivize key employees to have them transferred from the supplier back to the customer or to the new outsourcing partner, because there may be uncertainty regarding availability of sufficient staff to deliver the services. One needs to consider the employment laws of the supplier's country. Appropriate measures must be included in the contract for termination assistance, ongoing service provision for a transitional period, and skills and knowledge transfer, because when services are transferred to a different country, there is real danger that key knowledge will be lost. Access to key subcontractors and ongoing licenses of intellectual property rights (IPR) are also essential.

Transitioning—Postcontract Termination

What you will need in order to make successful transition can be identified through a well-considered termination plan. In such situations the relationship with the service provider usually gets strained, and the service provider will do the very minimum required to comply with the contract. Hence the exit provisions as specified in the contract are very likely to be invoked, unlike many provisions existing during regular working. Having specific people, processes, and infrastructure is a requisite before initiating termination, and the service provider should also have the suitable resources needed to perform the transition. *Smooth and quick transition from the vendor is important, and there should be suitable planning and execution for transition planning assistance, transfer of data, procedures, error logs, documentation, and other information.* Similarly, services like the hiring, assets purchase, software licensing, and assumption of subcontracts need to be executed efficiently before the final cutover to the new vendor or the outsourcing customer's internal personnel. Parallel processing runs for suitable duration after transition is complete and the continued use of shared networks for the same duration are generally advisable. General clauses such as "service provider shall provide such termination assistance as reasonably requested by customer" should also be included. The service provider may take the general nature of the provision as an excuse, but the provision can be helpful in filling the gap. To provide termination assistance, one should decide how to give service provider incentives. Only if you are lucky will your jilted service provider decide to provide high-quality service until the end of the outsourcing agreement. Instead of helping their departed customers, some service providers have hard feelings about termination or decide to focus their energy on serving their continuing customers. Therefore, to provide motivation, you cannot rely on the relationship. However, in the contract you can build both carrots and sticks. For providing termination assistance service, the most common carrot is a substantial fee. Only upon successful completion of termination should payout of the termination fee be made. A capable service provider will get motivated and do its best. If transition services are not possible in some cases, or the service provider has imploded, then the customer may have to face severe difficulties. There are some service providers who cannot properly focus on providing termination assistance because, although they are still afloat, they are circling the drain very fast. Structure the deal to allow an easy exit without termination assistance to reduce this risk. At the exit stage, it may be required of the service provider to provide the same services that the outsourcer provides and cooperate in building internal capability. If the service provider's facility were to be destroyed, safeguard yourself by implementing a mirrored disaster recovery site for your work specifically along with a disaster recovery plan. Home phone numbers and other traditionally internal information of any key personnel should be provided by the service provider at the exit stage. Some of the benefits of outsourcing will be lost, if one follows any of the above-stated alternatives. One cannot take benefit of the provider's presumably superior technology if one makes the service provider use one's own facilities and technology. The economies of scale will be lost if one's work is broken out from the rest of the provider's work or one's work is broken into separate pieces. To reduce damage, one can use early termination assistance and get the right to obtain key termination services before giving a termination notice. Developing and maintaining a procedure manual detailing how services will be performed by the service provider should be a requirement in the contract. A well-documented procedure manual can be the basis of a request for proposal (RFP) for a successor service provider or a template for building an internal capability, in addition to being a useful outsourcing management tool. The outsourcing organization should exude suitable control over operations like audits, technology roadmap, periodic data downloads, source code escrows, and efficient control over services availed. Transition and assignment of future supplier vendors and service to customers are important drivers.

Example—Antidumping U.S. Law

As practices change over time and laws fade giving way to new.

To protect local business from foreign competition, laws like the antidumping legislation exist in the United States. The buyer should be abreast of related laws that exist. These are some factors that should be properly understood before arriving at a decision to contract/outsource. In this age of information/knowledge, the buyer and organization should constantly update themselves and assimilate information so that there is greater prudence in their strategic decisions toward outsourcing.

Gazing out into the prism of time, at the unexplored frontiers.

Chapter 8

Operations—Execution, Challenges, Quality, Etc.

The waves (read: competitors) beside them danced,
but they outdid the waves in glee.

Operations Optimization

The deeds of those that reverberate through space and time.

Many businesses are starting to take a long, hard look at their own systems, processes, and structures as an alternative route to increased profitability and market share. They are spurred on by waves of additional regulations, demanding significant improvements in transparency and reporting standards, improvements that can be achieved through greater operational efficiency and clarity. In augmenting operational performance, skills of employees play an important role. Thus employee skill sets need to be continuously honed through adequate monitoring and training.

In enterprise application integration, vendor suppliers provide reductions in systems and IT total cost of ownership (TCO) by maximizing existing investments in systems, implementing business changes through underlying information technology solutions. Global enterprise visibility of information and business processes is enabled, often by extending the supply chain visibility. To maximize performance while maintaining the highest standards of service and safety is the strategic focus of any company. To improve profitability and performance, a focus on operational efficiency is a must, which can be taken care of by improving the analytical architectures and business intelligence solutions. *The business reporting solutions are enabled through standardization in data representation, data availability, nonduplication of information, adequate drill-down analysis capabilities, etc.* This plugs the information gap and keeps one updated to achieve operational efficiency.

Companies that have a heritage in the IT product side are referred to as technology owners, and companies in this category include those that provide infrastructure and front office applications as well as those that specialize in contact center technology. These include companies such as IBM, Oracle, Lucent, and Nortel. Most involved with the contact center–focused services are the companies with a telecommunications heritage, and in the past these companies were the primary source for call center technology and services, especially in the area of call routing and switching technology. The contact centers are affected by the telecommunication providers in ways like providing toll free phone service and intelligent network–based call routing and management services. Systems integration and consulting services help to achieve intelligent network–based call routing and management services.

To create a lower operating cost model, management has to overcome several strategic dilemmas and challenges. Employee retention is an issue that may come up as a result of the decision to outsource to an offshore vendor. This may increase unionization in various employee groups which perceive that additional positions will be offshored. Therefore senior management should effectively communicate and commit to avoid involuntary job reductions. There should be a proper mechanism to control operations, because service quality may not be up to the mark and offshoring makes it difficult to measure and correct performance failures, and it may be difficult to seek prompt redress of contract issues due to the offshore country's legal system. Therefore the client should select a vendor with a proven track record, monitor vendor performance constantly, include hiring and training criteria in the contract, and put some of its employees in the offshore center.

Operations Optimization through Vendor Expertise

Queen to the strike, as pawns fall by in the game of life and chess.

Organizations seeking cost reduction or the ability to handle capacity fluctuations often use outsourcing by leveraging from their vendors' abilities. The aim is to achieve maximum integration with the firm's internal processes and systems and to cause minimal disruption. *The provider's way of doing things is usually adopted by organizations that seek best-in-class processes or new technologies without capital investment.* By adopting such a provider's way of working, often an organization can achieve value by changing their own internal processes and the behavior of their own employees. At times it can be harder than ever to follow a well-trodden path to value, due to the expanded nature of what is possible to accomplish with outsourcing. On the other hand, stunning results can be achieved by organizations that carefully craft the right relationship to meet their needs and learn valuable lessons from the experience of others that have tried new and different ways of outsourcing arrangements. A wide range of strategic goals can be achieved, and the rewards can be significant.

To ensure that operational and developmental issues can be tackled, flexibility will continue to be a key issue. Valuable information and knowledgeable speakers at conferences can increase the understanding of key industry issues.

Operations Execution

The passion to give, whatever the challenges, a defining individual trait.

Global outsourcing may involve delegation and segregation of responsibilities. Staff may assist in tasks like ensuring correct specifications. The specifications may be technical or nontechnical. A good deal of accuracy may be required so that specifications are precise. Approximations or incorrect specifications may prove costly. Process knowledge and past experience may prove very handy, yet the task of process audits needs the services of auditors. This ensures greater clarity and presents the correct picture. A proper evaluation needs to be done so that there is correct estimation of cost and price. Qualified and experienced staff is required to select the supplier who can meet the requirements. This is an important task and can be the turning point in business. An expert and adroit supplier knows and performs its work well, which is beneficial to both the parties. Just like selecting an expert supplier can have very far-reaching consequences, similarly selecting one who is not skilled in the job can also have very far-reaching consequences. Global outsourcing may require training in some aspects.

To gain experience with technology, identify issues and develop a prototype of appropriate standards which serve as a working prototype.

An outsourcing relationship is helped by a few measures like saving of cost and time, updates on mandatory practices, satisfaction levels, mechanisms for continuous feedbacks, implementation of workflows, and effective policy changes. Outsourcing work is enhanced due to the constant advances in computers and technology, and providers are abreast of these changes and can offer high quality services. In fact, many Indian providers are becoming more advanced than their Western counterparts because of the sheer volume and diversity of work being outsourced to India, thereby causing some companies to grow larger in size, and thus becoming broader in their knowledge and experience. Customers and vendors can use a common platform to make outsourcing simple, thus enabling an easy flow of documents back and forth without having any glitches or incompatibility problems.

The creation of relationships between the various organizations, which include the buyer, supplier, and all intermediaries, is critical to the success of any contracting/outsourcing assignment. The assessment of the skills and the knowledge base of the supplier and other intermediaries is an important task. Also the time and distance factors, along with the language and culture factors should be kept in mind. Proper execution and management are of paramount importance. It is easy to manage a small organization or a small project. As the organization grows in size or the project becomes more and more complex, the degree of dexterity needed for management increases. The delegation and segregation of duties and tasks should be proper. Thus leadership skills and managerial capabilities come into play. This includes the identification of personnel best suited for a particular task and delegation of responsibility to them with regular reviews and supervision.

Example—Operations

Without the expense of establishing a shared service center, outsourcing can also be the answer for a company wishing to get control and oversight of a process at a regional level. *In the Asia Pacific region, in-country regulations and banking conventions are particularly complex, and here as an example, Deutsche bank has developed the capability to centrally match funds with the invoice data supplied by corporate customers of various countries.* By outsourcing check collection to a third-party provider, a corporation can benefit from a more efficient process and lower total costs, because there can be a considerable time lag between receiving paper checks and getting visibility and use of funds, especially when payments are coming into different countries in several currencies. One collection point can be provided together with high-speed processing of incoming checks. Information is available via a secure online archive as soon as the check is processed and can also be downloaded to your internal systems in a choice of file formats. Once again the easy interchange of data with the outsourcing partner is a critical element of the solution. By enhancing the visibility of data associated with it, a traditional process can be improved. A variety of payment terms can be handled along with rebates and penalties, thereby helping to make functions responsive and highly efficient to the needs of the business. From local knowledge and expertise, added value comes.

Example—BPO Operations—Mentor–Mentee Concept

The knowing strokes from the masters of the game.

Many international call centers work at night, and some staff find it difficult to remain awake all night. For some, concentrating on work and customer problem resolution becomes more difficult at night, even if the work load is the same or less than that in a day shift. *Biologically with regard to sleep patterns, human beings are of two types—diurnal and nocturnal.* A diurnal person is more active during the day and can perform well during daytime, whereas a nocturnal person is more active at night and his or her performance at night is better. It is probably the diurnal type who will quit a job sooner when working night shifts. It has also been found that some staff fall ill after working for a couple of nights, while some others start suffering from stress, strain, and depression, which soon becomes unmanageable and takes its toll. To alleviate stress, some companies have introduced the mentor–mentee concept wherein the mentee can discuss problems with the mentor, who can try to provide a solution. The mentor can be from within a company or from outside, and if he or she is from within the organization, usually a senior person or one with a good performance track record. For instance, in a company handling a sales process, a person who cracks many sales and has been a consistent performer can be asked to mentor another person who is unable to crack as many sales. The mentor may give tips regarding sales, communication, process skills, etc., to aid the mentee to perform better. Moreover, if the mentee has any personal problems, he or she can discuss them also with the mentor, who can give suggestions. The mentor can also be an experienced person from outside the organization who understands the psychological problems of the staff.

Operational Costs

Costs, usually driven by needs, work and otherwise.

All costs need to be properly estimated so that an inflated budget is avoided and the benefits of a global contract are reaped. Consider, for example, travel to office, a tangible expense incurred by business process outsourcing (BPO) companies. Some companies provide a pick and drop facility for their employees wherein a cab picks them up from their houses and takes them to office and then drops them back home after work. Those employees who commute on their own may be disbursed money for the expense incurred on fuel. Expenses for business-related travel to other cities in the same country and to other countries should be calculated. The technological and telecommunication services being made use of by the company have a price. Computers, printers, stationery, broadband services, and upgrades of technology in case some new cutting edge technology has come in the market, etc., can cost a tidy sum. The taxes that have to be paid to the government should be considered while calculating the total expense incurred by the company. Some work may require legal assistance. *Apart from the tangible expenses, the intangible expenses (e.g., delays in an issue resolution) exist.* This can have an impact on certain tangible expenses also. For instance, a problem not getting solved may require a face-to-face meeting between the client and the supplier, who may be located in a different country in a global outsourcing contract. So the buyer may have to travel to another country and may need to stay there for a couple of days, giving rise to boarding and lodging expense. Travel, boarding, and lodging are tangible expenses which are the result of an intangible issue. Similarly gaps in communication and inability to forecast errors can lead to further expenses. Therefore, all these costs have to be properly estimated.

In any global outsourcing assignment, both tangible and intangible costs should be considered, and the revenue generated should be calculated after deducting both types of costs incurred. The total expense or total cost incurred is the sum total of the tangible and intangible costs. Tangible costs, among others, may consist of the personnel needed to perform work. Some personnel will be experienced and knowledgeable, while others may require adequate training. In most of the outsourced processes to BPO/international call centers, proper training is required to deliver services. Companies may spend huge sums of money on training new recruits. The training may last for a period of one to three months in most cases, depending on the type of process that has been outsourced. Then there is the huge problem of attrition in the ITES/BPO industry. Some trainees quit before the training is over, while others complete their training, picking up their salaries for the training period, and then quit the job. There are still others who work for a very short duration, a couple of months or so, after completing training and then leave. In all these cases, a lot of money and resources of the company that has been spent on the recruits goes to waste. Companies still have to devise effective methods to control this issue. This does not mean that recruits are responsible or at fault for attrition, because the repetitive nature of work and night shift working hours just do not suit many, causing them to quit.

Cash flow difficulties can be created by inexperienced and improperly trained personnel. The outsourcing process consists of a number of steps beginning with the sending of capabilities by the supplier to the client in response to a query. The last step is the finalization of the price and reference check.

Example—Chief Financial Officer (CFO)—Role and Operations

A master's touch, life defining.

At the center of a complex web of internal and external relationships, the chief financial officer (CFO) operates where relationships are carefully orchestrated and integrated. *The CFO must balance, as integrator, and control internal financial operations, processes, and transactions. The CFO also manages external relationships, needs, expectations, and competition.* The finance functions are driven in a clearly distinctive manner to derive differentiation by high-performance businesses that demonstrate this mastery. High-performance businesses develop their finance organizations by focusing on key sets of capabilities, one of which is finance operations. The use of technologies, organizational structures, and process best practices are required for excellence in finance operations to enable high-quality, effective service delivery while adopting a low-cost operating model. High-performance financial functions can be achieved by outsourcing routine, focus-consuming tasks. Help is needed to evaluate what processes are outsourcing candidates, as well as how to break down finance functions into entities suitable for outsourcing, although most CFOs are aware of the opportunities of cost savings and process improvements from outsourcing financial operations.

Example—Bearings of Office Location

Most of life is lived traveling a few routes.

Despite the recent economic downturn, a tangible expenditure for companies is their workplace, and prices of real estate have spiraled up. Purchasing an office or renting one is an expensive proposition these days, especially in the metropolitan cities where the price of land is at a premium. In a bid to reduce the expense incurred on office space, some companies have purchased large tracts of land outside city limits at comparatively lower rates. *Such out-of-city locations usually lead to higher employee focus, higher operational efficiencies, better ambience, space, and better personal–work life balance.* Employees know that they need to complete their work on time and catch a bus back to the city on time. The issue of staff commuting is relatively less expensive when weighed against the many advantages. Miscellaneous expenses like electricity bills, water bills, and refreshments like tea, coffee, milk, etc., tend to be independent of office location. When purchasing or renting an office, its location should be carefully taken into consideration.

Vendor Management

Transparency that permeates forward and aft.

Regarding transactions processed or funds handled by the service provider on behalf of the institution, appropriate controls should be placed. The policies and procedures of the service provider should be reviewed by the client institution. The operational and financial performance of the service provider should be reviewed by the client institution on an ongoing basis to ensure that the service provider is meeting and can continue to meet the terms of the arrangement. To review the service provider's performance and risk control, the institution's staff should have sufficient training. It must be ensured by the institution that it has complete and immediate access to the information critical to its operations that is maintained or processed by a service provider. At the institution, the records maintained should be adequate to enable the examiner to review its operations fully and effectively, even if a function is outsourced. The audit function of the institution should review the oversight of critical service providers. According to the scope and frequency appropriate to a particular function, audits of the outsourced functions should be conducted. Audits of service providers should be conducted by serviced institutions, or the service provider's internal and external audit scope and findings should be regularly reviewed. An effective internal audit system should be developed by service providers, or it should commission comprehensive, regular audits from third-party organizations. *Management responses and audit results must be available to examiners on request.*

Adequate business resumption planning and testing by the service provider should be ensured by the serviced institution. Based on the scope and risks of the outsourced function, and the condition and performance of the service provider, the serviced institution's contingency plan may also include plans for the continuance of processing activities, either in house or with another provider, in the event that the service provider is no longer able to provide the contracted service or the arrangement is otherwise terminated unexpectedly. For outsourcing of critical information, the arrangements for transaction processing functions to service providers located outside the United States should be conducted according to the risk management guidelines described.

During the long-term relationship, one of the most important issues for outsourcing companies is how to ensure that the supplier is operating efficiently and cost effectively. *To ensure that the supplier remains competitive, periodic benchmarking against existing best practices is the most popular way of subjecting the vendor to greater scrutiny.* On a periodic basis, price paid by the customer for the service performed and the relevant service levels can be compared with the performance of competitors, with a procedure for varying the contract where this is not competitive. Detailed management information and extensive auditing provisions will be needed by the customer who should monitor the offshore services very carefully. Regular communication between the outsourcing customer and the vendor is critical for day-to-day operations. Organizational politics and the culture may be very different in the offshore location, with different national holidays and political regimes and higher bureaucracy levels. Appropriate handling mechanisms should be set out in the contract to manage the same.

Example—Outsourcing BPO Operations to India

As players continuously reposition for all-around value propositions.

An integral part of organizational success is customer support, and that is why outsourcing has an impetus, with call centers making a niche for themselves. A flawless customer support service is of paramount importance in today's world of ruthless competition. The response to customers' queries should be in a polite, timely, and professional manner, thereby infusing confidence in the client. Communication services offered need to maximize business output, resulting in a long-lasting relationship with customers. World-class facilities, a large pool of highly educated professionals who speak English, increasingly good telecom connectivity, and capabilities to handle a range of services make India one of the most popular outsourcing destinations. The advantage of language capability in India goes a long way, and it has the largest English-speaking population in the world, along with the second largest and the fastest growing pool of technical manpower. Often call center agents in India are more computer literate and educated than their counterparts in the parent outsourcing organization. Hence rapid service delivery is ensured by a reliable work force of world-class quality.

The IT/BPOs in India have increasingly adapted to international quality and security standards. Instantaneous high-speed transfer of voice and data across the globe is ensured by the Indian telecommunication network. Regardless of the customer's private automatic branch exchange (PABX), automatic call distributor (ACD), computer, or database, the ability to provide critical telephony integration and interactive voice response systems exists. Uptime commitments of over 99% are provided with the deployment of the best of telecom infrastructure with various redundancies at every critical juncture. Frequently changing information is accurately driven with intelligent scripting programs, advanced learning and development teams, and quality first processes. Direct Internet access allows tracking online problems, and continued reception takes place due to flawless duplicated systems. Further boost to outsourcing is provided by the highly liberal policies of the government of India. Services in India are provided at competitive costs as compared to the costs in other countries. By reducing the prices of high-speed international private leased circuits, the government of India has given a special thrust to the industry. In most IT-enabled services, potentially 50% to 80% of total process costs can be outsourced offshore, and as much as 70% to 80% of the costs can be reduced, primarily because of wage differentials. But expatriate management may be required to initially support operations in remote locations, and this would result in an additional cost of 10% to 20%, together with higher telecom costs. The skill set of the staff of the supplier should consist of conversation skills and competency, education along with technical skills and outsourcing etiquette, experience in work-related domain and Internet skills. Good infrastructure, highly qualified agents, state-of-the-art technology and security solutions, and significant investment in the training of agents make outsourcing a lucrative option. Multimedia channel interaction is delivered with state-of-the-art multimedia centers. Through strategic tie-ups with other centers, the business continuity sites are established to provide disaster recovery (DR) services. In a rapidly changing global business environment, the need to comply with the international standards is understood, and the aim is that the processes should meet the International Organization of Standardization (ISO) compliance standards.

Example—Outsourcing Customer Support

The operations that must function around the clock, a business need.

Providing quality customer support has become a critical component in maintaining the trust and reliability in a relationship, given the fact that many institutions have to be accessible to their customers on a 24/7 basis. Institutions are burdened with customer support issues and spiraling support costs, with the perceptible increase in client interaction in recent times and with the limited scope of conventional customer service. To match the current operations of a firm, the provider can address the problem by delivering dependable customer service. Customer service initiatives can be raised to greater heights by the implementation of customer service best practices by the provider. *There can be savings of more than 50% over time with higher quality, elimination of peak staffing needs, payment based on usage, paperless environment, 24/7 access, and faster turnaround time.* The provider has highly competent and experienced professionals, secure environment with firewalls, intrusion detection, and monitoring, daily backup, and audits to meet client needs. Companies are constantly under pressure to reduce timelines and produce more out of less, and providers use various tools to fulfill customer needs.

Operational Challenges

Even down to the last man, such to be the approach and reach.

Global outsourcing is not the panacea for all problems, and there are some risks associated with it like overexpectation of cost reduction. The buyer giving the contract to the supplier may wrongly assume that the cost savings are more, without considering the hidden costs. Business estimates may wrongly assume initial cost savings in the range of 40%. *In reality it has been generally found that savings are about 15% to 25% during the first year, and it is only by the third year that cost savings reach up to 35% to 40%.*

Despite using the best methodology and in spite of the dexterity of the vendor, failures can occur. The ramifications of any such failure should be properly assessed, and if the business failure implications are severe, then it may sometimes be advisable to outsource to multiple vendors instead of one or outsource to a vendor with specific skills to mitigate risk of failure. Therefore an in-depth risk analysis should be done, especially if the consequences can be disastrous in the case of business failure on the part of the vendor. Though contracts may be fixed price, most projects undergo changes by 10% to 15% during their development cycles, and vendors expect payment for incremental scope changes. The vendor must adhere to government regulations as it may face various degrees of government oversight and therefore should be sensitive to the rules. There should be compliance with regulations and adequate transparency and accountability during audits. *The USA Patriot Act and the Sarbanes–Oxley Act call for greater accountability on all American corporations.*

Culture is another issue, and although English may be the official language of the country in which the supplier is located, pronunciations and accents may vary tremendously. Cultural differences may include the way questions are answered. Therefore accent training may be required for the employees.

Global outsourcing has created a rapid vendor base in certain cities of some countries, and this has led to an increase in the pay package of some key employees who have an appetite for new high-profile projects, and these employees can either switch jobs or be recruited by other vendors. Therefore the turnover of key personnel needs to be properly managed by the vendor. It has been found that turnover levels range between 15% and 20%. Key personnel turnover has an impact on the cost, and organizations have to spend more time on knowledge transfer and training of new individuals. The time and effort for knowledge transfer by the vendor is rarely accounted for by the IT organization, and this may lead to about 20% decline in productivity during the first year due to time spent on transferring technical and business knowledge. Video conferencing, teleconferencing, Internet chats/e-mails, and classroom modes may be used to disseminate knowledge.

In order to ensure proper and efficient management of their income, capital, and investment streams, until recently, the multiplicity of systems required by organizations and local government has been a major burden on their resources. The challenges of e-government and the cost of having multiple technical platforms, complex interfacing, and integrating issues have been traditionally high. Over and above the problems around information delivery, decision support, and user ergonomics, achieving process efficiencies means that the raft of income, investment/loan, and transaction generation systems have been a real barrier to driving costs out of management processes and improving service delivery. Providing an integrated single environment to address the issues of local government, education, and health sectors could be of real benefit to customers.

The decision to outsource and transfer jobs may cause a negative public perception, and so the senior management should address any such negative publicity. Process quality may be compromised due to aggressive implementation and deadlines. Resource constraint may lead to mishandling of the process by the vendor, and this may need more supervision on the part of the client. To support implementation and transition, it is necessary to utilize temporary resources and prioritize initiatives. Noncritical initiatives should be deferred to a later period, and realistic time lines should be developed and followed. Customer frustration with the offshore vendor may cause loss of revenue, unrecovered sunk costs may arise due to technology improvements which increase efficiency, and low U.S. employee morale may result in a fall in productivity. So, a vendor with a proven track record should be chosen, the contract should include ramp down and exit clauses, and senior management should not lack in effective communication. Offshore operations may get disrupted due to geopolitical reasons, and local strikes or financial problems of the vendor may cause operations to cease. Therefore an effective exit strategy should be built and maintained to mitigate risk and follow a multivendor sourcing strategy. In the event of business continuity problems, negotiate enough financial resources and select a vendor that is financially sound and has an established client base.

Many offshore businesses lack creativity and innovation, and clients have often complained about it. Bank on some heavy lifting when switching to offshore and do not bank on immediate payoff. Costs can actually increase during ramp up of offshore projects. Lags in productivity can add as much as 20% in costs to offshore contracts according to Meta Group. Staffing overlap as the home team hands off to the offshore programmers forms a part of the lag. Two rate schedules exist whenever work is outsourced to an offshore provider—offshore, which is the rate charged for work done overseas, and onshore, which means the rates charged for the consultants that must come on-site during the transition period. Onshore rates are significantly higher and usually rival internal IT costs. It has been found that clients invariably underestimate the number of onshore staff required for making a project successful. Therefore at the onset of the project, this leads to inflated expectations about savings. Indian offshore companies derive more than half of the revenue generated from onshore staff augmentation. Advances in technology have aided immensely in generating revenue and profitability.

Improper alignment between the ambitions of the buyer and the supplier can give rise to problems. *There should be shared vision and compatibility; otherwise the contract is more likely to fail than succeed. Gaps in communication can further exacerbate the issue.* It is possible that the vendor may be devoting more time to contracts awarded to it by other companies, thereby neglecting the work given by some other buyers. Compatibility and effective management are crucial for the relationship to succeed, and the operating styles should be in consonance. An effective management mechanism consisting of management committees, advisory boards, work groups, problem-solving teams, and relationship managers needs to be in place to ensure the success of the relationship.

Managers are constantly striving to meet challenges of keeping on-site and offshore teams motivated, maintaining on-time delivery, meeting service level commitments (SLAs), and staying within initial budgeted estimates. Offshore program and project management involve four basic categories of work. *These challenger project transition management, project governance, performance management, and quality compliance.* The real work begins only after the contract is signed, despite rigorous diligence, vendor reviews, and test projects. The next issue to tackle is smooth transition management, considered to be a critical success factor of offshore initiatives. The detailed, desk-level knowledge transfer and documentation of all phases, technologies used, business processes, and functions is called transition management. It may take a short or long time to complete the transition, which is perhaps the most difficult stage of an offshore endeavor. Transition management involves improving the vendor management by documenting the lessons learned; managing employees by redeploying, transferring, or terminating; managing strategic and operational communications; transferring knowledge of internal procedure and processes; initiating projects and facilitating transition operations; and developing transition plans such as key activities, milestones, resources, and dependencies. It is time to govern the offshore relationship—captive center, joint venture, or external vendor—after one has begun managing the transition. This goes beyond merely monitoring contractual obligations such as the evolution of services provided; focus on proactive and collaborative management, ongoing communication process, performance review standards, and overall project management. The importance of governance cannot be underestimated, and in offshoring it can either make or break a project. Governance may consist of risk management which entails identifying, analyzing, and responding to outsourcing partnership risks; change management involving standardized procedures being used for efficient and prompt handling of all changes; relationship management to compensate for the loss of direct interaction between stakeholders, managers, and team members; and project management to communicate, collaborate, and monitor the vendor.

To define, manage, and communicate service level results against each client's defined service agreements, Computer Science Corporation (CSC) has developed an innovative tool—STARS. Personnel can constantly monitor and report on service level status and initiate escalation and improvement procedures as necessary.

Data theft occupational risks exist in outsourcing, says Verizon. Verizon's unit investigates a large proportion (25% to 30%) of large data breaches every year and many smaller cases. *In the past few years, restaurant and retail business areas made up about half of Verizon's total of about 250 data theft cases per year.* Outsourcing by restaurants and retail businesses of credit card processing technical functions is also partly responsible for consumer data thefts, according to data investigations at Verizon Communications Inc. Even very large restaurants usually hire very few employees for their technology needs. More often than not external vendors would be used to manage most of these functions, said Bryan Sartin, director of investigative response team at Verizon Business. "What happens is there's a lack of accountability on the third party," Sartin said. It often finds that insiders at service vendors are part of heists.

Example—Operational Challenges of Banks and Financial Organizations

Financial institutions are facing the need to deliver improved shareholder value from ever-increasing competitive markets. Increases in costs are generated by duplicated structures and inflexible technological/service solutions. Business flexibility is reduced by them and service quality damaged through inconsistency. In order to identify each individual component in the financial service value chain, banks need to adopt a whole new way of looking at operations, one that breaks through artificial boundaries that have been drawn around discrete business units. The wholesale and capital markets institutions are one group of banks that particularly stands out here. These have been historically organized along the lines of separate operations supporting their banking, fixed income, and equity lines of business.

Rapid innovation in individual product development has provided much of the competitive edge. Factors like consistency, integration, and control of duplicated costs become major competitive concerns. *Thus banks need to integrate banking and capital markets by being able to offer a unified solution to their corporate customers.* To remain competitive, identifying common processes and achieving greater efficiency from them is vital. Each business process transformation initiative should not only identify common components but even common subcomponents. The need to achieve integration between operations and processes by banks is necessary to deliver and manage those integrated operations. Operations are being restructured increasingly by banks to supply the entire organization, delivering systems, process, and complete operational environments to business units through a single integrated manufacturing unit. By exploiting overlaps in the operations needed to support each product line and geography, the internal shared-service approach delivers economies of scale. In implementing such an approach, however, the challenges are considerable along with the need to overcome entrenched business attitudes.

In outsourcing decisions, cost reduction has long been a major factor, yet many banks are largely unaware of the real costs of certain functions. Complaints about costs and time taken for development will continue, unless this is made clear from the start. If application development is handed over to a third party, it can leave the financial institution in a position where it no longer has certain skill sets in house, a problem if the function needs to be brought back in house. Problems of remoteness can be presented by offshore outsourcing, resulting in misunderstandings. Lack of business knowledge and cultural barriers go hand in hand. The relationship between bank and outsourcer is often time intensive, and there needs to be a good working relationship. It becomes much more difficult to establish a close working relationship if the cultures of the two organizations clash. The outsourcing project will struggle to succeed if the outsourcer does not have a clear understanding of the bank's business. Employee support is necessary because in-house staff often transfer over to the outsourcer company.

Risk Management

Opening the game to reviews, critics, all.

Risk management measures are commonly used to address the operational control of the service provider under outsourcing arrangements rather than the serviced institution that would bear the associated risk of financial loss, reputational damage, or other adverse consequences. Before outsourcing projects, the client should ascertain the risk mitigation mechanism of the supplier. Transaction of information and information outsourcing involve operational risks (some similar in both cases) that arise when these functions are performed internally, such as threats to availability of systems used to support customer transactions, the integrity and security of customer account information, or the integrity of risk management information systems.

Companies should seek out risk management partners, specialists that focus on reducing program costs through use of managed care and improved productivity. To pay the appropriate amount and no more is the goal, and more innovative specialists take an attitude that the client's money is their own and make decisions accordingly. To set goals such as reducing the number of lost days, increasing modified duty, getting consistent control of reserves, and increasing the number of recoveries, specialists should work with the employer. The employer can rate how well the administrator addresses both high-severity and high-frequency claims over time, by stratifying claims by dollar value (e.g., small, middle, and large) and then compare the results with the goals.

Risk and reward clauses should be part of the contract if the company is serious about measuring results. Also, the best partners have the state-of-the-art administration technology. Dramatic reduction in administrative tasks can be achieved by having workers submit tasks electronically, integrating systems, having pull-down menus that contain client-approved vendors and client-specific service instructions, and looking for red flags on tasks that are outside normal dollar or timeframe criteria. From their desks, in addition, employers should be able to perform data analysis. They should have Web-based systems that allow them to manipulate the data in virtually any manner, instead of receiving paper loss runs.

Operations—Contingency—Disaster Recovery (DR)

Of risks and those who take them head on.

Once work has been outsourced, it is important that continuity of services takes place. What would happen if one were unable to reach one's customers, or if the service provider's center is inaccessible for a certain period of time due to unavoidable circumstances? For an outsourced service provider/BPO/call center, disaster recovery is indispensable if one wants to keep connected at all times. The disaster recovery plans can be based either on geography or on operations. On geography, the disaster recovery plan can be at the site or state or national or international level, with additional infrastructure accordingly in the same facility, or in the same city/state, or a different city/state, or same/different country, which is used to maintain business continuity in case of emergency and disruption of work.

Based on operations, disaster recovery could be cold DR or warm DR or hot DR. In case of cold DR, the service provider maintains an additional center consisting of extra furniture and structured cabling so that in case the existing center closes down, operations can be shifted to this one. Computers will have to be set up and the WAN links redirected, and this could take a few days. In case of warm DR, furniture and cabling, computers, and WAN links already exist at the contingency site, and in an emergency only data needs to be synchronized, applications installed, and the WAN link redirected. This could take up to 24 hours. The hot DR is the costliest option. In an emergency, only the staff needs to be moved into this center, which is always online and kept synchronized with production.

Through strategic tie-ups with other centers to provide disaster recovery services, Indian service providers have established business continuity sites in India and overseas. In their entire technological infrastructure, they have ensured backups—from servers, processors, leased lines, and storage systems to fully backed-up UPS and generator systems. Customers will not be able to tell the difference because these disaster recovery centers work just like the actual functioning center, with facilities such as computer systems, network connectivity, peripherals, and communications equipment. It is ensured that business is recovered very quickly with these facilities and agents' expertise.

Quality Imperative

Continuous relearning, through work and life.

The BPO industries cannot sustain themselves merely by positioning as lower-cost alternatives with English-speaking abilities. So the Indian players are moving at a frenetic pace toward achieving internationally recognized quality control standards. Never before has the importance of consistency, low error rates, and customer satisfaction been felt as strongly as right now. Therefore, no holds are barred in the efforts of governing bodies like the National Association of Software and Service Companies (NASSCOM) to improve quality regulations. In terms of skills and knowledge required by the BPO industry, NASSCOM plans to introduce common certification programs across India. Initiatives toward controlling issues like copyright infringement are being made by the organization for ensuring quality. To ensure information security and control data piracy, there are plans to formulate a comprehensive draft proposal. Both the internal senior management team as well as the client team will perform internal checks and continuous quality reviews. Creation of a common yardstick for BPO organizations is being planned by NASSCOM.

Carnegie Mellon University was involved in developing E-SCM (the E-services capability model) to create such a yardstick. Clients who are selecting a suitable service provider will benefit extremely from the model because it allows them to compare the capabilities of different service providers and also compare issues associated with the initiation and completion of the project. Now the concept of benchmarking is being used on a more regular basis. *The continuous process of comparing an organization's performance with a recognized industry leader is benchmarking.* Where a particular company stands in relation to its competitors can be assessed and known from benchmarking. Various training programs in Six Sigma, COPC (Customer Operations Performance Center) implementation, and support and non-certified skills like maintaining customer satisfaction, people management, service levels, and transaction monitoring are held by the Quality Assurance Institute. Ignoring quality in today's world is a call to certain extinction for a company, for now quality is the only choice and no longer an option.

A straightforward approach to identifying the areas that require quality control is resorted to by the quality departments. *Identification of parameters that are "critical to quality"* is the first step. Client's expectations and requirements are included in the parameters. Accuracy, productivity, and turnaround time are the other factors. The process approach is now being followed by many companies. The process approach is a description of the linkages between all the activities that work toward meeting the finest quality standards that have been identified by prevalent quality norms and the client's expectations.

In order to win the battle of customers, a lot of emphasis is being laid on quality. Two popular certifications are offered by Quality Assurance Institute, an international body in the ITES industry, which are the Certified Software Quality Analyst (CSQA) and the Certified Software Test Engineer (CSTE). But most authorities largely consider both these certifications as inadequate. The use of incorrect accent and grammar is another problem concerning industries like the customer contact center which relies on verbal one-on-one communication. Because of misunderstandings or the customer's inability to understand an Indian accent, quality lapses are strongly felt. Specific bodies are being deployed that evaluate prospective employees on English-speaking capabilities such as accent, grammar, fluency, and overall communication skills, and efforts are being made to improve the quality standards in these areas. In great demand among the Indian contact centers is the COPC certification for international standard in contact center operations. Many Indian contact centers already have COPC certifications, and others are in the process of being certified.

In a bid to give impetus to the entrepreneurship activity, many academic institutions like Babson College (United States), Emloyn Business School (France), University of Essex Business School (United Kingdom), and Europe Asia Business School (EABS; India) are providing entrepreneurship education. To boost the spirit of entrepreneurship, a club has been started by EABS, wherein an enterprise can be started by students in a monitored environment with faculty members as consultants. The enterprise can then be taken to the next level of venture capital funding if progress is satisfactory during the year. Apart from helping in comprehending the issues pertaining to business, such ventures also aid in creating wealth and environment.

The types and complexity of contracts and sourcing alliances are bound to explode as offshore outsourcing becomes viable for multiple business processes. The challenges involved are coordinate interactions, managing performance across teams, monitoring contractual obligations, tracking financials, and maintaining alignments in cases where organizations have outsourced almost every aspect of their operations to multiple vendors and with business users and governance teams residing across disparate geographic locations and activities occurring around the clock. For long-term success, a disciplined, continuous improvement is a necessity.

Ongoing governance consists of measuring outsourcing effectiveness using appropriate metrics, SLAs, and business case and continuous performance reporting. Improvements and adjustments are quickly implemented, and based on industry and business changes and lessons learned, outsourcing is reevaluated versus the in-house decision, and the feasibility of additional outsourcing is evaluated.

Quality management is of paramount importance, and it is more costly to fix defects compared to requirement problems. A strict quality assurance and control program forms an integral part of every offshore delivery model. Different methodologies are used to assess offshore projects and delivery centers. To measure the quality of an organization's management and software engineering practices, SEI-CMM (Capability Maturity Model) can be used. The Software Engineering Institute (SEI) of Carnegie Mellon University offers P-CMM, the People Certification, and the International Organization of Standardization offers ISO 9001-2000 certification, an international standard for quality management systems. Six Sigma improvement methodologies can be used. Such approaches involve sustained review and continuous improvement of software development life cycles and business processes, regular monitoring of work and outputs, and regular internal and external quality audits. Customized status reports are submitted for senior management review.

The risk of data security cannot be overlooked. An evaluation of the security and protection mechanism of the vendor needs to be done. Many offshore vendors have impressive security and intellectual property protection practices, thereby addressing many privacy concerns. The Capability Maturity Model (CMM) is an important measure, with CMM level 5 becoming a common characteristic, although it was observed by Meta Group that approximately 70% of the companies are at CMM level 1, a gap that is compensated by additional vendor resources on site. A global outsourcing assignment may lead to compromising company practices and loss of business knowledge, and in some cases the business knowledge/expertise may be proprietary or of competitive advantage.

India still remains at a disadvantage when it comes to certifications for quality professionals, despite having highly academically qualified professionals with high performance levels. Most international certifications available are either U.S. or U.K. based, and few reputed quality certifications are based in India. In order to provide quality work, vendors should gain a better understanding of the issues affecting the development of outsourcing. Contracting/outsourcing is a powerful tool, and buyers and suppliers both must understand the relative scope of contracting services that will be utilized. Key business challenges and the traditional obstacles and the leading market dynamics are accelerating the acceptance and utilization of outsourcing services. Education and technical qualifications of vendor personnel are a key factor, and vendors should strive to hire personnel who are often more qualified than the outsourcing customer organization.

People and resources an intertwined web.

WEB-BASED OUTSOURCING

Chapter 9

Web Outsourcing— Introduction

The Web shall be the other timeless entity, like God.

Internet—Brief Background

The Web, the marketplace universe.

The advent of the Internet is almost as significant as electricity, the assembly line, the telephone, and the steam engine. Other than the Internet, few concepts have caught the attention of financial markets, news media, government bureaucrats, and the public at large with so much sound and fury. The Internet has become the leading buzzword that has so many definitions and is known variously as the electronic, interactive, or multimedia information superhighway.

The Internet is a large group of millions of computers (greater than 6 million computers currently) located around the world that are all connected to one another over a maze of networks. Thus the Internet is a global network of networks. It actually consists of many networks. The number of computers in such a network can range from two or three in a small intranet to several thousands in large organizations. *It has over 50 million users currently.*

Tools and programs are being built by software companies to make the various heterogeneous pieces work together. To prepare for the future, we do see billion-dollar companies and global conglomerates (e.g., Microsoft, Viacom, AT&T, Sony, Time Warner) accelerate, align, and leverage from the Internet. The interest in the Internet is diffusing to all industries. This has led to maneuvering through mergers, acquisitions, and joint ventures. To construct new infrastructure, firms have begun making sustainable investments in technology. Over the next 10 to 15 years, projections indicate that anywhere from $100 to $200 billion will be spent on constructing the Internet infrastructure. In all spheres, the pace of activity is frantic. To better prepare for life on the Internet, companies are constantly upgrading their network infrastructures, repositioning products and services, etc.

On the nontechnology front, courts are stepping in, declaring certain regulatory statutes. To eliminate restrictions on competition worldwide, governments jointly are proposing new laws to keep the Web free and fair.

History of the Internet

The history of the Internet starts in the 1950s and 1960s with the development of computers. This began with point-to-point communication between mainframe computers and terminals, expanded to point-to-point connections between computers and then early research into packet switching. The idea of the World Wide Web (www) was later introduced in 1989 by Sir Tim Berners-Lee, considered the father of the Internet. Since then the growth of the Internet was rapid. Tim Berners-Lee himself introduced terms like URL and http. He is currently the chairman of w3c (World Wide Web consortium), which is the governing body of the Web.

The history of the Internet can be divided into three stages:

1. Initial stage: Internet is generally used for file transfer purposes based on FTP protocol.
2. Second stage: GOPHER is introduced. Web pages contain text only.
3. Third stage: HTML is introduced. Multimedia features are introduced in Web pages.

For additional details, see http://en.wikipedia.org/wiki/Internet.

How People Discover Web Sites

Search ranks second (e-mail is first) as the top online activity. Web users of, 85% use search engines to find solutions and vendors.

- Search engines 87%
- Links from other sites 85%
- Printed media 65%
- Word of mouth 58%
- New groups 32%
- e-mail 32%

- Television 32%
- Others 28%
- Books 28%

Marketing strategies include

- Search engines and directories
- Advertising banners
- Online classified advertisements
- Message boards
- Registering users and sending e-mails
- Links on other Web sites
- News groups, discussion lists, press releases
- Traditional media
- Trademark and branding

Search engine market share—2009:

- Google 83%
- Yahoo 7%
- Baidu 3%
- Bing 3%
- AOL 0.6%
- Ask 0.6%
- Others 1% (balance)

Web-Based Outsourcing

The Internet encompasses almost every field of modern-day life, some fields being:

- **Empowering the user**—The Net users resort to increased self-help and individual effort through Internet usage toward achievement of required needs.
- **Jobs**—As a key economic factor and a vector in globalization, the Net drives multifarious jobs, new businesses, and trade.
- **Services**—Providing ever-improving end user information and experience to the customer by public authorities and private enterprises.
- **Education**—The Net is the superstore of knowledge, and by extension diversified education across various fields is driven by it.
- **Entertainment**—Audio, video, leisure, shopping, and gaming are some commonplace applications.
- **People-to-people interactions**—E-mail (the most prevalent usage), chatting using text, voice, images, video, etc., are some related uses of the Net.

- **Mobility**—Three billion mobile devices use the Internet currently (2009). This is an exploding market with high future potential.
- **A public good**—The Internet is slowly growing into a critical infrastructure providing support to various core aspects of society.

The way for a more competitive market is thus being paved, and Web-based outsourcing is one such business approach which uses the underlying World Wide Web framework of public and dedicated wide area networks. People, teams, and organizations work together across multiple geographies to buy, sell, and deliver products and services using online Web-based outsourcing.

In online outsourcing, speed is the essence. By using fast-paced enablers, the online idea should be set up and executed by vendors, with its results evaluated. Quick changes (big or small) or exiting altogether should follow suit. The cycle is quickly repeated for succeeding ideas and products over the Web until desirable results are achieved. *Online outsourcing setups should follow the approach "Load, fire, aim" (in that order) versus traditional businesses, which follow the approach "Aim, load, fire" (in that order). The aim can be quickly readjusted from the results quickly achieved by using online vendors.* The question needs to be sufficiently deliberated. Traditional outsourcing follows the simile of the "manual handgun." Each bullet needs to be manually loaded by hand, the aim taken, followed by firing of the handgun, in that order. The cost, effort, and time involved in manual firing of every single bullet is significant and counts. Online outsourcing follows the simile of the "automatic machine gun." The magazine containing a few hundred bullets is loaded and fired off with only an approximate aim, in that order. The aim may be adjusted while firing is under way to hit the target. Since the automatic weapon fires hundreds of bullets in a short span of time, aim taking is not of paramount importance and can be readjusted on the fly. The cost of a single bullet from the many fired off is negligible. Similarly, in the virtual world, outsourcing strategies and goals need to be just realistic in nature with sufficient room for experimentation and innovation, even exit. This is almost in line with the general human behavior, according to which more than 90% of the people do not have a clear long-term goal in life and take up whatever potential opportunity presents itself, making adjustments as they proceed in life. Thus minimal time and effort should be invested in long-term strategy planning in Web-based outsourcing business ventures. *The foresight to sense emerging trends online and the agility to react swiftly through suitable actions to ride the wave is needed in the virtual landscape of online outsourcing.* Agility and speed of execution to close a potential outsourcing business opportunity on the Internet are essential, necessary traits.

Chapter 10

Web Outsourcing Models and Frameworks

Practices endure, till innovation comes knocking.

The business models in the sections that follow suggest ideas, concepts, designs, and frameworks which add innovation to Web-based outsourcing. These are new approaches which can mostly be deployed with relatively small investments across the online outsourcing businessscape.

Business Model 1—Outsourcing over the Web Using Well-Defined Contracts

Net, the new delivery messengers.

Outsourcing organizations and project buyer(s), individually or jointly, may put projects (software, etc.,) needing execution on a Web portal with related information and related expected timelines. Interested, multiple vendors, project sellers, even individuals (as applicable) would compete for the same through respective bids or filled request for proposal (RFP), as required. An online auction could be set up for the project on the respective Web portal. A project order may be awarded suitably to one or more online vendors/project sellers by the project buyer, depending on bid value, project complexity, profile and past performance record of project seller, geographic proximity (if needed), etc. On mutual agreement between the project buyer(s) and project seller(s) based on achievement of project milestones, corresponding payout is made by the project buyer(s) to the vendors/project seller(s).

For example, if agreeable to all concerned parties, the project amount can be transferred in advance to an escrow account of an impartial intermediary organization (which could be a bank, the Web portal administrator, etc.). On achievement of related project milestones, the project buyer can send a confirmation to the intermediary to release appropriate amounts from the escrow account to the project seller(s).

The organization owning the Web portal may become an intermediary allowing other organizations or groups of organizations to put up (i.e., add) new project requests for buying.

Compensation Principle

Actual project value may be subjected to negotiations over and above the initial bid submissions between the project buyer and project sellers before reaching an agreement. Thus actual value is decided as part of a formal contract before initiation of project effort by the seller. This is based on the classical contract model which is commonly prevalent.

1. Financial intermediary (e.g., bank, webmaster, portal administrator) may hold the project value in custody in an escrow account during the execution phase of the project. Such a financial intermediary may in turn charge a certain percentage of the project value or a fixed service charge (as appropriate) and pass the balance amount to the project seller on project closure. This normally applies to small-scale projects.
2. For medium and large-scale projects, for a fixed or variable fee, the Web portal administrator could introduce the project buyer to the vendor project sellers and allow them to enter into an independent contract.

Working Framework 1

Assume today's date is <Date1>. Assume an applicable "project" is planned to complete tentatively on <Date2> (<Date 2> is the same or later than <Date 1>). This is traditional outsourcing framework.

Model suggests today (i.e., on <Date1> itself) to put the "full" project on the the centralized Web portal:

■ Specify project details, the deadline for receiving submissions as <Date2>. This is also the date of completion of project, etc.
■ Float request for proposals (RFP) from potential sellers. Sellers may compete on price, quality, past track record/past projects' history, ratings (if maintained by the portal).

- Award of project order suitably to one or more sellers, specifying respectively the contract and compensation policies.
- Periodically by <Date2>, assimilate the intermediate and final submissions received via the portal. On completion of the project, pay the final contracted amount, as applicable.
- Project ready for further resale from <Date3> onward, if applicable.

Working Framework 2

Assume today's date is <Date1>. Assume an applicable "project" is internally planned to start on date <Date2> (<Date 2> same as or later than today <Date1>) and complete tentatively on <Date3> (<Date 3> same or later than <Date 2>).

This framework suggests today (i.e., on <Date1> itself) to outsource the project in "part" or full on the centralized Web portal:

- Specify the project module details, the deadline for receiving submissions as <Date2>, etc.
- Float request for proposals (RFP) for the part project module from potential sellers. Sellers will compete on reuse of already existing similar past projects/products, price, quality, past track record/past projects' history, ratings (if maintained by the portal).
- Award the project (in part or full) suitably to one or more sellers, specifying respectively the contract and compensation policies.
- Periodically by <Date2>, assimilate the intermediate and final submissions received via the portal. On completion of the project, pay the final contracted amount, as applicable.
- Initiate internal (further) execution of the project on <Date2> and complete by <Date3>.
- Project ready for sale/freeware from <Date3> onward, if applicable.

Salient Feature of This Framework

In the case where the project is planned to be executed internally from a certain future date (<Date2>), the time period for receipt of finished project from the external vendors should deliberately be kept much smaller than the actual time period needed to execute the same from scratch, because this approach targets an already existing similar body of work done previously. Thus this aims to reuse already existing similar work. This would usually reduce the overall final project deadline of <Date3> and possibly a much lower cost is incurred than when attempting to do the whole project from scratch.

Engagement modus—Contractually binding agreements are signed before initiation of project. Respective contract templates can be also made visible on the portal for perusal by the respective potential project sellers.

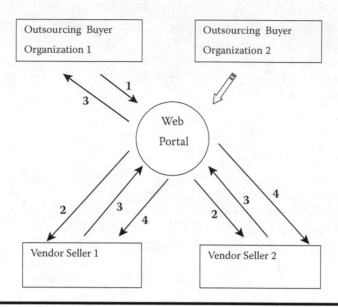

Figure 10.1   Working framework—outsourcing over the Web using well-defined contracts.

Barter—The oldest form of exchange.

In the flow chart in Figure 10.1:

Step 1: Project requirements, miscellaneous project information, the deadline for receiving submissions <Date2>, etc., are put up by the outsourcing buyer on the Web portal. Request for proposals (RFP) may be initiated.

Step 2: Project requirements viewed by multiple potential project seller vendors who respond to the RFP on the Web portal. Award of project order suitably to one or more sellers, specifying respectively the contract and compensation policies.

Step 3: Submissions are made periodically by one or multiple project seller vendors to the outsourcing organization (via the portal).

Step 4: Payout of compensation and project closure.

Related Examples

Framework 1 is a *new* concept with few known existing players. Thus the pioneer advantage can be reaped.

A large number of Internet Web portals exist which use Framework 2 to buy and sell projects online.

Some related examples of these Web portals which cover the fields of software, information technology, BPO, accounts, finance, legal, personnel, administration support, writing, etc.:

http://www.allfreelance.com/ (master site containing links to multiple sites)
http://www.vworker.com/
http://www.freelanceauction.com/
http://www.freelancecentral.net/
http://www.freelance-work.net/
http://www.freelancecenter.com/

A portal example for industrial applications in the fields of business and entrepreneurship, computer science and IT, engineering and design, mathematics and statistics, chemistry, physical sciences, food and agriculture, life sciences, requests for partners/suppliers, etc.:

http://www.innocentive.com

Thus the outsourcing model may be used for any industry and is *not* limited to IT and BPO industries only.

As subnets add to the vast Internet expanses.

Business Model 2—Outsourcing over the Web without Contracts

The networks silently beep with the traffic rushes, day and night.

This model suggests that any required "project" (software, etc. should be put on a centralized Web portal specifying up front an indicative budgeted payout (compensation) which the outsourcing organization/project buyer can pay for the same. Related details of the project, the deadlines for receiving the contributions for the same, the expected date of completion, and legal guidelines (if any) are also put up. *Submissions thus expected and received need "not" be an exact fit of the actual requirements but may be related in some manner, depending on the nature of the respective project. Deadlines should be set such that only sellers having already existing, similar work or projects would be able to successfully meet these timelines.*

Related submissions from multiple sellers would yield an exponential value when assimilated by the project buyer. Multiple submissions/inputs thus received, together reduce the actual effort and project execution time manyfold (a guesstimate being 10 times) which the outsourcing organization/project buyer will subsequently initiate internally. It also adds to faster knowledge buildup and higher quality of project deliverables. This also allows the project buyer/initiating organization to change the received submissions suitably and quickly, as applicable.

Thus from related contributions from as many project sellers as possible, speed is the essence of this model. Hence no contracts whatsoever are drawn up by the outsourcing organization/project buyer organization with any of the vendor project sellers during the entire life cycle.

Additionally, internal effort for evaluation and incorporation of received contributions and further additional effort needed to take the project to completion by the organization putting up the project request needs also to be considered. A gradual buildup of a knowledge and projects repository is one of the value adds of this model.

Projects across various fileds like software, information technology, business process outsourcing (BPO), accounting finance, legal, personnel, administration support, writing, etc., may be put up on the Web portal. Examples of software projects may be design reviews of projects, pieces of programs for doing certain functions, and applicable best practices of similar projects.

Compensation Principle

Budgeted compensation for respective project is indicative in nature. *Actual disbursement paid may not be subject to negotiations between the project buyer and vendor project seller(s), but may involve discussions between the project buyer and an independent evaluating third party which is mutually acceptable to both the project buyer and the project sellers.*

Note: Project seller(s) may nevertheless be allowed to submit an expected disbursement for their respective submissions.

Distribution of compensation may be based on parameters like quality, speed of submission, and profile of project seller (if doing repeat business with the organization).

Actual compensation amount thus disbursed may vary from the previously published, budgeted compensation, depending on the quality value of the contribution.

Contributions are rated by the project buyer(s)/evaluators. Even after publishing a proposed budgeted compensation for a respective project, it is subject to the discretion of the owner and project evaluator. At best, actual compensation payout can be higher than the previously indicat budget.

If needed, payout of compensation may be done in close tandem with the executed project contributions, along with periodic updates of balance compensation available for the respective project before closure of the deadline. This may be resorted to at a high level of practice maturity where speed is the essence.

Working Framework

Assume today's date is <Date1>. Assume an applicable "project" is internally planned to start on date <Date2> (<Date 2> same or later than <Date1>) and complete tentatively on <Date3> (<Date 3> same or later than <Date 2>).

Model suggests today (i.e., on <Date1> itself) to put the project on the centralized Web portal specifying:

- The deadline for receiving contributions as <Date2>.
- The budgeted compensation (indicative).
- The tentative date of completion of project (i.e., <Date3>).
- If project after completion is further available for sale or as freeware or not, if applicable.
- Contributions or salient points thereof by different project sellers can be visible to each other so as to allow one project seller to add value over and above the work done by another project seller.
- On <Date2> assimilate the various contributions received over the portal.
- Distribute compensation/incentive for appropriate contributions based on respective weights/criterion for payment.
- Initiate internal execution of the project on <Date2> and complete by <Date3>.
- Project ready for sale/freeware from <Date3> onward, if applicable.

Engagement modus   Contributions submitted in response are voluntary with no initial contractual bindings. Hence the model is christened as a *"flexi engagement"* model.

The unique selling proposition (USP) of this model is its applicability to almost all natures of business domains and competencies. It cuts across all units, verticals, and competencies.

In the flow chart in Figure 10.2:

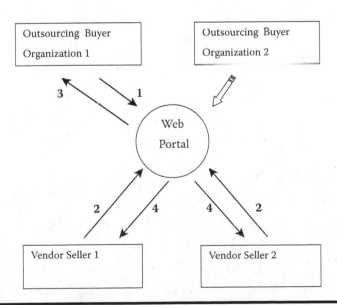

Figure 10.2   Working framework—outsourcing over the Web without contracts.

Step 1: Project requirements, miscellaneous project information, the deadline for receiving submissions <Date2>, etc., are put up by the outsourcing buyer on the Web portal. Importantly the budgeted compensation (indicative) for the project is stated up front.

Step 2: Project requirements viewed by multiple competing project seller vendors who respond with their submissions on the Web portal. Thus various seller vendors make their contributions without any contractual tie-up with the outsourcing buyer, just going by the initially declared budgeted compensation (in Step 1). Speed and quality becomes the differentiating factor between various similar submissions by different vendor sellers.

Step 3: Collection and evaluation of various received submissions is done by the outsourcing buyer.

Step 4: Distribution of compensation is done to different vendor sellers based on the evaluation results followed by project closure online.

Salient Feature of This Model

*Though multitudes traveled over the eons,
only a few left their mark over time.*

In the case where the project is planned to be executed internally from a certain future date (<Date2>), the time period for receipt of project contributions from the external vendors should deliberately be much smaller than the actual time period needed to execute the same from scratch, because this targets already existing similar work done in the past. *This aims to target "reuse" of similar work already existing elsewhere in the world.* This may greatly in turn reduce the overall final project deadline of <date3>, and possibly a much lower cost is incurred than when attempting to do the whole project from scratch.

Movement of Projects between Models 1 and 2

Parts of the project may use and even move between the models 1 and 2, depending on time, nature, size, complexity, magnitude, and expenses of the respective project.

The Models—Roles

Five different roles are engaged in the above models:

- Web portal owner, administrator
- Outsourcing buyer
- Project evaluator
- Vendor seller
- Financial intermediary enabling the financial transaction

These roles target a worldwide pool of professionals.

Web Portal Owner, Administrator

Web portal owner, administrator role would target organization/software profes-sionals who set up and manage the Web portal on which project requests are put up. This is a specialized role.

Outsourcing Buyer

Project buyer role would commonly apply in the software field to

- Any organization
- Individuals or set of professionals

Those in this generic role are in need of execution of their project(s) partly or fully. Age, educational background, geographic location, etc., may not have strong depen-dencies on this role.

Project Evaluator

Project evaluator is any organization or set of software, business, and domain experts who evaluate the nature of the project, correlating complexity, effort, resources needed, and quality of contributions made by the project sellers to decide the compensation value. This is a new specialized role, which has the potential for rapid growth in the respective business models.

Vendor Seller

Project seller role is the large pool of professionals, organizations, and communities worldwide who can execute the project. Age, educational background, geographic location, etc., may not have strong dependencies on the role. This is a generic role. A project seller, instead of executing a project, may in turn point to another ready solution, freeware, or seller depending on the nature of the project request.

Financial Intermediary

Banks, financial institutions, or even the Web portal administrator can play the role of financial intermediary.

Example—An escrow account may be used as a mechanism of payment from the project buyer to the vendor seller via a financial intermediary. At the start of the project, if agreed contractually, the project buyer deposits the contracted com-pensation amount in advance with the financial intermediary. The same amount is disbursed by the financial intermediary to the project seller(s) subsequently on completion of related contracted project milestones. This is a specialized role.

Criteria for Success of These Models

The rate/speed of proliferation of such projects depends on the Web portal's total user population and value reaped.

Submissions thus received may possibly be of little or no value to the buyer, at times, depending on the nature, complexity, scope, etc., of the project.

The seller vendor organization making such offers should do sufficient homework regarding value proposition, issue pricing, marketing dynamics, etc.

The governing laws of the respective country would be detrimental toward various factors like pricing offer, marketing dynamics, etc.

Buyers and sellers should check past history of projects and timely payments before initiating contracts.

Vendor sellers dealing in similar products or services will need to compete with each other on issues like value, price, quality etc. **Note:** Lowest pricing is not a guarantee of success.

Such models have some inherent degree of risk attached.

The Models "1 and 2" Value Proposition

Following is the value proposition of these models:

- **Reuse of tools, resources, experiences**—"Reuse" of already existing similar projects, work, knowledge, etc., leads to exponential gains in time, cost, and effort for the buyer. Options of customizing the same and integrating with related products to meet specific needs leads to a significant advantage.

    For most of life is lived in a few repeated strokes, work or otherwise.

- **Pioneer concepts**—The models explore largely unexplored business opportunities for outsourcing projects using the Web.

    The highs felt by first-time achievers.

- **Customization**—To meet individual buyer's needs, solutions are tailored by the seller vendors. Customization is the key because vendors display operational versatility and flexibility of execution.

    The individual's need for personalized things.

- **Project budgets**—Online outsourcing budgets range from very low to high depending on the nature of work. Small jobs and large complex projects can be bought and sold over the Web.

    For the many who play for financial ends and the few
    who play for sustaining value and passion.

- **Expert vendor knowledge**—Expertise available in other geographic location can be tapped by the buyer. An experienced online provider enables the client to achieve measurable business value, exceeding service level requirements, delivering on time and on budget, and offering creative and innovative solutions to customer needs.

Sifting the information of value from the dross.

- **Quality**—Seller vendors in similar products making such offers would need to compete on factors like delivered value, issue pricing, market share, returns, etc. This would lead a high benchmark in quality and value of such offers over time.

And prevalent standards turn into protocols.

- **Cross-currency conversion**—Models leverage cross-currency conversion synergies if buyers and sellers exist in different geographic location, preferably with the buyer located in a strong currency and the seller located in a weaker currency. This result in a win–win advantage for both the buyer and seller.

The changing prints of notes and their respective values.

- All sellers' and buyers' accounts are tracked centrally by the application.

Connecting across the time zones, as night and day coexist.

Business Model 3—Strategic Tie-Ups— The Time Shares—Selling Time

The time barrier, still the unbroken frontier.

Time—The most precious commodity of all for people and organizations.

Time shares have been commonly sold in the travel industry, where people use the same accommodation at different spaces of time at various locations across the globe. The concept of time shares is here extended to outsourcing, other industries, and even to individuals. This is an approach by which either the outsourcing organization or their respective vendors/providers allow each other, and also other potential organizations/individuals, to invest in and share their end business revenues.

The initiator/proposer is usually either of the players (the outsourcing organization or the vendor provider), though it may be extended to a potential individual candidate too who may sell time. *The proposer puts up "time shares" for sale (through auction or any other suitable means) of a "future" time period, possibly using a Web portal.* The time shares put up may be a time period of days, months, or even complete financial years of the future. The proposer may specify a minimum qualifying investment amount and other conditions of eligibility for potential applicants. Such eligibility conditions may allow only existing business associates (e.g., outsourcing customer, vendor provider, suppliers, etc.) to qualify. Proposer provides details of various projects under way during the respective time period (put up for sale), expected returns, guidance values, profiles of various stakeholders, etc. Importantly, the proposer specifies up front the revenue sharing mechanism and revenue percentage which will be shared with the respective time share holders.

Auction or any suitable means may be used for the first time sale of time shares by the proposer. Investors buy/bid for the same.

Buyers/investors may be decided by the proposer/initiator (some sample criteria given below):

- Highest bid
- Quantum of existing business relationship
- Strategic control and revenue sharing
- Proposer's choice

On successful selection, money is transferred to the proposer by the selected buyer/investor.

Periodically, with the passage of time, say quarterly, annually, etc., financial results are declared by the proposer. This is translated into financial revenues made over the respective period for which time shares were sold. The investor is paid as per the originally specified percentages of revenue sharing settled during contract drawing. Payout results in the closure of the respective time share. Thus investors (shareholders) may gain or loose money based on the final revenues actually made by the proposer over the respective time period.

Subject to legal and contractual permissibility, the concept may be extended, and time shares may additionally be traded over suitable portals by the holders. The principles of this time share trading essentially remain the same as regular stock trading. As demand rises, and more buyers purchase a particular time share, its price rises. Time share values will rise or fall as the respective time period (of sold time shares) approaches (in real) and finally draws to a close. Time shares may continue to be traded after the respective date has passed until payout by the proposer, assuming there is an interval between the end of the time share period and initiation of payout by the proposer organization. Such may happen if results declaration and payouts are made at fixed periodicity by the proposer organization. After payout, the time share thereafter is no longer valid. The challenge here is to be able to estimate the cost incurred versus the returns.

How It Works

Explaining with a simple example, proposer is a vendor/provider organization which puts up a time share of 1 day for sale in the next (forthcoming) financial year, say April 1. Additionally proposer agrees to share 10% of the returns with the time share holder at the close of the respective (next) financial year.

Assume only business associates are eligible to invest, and its outsourcing customer makes an investment (say bid) of say $1 and is accepted.

As "April 1" date approaches in real time, due to demand the price of the time share rises to $2. On March 31 the original investor customer (as allowed as per contract) sells the time share to a second investor for $2 on the portal, thus making a profit of $1.

After April 2, the price of share continues to rise based on the quarterly performance results of the proposer organization's performance. Near the close of the financial year, because results of the previous three quarters are already known, assume the price of the time share has gone up to $3, and the second investor sells the same off to a third investor, again for a profit of $1.

After closure of the financial year, assume the proposer organization makes a profit. The annual revenue is translated into revenue for 1 day (i.e., April 1). This may be calculated based on earnings from only those projects covering the date of the time share (i.e., April 1), or the entire year's earnings may simply be equally split up to give the per day earning of any day of the respective financial year. Even some other calculation mechanisms may be used. Whatever the mechanism, assume the revenue for the day of April 1 is $100.

As per the initial declaration, proposer pays 10% of $100 (i.e., $10) to the current time share holder (which is investor 3). The third investor thus makes a profit of $7.

If say, due to loss, the revenue calculated for April 1 was say $10. The proposer organizer would pay $1 (10%) to the third investor. The third investor would thus incur a loss of $2.

After declaration of results and payout by the proposer organization to the share holder, the time share lapses.

In the flow chart in Figure 10.3:

Step 1: Proposer organization/individual 1 puts up its time share on the Web portal with related supporting financial and miscellaneous information.

Step 2: Investor 2 buys the time share from the portal.

Step 3: Investor 2 further sells the time share in part or full at the stock price existing at that respective point in time.

Step 4: Investor 1 buys the time share and continues to hold it until the date of results declaration.

Step 5: Proposer 1 pays investor 1 based on its initial offer.

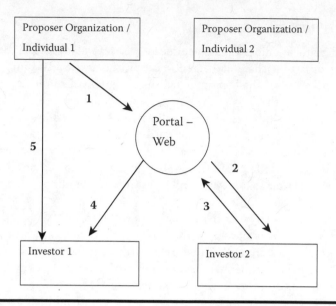

Figure 10.3 Working framework—strategic tie-ups—the time shares—selling time.

The Models—Roles

Four different roles are engaged in the above models:

- Portal owner, administrator
- Proposer
- Investors
- Financial intermediary enabling the financial transaction

These roles target a worldwide pool of professionals.

Web Portal Owner, Administrator

Portal owner, administrator role could be any organization who sets up and manages the portal. This is a specialized role.

Proposer

This may be organizations or individuals who initiate the proposal for sale of time shares.

Investors

Investors could be any organizations or individuals.

Financial Intermediary

Banks, financial institutions, or even the Web portal which enables the process buying, selling, trading, and closure of the time shares, can be the financial intermediary.

The Web Portal Setup and Features

Portal setup prerequisites:

- Portal setup—suitable software and hardware infrastructure.
- Common centralized database to contain required information, trading and other transactions' history details, etc. Store participating proposer's profile details, credit ratings, offer declaration, payout date, etc. It may store investor profiles too, if needed for facilitation of transactions.
- Enabling features for end-to-end life cycle (i.e., purchase, sale, trading, closure).
- Archiving data which is no longer needed. History of past transactions, etc., is maintained in archives. This may be studied to understand the behavior of the time share over time.
- Periodic housekeeping and maintenance activities.

Related Examples

Individual movie celebrity time share—*This is an extension of the same concept to individuals, though not strictly related to outsourcing.* An individual movie celebrity auctions time shares for various time periods of the future. Investors evaluate the various movie projects under production or draw estimates for future periods based on past projects for the respective time share's period and accordingly buy time shares. After the passage of the respective time period, periodically the total earnings of the celebrity are translated into earnings made over the respective time share period. The earnings are then shared with the respective time share holders.

The closest to this are seemingly gaming sites which trade in Hollywood celebrities—http://www.hsx.com/, http://www.bbc.co.uk/celebdaq/index.shtml.

On signing up, players are given a startup capital of virtual money (i.e., 10,000 Celebdaq pounds). The aim is to make as much money as possible by investing in a set of listed celebrities. Money is made through dividends, which are paid out weekly based on how much relative "press coverage" the listed celebrities receive weekly, and also through capital gains by buying low and selling high. Since celebrity share are updated every 20 minutes, money can be made or lost rather quickly. Press coverage received is taken from feeds from various publications: *Daily Mirror, The Sun, Daily Star, Daily Express, Daily Mail, The Times, The Independent, The Guardian, The Telegraph,* etc. The game also allows users to set up alerts for percentage variances in prices.

Criteria for Success of These Models

Financial risks similar to stock trading exist. Investors should have done sufficient homework and study about the proposer when attempting to trade in the respective time shares. Time share prices may fluctuate on the portal based on various factors like organization track record, performance, demand and supply, etc.

Large numbers of proposers and investors trading over such portals.

Selection of service provider need not be based on lowest price but on highest value addition and best cultural fit (cheapest service provider is not necessarily the best one).

If the proposer and investor exist in different countries, then both are subject to the currency conversion dependencies existing at the respective point in time.

Dispute resolution may become even more difficult if the various stakeholders (proposer and investors) exist in different countries.

Suitable contractual and legal systems to ensure that all stakeholders honor their respective obligations.

Investors may possibly be able to influence the decisions and actions of respective proposers.

Changes in inflation rates, inflation differential, consumer price index (CPI), purchasing power parity, interest rates, money supply, GDP growth, etc,. may impact proposition suitability.

The portal assumes the necessary resources (i.e., financial, infrastructure, etc.) are somehow available to the investors.

The Model Value Proposition

Following is the value proposition to the various players involved including the market, clients, etc.:

Of market principles and personal values.

■ This is a pioneer concept of sorts, which applies across industries and individuals.

Those that shall learn to ride the crest of change,
shall be the ones to lead the future.

■ Investors can trade in time shares on the portal in much the same way as traditional stock trading.

Of finding the gaps and filling them first.

■ The proposer receives an investment for a future time period, for which returns are to be paid out subsequently. The proposer thus raises funds suitably for the respective time period so as to generate maximum returns.

Futures and options and the risks therewith.

Business Model 4—Strategic Tie-Ups—Making Customers and Employees Shareholders

The enabling means through sustaining deeds, in life and beyond.

Model 4a—Making Outsourcing Customers Shareholders

Prerequisite—The seller vendor organization needs to be listed with the stock exchange.

This is a strategic approach whereby the seller vendor organizations allow their outsourcing customers to become shareholders and hence partners in business. The seller vendor organization, on sale of its goods and services beyond a specified threshold value, offers to issue a corresponding number of preferential shares/stock to the customer. Such may be envisaged in the business contract between the seller vendor and the outsourcing organizations.

Buyer outsourcing organizations who initiate an outsourcing business relationship with the seller vendor are managed as an account on the vendor's portal, which maintains a history of their purchase transactions of respective products and services. Such is maintained for all the outsourcing customer organizations of the seller vendor.

This threshold sale value, which qualifies for issue of preferential shares, may need to factor in the market price of the shares being issued, etc. Simply speaking, the smaller the market price per share as compared to the qualifying sale value, the larger the number of shares which may be issued.

Such issue is, however, subject to the laws of preferential share allotment of the respective country. There needs to be a suitable legal basis for pricing the issue of such stock. For example, as per Indian laws, the price of a preferential issue is the higher of the average of the weekly high and low of the closing market prices during the six months or last two weeks preceding the relevant date of issue. Such issue may be also subject to suitable mandatory legal reporting and audits. The organization may need to maintain miscellaneous related details of numbers of such shares issued, allottee details, and suitable justification for such an issue.

Care may also need to be taken that such an issue "offer" is not construed as a malpractice act by the recipient, as per their internal policies of interaction with the organization.

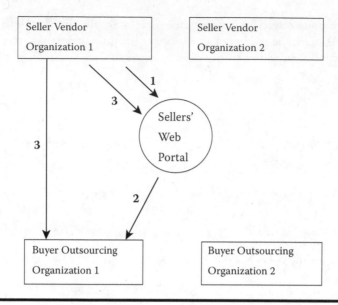

Figure 10.4 Working framework—strategic tie-ups, making customers shareholders.

In the flow chart in Figure 10.4:

Step 1: Seller vendors declare their offers of minimum threshold value of goods and services which qualify for issue of corresponding number of preferential shares.

Step 2: Subject to the agreed terms of issue of preferential shares the buyer customer's account is maintained by the seller vendor, possibly on a Web portal. As buyer outsourcing organization buys goods and services, their account is accordingly updated periodically with the respective purchase transaction value.

Step 3: Over time when the total value of the outsourcing customer's purchases sums up to a certain qualifying balance, the respective seller vendor issues a corresponding number of shares as per the initially declared offer. The outsourcing customer's account is accordingly updated with the corresponding number of shares issued.

Roles

The different roles engaged in the above setup:

- Web portal owner, administrator—Any person/organization that set up the portal for implementing this concept.
- Seller vendor's organization—It declares its offer of minimum threshold value of goods and services which qualify for issue of corresponding number of preferential shares.

- Outsourcing buyer's organization—It does repeat business with the seller vendor until the sum total of its business transactions reaches the required threshold needed for receipt of preferential shares.

The Web Portal Setup and Features

Portal setup prerequisites:

- Portal setup—Suitable software and hardware infrastructure.
- Common centralized database to contain transaction details and store buyer's account details. Portal to maintain transaction details, history, etc.
- Archiving data which is no longer needed. History of past products, transaction, etc., is maintained in archives. This may be studied to understand the behavior of prices over time.
- Periodic housekeeping and maintenance activities.

Model 4b—Making Employees Shareholders

Outsourcing organizations may offer to periodically issue employee stock options (ESOP) to employees. Such stock options, essentially preferential shares, may be issued based on various criteria like:

- *Issued on joining to new employees at senior/experienced positions who are of perceived potentially strategic value to the organization*
- *Issued periodically (e.g., annually) based on employee performance*
- *Issued periodically to all employees based on seniority (number of years) in the organization*

Such issued options usually have some lock-in period. This would be specific to the issuing organization.

Organization issues say 100 ESOPs (shares) to an employee on <Date1>. The issue price of this option is dependent on this date of issue (i.e., <date1>). Repeating, as per Indian laws, the price of a preferential issue is the higher of the average of the weekly high and low of the closing market prices during the six months or last two weeks preceding the relevant date of issue. This, however, may differ from country to country based on the respective governing laws. Assume the issue price per stock option (1 share) is 100 INR (Indian Rupees).

Such issue may be locked in for a period of time and be vested (made available to the employee for exercise/purchase) only after periodic intervals. An example (as was used at Infosys Technologies Limited) is 10% of the initial issue are unlocked/freed 1 year after the issue date <date1>; 20% of the initial issue are unlocked/freed 2 years after the issue date <date1>; 30% of the initial issue are unlocked/freed 3 years after the issue date <date1>; 40% of the initial issue are unlocked/freed 4 years after the issue date <date1>. This makes up the total of 100% of the initial issue. This procedure may differ from organization to organization.

After vestment, the employee may further be allowed an additional time period to initiate purchase. Quoting from Infosys Technologies Limited, this available period for purchase of vested stock options was 5 years. Thus the employee has another 5 years from the date of vestment for purchase of the free (unlocked) shares. Assume the market price rises to 200 INR per share in this time period. The customer can purchase the stock option for 100 INR per share, and if sold thereafter makes a profit of 100 INR per share.

Optionally if the market price of the share falls and persists at a value below 100 INR (the issue price) for the entire 5-year period after vestment, the employee need not exercise (purchase) the stock option. Hence such offerings are rightly termed as stock options.

In the flow chart in Figure 10.5:

Step 1: Organizations declare their intent to distribute employee stock options (ESOP) with respective qualifying criteria on the internal organization portal (intranet).

Step 2: Periodically organizations grant ESOP to selected employees, specifying related details of the number of issued stock options, the issue price per option, the lock-in periods, other related conditions, etc. The respective employee's account on the portal is updated with the corresponding number of issued stock options.

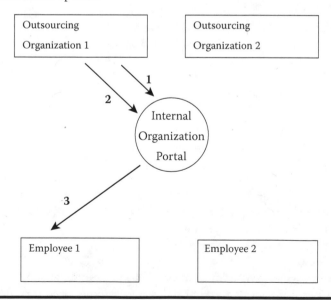

Figure 10.5 Working framework—strategic tie-ups, making employees shareholders.

Step 3: Employees exercise these options periodically after their vestment (availability) based on factors like option issue price versus the existing market price per share, possibility of reaping bonus, dividends, etc.

Roles

The different roles engaged in the above setup:

- Portal—An internal portal set up on the organization's intranet for implementing this concept.
- Organization—Declares its policy of issue of ESOP with corresponding qualifying criteria.
- Outsourcing buyer's organization—It does repeat business with the seller vendor until the sum total of its business transactions reaches the required threshold needed for receipt of preferential shares.
- Employees—Potential recipients of preferential stock.

The Web Portal Setup and Features

Portal setup prerequisites:

- Portal setup—Suitable software and hardware infrastructure over the organization's intranet.
- Common centralized database to contain transaction details. Stores employees' account details. Portal to maintain transaction details, history, etc.
- Archiving data which is no longer needed. History of transactions, ESOP issues, etc., is maintained in archives. This may be studied to understand issues like employee attrition, etc., over time.
- Periodic housekeeping and maintenance activities.

Examples

This could apply to any industry (e.g., software, food, construction, commodities, etc.). Software organizations like Infosys, Tata Consultancy Services, and Wipro could potentially leverage from this model.

Criteria for Success of These Models

The rate/speed of proliferation of such outsourcing propositions for issue of preferential stock.

Buyer outsourcing organization may need to buy seller products or services over a sustained period/duration to reach the qualifying threshold for issue of stock.

The seller vendor organization making such offers should have done sufficient homework regarding value proposition, issue pricing, threshold amount setting and periodic revision, marketing dynamics, etc.

The governing laws of the respective country would be detrimental toward various factors of preferential issue pricing, threshold amount setting and periodic revision, marketing dynamics, etc. Seller vendor must understand the legal issues before proposing the offer. Similarly the organization planning to issue ESOPs must also understand the respective pertaining laws before initiating the offer. Such offers have related tax implications. Such would be further subject to change with change in laws periodically.

Seller vendors may limit such offers to only certain products, services, and customers. This may be influenced by factors like feasibility, institutional investor's core business needs, customer distribution, desire to enter a particular segment, strategic relationship, etc.

Seller organization's market price of shares would be influenced by various factors like profile, performance track records, history, nature of business, change management capability, delivery, execution, financial strength, etc.

Seller vendor may need to set up long-term processes toward monitoring buyer's purchase history over the portal and issuing shares to those qualifying.

Sellers dealing in similar products or services may need to compete with each other for issue of preferential stock.

Sellers may need to do sufficient estimation of market pulse, future stock market trends, impact on market price, etc., before putting forth such offers. Such offers come with respective risk. Learning from such failures would gradually mature the process.

Limitations

What does not qualify for this model—the following seller organizations may not qualify for usage of this model:

■ Organizations which are subject to laws which prohibit issue of such preferential stock to customers and employees

The Models Value Proposition

Following is the value proposition of these models:

■ Builds organization's *brand loyalty*. Seller vendors can use this as a unique sales strategy to gain customer loyalty toward long-term business. Likewise, organizations issuing ESOPs to employees mostly stand to retain employees for the period that part of the options are in locked status.

A sense of belonging over time, to values, systems, and organizations.

■ Seller vendors in similar products making such offers would need to compete on factors like delivered value, issue pricing, market share, returns, etc. This would lead a high benchmark in quality and value of such offers over time. Small organizations may offset the market shares of established players by using such strategies of issue of preferential stock.

The USP sets the winning position, between competing players.

■ Makes customers stakeholders in the organization.

The inclusive strokes, to reach and engulf.

■ Supports a long-term vision of the organization and customer relationship.

Playing for long-term aims, not short-term gains.

■ Creates a synergic relationship between an outsourcing vendor organization, its customers, and employees.

Building bonds through inclusive strokes.

■ Seller vendors and organizations through issue of such preferential stock take the business relationship to a higher level.

Differentiation through leaps and timelines.

■ The models explore largely hitherto unexplored business opportunities for potential and successful business ventures.

Changing the rules of the game, to leapfrog over the crowd.

■ Additional capital may be created through issue of such preferential stock.

Infusing capital through strong relationships.

■ It leverages cross-currency conversion synergies if buyers exist in multiple geographic locations and the seller's organization is listed on stock exchanges in multiple countries. For example, seller vendors may give selected American dollar shares to Indian buyers. Similarly an organization may give American dollar shares to its Indian employees. Infosys Technologies had issued American depositary receipts (ADR) to its Indian employees by way of ESOP. Thus geographic and location dependencies of the various players (the seller organization, buyers, employees, portal organization, etc.) are greatly alleviated. The physical geographic locations of the various players become relatively meaningless, if the respective processes are streamlined to accomplish the same. This is, however, subject to the governing laws of the two countries involved.

As systems explore multinational practices, permissible interchanges.

■ The value proposition is both direct and indirect. Seller vendor organizations leverage from long-term product/brand loyalty, and buyers reap value from becoming shareholders.

Expanding the scope to change the business playing field.

■ The portal provides a high degree of automation through the entire offer life cycle. Buyer accounts are updated for each purchase transaction through the portal. Transparency in procedures and processes allows seamless operations.

Automation, a necessity for survival, in current times.

■ All buyers' accounts are tracked centrally by the application, and whenever the balance reaches the qualifying threshold, suitable intimation is sent to the seller vendor organization (for issue of preferential stock) and the respective buyer account holders.

The natural potential of the machines to process large data volumes.

■ Primary/large customers (buying organizations) of respective seller vendors may gain suitable official influence in the decision-making process of the seller organization through issue of such preferential stock. This would result in buyer outsourcing organizations becoming partners as the sellers' stock-linked offers mature over time.

As customers ascend to influence the business.

■ Model 4b of issuing preferential stock to employees, when used internally within a large organization, leverages complementary synergies between employees and resources across various levels, roles, and functions. Employees who have been issued options become role models for other potential aspirants.

As some within the system rise to carry the baton forth.

■ Model 4b of issuing preferential stock to employees, when used internally within a large software organization, improves employee motivation and morale.

A bond strong, not just a professional relationship, for long-term gains.

■ Models 4b of issuing preferential stock to employees allows talent, skills, etc. to be tapped from within the organization using the in-house intranet.

Of making people rise and stretch their very limits.

Business Model 5—Time-Based Costs for Services and Products in Outsourcing

Relationships that stand the test of time—business or pleasure.

Both outsourcing services and products delivered by the seller vendor to the buying outsourcing organization may qualify for costs linked to time factors, depending on their nature, like some of the following:

■ **Age of the business relationship between provider vendor and outsourcing organization**—Pricing may be linked to the duration of the relationship. Charges and pricing may be set proportional to the age of the business relationship. New business relationships are priced higher, while long-standing, old business relationships are charged correspondingly lower rates.
■ **Duration of advance booking**—Services and products booked well in advance qualify for cost-based benefits.
■ **Frequency of use by outsourcing customer**—Frequent users of services may be given suitable cost benefits versus infrequent users.
■ **Seasonal fluctuation in demand and supply**—Such seasonal fluctuations may occur due to fluctuations in prices of materials and other seasonal factors procured externally by the seller vendor. This would lead to corresponding variance in sale of products and services to the buying outsourcing organization.
■ **Periodic fluctuation in transaction load/volumes**—Certain outsourcing businesses may have lean/peak periods of transaction load. The seller vendor accordingly offers reduced/increased rates, respectively, of service or products during such periods.

In the flow chart in Figure 10.6:

Step 1: Seller vendor declare their policy and offers (as applicable) of time-based cost of services and products (as applicable), both on the Web portal and in real (from its shop) with related supporting information and details.
Step 2: Buyer outsourcing organizations initiate business with the seller vendor based on the available offers, leveraging from the applicable time-based offers.
Step 3: Seller executes the required service or product and bills the outsourcing buyer accordingly.

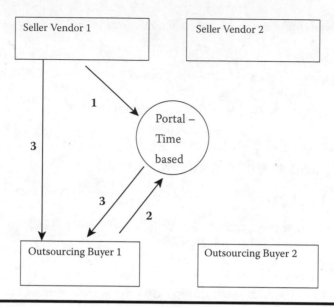

Figure 10.6 Working framework—time-based costs for services and products in outsourcing.

Roles

The different roles engaged in the above setup:

- Web portal owner, administrator—Any person/organization that sets up the portal for implementing this concept.
- Seller vendors—Seller vendors declare their policy and offers (as applicable) of time-based cost of services and products (as applicable).
- Outsourcing buyers—Initiate business based on the applicable offers, leveraging from suitable time-based offers.

The Web Portal Setup and Features

Portal setup prerequisites:

- Portal setup—Suitable software and hardware infrastructure.
- Common centralized database to contain transaction details. Stores buyers' account details. Portal to maintain transaction details, history, etc.
- Archiving data which is no longer needed. History of past products, transaction, etc., is maintained in archives. This may be studied to understand the behavior of prices over time.
- Periodic housekeeping and maintenance activities.

Application Examples

This concept exists in very limited measure and can be extended and applied to different businesses, services, products, and opportunities.

- **Example—Seasonal fluctuation in demand and supply during holiday season:** Mission-critical operations provided by a vendor during periods of low employee attendance at the outsourcing organization (e.g., the Christmas holiday season) may be charged higher due to deployment of additional resources or people by the provider vendor, as also their working during the holiday season.
- **Example—Tourism:** Travel and tourism agents should receive duration-based pricing from the respective seller organizations and pass on the same to the end user traveler. *Such duration-linked pricing and discounts may be offered in areas like hotel stay, travel (by air, rail, road, ferries), restaurants, vehicle car/taxi charges, tourist tickets to various landmarks, package tours, etc.* As the duration increases, the discounts should proportionately increase.

Many ultra-low cost air carriers through their travel agents reward customers with free air tickets. Such may be based on factors like frequent flying, booking sufficiently in advance, etc. European ULCC Ryanair gives free fares to a quarter of its customers. Ryanair's CEO Michael O'Leary feels eventually more than half of the passengers will fly free.

End-user tourists would also get good deals and lower rates during off-season periods. Furthermore, during off-peak, low-usage hours, buses and trains may allow customers to use such travel services free, based on factors like frequency of past usage, senior citizen, students, etc.

Hotels through a network of agents may offer room tariffs based on the duration of guest's stay. Rates may also be subject to seasonal fluctuations based on occupancy. Hotels may even offer the night's stay free to customers dining at their restaurants, subject to availability on that particular night, frequent visitor case, etc.

Criteria for Success of These Models

Large numbers of sellers offering such time-based cost offers are needed, until it becomes an established business practice in various fields.

The Model Value Proposition

Following is the value proposition to the various players involved including the market, clients, etc.:

- Sellers can maximize usage of their services and maximize revenue by pricing their services and products based on lean, peak business hours, seasonal changes, etc.

Seasonal fluctuations of demand and supply.

■ Costs are set based on the respective dependencies of time, usage, and availability and not a standard fixed rate.

Of costs in tune with time and demand.

Business Model 6—For Every "n" Units Sold, Giving "m" Units Free

In simple values, often core concepts rest.

Seller provider vendors declare their policy that, on sale of every "n" units of specified products or services, it pledges to give "m" units free to the respective outsourcing organization or optionally to a recipient chosen by the outsourcing organization. Products and services sold may or may not be the same as the those given free, though same (sold and given free) may be advisable because the seller provider has a business expertise in the same. Units of products may be defined by value, number of pieces, weight, etc., whichever is suitable/applicable. Units of services may be defined by value, number of business transactions, elapsed time, person hours, duration of service provided, etc. Recipients of free units may be individuals, communities, or organizations in need. Seller providers may be small and big organizations, shops, business and social communities, etc.

Sellers may sell products and services both online (over its Internet portal) and also through their retail stores.

This threshold number of units which qualify for free units may also depend on issues like the nature of products, the number recipients of free units, the urgency of need, etc.

Buyer outsourcing organizations may further be encouraged to volunteer participation in delivery and distribution if they choose to select some third party as a recipient of the free units.

Seller providers and buyer organizations may group together, where possible, for delivery, distribution of units of similar nature, same target recipients, etc.

As business concepts extend into humane domains.

In the flow chart in Figure 10.7:

Step 1: Various sellers providers may put up products and services with suitable offers on the Web portal for sale. Sellers publicly declare their policies for specified products or services—On sale of every "n" units, seller(s) pledge to give free "m" units of specified products or services.

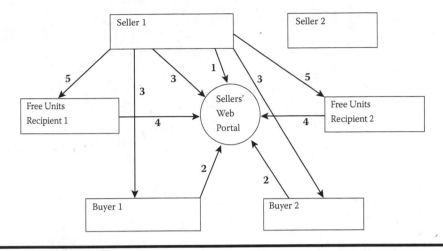

Figure 10.7 Working framework—for every "n" units sold, giving "m" units free.

Step 2: Buyer outsourcing organizations initiate business with the seller vendor. Based on suitable offers coupled with sellers' policies of donation, buyers make purchases from the seller.

Step 3: Shipping/delivery of products or services to the buyer outsourcing organization by the seller provider is carried out. The buyer's account (with the seller portal) is concurrently updated with the transaction status. Thus a history of orders and purchase transactions made by the buyer is maintained.

Step 4: Potential recipients may even apply and put forth their case with suitable supporting details on the portal. This step is optional. Buyers and sellers may use any alternate means of identifying suitable recipients for the free products and services.

Step 5: Delivery of products or services is carried out to suitable free recipients.

Roles

The different roles engaged in the above setup:

- Web portal owner, administrator—Any person/organization that sets up the portal for implementing this concept.
- Sellers—Update the products available and policies of donations linked to sales.
- Support groups—These are individuals or organizations who work with the seller toward delivery and distribution of the free units periodically.
- Buyers—Register and open accounts on the portal, which maintains their respective transactions and up-to-date balances and history.
- Free recipients—These may be individuals, communities, or the same buyer outsourcing organization itself.

The Web Portal Setup and Features

Portal setup prerequisites:

- Portal setup—Suitable software and hardware infrastructure.
- Common centralized database to contain transaction details.
- Store buyer's account details. Portal to maintain transaction details, history, etc.
- Archiving data which is no longer needed. History of past products, transaction, etc., is maintained in archives. This may be studied to understand the behavior of prices over time.
- Periodic housekeeping and maintenance activities.

Application Examples

Sellers pledge policy toward donation may include (but may not be limited to) fields like software products and services, business process outsourcing, clothing, education, charity, funding, environmental protection, medicines, medical support, insurance, etc.

Example—TOMS Shoes (http://friendsoftoms.org/; http://www.tomsshoes.com/) has the policy that on sale of every pair of shoes, it shall donate one pair of new shoes to a deserving child. The organization's aim is to prevent podoconiosis (Podo) disease. This causes extreme swelling, ulcers, and deformity in the feet and legs. It is preventable by wearing shoes.

TOMS (brand name) shoes are sold both online from their Web site and also from retail stores worldwide (e.g., across the United States, Mexico, Australia, most European countries, Hong Kong, Philippines, Singapore, Japan, South Korea, etc.). Buyers open user accounts online on their Internet Web site portal.

The shoes are manufactured and purchased from factories in Argentina, China, and Ethiopia. By policy, the factories involved in the manufacture need to follow and operate under sound labor conditions, pay fair wages, and follow local labor standards. Yearly third-party audits ensure the same.

Periodic shoe donations known as shoe drops are carried out across various countries like the United States, Argentina, and South Africa. Since its inception in 1996, the organization has donated over 1 million pairs of shoes. Buyers are encouraged to volunteer in delivery and distribution of the shoe donations. Individuals and organizations may additionally donate money toward this cause through credit cards.

Of making a difference, howsoever small.

Criteria for Success of These Models

Buyers may need to do some homework on seller's policies of free units, commitment, honor of past pledges, etc.

Only appropriate nature of products and services may be sold through this
model. Selection of projects should be judiciously done after due evaluation
and deliberation.

In case of third-party recipients, buying outsourcing organizations and sellers
may need to set up a suitable mechanism for verification of recipient credentials and delivery and distribution of free units.

In case of time-critical nature of products and services, consistent timely delivery
on schedule by sellers is a must. Thus seller must set up suitable mechanisms
to estimate buyer's consumption patterns and dependency on such critical
products and services.

The Model Value Proposition

■ Sellers from different fields, domains, and products can put up their offers
on the Web portal. Seller may make donation-linked sales in various fields
of software products, services, business process outsourcing, clothing, food,
education, charity, funding, environmental protection, medicines, medical
support, insurance, etc.

The spirit to give and the decision to back it.

■ Cost-effective delivery of free units. Sellers may carry out delivery/distribu-
tion of free units periodically only after sufficient threshold value or numbers
have been sold.

When and where, at the right time and place, for maximum impact.

Business Model 7—Prepurchase of Outsourced Products and Service in Bulk with Delivery Spread Out in Parts at a Later Period of Time

The inherent concept, a winning position.

Sellers and provider vendors may use this system, which allows prepurchase of
goods and services in bulk at a fixed bulk rate with delivery spread out over a period
of time into the future to outsourcing organizations.

Seller vendors may offer this at their stores and also set up a Web portal putting all available products and services which qualify for prepurchase,
along with related details of minimum threshold value or quantity which qualify for prepurchase. A basket of products and services may also qualify for
prepurchase.

Seller vendors specify a certain minimum value or quantity of goods and services which qualify for prepurchase. **Example**—Goods and services worth a minimum value of say $10,000 qualify for prepurchase. Or a minimum of 1,000 units of a basket of products qualify for prepurchase. Units of goods may be value, number of pieces or weight, etc., as applicable. Units of services may be defined by value, number of business transactions, elapsed time, person hours, duration of service provided, etc.

The delivery of respective goods, however, is spread out over a mutually agreed period of time into the future (i.e., not immediately at time of prepurchase) to the buyer. This period of time would usually be limited to a specified period agreed between the buyer outsourcing organization and the seller vendor.

The buyer outsourcing organization would usually set up a schedule for delivery of such prepurchased goods and services after prepurchase through suitable communication channels (e.g., online via the Web portal, etc.). Alternately the buyer outsourcing organization can also request for an achievable delivery of goods and services whenever needed, quoting the earlier prepurchase transaction.

As delivery of goods and services is periodically taken by the buyer outsourcing organization, the corresponding balance is updated concurrently.

Buyer outsourcing organizations may automate repeat prepurchases with suitable delivery schedules over a future period based on the balance left in their account. **Example**—Should the balance of a particular product or service fall below a certain threshold value or quantity, it may qualify for repeat prepurchase for a certain value, quantity, and schedule. Buyers would need to provide suitable credit card, debit card, or other financial transaction mechanisms for such automated prepurchases.

Should the buyer outsourcing organization request immediate delivery of a product value or quantity which is lower than the specified minimum purchase threshold, current market price may be levied for the respective transaction.

Should the buyer request for delivery of a product or service which has not been prepurchased by it, regular contractual negotiations and policies will apply.

Groups of sellers may team up to use a common Web portal. Sellers may be small individual people or big organizations.

The seller additionally needs to invest this money received as down payment suitably so as to reap suitable returns. This would be needed for providing goods and services over a future period of time at the initial prepurchase price; that is, at a constant rate as against (irrespective of) the rise in market price of the respective goods and services, if it occurs. This may place the seller vendor at some risk if the market price of respective goods inherently fluctuates significantly over time. Thus sellers need to do suitable study into the behavior and fluctuations of prices of goods and services before offering them for prepurchase.

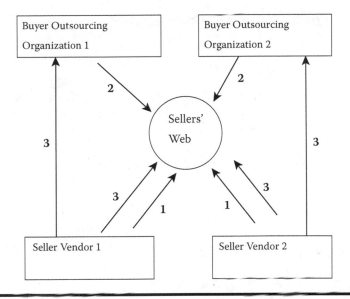

Figure 10.8 Working framework—prepurchase of outsourced products and services in bulk with delivery spread out in parts at a later period of time.

In the flow chart in Figure 10.8:

Step 1: Various seller vendors may put up offers on a Web portal specifying the minimum threshold value or quantity for sets of goods which qualify for prepurchase (with deferred periodic delivery in parts).

Step 2: Based on available offers, buyer outsourcing organizations negotiate and prepurchase goods and services. Thus the buyer's account balance (with the seller portal) is suitably credited. Buyer would need to specify a delivery schedule for delivery of the goods and services periodically.

Step 3: Based on the delivery schedule mutually agreed upon, delivery of goods and services are done by the seller to the buyer outsourcing organization. Concurrently the buyer's account balance is updated on the portal.

Roles

The different roles engaged in the above setup:

- Web portal owner, administrator—Any person/organization that set up the portal for implementing this concept.
- Sellers—Update the products available for prepurchase with related threshold details and any other clauses.
- Buyers—Register and open accounts on the portal which maintains their respective balances of prepurchase and delivered goods.

The Web Portal Setup and Features

Portal setup prerequisites:

- Portal setup—Suitable software and hardware infrastructure.
- Common centralized database to contain details of inventory available, prepurchase offers of respective goods, accounts, and transaction details.
- Archiving data which is no longer needed. This may be studied to understand the behavior of prices over time.
- Periodic housekeeping and maintenance activities.

Application Example

http://www.mygallons.com, though the same concept, is not strictly an outsourcing example.

Criteria for Success of These Models

Only appropriate nature of goods and services may be sold through this model. Selection of projects should be judiciously done after due evaluation and deliberation.

Consistent timely delivery on schedule by sellers is a must for the success of this model. Thus seller and buyer must set up suitable delivery mechanisms based on estimates of buyer's outsourcing organizations need patterns.

Sellers, if awarded repeat business by buyer, should set up some mechanisms for additional loyalty discounts, rewards, etc.

Seller lead times—Sellers need to be able to deliver to unexpected, sudden fluctuating demands by the buyers outsourcing organizations. These may occur depending on the nature of goods and services.

The Model Value Proposition

- Seller vendor makes a certain minimum lump sum on every prepurchase transaction. Seller has the large cash flows.

Of aims big and exponential growth paths.

- Buyer is able to get lower bulk rates and fixed-price benefits. Buyer may be able to get discounts, bulk/wholesale rates of purchase, etc. Hence the probability that the per unit market price of the respective product over time will fall below the prepurchase price is very low. In such an event, the seller may possibly offer a prepurchase price on another product in place of this product, which is lower than the current market price. Also customer is free to purchase that product directly from the market instead of using the higher prepurchase price.

Businesses driven by customer-centric gains.

■ Small and medium-sized sellers may get a better wholesale price by selling directly to the end consumer buyers.

Changing the rules of the game and the players therewith.

■ The value proposition is both direct and indirect. Buyers make purchases at a reduced wholesale price and are buffered from price fluctuations. Sellers receive a higher cash flow per transaction, which can be suitably invested.

A mass in motion, near unstoppable,
hence the guiding direction so important.

■ Competing sellers will learn (from each other) how to optimize on offers, quality, costs, delivery, etc.

Continuous relearning, in work and life.

■ The Web portal will thus become an enabling mechanism for very diverse sets of products, goods, buyers, and sellers. Any purchase transaction can be tracked centrally over the Web portal.

Myriad products, united in a common selling approach.

■ Such enabling Web portal needs low initial investment for setup, maintenance, and working.

The Web businesses, quick in setup, vast in reach.

■ Sellers may turn buyers, buying goods at wholesale rates from sellers over the portal and further selling through their stores in regional markets where Internet penetration is low.

The middleman's role and existence, always seasonal, usually short term.

Business Model 8—Big Projects Outsourcing to a Consortium

Small and big, all pieces make work and life.

A consortium is entered into by multiple vendor organizations, usually in response to a call by an outsourcing organization toward a large specific target project or a long-term business relationship.

Such business projects are usually very large in size and need multiple organizations with corresponding "diverse" complementary skills, all of which may not exist with in one organization. The outsourcing organization may nevertheless prefer to have the contractual agreement with only one vendor organization for the overall project. The vendor organization in turn does back-to-back tie-ups with other organizations for skills and deliverables which it does not possess. It is internally the responsibility of this vendor organization to manage and ensure delivery from the multiple partner organizations in the consortium. The multiple vendor organizations referred to as partners (or parties) in the consortium are usually independent organizations. The outsourcing organization thus has a single point of contact which enables a more efficient system of working. A single point of responsibility often prevents multiple vendors from blaming each other for the cause of a somewhat ambiguous problem. The target project may involve delivery of a set of products and services to the outsourcing organization.

Consortium Contract Basics between Partners

The consortium contract(s) between the partners defines in detail for each partner:

- The respective tasks to be executed with corresponding specifications
- The end results and deliverables and respective schedules
- The funding and sharing of financial revenues

Operations

Designation of Project Managers

For their respective tasks, each of the partners will designate a project manager (PM).

The PM is responsible for overall project execution including monitoring day-to-day activities of the respective partner. Usually the same PM continues until the completion of the project unless it is exceptionally long term in nature. In the event of a change of the PM, the transition should be smooth and should not affect the progress and deliverables of the respective partner.

Monitoring and Coordination Committee

The coordination committee is usually constituted by senior management overlooking the respective project. The frequency of such meetings depends on the nature of the project, sudden escalation issues, etc.

The meeting is anchored by one of the partners. The anchor handles the meetings execution (setup of agenda, etc.), preparation, and distribution of the minutes of meeting.

The coordination committee's periodic responsibilities include:

- Review of project status and progress
- Discussion on issues raised by various partners
- Periodic decision making which is needed to move the project forward.
- Resolution of any conflicts arising, and ensuring smooth operational interactions between partners. Any partner is formally bound to inform other partners as soon as possible of any events of interest, risk, etc., arising during the project tenure.

In the flow chart in Figure 10.9:

Step 1: Prospective outsourcing organization declares the project agenda and invites proposals from consortium partners.

Step 2: Various consortium partners team up for delivery of required products and services.

Step 3: Consortiums respond by submitting proposals to the outsourcing organization with highlights, deliverables, strengths, financial details, etc.

Step 4: Outsourcing organization awards project to suitable organization, which forms a consortium.

Step 5: Consortium partner organizations deliver project to required specifications and schedule leading to project closure.

Step 6: The consortium ceases to exist after contractual closure.

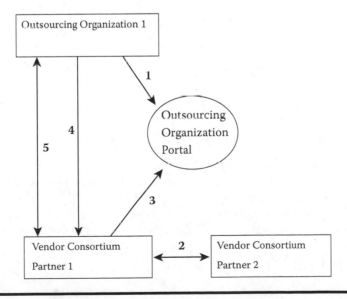

Figure 10.9   Working framework—big projects outsourcing to a consortium.

Roles

The different roles engaged in the above setup:

- Outsourcing organization—It needs execution of a large and complex outsourcing project.
- Vendor consortium partners—Together they manage delivery of the contracted deliverables.

Example 1

Huawei Symantec Technologies Co. Ltd.—Huawei Symantec is a joint venture between Huawei and Symantec. Huawei owns a 51% stake, while Symantec owns 49%. Symantec, Huawei, and Symantec Corporation are separate entities. John W. Thompson is the chairman of Huawei Symantec. Ren Zhengfei, the CEO of Huawei, is the CEO of Huawei Symantec. Its headquarters are located in Chengdu, China. Its business interests include network security, storage, and computing solutions with a specialization in technological standards.

Example 2

Airbus is owned by *European Aeronautic Defence and Space Company* (EADS). EADS is a merger of the following partners, who originally owned the below respective stakes:

Aérospatiale-Matra of France—37.9%,
Daimler-Chrysler Aerospace of Germany—37.9%,
Construcciones Aeronáuticas of Spain—4.2%
BAE Systems—20%, but sold this in 2006 to EADS

The profits accrue to the partner companies based on corresponding stakes. Work allocation is done on a similar basis.

Criteria for Success of These Models

Consistent timely delivery on schedule by consortium partners is a must for the success of this model. Thus consortium partners must set up well-defined mechanisms and processes for delivery.

Only appropriate nature of products and services may qualify for consortium delivery, and where possible, such may be avoided because it has a relatively higher risk.

The Model Value Proposition

- The outsourcing organization may have the contractual agreement with only one organization for the overall project. It is internally the responsibility of this organization to manage and ensure delivery from the multiple partners in the consortium. This concept frees the outsourcing organization from interacting with multiple vendors and reduces its management overheads significantly which accrue from the same. A single point of responsibility often prevents multiple vendors from blaming each other for the cause of a somewhat ambiguous problem.

Aiming and positioning for a 360-degree approach.

Business Model 9—Using Online Provider/ Vendor to Manage the Internet Business (E-Business) Part/Component

As traffic, real and virtual, converges into a gateway for passage across the globe.

This model envisages using an online service provider (external or internal) for setup and management of the Internet-based component of the business process cycle. The complete set of operations which are part of this Internet-based business component are envisaged as part of this Web-based outsourcing model. Attempts at enabling such competence in house may have been unsuccessful versus the level of efficiency that such online outsourcing providers could engender.

Many pressures and drivers exist that lend relevance to outsourcing online for cost containment and cost reduction. Such models, in principle, can be traced back to the Industrial Revolution. This business model initially used in the United States has been increasingly adopted in the European and the Asia Pacific regions. Subject to the terms of the agreement, the online provider truly takes control of all the process and operations related to the Internet-based component of the business. The outsourcing buyer organization will consider solely the outputs as per agreed service level agreements (SLAs). The online provider is focused on delivering the service in an efficient manner sustainably and meeting the time and quality requirements.

Such business models are adopted by organizations with a view to reduce operating costs, focus activities and resources on core business needs, and possibly obtain access to technology capabilities that may not be available internally. There usually is improvement in quality. Exceptional growth of the Internet and outsourcing market has followed the startling growth within the IT sector.

In the flow chart in Figure 10.10:

- Step 1—Organization outsources the setup and management of the Internet-based component of its business cycle.

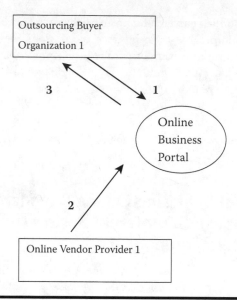

Figure 10.10 Working framework—using online provider/vendor to manage the Internet business (e-business) part/component.

- Step 2—The online vendor provider delivers the required services as laid out in the contract.
- Step 3—Outsourcing organization uses the outputs (deliverables) from the Internet-based component to complete its business cycle.

Roles

The different roles engaged in the above setup:

- Online business portal—This envisages Internet-based components of the outsourcing organization's business.
- Outsourcing buyer—Outsources the management of the Internet-based component of its business cycle.
- Online vendor provider—Delivers required services as per the contracted SLAs to the outsourcing buyer.

The Web Portal Setup and Features

Portal setup prerequisites:

- Portal setup—Suitable software and hardware infrastructure.
- Common centralized database to contain details of accounts and transactions.

- Archiving data which is no longer needed. This may be studied to understand the performance and SLA history over time.
- Periodic housekeeping and maintenance activities.

Criteria for Success of These Models

Only appropriate Internet-based component of the business process cycle should be outsourced, keeping the overall efficiency of operations execution in mind.

The Model Value Proposition

- Cost containment and reduction accrue usually from such outsourcing of noncore Internet business components.

As the networks make distances irrelevant.

- The outsourcing organization is freed up to focus on key "in-house" core business aspects in line with their expertise by outsourcing Internet business components to external experts.

Purpose, not just distance defines a journey, business or pleasure.

Business Model 10—Automated Outsourcing Using Software Agents

Of self-sustaining mechanisms and self-actualizing means and ends.

Software agent, are a new breed of software-based products that will act as the organization's personal outsourcing assistants. In dealing with the voluminous amounts of information on the networks, agents are fast becoming a necessity. What is available with whom, how does one use it, and how much is charged for it? Keeping track of files of interest on one or two database services is quite troublesome for most professionals. It is impossible for humans to do the searching, with all the complexity associated with large numbers of online databases and service bureaus. On the searcher's behalf, it will have to be software programs, information brokers, or software agents. The increasing information resource fragmentation has necessitated the development of information brokerage software agents. Given criteria like price range, fast service, or profit maximization for a client, the agent represents an intermediary which provides service integration between customers and information providers.

In the workplace, there are two types of human agents' functions—office-bound workers and mobile field workers. *In the same way, the two types of software agents functions are static (computer bound) and mobile.* To actively monitor the environment, the static software agent simply sits on the server or the computer. In the background, for instance, the user's mail agent executes and gets activated when there is incoming applicable data (e.g., a mail message). After processing the data, the agent becomes dormant again until another event requires processing. To assist in filtering and processing the volume of incoming information, the stationary agents do not roam around the online world but use embedded knowledge.

Mobility is incorporated in advanced forms of agents, which allows a software agent to execute commands while living on a remote server, only reporting back to its home base when the given task is accomplished. A new computing environment will be created by the mobile or roaming agents in which software agents perform a plethora of tasks for organizations. A PDA or computer client could be used to launch the agent into the network with suitable instructions to accomplish required tasks.

To accomplish an activity, agents can also cooperate with other agents. Static agents and mobile agents may actually work together to accomplish complex tasks. Incoming messages need to be filtered and routed intelligently to recipients on the move in the case of "'intelligent messaging."

On the searcher's behalf, information brokers in the form of software programs, software agents, etc., come into play in the vast borderless virtual world. Such agents sift through the volumes of unwanted information, gather the needed bits, and communicate the same by integrating with other related applications. Value is added to the information that is retrieved, and so information brokerage does more than just searching. The ability to structure, manage, channelize, filter, and leverage from the flow of information is one of the most powerful competencies. To sort and filter an incoming data stream automatically into a manageable amount of high-value information, the support of an agent is needed.

Technological advancements have immensely enhanced quality with the growing complexity of work and personal lives and the competitive business environment creating demands to perform many and often simultaneous tasks efficiently and promptly. New computing tools are needed to support these imperatives. The notion of an intelligent autonomous software agent is one such approach. Behind the development of software agents the underlying vision involves a paradigm shift from the traditional software as tool to software as assistant. A user initiates various actions that are passively facilitated by the software, in the existing tool-based model. A user instructs the software program to download files from the Internet, browse the WWW, or compute a spreadsheet column in a more efficient fashion, but the commands themselves issue directly from the user's mouse or keyboard input, and this is called a "do what I say" model. The user informs the agent about the various actions to be performed or tasks to be accomplished in the new agent-based model. On behalf of the user, the agent takes these requests and actively performs tasks, such as comparing prices in online shopping malls or monitoring incoming electronic mail messages and organizing an agenda even when the user is on vacation. Thus, the new model is proactive, and the traditional model is reactive.

The huge amount of information available has overwhelmed users, and the effort, time, and cost required to find the specific information they need is immense. To sort and filter an incoming data stream automatically into a manageable amount of high-value information, the support of agents is very much a necessity. Software agents are needed for decision support toward tasks performed by "knowledge workers" such as managers, technical professionals, and marketing personnel. In the marketplace, timely and knowledgeable decisions made by these professionals impact their effectiveness and the success of their businesses. To manage the huge information load and deliver quality service, use of software agents is the certain fast-approaching future.

The lives of the people can be affected in many ways by the software agent technology. Radical alteration will be induced by agent technology, not only in the way we interact with computers but also the way we conceptualize and build complex systems. Software agents are needed for multifarious reasons, and the basic premise is that software agents are autonomous, background software processes that execute on behalf of the user.

Related Examples

Example—Message redirection—Suppose an important message arrives when you are out of the office. The incoming message is processed by the agent on the computer, and it understands the significance of the message. *Several mobile agents are immediately initiated by it to track you and deliver the message content in the most appropriate way through a digitized voice over the phone or the cellular car phone, by fax or via electronic mail to the home, or even by paging you.*

Software agents using the organization's requirement criteria will navigate across a number of computer systems and networks gathering required information.

Example—Stock trading—The agent can also be programmed to make purchase decisions. After being unleashed, the mobile agents can carry out transactions without further input from the consumer and can do so hours or even days later. Consider the case in which a user dispatches a software agent off to a financial service to monitor the fluctuations of a given stock, instructing the agent to sell once the stock reaches a certain price threshold. *The agent may not communicate back to the customer for weeks or months after the agent attaches itself to the financial server, where it follows the stock.* Once the preordained value of the stock is reached, the agent executes the sell command and deposits the proceeds into the user's bank account.

Example—Knowledge assistants—To describe everything from a spreadsheet's macro functions to complex mobile code that can roam networks to do our bidding, the term software agent has become a marketing buzzword. The emerging understanding of the software agent nature can help solve business and scientific problems.

Example—Value-added information—Value is added to the information that is retrieved, and so the software agent does more than just searching. Information is retrieved about the latest currency exchange rates, for instance, in foreign exchange trading, in order to hedge currency holdings to minimize risk and maximize profit. Execution of transactions involves retrieval and processing of data and information—information searches like finding the cheapest flight tickets to a certain destination or all recent news stories pertaining to a particular issue.

Example—Integration—Services' integration becomes very much needed because multiple concurrent transactions may need to be executed. Service integration allows one to link the hedging program with the search program that finds the currency rates from the cheapest online service to automatically send trades to the bank or financial services company. Without having to go into any financial institution, in effect, personalized automated trading system can be created. Thus value has been added in this way by the software agent toward enhancing data management and traditional transaction services.

Example—Decision support—Software agents are needed for decision support. Especially in decision-making areas, there is a need for increased support for tasks performed by "knowledge workers" such as managers, technical professionals, and marketing personnel. In the marketplace, timely and knowledgeable decisions made by these vendor professionals greatly impact their effectiveness and the success of their businesses.

Miscellaneous examples—*Software agents in many ways mimic the real-world roles of highly competent secretary, reference librarian, personal and relentless world events watcher, news clip agency, office and personal assistant, personal online shopper, personal investment advisor, or decision making counselor.* In the software world, these capabilities of indisputable value will bring about a service model shift that will touch and shape all of our lives significantly.

To make costly niche expertise widely available, it needs to be modeled through automation. Exert software agents could be models of real-world professionals such as translators, lawyers, diplomats, union negotiators, stockbrokers, and even priests.

The Model Value Proposition

■ Software agents are useful to tackle repetitive office activity. To automate tasks performed by administrative and clerical personnel in functions such as sales or customer support, to reduce labor costs and increase office productivity, there is need for processing. Of the total cost of information delivery today, labor costs are estimated to be as much as 60%. Software agents are required for mundane personal activity. Time-strapped individuals, in a fast-paced society, need new ways to minimize the time spent on routine personal tasks like booking airline tickets so that they can devote more time to other activities. Voice-activated interface agent is one specific form of smart agent that reduces the user's burden of having to explicitly command the computer.

Users will have to relegate the task of searching and cost comparison to agents, because it is not possible to directly manipulate a distributed database system in an electronic commerce setting with millions of data objects, and therefore for search and retrieval, software agents prove very handy. The tedious, time-consuming, and repetitive tasks of searching databases, retrieving and filtering information, and delivering it back to the user is performed by these agents.

Repeatable tasks, a natural potential of the machines.

■ Therefore the productivity of the end user can be improved by software agents performing various tasks, the most important being gathering information, filtering information, and using it for decision making. Irrespective of whether a process is insourced or outsourced, software agents are needed for multifarious tasks. A generation ago, outsourcing entered the vocabulary of business. Today it is used widely in various industries like finance, banking, etc., as they seek to increase their strategic transaction business from their clients and optimize their high cost infrastructure. Corporations and financial institutions too, for their part, are looking for cost reduction projects that will bring rapid yet lasting returns. That a whole menu of outsourcing solutions is on offer is hardly surprising, and they range from single process options to the fully outsourced regional banking operation.

As change knocks on the frontiers of time and so-called impossibles.

Chapter 11

Web Outsourcing Examples

As the Web explodes in myriad hues, approaches, and means.

Ease of radio operation and cost was the argument advanced initially by radio manufacturers after TV was introduced about 50 years ago. Improvements in TV made it far more appealing than the radio though, in time.

In outsourcing online, the success of the two organizations is dependent on each other's success. To deal with the changing business conditions, the relationship requires a moderate amount of dialogue. In traditional outsourcing, contracting with an external entity to take primary responsibility for providing specified deliverables, business process, and functions is not new. Online outsourcing has helped to cope effectively with the management burden, thereby reducing the costs by shifting operations to less expensive locations, thus taking care of high-turnover, high-touch, and people-intensive processes. A much broader range of projects, deliverables, products, and services are being outsourced today over the Internet and other dedicated networks.

Projects That Are Good Candidates of These Models

- Repetitive
- Labor intensive
- Easily defined

- Non-proprietary
- Predictable in volume and delivery date
- Knowledge exchange

General Category of Applicable Projects

- Coding work
- Design of application and/or respective reviews
- Software tools development
- In-house requirements
- Technical consulting for problem resolution
- Inviting experts for training
- Simple documentation work
- Research and development, product development
- Internal IT
- Customer service and support
- Back office operations
- Buying of physical goods (nonsoftware)
- Consultancy services
- Project planning and management services
- Back office services (i.e., transaction processing such as data entry, processing)
- Web catalog and content management services
- Technology services—software verification and validation

Note: Thus projects of any nature and at all levels of the value chain can be put up on the portal.

Not just mass production, but production
for the masses, by the masses.

Miscellaneous Examples

The vast fields of creation, to build upon.

Considerable types of creative services can be outsourced online, such as animation, business writing, music composition, illustrations, photography, instructional design, editing, textbook manuscript layout, screenwriting, video editing, photo editing, storyboarding, creative writing, graphic design, proofreading, technical writing, cover design, art, white paper development, and so many more. Individual examples are discussed in detail in the following sections.

Example—Design of Application and/or Respective Reviews

The core and its underlying framework.

Consider the need for designing a software application. This would involve issues relating to design, number of underlying tables, fields, their normalization, etc.

Note: An inappropriate design could affect the robustness of application, and data integrity, cause excessive coding, and lead to bugs, unanticipated future problems, enhancement bottlenecks, etc.

Such an issue, if outsourced with inputs from many sources and experts would yield an optimal design. This would lead to savings in time, effort, resources, quality, etc.

Example—Technical Consulting for Problem Resolution

The expert and his word, a decision enabler.

Consider the occurrence of slow performance issue for an application software batch process that periodically processes a large volume of data. This may have become a problem *gradually* due to the common ever-increasing volume of data over time. The batch processing may have been within acceptable limits initially due to lower data volume.

Note: Such a request can affect the contracted service level agreements (SLAS) with customers and affect regular service adversely.

Such an issue, if outsourced with inputs from many sources and experts would yield an optimal result.

Example—Application Development

Sourcing from a ready source or building anew.

Consider the need to develop a software application which has a certain functionality set. Developing the same in-house needs, say, 100 person-days.

Vendor organizations which already have similar applications can deliver the same in much less time and at a much lower cost versus that incurred by the organization developing it internally.

Example—Web Site Content Writing

Not just building content but also adding value.

Here are some of the services related to the Internet that can be outsourced. Web site content writing is one of them, because it is known that a Web site is essential, but all your business requirements cannot be taken care of by a Web site, nor can it generate business alone. Appropriate content writing of superior quality that stands out from the rest is necessary, and that can help generate more traffic and consequently more business. When wanting to outsource Web site content development, there are some who want to add content with valuable insight, while there are others who want to put volumes of content. Firms who want to outsource Web site content development can benefit from the experience of the provider who can deliver a range of content, from technical white papers, to FAQs about automobiles, to reviews of tourist spots. The provider will achieve the results once briefed about the objectives, topic, style, and audience needed. *Along with search engine optimization, Web site content development involves typical writing capability and skills and is not just a replication of the writing process followed for print media.* For ranking your Web site, search engines use algorithms, and if you desire to be ranked high, high-quality content is required on your Web site, and a strategic understanding of how to write, keeping the search engines in mind. It can be quite a daunting task to write and compile content for a Web site, yet this service can be effortlessly outsourced, thereby adding significant value to the project. One can be assured that the Web site will produce desired results, because established Web site content management providers are experienced at writing specifically for the Web. The writers try hard to meet your needs. For instance, if a customer wants a summary of the 10 volumes of the history of a university, then they will try to find someone who knows the history and is experienced in summary writing. There is a vast talent pool, and if a customer wants engineering writing, the provider can assign an engineer to the task, and they can even assign teams to projects, say an expert engineer, a writer, and an editor. On an ongoing basis or on a project basis, a writer, an assistant writer, or an editor can be assigned to the work, and the charges are either a monthly fee or by the article or number of words. Depending upon the amount of research and skill required, the provider can quote the cost once it receives the project details.

For instance, a casual article, a summary, and a press release can be developed from a formal white paper. The tiresome task of organizing and preparing content for use on the Web can be outsourced, if one already has the necessary content. To meet your needs, service providers can modify existing content or reorganize it, whether it is an electronic, paper-based, or idea content. Content developers can distribute information on the appropriate pages of your Web site after understanding your products, services, and other needs. A major function of any Web site is to communicate clearly and powerfully and create an impact through content.

Example—Marketing and Consulting Online

Being present there without having a presence.

Internet marketing strategy and consulting is one example. Despite being controversial, there are reasons to outsource at least a part of it to India. To acquire customers, many organizations (significantly Indian companies) are increasingly depending on the Internet, because for the majority, opening an office in the United States or Europe may not be feasible. Therefore such companies have achieved great mastery over the medium. The niche skills to market products and provide consultation services over the Net are possessed by a large pool of Indian professionals.

Example—Search Engine Marketing (SEM)

The charmed pied piper of Hamelin, driving the hordes.

Another service is search engine marketing (SEM) wherein search engines are used to drive traffic to your Web site, and SEM is very intensive. Automatic submissions are not approved of by most of the directories and search engines, and they prefer manual submission where a person submits a site for approval. Someone is required to read up on the tips and tricks and constantly be at it to implement SEM in house, although it may not be necessary to hire a full-time person. With very little investment, this service can be outsourced to professional Internet marketing firms. But a monitoring mechanism should be in place to know the way the outsourcing partner implements this service. There is no dearth of individuals and companies in the industry who spam the search engine for quick results, and it would be prudent to avoid dealing with these companies to avoid your Web site getting blacklisted.

Example—Web Link Building Service

Knitting the links of your Web world together.

Closely associated with search engine marketing is the link building service, and it requires someone to continuously write to webmasters and request them to link to your Web site. It may take considerable time if one does it the right way, so it should be first figured out why people should link to your Web site. Then one should proceed to procure links for the Web site. Although it may be easy to monitor, measure, and outsource the service, it could be very time consuming.

There are a huge number of services that can be outsourced, because the outsourcing boom, which started with software and expanded to call centers, is now moving to other high-end services like engineering, architecture, research technical writing, creative writing, and creative services.

Example—Data Collection

Providing the critical basics to help make informed decisions.

Web analytics involves using data to make a decision, but spending time to collect that data is a different ball game altogether. The vendor who has been outsourced the service of Web analytics is responsible for collecting and analyzing data and making suggestions to you based on the analysis. As a business owner, it makes sense to spend time looking at data and reports, rather than spending time collecting this information.

Example—Web Site Marketing

The value of a few words often more than umpteen volumes.

In Web site marketing, content is the king, and firms should be prepared to invest in original and persuasive quality content if they want their Web sites to do well. Immediate benefits can be reaped by outsourcing content to a professional writer, and your existing Web site content can be used by the writer along with your brochure, memos, telephone conversations, e-mails, etc., to either tweak an existing article or produce an original one.

Example—Newsletters

As news circulates around the world taking an increasingly virtual form.

In spite of the spam menace, newsletters are still known to be effective. A few things are required to churn out a newsletter, and they consist of a system to collect e-mails, content, good design, a tool or service to send e-mails, and a system to monitor the effectiveness of the newsletter. Writing, design, and technology skills are required for this service, and outsourcing it can make the newsletter campaign extremely effective.

Example—Online Newspapers and Magazines

The virtual stands, continuously updatable.

Beginning with online newspapers and magazines, to illustrate the difficulties in interface design in e-commerce applications, let us look at some specifics. Many publications like *Time, The New York Times,* etc., have gone online. Rather than browsing or skimming as done with normal reading, at this point, they are best used for looking up specific information they are known to contain. All within seconds, readers of printed magazines can browse the headlines, the subheads, the photos, the captions, or perhaps read three paragraphs and then hop to another story. Graphical user interfaces provide ease of navigation. However, the generation of online publications is constantly evolving and improving. At this point, this area is nascent, with tremendous potential.

Examples—Merging of Fields—Advertisements, Entertainment, Education, and Service

Convergence enabled through a common delivery platform.

The idea of convergence of industries centered on information and e-commerce has irrevocably linked what until today have been isolated content, storage, networks, business applications, and consumer devices. Broadly defined, convergence is the merging of computers for the purpose of facilitating new forms of information-based commerce. Because the popular press uses the terms multimedia and cross-media interchangeably, the public can be forgiven for finding the concept perplexing. *The conversion of text, voice, data, image, graphics, and full motion video into digital content is multimedia convergence.* The integration of various industries—entertainments, publication, and communication media based on multimedia content is cross-media convergence. Often, these two types of convergence are closely linked. For example, the lines between advertisements, entertainment, education, and service are often blurred in the new era of interactive TV. You may develop an urge to know more about Australia while watching a cricket match between India and Australia. You can link to an online database and search, while not missing the match, instead of running to the local bookstore and purchasing a book. Therefore removing barriers between telecommunications, broadcasting, computing, movies, electronic games, and publishing industries to facilitate interoperability is convergence. Some simple technological advances are driving the phenomenon of convergence. All types of information—content books, business documents, videos, movies, music—are translated into digital information in convergence of content. The information can be easily processed, once it is converted into digital form. This allows easier searching, sorting, enhancing, conversion, compression, encryption, replication, and transmission in ways that are conveniently matched to today's information processing systems. Compression and storage of digitized information so that it can travel through existing phone and cable wiring is achieved through convergence of transmission. Technological breakthroughs and new switching techniques enable all types of information to travel to home. "Pipelines" are provided through convergence of communication equipment to transmit voice, data, image, and video all without rewiring the neighborhood. Devices that have the sophistication to function as both computers and televisions are accessed through convergence of information. The telephone with internal fax machine, modem, and video capable of receiving fax, e-mail, and video are other examples.

Example of Outsourcing Online—Tax Preparation Services

As they say in the United States,
"There is no escape from death and taxes."

Greater speed along with reduced costs and turnaround time are the hallmarks of outsourcing. Client cost can be cut by up to 50% over a period of time, if tax preparation service is outsourced, and the client's source documents can be electronically and securely shared with the provider's accounting professionals using Internet-based document management tools. Client records are converted to electronic files and stored on servers so that they can be accessed from anywhere on the Internet, and the original client records never leave the premises.

Example—Desktop Publishing (DTP) Outsourcing Online

Of geographically scattered roles in a virtual team.

Suppose the outsourcer and the vendor are working together online on a DTP project. Then they should both be using the compatible computers and applications (e.g., Mac), so that the fonts are compatible.

Example—Outsourcing Training and E-Learning Products Development Online

*Quality learning anytime, anywhere,
faster and cheaper from the virtual masters.*

World-class training products can be created by combining the latest technology with the best talent, as in the case of Macromedia Captivate, a great e-learning development tool. In e-learning products, training can be designed to make learning fun and easy, faster and better. The product can be built from scratch, depending on customer needs, or just a portion of the work can be outsourced. Company orientation and training can be imparted to new employees sitting at a computer, with the training CD or online course being effective and costing less per person. Training CDs with workbooks enable effective training and generate revenue. The learning of the employees can be evaluated after giving them a training CD, and this kind of training can be made available across distances, thereby boosting the knowledge level and revenue. For large and mid-size companies, it is a cost effective method. Training products can be sold by entrepreneurs, so that people can learn almost anything like company policies, accounting, cricket, leadership, writing, factory safety, PowerPoint, company policies, and more. The return on investment (ROI) will be high, because the production cost of a training product is very low, and it is a great digital product to sell online. In creating a training CD, there are four steps involved, which are content, instructional design, develop, and publish. The content part involves the writing of training content from scratch or redesigning existing training. The instructional design step involves design and development of script to maximize learning according to your objectives. In the develop step audio, animation, tests, interaction, simulations, or other elements can be included. Finally, the training is published for delivery on the CD or over the Internet.

Outsourcing training development to India can be a great opportunity because there are plenty of talented and experienced people familiar with working global customers.

Example—Home and Business Shopping

Those everyday chores of little value that eat up all the time.

Online outsourcing enables execution of operations like home and business shopping, etc., over the Internet.

Example—Outsourcing of Small Web-Based Businesses (e.g., Online Video Rentals)

Never too small to outsource.

Development, deployment, even operation of such relatively small Web-based applications can be outsourced over the Web. Consider video on demand choices presented to a prospective virtual customer over the Web. Suitable enabling criteria should allow the virtual customer to search and pick up the required product and services with minimum effort.

Example—Insourcing Online over the Organization's Internal Intranet Network

There are some areas that are best suited for insourcing internally over the organization's intranet web. The areas are application updates, troubleshooting (tax, audit, etc.), workstation and server security updates, security and event log review, end user help desk and support, tape back up team (backups, restores) and general day-to-day administration.

Example—Usage of Online Software Agents

Information may be retrieved over the Internet from suitable resources about the latest currency exchange rates, for instance, in foreign exchange trading, in order to hedge currency holdings to minimize risk and maximize profit. *Service integration links the hedging program with the search program that finds the currency rates from the cheapest online service to automatically send trades to the bank or financial services company.* Without having to go into any financial institution, in effect, a personalized automated trading system can be created. Thus value can be added in this way by information brokerages and also to support data management and traditional transaction services.

Examples in E-Commerce

The abstract values of thoughts and things.

E-Commerce Applications—Order Management

The new approach of computerizing and subsequently outsourcing online includes traditional functions such as payment and funds transfer, order entry and processing, invoicing, inventory management, cargo tracking, electronic catalogs, and point of sale data gathering. Advertising, marketing, and customer support functions are also part of the online outsourcing domain. The entire order management cycle is integrated online through a suitable blend of people, resources, machines, and networks. We are witnessing online integration of a wide range of new and old applications.

Examples of E-Commerce Applications—Content Ownership

Value built over time, some sustaining, some transient.

Application software rich in multimedia content includes electronic books, real-time information, movies, video, and interactive services. Online outsourcing organizations, even telecommunication and cable companies, understand the importance of content and have begun to acquire rights to the content they believe will have great value. Programming content theme has been picked up by the press with a vengeance, painting all content providers as winners and differentiating very little between possession and application. Traditionally the type of content produced via online outsourcing varies from industry to industry (e.g., cartoons, games). The media broadcast productions industry outsources relevant parts of production of documentaries and entertainment programs. *Production of online books, reference collections, Web maps, and Web catalogs is outsourced online by Web-based publishing houses.*

The protracted bidding war, which ran into several billions of dollars, between Viacom and QVC for Paramount studios is evidence in this direction of the value attached to content. Paramount's library of movies, television series, and copyrights was the target.

Examples of E-Commerce Applications—Interactive Multimedia Online

Services that address the myriad individual choices.

A range of interactive services such as shopping, video navigation, interactive TV guides and directories, interactive telephone yellow pages, and video on demand may be outsourced online.

Such businesses need underlying telecommunication networks, multimedia applications, geographical information systems, computers, storage, production studios, shopping kiosks, etc. This has led to a unique business partnership between technology/transport and media companies. This tie-up between the content providers business (entertainment/media), transport providers (telecos/wireless/cable operators) and online content developers, vendors, and support has grown significantly.

Example—Interactive Communications Online

Communications, the backbone of business conduct.

Interactive communications worldwide are much easier, much more useful, and much less expensive due to advances in computers, online applications, and communications. Centralized online outsourcing of setup, maintenance, and operation of such communications is advantageous, because a small dedicated virtual service team can virtually manage large networks.

EDI Example—Medical Field

End-to-end delivery made simple.

Let us consider the claims process, to understand the role of Web-based outsourcing and electronic data interchange (EDI). With a claim filed manually by the health care provider, the normal process executed without EDI begins. After that it is photocopied, filed, placed in an envelope, and mailed via regular postal service to the insurance company. The envelope is then opened manually along with thousands of other claims, and the claim is microfilmed and keyed into the insurer's database system. If the provider wants to find the status of the claim, in the meantime, he would have to phone the company and wait till the customer service representative locates the claim (assuming that it was entered into the database) and checks on its status. The process would start all over again, if a discrepancy or error arises. The form handling complexity is further increased when we take into account the fact that each provider has many subsets of claims—hospital claims (in patient care, emergency care, outpatient care) and medical claims (surgery and other types such as optical and dental). In a paper environment, the initial processing would alone take 10 to 15 days.

Using EDI, now let us look at the process. Online service providers working with the health providers prepare the necessary forms using the EDI software and submit claims via telecommunication lines to the value-added network service providers. Properly formatted forms are then passed on to the appropriate payer organizations for suitable editing and sorting. Prior to sending it to the payer, for certain criteria, the insurance company computer can automate and electronically route the transactions to a third-party organization for price evaluation, additional review of case, and so forth. Acceptance/rejection reports are also received by claims submission that may contain payer-initiated messages regarding claim status and requests for additional information, unprocessed claims, and zero balances and settlements. There are many advantages of using online service providers coupled with the EDI process. Claims are received in a standard data format, on the payer side, which increases quality and eliminates the extra data entry of claims office and mailroom mess that is part of the manual process. *For online-processed EDI-based claims, turnaround is estimated at two to four working days.* Because payment settlements are done either weekly or fortnightly, actual payment takes longer, so health providers may receive payment about 14 to 20 days after the claim was submitted electronically. The health care community must adopt EDI to achieve significant cost reductions.

The health care community had been reluctant to migrate to EDI because guidelines defining specific data requirements had not been developed, although the business and operational efficiencies achieved using integrated service providers and EDI produced significant savings. There has now been full acceptance by all health care providers to implement standardized EDI. With the creation of EDI standards for the health care industry, this situation is changing for patient information, certification, utilization management, expanded claims formats, coordination of benefits, and claims status.

Online service providers coupled with EDI are rapidly becoming a permanent fixture, as medical providers, patients, and payers increasingly process claims via electronic networks. The administrative cost of health care is reduced because electronic claim processing is quick. Claims can be sent to the payers within 24 hours, in most cases, and there are fewer errors, and this translates into decreased turnaround time. Online service providers and EDI enable physicians, laboratories, and hospitals and other health care settings to communicate with each other, in addition to processing claims for billing purposes; thus there is better managed care.

EDI Example—Usage in Manufacturing and Retail Procurement

Supply that follows the demand patterns.

Both manufacturing and retail procurement are heavy users of online outsourcing and EDI. *Thousands of large parts are no longer stocked in advance for their use by companies using "just in time" (JIT) and online outsourcing.* How many parts are needed each day is calculated instead based on the production schedule and orders. Schedules are electronically transmitted to suppliers online every day, or in certain cases every 30 minutes. For production activity, the parts are delivered to the plant "just in time." The whole manufacturing environment has been changed by online outsourcing using EDI. For instance, stock holding used to be planned months ahead. This is no longer feasible today, and delivery has to be responsive or it will cost too much in money and time. As opposed to previous massive shipments, small quantities must be delivered more frequently, and that means getting data to online suppliers quickly. Immediacy of EDI may not be required by all parts, depending on their nature. Different delivery schedules are dictated by different parts, in other words. Small fixings like nuts do not need to be delivered just in time or even close, for instance, in the automobile industry. A streamlined cash flow is a major benefit of JIT and EDI. When an invoice is received by a company, it pays for parts that are actually in use, in a product ready to be sold, instead of paying for large costly items stored in the inventory. Online retailers are defining practices through the entire supply chain using quick response (QR) systems and taking their cue from the efficiencies manufacturers have gained from just in time manufacturing techniques. QR means better service and availability of a wider range of products for the customer. QR may mean survival in a competitive marketplace for retailers and suppliers. Using event-driven online outsourcing, much of the focus of QR is in reduction of lead times and occurrences. For example, inventories falling below a specified level immediately trigger a chain of events including automatic ordering from one company's application directly into the other's application. In order to save money, batch EDI, whereby an organization may group a set of transactions from various departments and mail them at one time, may no longer suffice under these time pressures. Online documents include purchase orders, shipping notices, invoices, inventory position, catalogs, and order status in QR. Effectiveness in other areas is also improving because of some of the innovations originally targeted for improving distribution. For example, the data generated can be used in customer information systems to provide better marketing. The starting point in this online networked chain of organizations is often the point of sale (POS) scanning that allows the retailer to track merchandise at the item level and provide detailed information for demand forecasting. The need to remark merchandise for discounts and promotion to reduce inventory levels can be eliminated by this way of managing inventory. Data is fed by point of sale systems to automatic replenishment systems that constantly monitor inventory levels and trigger transactions online to respective players. Smaller, more frequent deliveries which improve in-stock position and reduce on-hand inventory are supported by these systems. Of the warehouse operations, scanning is a valuable part, because this expedites the rapid flow of goods through the distribution center by reducing manual receiving and checking procedures. Merchandise can be cross-docked within the distribution center or be sent directly to the store, when scanning is used with predistribution techniques such as packing directly for an individual store.

EDI Examples—Miscellaneous Usages

Making in-roads into ever growing vistas.

Online outsourcing has spread everywhere, although it was developed to improve transaction and trade. From a sample of online outsourcing applications currently in development or under consideration, some idea of its breadth of coverage may be obtained. *It includes railway rolling stock monitoring, ship bay plans (cargo plans for container ships), ship berthing and scheduling notices, notifications of presence of dangerous/ hazardous goods on ships/trains/planes, the exchange of CAD/CAM documents, tender tracking, lodgment of law court documents, notification of lodgment of archive documents, the exchange and lodgment of trade documents such as ship manifests/airway bills/ customs clearances, airline ticket settlements, in addition to the more commonly considered exchange of documents concerned with the purchase and supply of goods (such as purchase orders or invoices).* From its original and somewhat limited use as expediter of the transfer of trade goods, EDI has grown to facilitate exchange of standard format data between any two computer systems. In various industries, an examination of online outsourcing usage provides insight into the business problems and solutions. In many different scenarios in industries, online outsourcing is used extensively, such as in international and cross-border trade, electronic funds transfer (EFT), in health care for insurance claims processing, and in manufacturing and retail procurement. To improve business process for both strategic and competitive advantages, companies have applied a number of online solutions. Operational aspects of a business have in some cases been transformed by Web-based online outsourcing. Industry standards of competition have changed significantly through increased quality and cost reductions as innovators exert greater pressure on competitors to meet new standards of customer satisfaction and productivity. A company's marketing and distribution efforts have been shaped by online outsourcing by helping to create new distribution channels, develop new merchandising and market research methods, and introduce better customer service. Thus companies can be more competitive due to major improvements in product manufacturing and customer service response time.

For electronic transmission, other transactions targeted include claims submission or billing, payment and payment posting, eligibility verification, and primary care member enrollment. Labor-intensive activities of providers and payers involved with submitting adjudicating, processing, and paying claims can be reduced by online outsourcing, and the most innovative efforts involving online outsourcing go considerably beyond claims administration. Retail procurement and manufacturing both are already heavy users of online outsourcing and EDI. Online outsourcing is used to support just in time in manufacturing and in retailing. It is used to support quick response systems.

EDI Example—International Trade

The ships transporting goods over the high seas across the virtual globe.

With international trade, online outsourcing has always been very closely linked. Significant progress has been made toward the establishment of more open and dynamic trade relations over the last few years. Long-standing trade restrictions have been lifted. Developing countries in particular and many other countries in general have made significant efforts to liberalize and adjust their trade policies. Thus, trade efficiency in this context is an utmost necessity which allows faster, simpler, broader and less costly transactions. Only by using online outsourcing as a widely global transactions medium can trade efficiency be accomplished. Smooth flow of information is facilitated by online outsourcing. Those not involved in international trade tend to think only of its physical aspects like the movement of goods, containers, vehicles, ships, and aircraft. The physical movement is controlled and regulated by a deluge of information handling and exchange manifested by a variety of documents or their electronic equivalents. The information flow does not merely provide data but also facilitates timely delivery. It is of little help if the best quality information arrives days after the cargo. Poorly designed documents, mistakes in document handling, or bad management upstream where a bureaucrat sits on documents can cause delays.

Paper had been the mainstay for carrying trade-related information, and online outsourcing coupled with EDI replaced it. Because of the labor involved, error delays, and other associated delays, paper-based communication is inefficient and costly. In national trade, the problem of paper is significant, but it becomes far more acute in international trade. In the simplest international trade transaction, it is estimated that a minimum of 12 participants are involved. Information of what is being moved or paid for is wanted by all of them, and the core of that information is the same. In transferring and checking information from one paper document to another, vast amounts of time and resources are often spent, and errors may occur frequently and unwittingly. It has been estimated by the United Nations that error rates in excess of 50% have been consistently recorded in letters of credit, and error rates of 30% are not uncommon in manual processing of customs entries. The cost of voluminous paperwork, complex formalities, and associated delays and errors amount to about 10% of the final value of goods according to the UN Conference on Trade and Development (UNCTAD). Large numbers of such transactions, if centralized by online outsourcing and through further use of automation and EDI, minimize such errors.

EDI

The virtual messengers that replaced the physical carriers.

In an online outsourcing arrangement, for reducing cycle and order fulfillment times, many industries see EDI (*electronic data interchange*) as essential. Businesses are looking at electronic data interchange in a new light, as a conscious, highly competitive e-commerce environment comes of age. The interprocess communication (application to application communication) of business information in standardized electronic form is known as EDI.

Huge volumes of paper orders and records used to crawl back and forth between manufacturers, agents, service providers, customers, and suppliers. Online outsourcing coupled with EDI provides vendors with a snapshot of what stores are selling in retailing, enabling them to recognize and meet the customer's needs much faster than in the past. Time and expense associated with paperwork are reduced, because it enables retailers and vendors to place orders and pay bills electronically. Online outsourcing benefits translate into reduced transaction costs, by improving the speed and efficiency of filling orders. It takes up to five times longer to process a purchase order manually than it does electronically, according to studies. Closer relationship, in addition, between trading partners can be fostered by the common interaction channel. This can lead to important competitive and strategic advantages.

Unfortunately, online outsourcing, automation, and EDI are not widely used despite all these advantages, although more than 90% of the Fortune 1000 companies are currently using them, and high growth is expected as online outsourcing and networking become pervasive. Online outsourcing and integration took off only in the 1990s, and the technique is used in a wide range of industries— automotive, retail, transportation, and international trade. It is set to become the standard as organizations adopt this practice worldwide.

Example—Shift over from Manual to Computerized Online Business

Make the virtual transition, for known and unknown benefits are many.

Information pertinent for business transactions, in short, is communicated by EDI, between the computer systems of companies, online service providers, government organizations, small businesses, and banks. Online outsourcing has changed the way firms do business, including with whom they do business in the current global marketplace. Prior to online outsourcing, various forms of communication like purchase orders, acknowledgments, invoices, etc., depended on traditional methods and postal systems, and communication with trading partners had to be restricted to those few hours of the workday that overlapped between different time zones. Communication, today, is simplified and enhanced through online service providers and computers, which enable new business practices. Computer-to-computer links are established by the organization, its online service providers, and trading partners, and this enables them to exchange information efficiently and electronically. Thus the growing avalanche of paperwork, purchase orders, invoices, confirmation notices, shipping receipts, and other documents are better matched up through automation and integration services by the online service providers. Such business process changes, with the aid of EDI, allow more work automation to occur and even alter the way business is done.

Example—Financial Organizations and Banks Using Online Service Providers

Leveraging from the means that make a significant difference.

Banks and big industrial and financial corporations use online service providers— first, for the fast transmission of critical information and regular financial information throughout the world, and second, for the movement of money internationally at rapid speed for settlement of debit/credit balances. Sophisticated cash management systems have been developed by banks on the back of these services, which essentially reduce the amount of money companies leave idly floating in low-earning accounts. The three principal types of noncash payment instruments currently used for business-to-business payments are checks, electronic funds transfer, and Automated Clearing House (ACH) transfers.

The Clearing House Interbank Payment System (CHIPS), one institution alone, currently moves an average of $1 trillion each day via wire and satellite. One of the biggest barriers to the widespread acceptance of financial EDI is the difficulty of handling various electronic payment and remittance formats. Some standards exist just for sending remittance information, others just for transferring funds, but fortunately new standards are emerging for moving information about financial instruments and data together. Suitable online service providers provide support in terms of networks, infrastructure, applications and transactions management, and consulting services. For communicating data to their corporate customers, some of these banks have developed their own networks, and some also contract with online service providers for secure networks to transmit remittance information to their corporate customer's trading partners. Between banks the growing volume of EFT has necessitated the increasing use of scrutiny and message authentication systems to determine whether a message has originated from its proper source and whether there have been any modifications. The banking industry has combined electronic payment formats with EDI formats for remittance data, in order to allow banks to automate payment processing fully. Some of the most commonly used formats in the industry are BAI, 820 and 823, CCD, CTP, CCD+, CTX, and EDIFACT.

Examples—Potential Fields for Outsourcing to India

As players jostle for space in the virtual marketplace.

There are a large number of technically competent software professionals, technical writers, script writers, artists, and many other professionals in India, combined with their natural talent. Global customers are dealing with professionals who are qualified to provide quality content for a variety of media. *A high level of education has produced very qualified professionals, and it would not be easy to find another country with a higher level of English writing and editing skills combined with understanding of literary nuances.*

Outsourcing to India is advisable for business content in the fields of opening new markets with the Internet, future Asian trends, labor arbitrage, media and communication, emerging Asian markets, cross-cultural communications, cross-cultural leadership, outsourcing case studies, Indian corporate governance, outsourcing to India, strategy in an global Internet economy, cultural insights for global marketing, business technology, business execution in a developing country, and more. Firms can safely outsource Internet marketing campaigns.

For outsourcing content development, travel writing, or lifestyle writing, some final editing of content may be required, but it is not required when outsourcing medical, scientific, or technical writing and other such similar writing/editing. India has a large population of expert writers who are well trained in English and its nuances. They can converse in English as comfortably as their American or British counterparts because English is their first language too. Hence the outsourcer need not bother about any issues regarding the differences in Indian and American English. Some of the features that Indian content developers offer include good research, best keywords, and content tailored according to your requirements. The types of Web site content that can be outsourced to India include photographs, articles, stories, audio, illustrations, animations, icons, and more. *A host of written content development services can be provided by the Indian content writers such as technical writing, brochures, tutorials, travel writing, academic writing, speech writing, presentations, fiction writing, news item writing, report writing, promotion leaflets, online help, copywriting, software and technical book writing, white papers, medical writing, book authoring, journalism, product description, game writing, grant writing, book summary, biography writing, news release writing, manuals, business writing, book reviews, script writing, and more.*

Apart from the global outlook of the Indian professionals, the experience and advantage that they have gained from dealing with global customers during the outsourcing boom has further honed their skills. A perspective of a merger of the East and the West has been created with the advent of the Internet, which has flooded India with a lot of information from the West. The output of the Indians becomes uniquely valuable, partly due to the bicultural global outlook giving them a keen insight into the global trends and markets.

Example—IBM's E-Business Strategy

Goals—IBM formed a division called Enterprise Content Management with the following four goals:

- To lead IBM's strategy to transform itself into e-business and to act as a catalyst to help facilitate that transformation
- To help out business units to become more effective in their use of the Internet/intranet, both internally and with their customers
- To establish a strategy for the corporate Internet site
- To leverage the wealth of e-business, to highlight the potential of e-business to IBM's customers

IBM's E-Business Approach

IBM created an independent e-business division, thereby introducing e-business as a corporate culture. Related processes were reengineered. IBM decided to be an e-business leader using ROI as the criteria for selecting e-business projects.

Key Focus Areas

e-commerce—selling more goods via the Web

e-care for customers—providing all kinds of customer support online

e-care for business partners—dedicated support services

e-procurement—working closely with IBM's customers and suppliers to improve the tendering process and to better administer the huge number of transactions involved

e-care for employees—for easier access to information and support

e-marketing communication—to better communicate IBM's marketing stance

Example—Mphasis' VTR (Virtual Tax Room) Tool

Mphasis' VTR (Virtual Tax Room) combines the latest Web technologies and outsourcing methodologies to offer a state-of-the-art solution for outsourcing tax preparation and processing. VTR tools consist of a lead sheet to summarize data from source document for comparison, a document management system, and an interaction tool to assist preparation and review process at back office and front office. The checklist ensures compliance; the grading tool evaluates and measures performance; the allocation and logic tool assigns work according to the skill sets of users and reports monitor and control operations. In an outsourcing arrangement, the provider ensures operational flexibility through access to multiple communication channels for knowledge sharing. There is improved efficiency, paperless environment, and leveraging time zone differences to operate on a virtual 24/7 model.

Better process control and quality are ensured by reviewing and monitoring performance metrics across parameters. Adequate security through the use of firewalls/protection from internal/external raids, audit trails and role-based user access result in increased customer and staff satisfaction, improved operational flexibility, and better control.

Service delivery offerings are thus driven by the convergence of technologies such as Web services, workflow software and business performance monitoring, business intelligence, and customer focus.

As competitors jostle in the virtual arena.

Chapter 12

Web Outsourcing— Criteria for Success, Challenges

Those limits that can be reached, stretched, and some even broken.

Web-based outsourcing is fraught with many challenges.

"Nature" of Business, Online

As new trends awaken and old fall away.

The nature of business defines everything else. All strategies, and business processes are dependent on this. Largely products and services are traded online between multiple entities. Some types of business lend themselves easily to the virtual world of online outsourcing, while some businesses do not. Only appropriate types of projects should be outsourced online. Selection of projects should be judiciously done after due evaluation and deliberation.

Evaluation of future trends and quick creation of products surround services to meet respective business and technological needs. Business trends may start slowly but leapfrog exponentially, building up to meet mass market demands. Trends usually surpass national and geographic boundaries and often have a life of five to ten years. Estimation of market pulse and customizing existing projects into products ahead of time to match the upcoming needs, this is in the nature of pioneering work in the respective domain.

189

Trends—Their essence usually in simplistic concepts.

The Internet revolution as it exists today is believed to have been invented by the Soviet Union in 1957 during the launch of Sputnik I. But the widely usable World Wide Web (WWW) was invented by Tim Berners-Lee in 1989 in Switzerland. Some more theories on its origin can be found at http://wiki.answers.com/Q/When_was_Internet_started.

The Internet will not replace the existing marketing. Rather it will be a new channel and a set of methods to improve the efficiency and productivity of marketing.

What Does Not Qualify for Online Outsourcing

The following types of work are not advisable for online outsourcing:

- Strategic planning
- Activities subject to massive business change
- Critical systems and processes
- IT customer relationship management
- Compliance management

Market Readiness

Those unexplored frontiers, offering an opportunity.

Some "limited" homework, including surveys of other players already using online outsourcing for similar products and services, may be needed to gauge the feasibility and readiness for initiating.

If the market is not ready for the proposed online outsourcing of the business idea, it is mostly doomed to fail, howsoever bright the idea may be. Customers learn about products and services differently in a virtual marketplace, buy them differently using electronic cash and secure payments systems, and have them delivered differently. There may also be a difference in how customers allocate their loyalty.

Remember the principle "load, fire, aim" (in that order) when it comes to Internet-based outsourcing business startups, as discussed earlier (see Chapter 9).

Target Geography for Online Outsourcing

Regional specialties spice up the global online menu.

Due to difference in currencies, applicable laws, economic development, cultural and social climate, etc., an online outsourcing business, though having a global reach, may often target regional competencies. An online outsourcing venture looking for large English-speaking competencies would do well to target India.

Vast Online Information Volumes

Imagine volumes unimaginable.

Information is power, and knowledge a still greater power. Knowledge is a byproduct of information and data. Mountainous volumes of data exist online. Information derived is much smaller in quantity than its source data, and information, when refined, produces knowledge which is far less in quantity than information. The increasing vast and voluminous information fragmentation online has necessitated the development of information brokerage. In dealing with the voluminous amounts of information on the Web, information brokers are rapidly becoming necessary. Customers and information professionals need to keep up with knowledge. They need to know things such as—What is available with whom, how does one use it, and how much is charged for it? *It is fast becoming impossible for humans (even in online outsourcing) to do the searching, with the large volumes online and all the complexity associated with large numbers of online information databases.* Manually searching, managing, and keeping track of information of value online is quite effort intensive and difficult.

Transparency and Interoperability between Networked Systems

Transparency no longer an alternative, but an imperative.

Transparency and interoperability over the network in the virtual world allows all stakeholders (the outsourcing organization, the online service provider, suppliers, customers, etc.) to access multiple systems without knowing the related technical intricacies. Transparency is needed to hide the underlying issues of the physical media working and network interconnection and traffic. "Virtual network" consists of various components like departments, servers, applications, and inter-enterprise LANs that work holistically for the user in a seamless manner. Using middleware, transparency is accomplished that facilitates a distributed computing environment. Across collections of multivendor, heterogeneous systems, this gives users and applications transparent access to data, computation, and other resources over the Internet. The strategic architectures of every major system vendor are now based on some form of middleware. Transparency is the key to realizing the theoretical benefit of a seamless interactive virtual world. The network of online servers should provide a holistic resource, and users interact through a single window. They need not know where individual resources are located in this collection of online servers. Running applications just need to send a request to the middleware layer, which will do what is needed by accessing required resources from their respective locations.

An increasing gap between the business needs and the technology solutions, if existing online, possibly because of integration issues, could be fatal. Interoperability allowing integration of disparate systems and providing centralized technology management is critical. Only thus is return on investment (ROI) realized on technology investments.

Quality

As peak standards turn into essential basics over time
and new ones take their place.

A major concern is the quality of products, even for services rendered in Web-based outsourcing. Ignoring quality in today's world is a call to certain extinction in the virtual world, for quality is the only choice and no longer an option. Therefore quality management is of paramount importance. Online vendors must realize that it is much more costly to fix quality shortcomings than delivering high-quality products and services. Quality issues are a certain ticket to failure, loss of face, and branding. Poor end-customer experiences and reviews could have catastrophic business effects on the outsourcing organization and the online service provider, because it is not possible to isolate such customers, and such feedbacks are visible to everyone online.

Strict quality assurance and control programs need to form an integral part of the transaction life cycle. *Various quality-related models and standards exist, like the International Organization of Standardization's ISO 9001-2000 certification, an international standard for quality management systems, Six Sigma improvement methodologies, and SEI CMM (capability maturity model, for management and software engineering practices).* The software engineering institute of Carnegie Mellon University offers P–CMM, the people certification. Such approaches involve sustained review and continuous improvement of business processes, regular monitoring of work and outputs, regular internal and external quality audits, etc.

Time, Speed, and Uncertainty

The charge of the light brigade, to do what must be done.

Uncertainty is the extent of difficulty with which one can foresee what might occur during the course of a transaction life cycle online. The greater the length of time for the transaction life cycle online, the greater the uncertainty factor; the shorter the time span, the lesser the uncertainty. Uncertainty is inbuilt in time. Failures and problems occur because it may not be possible to foresee and predict all the uncertainties over a period of time. Hence risk is greatly reduced if the length of time is less. Lack of information, information asymmetry, and opportunism also cause uncertainty. Another factor is specificity. If a transaction is highly specific, transaction life cycles usually have lower costs.

Online outsourcing service can "never" be too fast.

Time—It is a process of rapidly delivering large-scale quality work online by organizations, institutions, and individual professionals. Achieving the ideal of instant, personalized and efficient service is the goal of most technologies and processes. Increase speed of delivery, response, service; for the customer, time is money, and the clock is ticking.

Business-to-business transactions use electronic data interchange (EDI), etc., for everyday transactions like purchasing goods, exchanging information, giving consulting services, and submitting and receiving proposals. Organizations, governments, and individuals increasingly depend on computers as a fast, economical, and dependable way for business and personal needs.

What would happen when an increasing number of players enter the online outsourcing space? It would:

- Deliver an equivalent value faster and more consistently to customers
- Provide higher levels of service
- Reduce transaction, project, and service costs online consistently
- Provide customized projects and services more efficiently

Note: Such issues are unavoidable as competition builds up with the passage of time.

Convenience and Self-Service

Space, to let their aspirations take to the wings.

Self-service by the outsourcing organization is the current most popular approach. Many teams within the outsourcing organization prefer to do their own homework online. Hence convenience, easy of use, navigation and availability of critical information often decide success or failure of the online outsourcing provider. Self-service also allows the team to work at their own time and pace. The adroit online outsourcing provider empowers the outsourcing customer to use 24/7 Web-based online systems for information, products, services, etc., through maximized automation and minimal manual support from its online back-end individuals.

A *single-window service must exist for all outsourcing organization and customer interactions with the online outsourcing provider.* Elicited support by a customer may be handed off from the customer to online partners or external vendors in a well-defined streamlined process. Otherwise this is a recipe for customer dissatisfaction.

Personalization and Customization

Customized services for the individual masses.

The ability of the online outsourcing vendor to provide personalized and customized service to meet individual customer needs is critical. The Internet world is replete with examples of outsourcing providers offering products and services online, customized to meet the needs of outsourcing organizations. Such range from ordering raw materials, travel information to different parts of the world, real-estate deals in various regions, etc.

Learn to Outsource, Even Online

The most defining trait of any organization is its learnability.

Organizations need to focus on their in-house key core business activities and outsource the rest. Organizations may lack online business deployment skills because they may not be in line with their core business nature. This also creates opportunities for using outsourcing of Internet-based services. It allows leveraging from subject matter experts, expert consultants, and seasoned organizations for access to world-class capabilities and technologies. This includes deploying enabling technology for extending the business online.

Organizations manage their relationships in a way that fits their unique needs and circumstances. These firms first select a capable provider for their Internet-based business needs, and the type of relationship needed to accomplish the objectives is formed. Selecting the wrong provider can spell disaster. By picking a service provider online based on low cost alone, success may not be achieved. Objectives can be achieved more effectively by choosing a provider that meets the unique needs of the organization. The relationship should be carefully managed once an appropriate provider is selected. In contractual relationships, most firms already have well-established methods of working with such service providers. How deep the relationship between the partners should be needs to be decided by the organization based on the nature of business, etc. Firms know how to set and assess minimum service levels and negotiate fee-for-service contracts. Additional management techniques can be used to substantially improve performance levels, such as inducing a competitive spirit among providers by pitting them against other providers or an organization's own internal center group. The director of a reputable firm said that by outsourcing online work to two separate providers and maintaining one center in house, the providers are kept sharp, and this way the service levels do not go down.

Therefore organizations will want to establish joint outcome-based business goals they can work on accomplishing together. To seal a close relationship, some firms even choose to take equity positions in their provider or establish a joint venture. Niche providers can be a viable choice, because outsourced work can be performed quite independently online by different organizations, as long as common systems and applications are used. It will be more difficult, if not impossible, for a niche provider to transform the entire function, if that is on the agenda. There is some dependence on the online provider and some risk if the online provider defaults, but such are usually manageable and quickly corrected, if suitable detection mechanisms exist. By starting small, clients can mitigate the risk, and as trust builds and the client–vendor relationship matures, they can shift additional work online to the service provider. As compared, the traditional relationship enjoyed between business and professional services firms is different in many ways. In an online outsourcing arrangement, there should be adequate preagreed service levels and the tight management of these service levels, along with the incorporation of emerging trends online as well as in the respective industry. There is an increasing need for the providers to demonstrate what they have value added to the gains.

High Demands of Online Users/Customers

Aiming and positioning for 360-degree value.

As business environments go online over the Web, outsourcing firms need to enable suitable mechanisms such that the online outsourcing provider exceeds end consumers' expectations and experiences. *End consumers now have more and more options to choose from; therefore both products/services and online suppliers have to find new ways to attract new customers, and constant innovation is imperative.* Since both the outsourcing provider and the outsourcing organization target repeat customer business, the relationship experience has significance. Evolving the business relationship hinges greatly on repeat business from past interactions of satisfaction. High repeat business leads to predictable revenue growth and lower marketing costs.

Organizations have to manage their businesses online and seamlessly integrate it with back-end management, in the face of ever-increasing competition and challenges. The changing role that information technology is increasingly assuming in the world of business and the global economy at large is illustrated by business solutions such as CRM (customer relationship management). Views will soon be adopted by society that will perceive technology as a merging of products and services that seamlessly enable new approaches to business activities and redefine how people work and interact with each other. E-business, e-supply chain management, enterprise relationship management, and e-customer relationship management are some of the excellent examples of this trend.

End consumer support and experience are critical in today's online business environment. Other than price and quality, factors like online support and service received from an Internet business organization are key factors in attracting new customers and retaining the loyalty of existing ones. One aspect of customer support is catering to general customer complaints and questions. Also technical issues concerning the product or service may arise. To deliver high value to customers, it requires a dedicated and experienced team, which will work at the back end, around the clock if needed. Such teams need to be officially given their due recognition.

Businesses, especially with Internet dependencies, are facing a constantly changing environment, requiring an immediate and proactive adaptability in operations, customer relationship management, and back office processes. End consumers demand fast and highly personalized services due to diminishing product and service offerings differentiation.

Outsourcing Approach Online and Confidentiality

There is tremendous potential in Web-based outsourcing, although there is a lot of uncertainty and skepticism about it. Before resorting to Web-based outsourcing, the outsourcer should assess if the outsourcing partner has the skills to do it or not, if financial benefits can be reaped immediately, and the mode of interacting with the vendor through the life cycle of the project. It is important to look into the nature of the service itself to determine if it is easy to outsource online. With the known limitations of interacting only over telephone and e-mail, it should still be possible to conceptualize, define, and execute the service. The range of the service fee could be between a few hundred and a few hundred thousand dollars. It should be possible to easily monitor online the results of the service. Online outsourced services generally require manual human effort and may often be difficult to automate.

Confidentiality, original content, and the promise not to reuse content should be assured by a good vendor because it boils down to the trust and reputation of the vendor. Although sometimes impractical to enforce, international agreements are useful for clarity. Hence the agreements between the outsourcer and the online vendor should be realistic; otherwise they will fail to meet expectations, and areas of dispute will surround quality and timing. It is imperative to communicate information clearly, which includes describing the target audience and what you aim to achieve.

Training

Emulation, ideas linkage, and conditioning,
the building blocks of human learning.

Suitable trained personnel, both with the outsourcing organization and with the online outsourcing provider who manage and support the online business at the back end, are critical to its smooth operations. Trainings may be formal, technical, business, and operational. Experience-driven on-the-job learning is very significant too.

Quality programs like Six Sigma or SEI CMM support mechanisms for maintaining and measuring customer satisfaction, people management, service levels, and transaction monitoring and give pointers to the need for additional training.

Online Vendor/Providers Specialized Domain, Business, and Technology Skills

Knowledge, that infinite life-defining resource.

When making a foray into the virtual world, sectors like banking, manufacturing, pharmaceuticals infrastructure, travel, etc., need online outsourcing providers with appropriate domain expertise, popularly known as subject matter experts, who understand the business processes and its integration online.

In order to implement the service, people with specific skills and knowledge are required. The skills required to implement the service should be possessed by the online provider in the region in which the service is being outsourced. Selection of sellers online should be based on "correct" criteria (e.g., selection not simply based on lowest price but selecting based on highest value addition and best cultural fit—cheapest project seller is not necessarily the best one). Past project execution track records, history, flexibility, change management capability, postdelivery support, and financial strength of competing prospective online sellers should be sufficiently evaluated before selection by an online buyer. Consistent delivery on schedule by the online service providers is imperative.

Use of technology merely in product creation is not enough. *It must be used in the entire product life cycle from design, manufacture, sale, delivery, service, even final disposal when it is no longer meant for use.* Thus technology should deliver an overall customer experience. Lack of enabling technology and manual approaches will result in the organization working harder and faster just to survive.

Customer lead times must be met above expectations. Enabling delivery ahead of expected schedule should be the constant aim of the online provider, with minimal lead times toward assimilation, execution, and closure of deliverables. Proactive and reactive methods of delivery must be systemized.

Sustained post-sale services, support, and periodic enhancement offers are essential to maintaining the existing customer base online.

Online Outsourcing Organization's Specialized Business Skills

In a virtual battleground, with David versus Goliath, the odds are equal.

Online outsourcing organization should also have sufficient experience in structured governance, project execution delivery processes, controls, mechanisms, and service level agreement (SLA) metrics in a globally distributed project environment. Sufficient communication and knowledge transfer channels need to exist between all the players.

Risk Management

Risks: Know them, and turn them into your decisive point of advantage.

Risks are both internal and external. Internal risks stem from business strategies including outsourcing strategies, shortcomings, etc. External risks stem from the competition. Online business operations have clearly scheduled deliverables. On one hand these set delivery expectations, but on the other hand they increase the risk of consequences in case of failure. To pay the appropriate amount and no more is the customer's goal online, and hence the business approach needs to treat the customer's money like one's own and make decisions accordingly.

Employee Retention

A jewel needs polish to glow.

The Web is a universe of opportunities, and the lures may be many for existing employees. Hence, resorting to innovative means for employee retention becomes imperative. Just best practices may not suffice, and this is needed on both sides of the online outsourcing business, both with the outsourcing organization and with the online provider. Innovative means may include giving employees preferred stock options, thereby allowing them to become stakeholders in the virtual business, encouraging employees to put forth new business ideas, and supporting such, as may be found suitable.

Variable Pay

Pay, they say, is based more on the capacity of the giver than the ability of the receiver.

People in the business enterprise who are not part of the core organization strategy may be paid lower salaries. Such people are counted as overheads. The reality is that the IT salaries are frequently inflated compared to many vocations. Therefore a clear business strategy and variable salaries are a must. Some businesses may inaptly expect the online outsourcing provider to act as technological visionaries and strategy architects. It is actually advisable to use experienced business professionals for this. Remember that the Internet is a means for some and an end for some, based on the nature of the business.

Access to Critical, Sensitive Data by Partners, Online Vendors, and Unauthorized Users

Some data are rarer than diamonds and, commonly, the wayside stones.

One should be aware of the "potentials" and "perils" of online outsourcing. One should be abreast of the privacy, copyright, intellectual property, and security issues, because data privacy and security issues have significant relevance. *Intellectual property capital (IP)/ownership issues of contributions received from outsourcing providers over the Web should be properly envisaged in contracts with the provider.*

Governments worldwide and other regulatory associations work with each other through international frameworks, legislation, and guidelines. India as a country has established its trustworthiness and is high on the value chain by offering complex services online.

Language Nuances Online

The written word and its many spoken nuances.

Recommendations to American customers intending to outsource work online over the Web are that they should be prepared for some minor differences in grammar, spelling, and style. In the case of India, although British English is common, the influence of American TV has helped many Indians understand the subtle differences and adapt accordingly. Suitable modifications in style, training, and some writing guidelines can bridge the gap. Some of these differences, however, are fading rapidly because the college students of today are very globalized. Nevertheless, expect to tweak the final work according to the target audience, if you outsource writing or other creative services online. Tweaking may be required because cultural nuances may appear more often when more creative services are outsourced.

Example—If outsourcing content online to India, the outsourcer need not bother much about issues regarding the differences in Indian and American English. A large set of expert writers who are well trained in English and its nuances is available when outsourcing content development to India. Indians can converse in English as comfortably as their American or British counterparts because English is the first language of many, and as a result, there are a large number of qualified people who are ready, willing, and able to work for global customers. To meet the exact requirements of the customer, some fine-tuning may be required, and this can be done in a final edit. For travel writing or lifestyle writing, this tweaking of content may be required, but it is not required for medical, scientific, or technical writing and other such similar writing/editing.

Recession and Low Market Economic Conditions

Money is the most common commodity in any exchange today.

In the 1990s and early 2000s huge numbers of middle management jobs, running into hundreds of thousands, were shed by the United States and the European Union. The economic downturn of 2008–2009 and corresponding recession had severe ramifications worldwide. This was triggered by the failure of key financial institutions across the globe. The impact on the economy worldwide was severe. Correspondingly business volumes over the Internet were also affected due to diminished buying power of the customers.

Through 2010, people anticipated another year of economic stagnation. Therefore in the last two years, things that had become a norm like five-star luncheons, off-site meetings abroad, and business-class travel had been done away with. Practices of switching off the lights when leaving one's room, domestic offsites, video conferencing, and black-and-white printing only if necessary have become the norm.

Layoffs

Make your move before they do.

Consequences of the global economic recession include massive layoffs by companies and unattractive salaries. Corridors were abuzz with discussions of employee retrenchment and poor salary hikes or even no hikes for those lucky enough to save their jobs. Bonuses were out of the question for some time as companies sought to cut costs. Excitement of working was replaced by fear and job uncertainty. The story held true for professionals across multiple sectors. Survival led to demotivation of employees and a fall in productivity, especially in the IT, information technology enabled service (ITES), and banking, financial services, and insurance (BFSI) sectors, which largely depend on outsourcing. The online outsourcing providers were in turn forced to layoff as a chain reaction to the plunge in the business of the outsourcing organizations.

Reverse Brain Drain

The return to one's roots, a safety net.

Flagging prospects in the United States and Europe due to the ongoing slowdown resulted in reverse brain drain. Burgeoning economies abroad caused talented immigrants to be homeward bound. For more than four decades, India and China suffered a major brain drain as many talented professionals left their homes for the United States. The dismal economic low caused many professionals with postgraduate and doctorate degrees in management, technology, or science to move back.

Reuse of Related Past Work, Knowledge, and Experience

The lingering whispers of those who had previously walked the path.

Reuse of existing tools, work from past projects of similar natures, past experience, and knowledge act as a great leverage toward effective delivery. Such knowledge could exist in structured documentation or be known to respective domain specialists through information and past experiences. Structured knowledge thus maintained reduces effort and results in optimum quality and successful delivery.

Presentation Challenges Online for Enabling Quick Decision Making in Web-Based Applications

The communication gaps in the World Wide Web.

The online outsourcing provider must make its online applications and delivery efficient, allowing the customer (whether the online outsourcing organization or its Internet end user customer) to *find the required information or make an informed decision within four "clicks"* (e.g., purchase, etc.), according to Bell Atlantic estimates. Using software agents that act on the consumer's behalf, a number of firms are tackling the challenge for the consumer in a world of many choices.

Readability Challenges Online

Those piles of needless information and the wee bit one seeks therein.

It may not be fun reading copy on a screen if the colors and layout are not attractive, even if the material is relevant. Additionally the reader's inability to immediately locate relevant matter is one major drawback. It is not easy to browse online, and often users are confronted with a menu of not so suitable headlines. To make an informed decision, often menus may not yield enough information, so time and effort is wasted navigating irrelevant screens and pages.

Personalization Challenges through Example—Video Rentals Survey

The personal touch, for one and all.

The need for personalized services both for the outsourcing organization and also its customers is a challenge for the online outsourcing provider. This is best explained through a video rentals survey. Customer technology interfaces were researched through surveys by Disney, a video rental service. Some interesting aspects of customer behavior were revealed. About 65% of the customers could not accurately remember the name of the video they rented a week or two before. *Consumers like to hold the video boxes/discs in their hands and read the labels when choosing viewing material.* The need for facilitating better recall is indicated by both observations. To provide some sort of memory by association, the online outsourcing providers and interfaces will need to be more effective at recreating the personal experience. Experiments and such surveys over time will improve such interactive virtual user and multimedia interactions.

Acceptance of the Concept

A bit of personal unconcern, the key to acceptance.

Online outsourcing is a management challenge. Resistance within the organization too is often an internal barrier. Online buyer organization needs to be culturally ready to outsource online.

Example—Toy giant Toys"R"Us took two years to meet the challenge by newbie "eToys" after setting up its e-business Internet subsidiary, Toysrus.com.

Online Payment Systems and Electronic Data Interface (EDI) Challenges

The one root to incorporate all off-shoots.

In the banking industry, for example, ATM networks required almost 20 years to progress from experimental ATM networks in the 1960s to the use of standard formats allowing for interconnection of networks in the 1980s. Similarly, enabling seamless communication between networks of computers for the development of and adoption of online payments and universal EDI formats takes many years.

"Business Transactions Challenges" of E-Commerce

As the multitudes network in a virtual universe.

Computers and networks are well suited for e-commerce processing jobs like data collection, processing, and transfer. The activity of information processing is usually in the form of business transactions. For the purpose of home shopping or home banking using encryption for security and electronic cash, credit, or debit tokens for payment, transactions can be between a company and the customer over public networks. In order to minimize the exposure to risk, from a managerial perspective—for information gathering, transactions with trading partners using EDI transactions for conducting market research using barcode scanners, information processing for managerial decision making or organizational problem solving, information manipulation for operations and supply chain management, interactive advertising, sales, and marketing transactions for information distribution with prospective customers—all of these transactions require tight coordination and control among many participating organizations. The complexity is compounded by long transportation distances, currencies, customs regulations, and language barriers, if we look at managing these transactions in light of global sourcing, an integral part of the increasingly global market. The complexity of the task can be reduced by codifying these transactions and coordinating them through software via the Internet To the operation of the information superhighway, the concept of convergence is essential, and also the way the business world is gearing up to deal with it. To make electronic marketplace a reality, many companies are pooling their resources and talents through alliances and mergers with other companies. Reducing their risk is a part of their motivation because of uncertainty about the final form the eventual global marketplace and e-commerce applications will take.

Technical Challenges in E-Commerce Applications

The many layers that make up the core.

In existing literature, the software framework necessary for building electronic commerce applications is little understood. Allowing the development of e-commerce applications, in general a framework is intended to define and create tools that integrate the information found in today's closed systems. The aim of the architectural framework, it is important to understand, is "not" to build new database management systems, data repository, computer languages, software agent–based transaction monitors, or communication protocols.

Organizations with diverse resources need to integrate them by focusing on their respective architecture. E-commerce applications usually have six primary layers of functionality. These are applications; brokerage services or data or transaction management; interface and support layers; secure messaging, security, and electronic document interchange; middleware and structured document interchange; and network infrastructure and basic communications services. By transparently integrating information access and exchange within the context of the chosen application, these layers cooperate to provide a seamless transition between today's computing resources and those of tomorrow. E-commerce applications are based on several elegant technologies, but only when they are integrated do they provide uniquely powerful solutions.

Troubleshooting and sustained maintenance of telecommunications and data infrastructure are needed on a long-term basis. Preventive measures like security of shared and individual physical assets (e.g., resources, data, facilities, etc.) from risk of sabotage, theft, etc., are additional issues.

The Rate of Proliferation of Internet/ Intranet Outsourcing Portals

As the movement explodes into a virtual phenomenon.

The rate/speed of proliferation of Internet/intranet outsourcing portals impacts the amount of outsourcing online. This is in turn linked to the corresponding growth of Internet and internal organizational intranet portals, the rate of addition of new outsourcing projects online, and the speed of new projects' addition and roll-over on the Internet/internal intranet portals. Success greatly depends on the growth, prominence, and popularity of the respective Internet and intranet portals.

General Challenges Faced by the Internet

Ye shall always exist, in one form or another.

The growth of Web-based outsourcing is directly linked to challenges faced by the underlying Internet which serves as its primary enabling and delivery mechanism.

The Internet growth has not been as easy as initially expected. The 30-odd-years-old current Internet architecture evolved on a best-effort basis driving the underlying design. It is now acknowledged that the Internet is being stretched beyond its abilities to deliver. This is admitted by the business moguls, intelligentsia, etc. Constructing the Internet is a painstakingly slow and arduous process, given the transition times of people, resources, and technology. Everyone involved realizes the technological complexity and the multiyear research and development (R&D) effort needed to make the Internet a sustainable reality. In early 1994, the $30 billion merger of Bell Atlantic/ TCI collapsed, which otherwise would have combined telephone and cable networks in the northeast to create a large segment of the Internet infrastructure. The development of the Internet as the next industrial revolution was initially the thesis and then the dismissive antithesis. Hence the initial euphoria about it is somewhat tempered.

The future Internet needs flexibility, management capabilities for multiple applications and environments, adaptability for new fields, complexity management, etc. These network infrastructures may be architected to integrate and execute dynamically evolving services over worldwide service delivery platforms.

Some of the tremendous challenges in areas of design, scalability, mobility, flexibility, security, governing policy, etc., of networks and services are discussed below.

Need for Standards

Practices that spread like wildfire set the standards of the future.

Online communication and interoperability between heterogeneous systems and networks essentially need technical standards as a prerequisite, which is one of the pillars on which the frameworks rest.

Similarly, railroads would not have flourished had each state established a separate track standard (e.g., meter gauge, broad gauge). Passengers and goods would have to be moved manually from one train to another every time the standard changes, as it does today at the Russian–Western Europe border, the Russian–Chinese border, and the Spanish–French border.

Worldwide, use of many products is limited because similar differences in standards exist today, (e.g., in electricity distribution, 110 volts versus 200 volts).

Another example Sony Beta versus VHS video distribution. To ensure not only seamless and harmonious integration across the network, standards are crucial in the virtual world in order to access information on any type of device the consumer chooses, including laser disc, computers, portable handheld devices, or television plus set-top boxes (cable converter boxes), and all types of operating systems. Video conferencing will never become widespread without the adoption of video standards, and rather than working toward customer goals such as interoperability, individual manufacturers attempt to develop equipment that maximizes their short-term profits.

Openness

A playing field open to one and all.

The Internet must continue to maintain its openness. *Open standards are a crucial characteristic.* Open interfaces and standards allow the markets to grow freely for one and all. Free entry of new players to the Internet prevents monopolistic royalties which could throttle innovation. An open Internet is a platform supporting myriad overlay services.

Global Governance

Uniting the nations into a single governing body.

The Net is global. The majority Internet populations will shift from the United States and Europe to other possible regions, hence the need for global Internet governance through suitable cooperation between various global players. *Internet governance and policy are based on "Net neutrality."* Business practices over the Net are subject to legal, ethical, and governance principles and may need respective regulation.

Design

A design so flexible as to cater to the unknown future evolution.

The evolving Internet must be architected for change. *The Internet should have the capability and flexibility to seamlessly support evolution in application, configurations, environments, new types of business models, relationships, etc.* Such technology changes will automatically drive changes in business practices, approaches, etc. *An integrated and interoperable communication and service framework should gradually replace the existing Internet, mobile, fixed, satellite, and audiovisual networks.* Such a framework needs to be pervasive, ubiquitous, and highly dynamic, supporting myriad formats, delivery modes, applications, environments, etc. It should be highly user customizable and deliver need-based unlimited capacities. Most traditional designs keep a separation between technical matters like congestion control, routing mechanisms, and business rules, policies, and practices. The current issues of naming, addressing, and querying hosts in the Internet world may need to be reviewed. New rearchitecting approaches may need to be pondered. Such a robust underlying control architectural design shall be the way to the future.

Investments

Playing for long-term aims, not short-term gains.

Forward looking investments in R&D innovation must be committed by nations, organizations, communities, even individuals. Such efforts would reap exponential changes, given the current state of technology dynamics. New technical information is doubling every two years currently.

Data Management

Innovation off-shoots sprout all over the fertile technological soil.

Massive amounts of data need to be managed, compressed, and archived into related logical pieces in a timely manner using the suitable media. An estimated 1.5 exabytes (i.e., 1.5×10^{18}) of "unique" new information was generated worldwide in the year 2009. That is estimated to be more than in the previous 5,000 years.

Security

A secure environment for every single one.

The Net must be a secure, trustworthy medium, reliable, resilient to attacks, guaranteeing desired levels of services, protecting user data, ensuring privacy, etc.

Almost 70% of the 200 billion daily e-mails currently (2009) are spam. About 20% of the online computer population is reported to be compromised by botnets. (A botnet is a collection of compromised computers connected to the Internet that are used for malicious purposes.) Users should be able to exercise sufficient control over their own privacy. Integration of privacy and security features must figure as part of the underlying design approach. Due to increased communication between complex large-scale heterogeneous networks with massive distributed data storage and management capacities, the vulnerability challenges have increased.

Strategic Cooperation

By inclusion do we all collectively grow.

Sustained interaction and close cooperation between organizations, technology developers, academia, scientists, and government must exist. Because the Internet has grown to become a critical infrastructure enabler for various economies and societies, there is a need for a closer bonding between the various driving communities.

Mobility

Mantra: Travel of the masses, for the masses, by the masses.

Mobility with constantly higher end-to-end data rates is also emerging as an important design driver. Efficiency of wireless network operations and exploring their full potential will be the way of the future. Potential growth areas include next-generation mobile radio technologies leveraging the heterogeneous radio eco-space, architectures exploring usage of the licensed, unlicensed, and unused radio spectrum.

Speed

Internet speed, still in the cave ages.

Currently (2009) typical speeds for home broadband access are in the 2 to 4 megabits/sec (MBPS) range. Currently over 2.7 billion searches are performed on Google each month (2009). Common local area network (LAN) speeds range from 100 MBPS to 1 GBPS and beyond. Thus there exists a big gap between Internet and LAN speeds. This is a severe constraint in limiting communication over the Internet. Internet speeds of 100 MBPS to 1 GBPS may require exploration of technologies like optical fiber lines, cable (CaTV), xDSL lines, satellite communications, powerline (PLC), etc. There is a continuous trend in demand for faster broadband access.

Limitations of Online Outsourcing

The many colors that constitute a rainbow.

- Online outsourcing can not fully remove the need for person-to-person interaction, on-site visits, etc., but can alleviate the same.
- Online outsourcing assumes the necessary resources (i.e., machines, hardware, network infrastructure) are somehow available to the various players who may be in a different geographic locations. This could be a limiting factor.
- Intellectual property rights (IPR) issues due to the sensitive nature of work may somewhat inhibit outsourcing work to remotely located project sellers.
- Top management's bias may sometimes inhibit too.
- Changes in inflation rates, inflation differential, consumer price index (CPI), purchasing power parity, interest rates, money supply, GDP growth, etc., impact outsourcing suitability.
- Legal handling of significant breach of contract and different applicable legal systems in different countries may make legal action tedious for Internet-based outsourcing projects.

The Net, a great leveling playground.

Chapter 13

Web Outsourcing— Advantages

Reaching out through the pulsating virtual spaces.

Online service providers provide a reduction in IT total cost of ownership; investments are maximized in existing systems; business change is implemented by integrating the overall life cycle, considering the virtual world dependencies; global enterprise visibility is provided online of information and business processes; and supply chain visibility is extended and brought online. To maximize performance while maintaining the highest standards of service and safety is a strategic focus of an organization operating in part or full in the virtual world. To improve profitability and performance, a focus on operational efficiency is a must, which can be taken care of by improving the analytical architectures and business intelligence solutions which are used online. The business reporting solutions should have standardization in data representation, data availability, nonduplication of information, adequate drill down analysis capabilities, etc. This plugs the information gaps and operational efficiency high in the virtual world. This would result in companies shifting from a focus on *economies of scale toward economies of scope.*

Online outsourcing businesses, whether of products or services, generally result in increased customer domain knowledge, shorter lead times, customer satisfaction, learnability, operational efficiencies, lower risk, and cost savings.

The spirit set to soar with the means to explore, the virtual spaces.

Business Advantages in the Virtual World of Web Outsourcing

Exploring the business scapes, unchartered.

Pioneer Advantage

Of finding the gaps and filling them first.

Since such models hardly exist currently. Pioneers can reap from an exponential increase in volumes before other players also compete to move into the same space.

Web outsourcing offers opportunity to launch new products and to purchase and sell finished projects and products worldwide.

Web outsourcing offers opportunities to find new ideas from interactions between participating players. Such interactions would foster lateral thinking, out-of-the box solutions, quick fixes, workarounds, and diverse approaches for executing a given project request.

This virtual world gives insights into existing and changing technology, business, and market trends. Unfavorable economics and rigidity of contracts are avoided.

Benjamin Franklin said, "Look before, or you will find yourself behind."

Pioneers using the Web can reap a rich domain knowledge and financial harvest from an exponential increase in volumes before other players also emulate to move into the same space. The Internet enables organizations to rapidly launch new products, capitalize on additional distribution channels, or segment specific markets. Tapping new markets across the globe is very possible over the Internet, even when the organization has no physical presence in that market/region. The Internet allows exploring largely hitherto unexplored business opportunities and virtual landscapes.

To keep pace with the rapidly changing business (including the legislative) environment through use of increasingly sophisticated bridging technology, the online world is adapting rapidly, with flexibility, and constantly reengineering to meet such new landslide changes, ideas, and norms.

Warren Buffet, famed investor, in a lighter related vein said, "The rearview mirror is always clearer than the windshield."

The online outsourcing business is expanding into largely hitherto unexplored business avenues.

Highly Skilled People and Resources

Learning from the gurus of the game.

Outsourcing organizations can handle peak periods of demand without hiring personnel that will not be needed later.

Specialized skills possessed by the online provider in a variety of products and deep business process knowledge improve revenue flow and customer satisfaction in the virtual world. Experienced professionals implement the best solution online for the given product/service needs and budgets. An experienced online provider enables the client to achieve measurable business value, exceeding service level requirements, delivering on time and on budget, and offering creative and innovative solutions to customer needs. Through the use of technology, online outsourcing businesses can help organizational clients to achieve strategic and operational results. Specific business challenges can be addressed by working collaboratively with all stakeholders to develop innovative technology strategies and solutions.

The provider uses highly competent and experienced professionals, secure environment with firewalls, intrusion detection, and monitoring, daily backup, and audits to meet the business needs suitably.

Combining the newest technology with capability can achieve startling results, and successful online businesses distinguish themselves through their ability to position, innovate, offer, plan, build, and operate highly reliable, efficient, and secure business solutions for the virtual marketplace.

Online outsourcing business offers tremendous benefits, given the exponential scale out in terms of customer volumes, with cost reduction, access to business best practices and expertise, performance enhancement, and focus on core business being some of them.

Talent and skills can be tapped within and outside the organization using the in-house intranet and Internet, respectively. It provides enterprise-wide access to corporate capabilities. Skills and resources available with the online provider are thus leveraged.

Reuse of Tools, Resources, Experiences

For most of life is lived in a few repeated strokes, work or otherwise.

Reuse can be cost effective, because similar projects may already have been done previously by individuals/organizations elsewhere in geographically dispersed locations. Similar projects already completed within the organization help new deliveries' completion in a much reduced time frame. Direct reduction in internal effort and cost is thus achieved due to past contributions from similar projects and deliveries. There is no need to repeatedly reinvent the wheel.

Tools and ready-to-use products can be additionally put up for sale by online providers, further augmenting their profits and brand. Options of customizing the same and integrating with other related products to meet specific needs may also be taken up.

Borderless World

> *As the Net knows no bounds, so does your target audience.*

The Internet and software products/services by nature transcend geographic boundaries. Geographic barriers have gotten blurred with the advent of the Internet. Organizations can penetrate markets using the Internet, where they have no physical presence. The physical geographic locations of the various players become relatively meaningless, if the respective processes are streamlined to accomplish the same, for the respective nature of the business. New markets and new sources of revenue can be explored and tapped.

The nature of products and services offered online, language/culture issues, and government policies often have some bearing on the target audience.

Project sellers/vendors have access to global markets via the Web without a need for an in-person presence in those markets.

24/7 × 365 Operations

> *Time and the virtual spaces, ticking endlessly with life.*

Round-the-clock operations allows people in different geographies and time zones to leverage the 24-hour window toward project execution. **Example**—Outsourcing organizations can raise issues/project work needing execution toward the "end" of their working day and retire for the day. The same is immediately actioned by online providers/vendors working in a different time zone window and delivered before the respective customer returns to work on the next working day. This results in a 24-hour workday.

Always open around the clock, the online outsourcing is always accessible. It results in improved operational efficiencies and customer satisfaction. Customers can access the Web at their own convenience, lending great flexibility.

Suitable back-end support is provided through skilled, customer-friendly, motivated, certified, and experienced support personnel and resources.

Speed

> *The speed to be and being, and omnipresence*
> *where speed is somewhat meaningless.*

Speed is the essence online, and instantaneous delivery the ideal. Any online outsourcing transaction (online or otherwise) has timelines and schedules attached to it. The colossal advancement in science and technology has increased the speed tremendously. The present-day computers can perform millions of computations per second. Speed and success go hand in hand. Online outsourcing constantly reduces timeframes, schedules products and services before time, tending toward an ideal of instantaneous service and delivery. Of course, this involves innovation, effort, resources, back-end support, etc., but helps in placing the organization head and shoulders above the competition, thus becoming the supplier of choice for many outsourcing organizations online. Reaction time of the online provider to the customer has radically reduced online. Greater speed along with reduced costs and turnaround time are the hallmarks of online outsourcing. On-time delivery every time is an achievable metric in the virtual world, given a stable set of predefined transactions. Faster turnaround times by leveraging the time zone differences are a significant feature.

Time to market (velocity) is a key competitive strategy of this model. Speed of execution, not just requisite competency, toward project execution will become the key differentiator of success between competing players in the twenty-first century. This will also become an entry barrier for new competitors.

Strategic Focus

The bird's-eye view.

The outsourcing organization can focus on its core capabilities, using the online outsourcing to outsource their nonstrategic activities. Clients can refocus current staff on higher-value tasks. Employee staffing is kept at optimal levels, with the online vendor providing and meeting periods of temporary demand spikes.

Vendors' Geographical Spread

Money is money, whatever the print.

Slumps in the U.S. and European markets drive online businesses to focus on economies like India, China, Japan, etc.

Online outsourcing can target vendor/providers from areas having high concentrations of respective competencies needed for a particular nature of business. This would lead a high benchmark in quality products due to their execution by vendors already mature in the respective nature of business.

The physical geographic locations of the various players in the project life cycle doing the various roles become relatively meaningless, if the respective processes are streamlined to accomplish the same. Organizations may need to change to match this multi-geo mode of the project life cycle.

Interaction between people with complementary skills in geographically similar or diverse locations results. Access to global human resource and global markets is achieved.

Personalized, Customized Services

Different strokes for different folks.

Microsoft CEO Bill Gates calls it the "What have you done for me lately" customer syndrome.

The business ideal—"What the customer wants, when and where it is wanted, and at the lowest possible cost"—also applies to the Web world.

Not merely surpassing customer expectation, but making them ecstatic is achievable by successful online businesses outsourcing. Customization is the catchword—hence versatility and flexibility are key factors. Increased control to the end customer/consumer induces higher operational efficiency. To meet individual needs, solutions can be tailored depending upon the complexity of delivery of the online product/service. Companies have turned to the Internet for virtually everything, because they are eager to focus on things they do best. Customer service initiatives can be raised to greater heights by the implementation of customer service best practices by the provider. Online outsourcing drives companies to raise the benchmark with respect to their customers and improves customer access to relevant information, skills, and expertise.

Referring to the online sale of cars, Robert Eaton, Chairman, Chrysler Corporation, in his speech at the annual meeting in New Orleans said, "The customer is going to grab control of the process, and we are going to salute smartly and do exactly what the customer tells us if we want to stay in business."

Through strategic and tactical decision making, the vendor management pays close attention to delivery and service to maintain the relationships that are critical to delivering superior customer value. A comprehensive understanding of its outsourcing customers' business, and how customers in the immediate and downstream markets perceive value, is enhanced by market-driven focus.

Example—The strengths of the Indian Web content writers include research at lower costs because 50% of most writing projects is research. One outsourcing team can do the research, and the other can do the writing/editing, and the Indian vendors can put more people on the task, thereby developing the content in a shorter time. Indian writers possess very high academic levels which include PhDs, MDs, MBAs, etc., thus providing top-quality documentation at lower cost. Value to content is added because Indians are global, and the outsourcer can benefit from the diverse network of talented writers with different styles, insights, and training. They have the talent to write on many subjects, and being well informed, they excel in scientific, medical, technical, and cultural writing in English and many other international languages. Due to their international work experience as Web content developers, engineers, software programmers, medical doctors, journalists, etc., Indian writers can develop a wide and diverse range of content.

Exponential Growth Prospects

Of tertiaries that sometimes have a defining effect on the primary.

The Web inherently lends itself to facilitate exponential growth. The Web's expansion itself has borne an explosion since inception in the 1980s. This has been fostered with the rise of the online outsourcing. The Internet phenomenon has stretched to previously untouched areas of business, and the rise of subject matter experts has begun to help organizations make strategic decisions.

Budgets for Setup and Working

Negotiations or haggling, *just different words.*

Online outsourcing budgets' range may vary from very low to very high depending on the nature of the work. Budget may have only a limited bearing on strategy. Online outsourcing budgets are often reduced by accessing skilled human resources from low-cost outsourcing geographies. Suitable contracting deliberation can further optimize processes and reduce costs.

Web—The Information Superhighway

As networks reach out, spreading their web.

The Internet encompasses all fields of life. Online outsourcing is used across fields like manufacturing, outsourcing, medicine, real estate, retail, etc. Suitable software agents and search engines enable users to meet their respective needs online.

Dematerialization—Migration of Manual/ Paper Records to Electronic Media, Online

The new age archives, from paper, wood, and stone to light and fire.

Outsourcing organizations' records are converted to electronic files and stored online on servers so that they can be accessed from anywhere on the Internet while the original paper records are archived for good. Changing to a paperless environment is the ideal. Making this transition is a one-time effort, whereafter subsequent records will be directly created online in their electronic form through suitable support and infrastructure. After automation, the organization can refocus such freed staff on higher value tasks.

Leveraging from Outsourcing, Online

Firms can focus on their in-house key core business by outsourcing online business deployment setup, operations, etc., and thereby shedding operating costs and retaining valuable customers. For the organization, gaining experience and expertise for online operations setup and execution may be time consuming, but the experienced outsourced vendors can optimize processes because they understand how to integrate people, process, and technology to deliver results that provide real business value. The outsourcing vendor anchoring the online deployment provides a diversified suite of proven applications coupled with proven expertise delivering tailored solutions, adding to significant customer and asset value.

Online outsourcing forays help transform traditional business models and achieve measurable results meeting customer service and quality standards. By turning static operations into dynamic online ones driven and complemented by the online outsourcing, companies are realizing greater financial flexibility.

The senior management is freed to do the creative thinking, once the noncore work is outsourced away. There is an increase in focus as outsourcing is a means of managing burden.

Service levels provided by the online vendor to the organization's customers can be monitored. Organization personnel can constantly monitor and report on service level status and initiate escalation and improvement procedures as necessary. An innovative tool like STARS developed by Computer Sciences Corporation (CSC) may be used for managing service level operations.

Financial Benefits

Passing financial benefits to the outsourcing vendor, who has demonstrated sustained ability to handle cost and capacity fluctuations, is commonly encountered in the online outsourcing world. This type of model is called gain sharing. Reduced costs and improvement in operating margins are derived from large volumes of transactions. In case of new markets' penetration over the Web by online providers, where speed and customer reach/capture are critical, gains are consciously shared with the outsourcing provider. Cost is one of the significant criteria on which products and services compete online.

Cross-Currency Conversion Benefits

The unit, value, and purchasing power.

Online outsourcing leverages cross-currency conversion synergies, with the outsourcing organization being in a stronger currency's geography and the online provider usually being in a weaker currency's geography. Thus the outsourcing organization gets the benefit of competitive rates for respective work, and the online provider gets a benefit from the currency conversion being physically located in a geography having a weaker local currency.

This leverages cross-currency conversion synergies of outsourcing, with project buyers being in a stronger currency's geography and project sellers being in a weaker currency's geography. Thus the project buyer gets the benefit of competitive rates for the respective project, and project seller gets a benefit from the currency conversion being in a geography having a weaker local currency.

Higher Integration

The evolving networks of men and machines.

Any organization that begins to outsource online (over the Web) automatically "induces" partners and interacting organizations in the business life cycle to follow suit, or risk being replaced. Various online means like the usage of similar business ecosystems, cooperative networks, virtual communities, and resources are prevalent. Technology often closely defines business strategy in the virtual world.

Integrating business strategies, outsourced processes, resources, and people together into a seamless operation is mandatory for an online transaction life cycle. This results in centralized access to information. The need for integrated planning has arisen with international cost reduction initiatives and globalization of online trading activities fueled by the e-commerce revolution. Sophisticated technologies enable access to critical information, which is indispensable for high-performance operations. For efficient delivery of a service online, the underlying technology for it is absolutely necessary, and access to information globally is critical for the virtual organization. The outsourcing organization and online provider should invest in the most contemporary technology solutions to deliver proficient service and deliver products and services consistently at the lowest possible cost to the customer.

Online outsourcing procedures and processes usually influence the back-end processes, which blend in suitably to accomplish the total transaction life cycle. The aim is to achieve maximum integration between the online and internal (back-end) processes and systems with minimal disruption. At times it can seem harder than ever to follow a previously well-trodden path to value, due to switching to the online mode of business. Such change needs to be assimilated. High levels of accuracy, quality, and management control result from suitable business processes.

Example—Dell computers—Dell needs to maintain no stocks of finished goods. It manufactures only the central processing unit, but internally purchases monitors and keyboards from other organizations. Dell has tied up with UPS Worldwide for delivery of all the three components to the customer. UPS assimilates the shipments of the processing unit, monitor, and keyboard from different sources at one of its facilities and finally delivers the complete package to the end customer.

Dell's computers come with the latest components. Dell uses the build-to-order model for manufacture of computers. A key element of Dell's operational excellence is its tight integration with its supply chain during the manufacturing process. This allows Dell to avoid significant depreciation, which applies to inventoried components.

> Transactions trend over time
> 1990: 95% build to stock
> 1995: 40% build to order
> Current: 95+% build to order

Dell interfaces with its customers primarily through its Web site. Dell sells directly to its customers. Hence it is able to sense, study, and monitor market pulse, trends, and practices very quickly. By selling directly to customers, there is no lag time from being paid by resellers. Its customers include some of the biggest organizations (e.g., Boeing).

Small orders for personal and business use are paid in advance. Thus Dell has reversed the common practice worldwide of payment after delivery of goods. Dell has a cash conversion cycle (the time difference between paying its creditors and getting paid itself) of eight days.

Dell's Outsourcing Strategy

Permitting partners to do work that otherwise might be done by employees.

Servicing is all done by other firm's employees under contract from Dell.

Mass Customization

Building paths to reach to the global masses.

Dell created an efficient order fulfillment process that provides rapid delivery and low prices while also providing important options related to power, storage, type of monitor, and other miscellaneous features.

Dell—Some Salient Points

The Net, a low-cost entry vehicle.

Dell is a leader in Web services for sales and information.
Dell has used technology to gain competitive edge.

Business through the Internet—It has cut out the middleman and sells directly to end customers.

Vendor managed inventory (VMI) on assembly—enabling Dell to build to order, thus reducing inventories and cutting costs.

Total time from customer order to shipments = 3.5 days.

Virtual integration through technology and integration with parts suppliers.

The Dell Web site has the following proposed roadmap:

- *Originally, in phase 1, the site presented potential customers with simple product models and corresponding prices, like an online product sales catalog.*
- *In phase 2, on the Web site, potential customers have the flexibility to customize by specifying the hardware and software components they require and receive corresponding prices that match the entered criteria.*
- *In phase 3, the Web site will have a more sophisticated customer support system, an order tracking system, and courier tracking system.* Hence customers, who have placed an order will be able to find out the status of their orders at any point between order placement and actual receipt of the computer.
- *In phase 4, the Dell customer will have a tag code located at the back of the machine. This tag code will be entered on the site to view related information, technical support, etc., pertaining to the corresponding model.* Increasingly, service will be a differentiator in this future phase.

Reduced Learning Curve for Online Organizations

When playing online, outsourcing organizations learn the rules of the game, the best practices, and the competition's unique selling propositions and positioning very fast. This is because information about online outsourcing businesses is out in the open for everyone, including competitors and customers, to see.

Brand Building

Respect, so critical for a sustaining brand.

Most organizations, small and big, online or offline, have a Web site, with possibly some business online too. This improves credibility and image, increases the operational rate, and serves larger markets. *With the online outsourcing making forays into newer areas, businesses which were once focused primarily on cost-centric sales are now leveraging the Internet to gain branding, penetration, operational flexibility, higher customer value, operational experience, etc.* As a result of online outsourcing (in some measure) organizations have reduced administrative costs, increased quality, improved accuracy, and reduced turnaround time significantly.

Small players in different geographic locations can thus team up to work with established industry leaders, adding value and brand to all.

Substantial Changes in the Environment

. Organic and inorganic growth.

Online outsourcing business is enhanced due to the constant advances in computers and technology, and virtual organizations abreast of these changes offer high-quality services. *In fact many regional online business providers become more advanced than their Western counterparts because of the sheer volume and diversity of work, causing some companies to grow larger in size and broader in their knowledge and experience.*

Integration solutions were challenged by technology, which gave existing and new competitors a new range of strategies based on sourcing and outsourcing that redefined supply chains, in respect of client capture and distribution.

Online outsourcing businesses have helped in measures like saving of cost and time, updates on mandatory practices, satisfaction levels, mechanisms for continuous feedbacks, and effective implementation of workflows and policy changes.

Some of the key trends include an increase in virtualization, a shift from product-centric to customer-centric strategies, and cost-cutting measures with an increase in focus and products/service positioning online as a key differentiator.

Proven approaches and technology enablers provide significant business performance improvements. Risks are mitigated and business continuity solutions are created, resulting in saving opportunities.

Interoperable Communications

As machines start taking over, humans get relegated to the background.

To allow interoperable communication between heterogeneous machines, systems, and applications online, various standards have evolved. Heterogeneous systems interact with one another by exchanging data, voice, and video.

Quality and Continuous Benchmarking

As times change and technology leapfrogs further,
concepts get extended in reach and width.

The value proposition is both direct and indirect. The quality of finished deliverables is better due to quality contributions. Quality deliveries by the outsourcing vendor optimize and minimize effort by the outsourcing organization. These reduce transaction timings, cycle time, and delivery times.

Contributions from diverse subject matter experts directly result in deliverables being of high quality. Use of best practices of the various complementing diverse players of the project team automatically lead to high-quality products.

Systemized and structured best practices and processes used by people toward execution reduce person dependency and automatically add to quality.

Technology, process, and operational efficiencies are constantly raising the benchmark in terms of quality, customer experience, speed of delivery, convenience, and customization to individual needs.

Key performance indicators (KPIs) or areas where improvement is needed are identified by benchmarking against the existing best practices and industry standards. Suitable changes are made by the online outsourcing business to imitate existing best practices and meet existing benchmarks.

Vendor sellers become "value-added partners" to their customers (outsourcing buyers) by propelling timely availability of quality products. Vendor sellers at the higher end of the value chain become business transformation agents helping their customers innovate through IT and thrive in this rapidly changing online world.

Long-Term Career Paths

Distances small or large each one of us must walk to fulfill our fate.

The online outsourcing industry has matured over time and is no longer a stopgap arrangement till another suitable job is found. With new business deliverables and verticals being added in their repertoire, the need for specialized skills and trained individuals has become mandatory. Employees have realized the importance of building a career and know what they are looking for when joining these businesses.

If used internally within a large software organization, it leverages complementary synergies between people and resources across various levels, roles, and functions through the use of the intermediate in-house intranet Web portal. This improves employee motivation and morale.

Large software companies may have people who are trained and waiting for projects to be assigned. These employees can be deployed on short-term deliveries.

Reduced Liability and Risk

Due to simplified procedures and transparency of processes, liabilities and risks are minimized. However, certain online outsourcing businesses, because of their inherent nature, may be more risky than others.

Knowledge Store

Knowledge, not wealth or fame, shall always be the key differentiator.

Online outsourcing serves as a medium of expert knowledge, constantly growing and encompassing new fields. It thus serves as an exceptional means for learning, training, and discovering best practices in myriad fields.

Linguistic Barrier Is Greatly Lowered

The concept, expressed through different tongues.

Individuals and organizations existing in different geographic locations with different prevalent regional languages interact online for personal and business reasons. Organizational teams of online businesses could easily include people from diverse linguistic backgrounds pursuing a common business aim. Team players (people and organizations) existing in different places with different prevalent regional languages could come together toward projects requested for execution and in actual projects' delivery and execution. Teams would thus consist of people from diverse linguistic backgrounds pursuing a common aim. This would in turn create a need for different regional language translators and interpreters.

Repetitive Tasks and Labor Costs—Software Agents

Means to an end.

Given a well-established process, most transaction life cycles online are repetitive in nature. Tasks performed by back-end, administrative, and support personnel in functions such as sales or customer support can be optimized and automated wherever possible to reduce labor costs and increase productivity. This is because labor is always very costly.

Suitable automation and software agents are useful for the same. Software agents are required for mundane repetitive nature of activity. Time-strapped customers, in a fast-paced society, need new ways to minimize the time spent online for personal and/or business needs like booking airline tickets, so that they can devote more time to other activities. Customers can relegate tasks like searching and cost comparison to agents, searching databases, retrieving, and filtering information because manual effort would be very intensive.

Automation—Software Agents

Sifting the information of value from the dross.

Online outsourcing inherently allows a high degree of automation. Software and data by its nature can traverse across national, physical, and geographic boundaries, transporting over the networked systems, unlike physical goods. There is a reduction in overall human resource and effort due to higher automation deliverables. It cuts the administrative overheads involved.

To make costly expertise widely and commonly available, it needs to be captured once and modeled through automated delivery mechanisms. Some examples of expert software agents could be models of online real-world agents such as translators, lawyers, diplomats, union negotiators, stockbrokers, and even priests. Therefore the value to the end user can be improved by software agents by performing various tasks, the most important being gathering information, filtering information, and using it for decision making. Software agents are used for multifarious tasks.

Behind the development of software agents the underlying vision involves a paradigm shift from the traditional software as tool to software as assistant online. An online user initiates various actions that are passively facilitated by the software, in the existing tool-based model. A user instructs the software program to download files from the Internet, browse the WWW, or compute a spreadsheet column in a more efficient fashion, but the commands themselves issue directly from the user's mouse or keyboard input, and this is a "do what I say" model. The user informs the agent about the various actions to be performed or tasks to be accomplished in the new agent-based model. On behalf of the user, the software agent takes these requests and actively performs tasks, such as comparing prices in online shopping malls or monitoring incoming electronic mail messages and organizing an agenda even when the user is on vacation. Thus, the new model is proactive, and the traditional model is reactive.

Deliverables can be tracked centrally using centralized monitoring and reporting systems and applications.

Online Payments

As the mode shifts to become the new standard.

All the components of monetary transfers can be effected through a network of Internet-based payment systems and supporting banks. These lead to the more superior cashless economy.

Operational Efficiency

The inherent capability, in itself a winning position.

End-to-end monitoring, tracking, and reporting improve efficiency and knowledge apart from cost savings, reduced overhead, and workload management. The confidentiality and security of the information shared is maintained through suitable people, process, and technology. Flexibility and teamwork aid in meeting client needs. Streamlining operations greatly reduces the learning curve. It helps in achieving integration with key business processes.

It is thus a source of competitive advantage leading to the following:

Doing things right—"operating efficiency"
Doing the right things—"value added strategies"

E-Commerce Benefits

The mobile networks and communication handshakes.

E-commerce is a modern business methodology that addresses the desire of firms, consumers, and management to cut costs while improving the quality of goods and increasing the speed of services. The demand within business and government to make better use of computing gives rise to the need for e-commerce, which is to better apply computer technology to improve business process and information exchange, both within an enterprise and across interacting organizations. *Hence it appears that e-commerce is an integrating force that represents the digital convergence of twenty-first century business applications and computing technologies.* Generation and exploitation of new business opportunities are emphasized by e-commerce and, to use the popular buzzword, "generate business value." Information is accessed, absorbed, arranged, and sold in different ways when buyer–seller transactions occur in the electronic marketplace. Information has become important on its own, and the information about a product or service has become separated from the physical product or service. In terms of its effect on a company's profit, in some cases this information can become as crucial as the actual product or service.

Electronic Data Interchange (EDI) Advantages

Of reaching out, far and wide, over spaces and time.

For many reasons, EDI can be cost and time saving because the automatic transfer of data between computers does away with the need to rekey information and, as such, reduces costly manual errors to nearly zero. Acknowledgments of receipts of data are produced by EDI transactions. These acknowledgments can make invoicing obsolete, as is now being found by many organizations, and it helps in saving many efforts that now can be devoted to acquiring, receiving, and paying for goods.

The savings from EDI are significant for companies dealing with thousands of suppliers and tens of thousands of purchase orders a year. It has been found that purchase orders that previously cost between $75 and $125 to process now cost about 93 cents. Through "automated receipts settlement" or financial EDI, companies can also pay each other, whereby electronic purchase order acknowledgments and shipping notices provide the data necessary for payment, further reducing paper. From improvements in paper-based systems, savings can accrue.

The effort and expense of a company can be impacted by EDI in terms of maintaining records, paper-related supplies, filing cabinets or other storage systems, and to the personnel requirement to maintain all these systems. Most of the functions of paper forms are taken over by electronic transactions, and through automation the time is drastically reduced to process them. Because of the amounts, EDI can also reduce postage bills of paper that no longer need to be sent. Then, there is improved customer service and problem resolution. The time companies spend to identify and resolve interbusiness problems can be minimized by EDI. Somewhere along the way, many such problems come from data entry errors, and EDI can eliminate many of them. Customer service can be improved by EDI by enabling the quick transfer of business documents and a marked decrease in errors (and so can fill orders faster) and by providing an automatic audit trail that frees accounting staff for more productive activities. Vendor stock replenishment (VSR) is an example of problem resolution and customer service facilitated by EDI and initiated by many retailers such as Walmart. Vendors should maintain appropriate inventory levels in all stores according to this program. Stores do not run out of product with VSR. As soon as the store EDI system reports that it is necessary, suppliers and distributors send stock and automatically bill the client. It cuts days and even weeks from the order fulfillment cycle and ensures that the product is always on the shelf. From not having to copy and fax/mail copies of invoices or purchase orders, saving of time takes place. Suppliers are being ordered by many large manufacturers and retailers to institute an EDI program. Because they are unable to build bridges to other companies, these are isolated islands of productivity. The ability to implement EDI is a big plus today, when evaluating a new product to carry or a new supplier to use, and these same companies tend to stop doing business with suppliers who do not comply.

For small traders EDI reduces an entry barrier. Because of the lack of efficient procedures, medium-sized traders are confined to the margins, and this is compounded by lack of access to information and information networks, or inadequate support services or trade logistics. From one country to the next, although the needs vary, most firms can generally benefit from efficient business practices and trade facilitation measures. Substantial benefits can be generated at all levels, because all such improvements need not be technology intensive. In international trade the EDI benefits include reduced transaction expenditure; quicker movement of imported and exported goods; improved customer service through track-and-trace programs that quickly identify, to the many participants in a trade deal, the companies, customs, banks, insurers, transport agents, etc., where things are located or being handled; and faster customs clearance and reduced opportunities for corruption, a huge problem in trade. Between a payer, payee, and their respective banks, financial EDI comprises the electronic transmission of payments and remittance information. Businesses, with the help of EDI, are able to replace labor-intensive manual activities associated with issuing, transportation, and delivery of checks through use of automated initiation, transmission, and processing of payment instructions. Thus manual delays inherent in processing paper instruments are eliminated. The certainty of payment flows between bank accounts is improved by financial EDI, because the payee's bank can credit its account on the scheduled payment date, and the payer's bank can debit its account on the same day.

Advantages of Outsourcing Online to India

As regions vie for dominance.

When outsourcing online to India, the outsourcer need not bother about any issues regarding the differences in Indian and American English. You are dealing with expert writers who are well trained in English and its nuances when you outsource your content development to India. They can converse in English as comfortably as their American or British counterparts because English is their first language, and as a result, there are a large number of qualified people who are ready, willing, and able to work for global customers. To meet the exact requirements of the customer, some fine-tuning may be required, and this can be done in a final edit.

Recommendations to American customers intending to outsource are that they should be prepared for some minor differences in grammar, spelling, and style. In India, although British English is common, the influence of American cinema and TV has helped many Indians understand the subtle differences and adapt accordingly. The customer can request some modifications in style and prepare some writing guidelines, because the Indian style can be more formal and wordy. Some of these differences, however, are fading rapidly because the college students of today are very globalized. Nevertheless, expect to tweak the final work according to the target audience if you outsource writing or other creative services. Tweaking may be required, because cultural nuances may appear more often when more creative services are outsourced.

Indian writers possess very high academic levels including PhDs, MDs, MBAs, etc., thus providing top-quality documentation at lower cost. Note that India graduates about 870,000 IT students annually. Value is added to content because Indians are global, and the outsourcer can benefit from the diverse network of talented writers with different styles, insights, and training. They have the talent to write on many subjects and, being well informed, they excel in scientific, medical, technical, and cultural writing in English and many other international languages. Due to their international work experience as Web content developers, engineers, software programmers, medical doctors, journalists, etc., Indian writers can develop a wide and diverse range of content.

The strengths of the Indian Web content writers include research at lower costs, and 50% of most writing projects is research. One team can do the research, and the other can do the writing/editing, and the Indian vendors can put more people on the task, thereby developing the content in a shorter time.

Chapter 14

Business-to-Business Payment Systems Online

Financial instruments change in form and value,
to meet the changing market needs.

E-Commerce—Internet Communications

The interactive web of machines, men, and their undying spirit.

The fascination with the future of e-commerce and the profit potential for the "first mover" companies are a potential source of media and business interest, which in time shall be answered. Many global networks will be propelled by e-commerce from the fringe into the core of business. E-commerce stands poised to make a momentous contribution to the way government, business, and individuals conduct business, despite the many unknowns in this rapidly changing area. It is clear from the way business activity already is taking place that e-commerce applications will be built on the existing technology infrastructure, a myriad of computers, communications networks, and communication software forming the nascent information superhighway. Buying and selling of information, products, and services via myriad computer networks today or in the future make up the information superhighway. E-commerce applications may be used in a variety of ways like buying and selling processes as part of common business services, for sending and receiving information through messaging and information distribution, and for creating a product and means to communicate about it such as multimedia content

229

and network publishing. All e-commerce must travel through the highway system provided by the superhighway, which is the very foundation. All e-commerce applications and infrastructure are supported by two pillars, namely, public policy and technical standards. Issues such as universal access, privacy, and information pricing are governed by public policy. The nature of information publishing, user interfaces, and transport in the interest of compatibility across the entire network are dictated by technical standards.

Let us use the analogy of a traditional transportation business to better understand the integration of the various infrastructure components. In the same way that regular commerce needs the interstate highway to carry goods from point to point, any e-commerce application requires the Internet network infrastructure. Business of all kinds, from an organization purchasing supplies to a customer buying movie tickets online, use the Internet highway. The Internet, however, is not one monolithic data highway designed according to long-standing, well-defined rules and regulations based on well-known needs. The Internet, which is still under construction, will be a mesh of interconnected data highways of many forms: telephone wires, radio-based wireless, cellular, and satellite. New ramps and small highway systems are being quickly acquired by Internet. To convince traffic to use their on-ramps or sections of the highway, numerous constructors are either in competition with or in alliance with one another. Revenues in e-commerce are based on vehicular traffic like tollways. In e-commerce it is the vehicles transporting information or multimedia content.

Similar to what the interstate highway system did for productivity in the nation's manufacturing, travel, and distribution systems, projections anticipate that the Internet will transform information transport technology for electronic commerce applications and provide economic windfall. As reflected by its various labels worldwide, the Internet is not a U.S. phenomenon but a global one. In the United States, for example, it is called National Information Infrastructure (NII), Data-Dori in Japan, and Jaring in Malaysia. The gamut of business process is run by factors fueling the avid interest in e-commerce.

Usage of electronic messaging technologies is a key feature of e-commerce which streamlines business processes, reduces paper, and increases automation. Electronic data interchange (EDI) is an effective medium to deliver electronic transactions between communicating computers.

The unique interplay among government, academia, and private commercial endeavors compounds the complexity in the nascent world of electronic commerce, and then there is also the challenge of integrating different technologies to allow a seamless data exchange. Very basic policy and legal questions are materializing in relation to e-commerce. Traditional businesses are governed by commercial law and codes and may have dependencies on matters like pollution, environmental impact, and consumer protection from fraud and taxation. Similarly e-commerce has related issues like cost of information access, legal measures to protect against fraud, right to privacy, and policing of global information traffic to foil pirating or pornography. As more and more people with variable intent enter the electronic marketplace, the issues themselves, let alone the solutions, are evolving and becoming increasingly important. In the same way, e-mail can be considered both a messaging infrastructure and a purchasable end product.

Electronic Payment Systems

Speed, never enough.

Companies are constantly endeavoring to serve customers faster, better, and at constantly reducing prices. In ancient times merchants of Asia and Europe, while trying to unlock the commercial potential of the expanding marketplace, faced many problems (e.g., conflicting laws and customs regarding commercial practices, incompatible and nonconvertible currencies that restricted trade). Traders invented various forms of payment instruments like promissory notes, bills of exchange, gold coins, and barter to circumvent some of these problems. Surrounding the use of these instruments, the merchants also developed commercial law that proved to be one of the turning points in the history of trade and commerce. A similar sort of development is taking place today, but one that is unlikely to take anywhere near the centuries it took for the traditional payment system to evolve. Electronic payment systems are rapidly becoming an inherent part of online business process innovation. Since customers pay online for goods and services, the enabling mechanisms of electronic payment systems and e-commerce play critical roles. Payment is an integral part of the mercantile process, and prompt payment (or account settlement) is crucial. The entire business chain is disrupted if the claims and debits of the various participants, individuals, companies, banks, and nonbanks are not balanced because of payments delay or, even worse, default. Prompt and secure payment, clearing, and settlement of credit or debit claims is an important aspect of e-commerce. In many ways, the current state of online electronic payments is reminiscent of the medieval ages. Conventional payment methods such as paper cash, checks, bank drafts, or bills of exchange have many limitations and bottlenecks. Though speed is a critical need of e-commerce purchase processing, electronic replicas of these are still in the evolving stage. A wide range of new business opportunities open up due to the current fast pace of emerging innovations, especially in areas of payment for goods and services online.

Anywhere money needs to change hands, electronic payment systems are proliferating (e.g., in banking, retail, health care, online markets, etc.), the need to deliver products and services more cost effectively, and to provide a higher quality of service to customers, motivates organizations. One can trace back to the 1940s, the research into electronic payment systems for customers and the first applications credit cards appeared soon after. The electronic payment technology was initially known as electronic funds transfer (EFT) in the early 1970s. Instructing a financial institution to debit or credit an account through any electronic medium, phone, or computer is known as EFT. Thus EFT as a mode differs fundamentally from traditional modes of cash and checks etc., which are transported by truck, train, or airplane, etc.

Payment Gateways

As means and mechanisms connect various delivery channels.

We are a long way though from a universal payment system, in spite of many prototypes developed. Moreover it is necessary that such a system should be robust and capable of handling a large number of transactions and will require extensive vetting and usage to iron out all the issues. This would be a boon to many e-commerce services and related payments. As corporate networks become more congested, qualities of e-cash such as anonymity are not major requirements. Widely accepted and secure means of transferring money online is still in an evolving stage and has enormous potential for growth.

Electronic Commerce and EDI

The machines at work, as humans sleep by.

Outsourcing organizations, online providers, and customers are moving toward a paperless exchange of business information using EDI, electronic mail (e-mail), electronic bulletin boards, electronic funds transfer (EFT), and other similar technologies. It is in high-payoff areas that these technologies are normally applied, recognizing that paper-handling activities usually increase expenses, effort, time, etc., without adding value.

The business-to-business transactions category is known as the market link transaction. Organizations, governments, and individuals increasingly depend on computers as a fast, economical, and dependable way for business and personal needs. The benefits of adopting the same methods has also begun to be seen by small companies. *Business-to-business transactions use EDI and electronic mail for everyday transactions like purchasing goods, exchanging information, giving consulting services, and submitting and receiving proposals.*

Limiting the deliverables and payments to small chunks until trust, quality, and reliability are established is the best way to avoid risk. Both the online buyers and providers should understand the scope, pricing, and contracting methodologies. Before entering into an agreement, a sample relatively small online deliverable is a common way of testing. To ensure quality, it is wise to determine a clear process, as in all outsourcing ventures. Confusion and misunderstanding can be prevented by having a detailed document spelling out exactly what is required. To help capture exactly what is wanted, a good vendor will have a questionnaire or checklist and will also outline some terms additionally.

In the business world, though electronic commerce and EDI may be often equated with each other, e-commerce is a superset and includes EDI and much more.

A popular example is structured document interchange using EDI. Data in the form of document content is exchanged between interacting software applications to process a business transaction. EDI only specifies the format for business information, but the actual transmission of information is handled by other underlying transport mechanisms like e-mail, point-to-point connections, etc. There is no consensus on the definition of EDI, because of the different approaches in development and implementation of EDI.

EDI—Some Definitions

Of messages blowing across the spaces.

One prevailing definition of electronic data interchange is the transmission, in a standard syntax, of unambiguous information of business or strategic significance between computers of independent organizations. This definition is per the accredited standards committee for EDI of the American National Standards Institute.

According to the UN/EDIFACT training guide, electronic data interchange (EDI) may also be defined as the interchange of data in a standard format between multiple participating computer applications with minimal manual intervention. According to Article 2.1 of the European Model EDI Agreement, electronic data interchange is the electronic transfer from computer to computer, of commercial and administrative data using an agreed standard to structure an EDI message.

Still another definition of EDI is that electronic data interchange is the electronic transfer from one computer to another of computer processable data using an agreed standard to structure the data. This is according to International Data Exchange Association's *The EDI Handbook: Trading in the 1990s.*

EDI has its usage in one context as a technological solution that focuses on the mechanical transport and assembly of business forms and in another context as a business methodology that focuses on the content and structure of forms. By examining the layered structure of EDI, this confusion can be cleared. In the case of EDI, the idea is very simple because EDI seeks to take what has been a manually prepared form or a form from a business application, translates that data into a standard electronic format, and transmits it. The standard format is converted back at the receiving end into a format that can be read by the recipient's application. Through computer-to-computer exchange of information, therefore, the output of one application becomes the input to another, and as a result there is an elimination of the delays and errors inherent in paper-to-paper based transactions. By comparing the flow of information between organizations before and after the implementation of EDI, its benefits can be seen.

An ideal example is provided by the purchasing application for this purpose. In the procurement function, EDI has been used extensively to streamline interaction between buyer and seller. There are many other uses of EDI. Universities use EDI to exchange information/transcripts quickly. Large complex engineering designs created on specialized computers are transmitted by auto manufacturers using EDI. Online price catalogs listing products, prices, discounts, and terms are sent to customer by large multinational firms using EDI. Prices and terms can be compared by EDI-capable businesses, and direct orders can be made by EDI.

Models which can benefit from such EDI transactions are just-in-time (JIT) manufacturing methods resulting in savings in inventory, warehousing, and handling costs. Firms can accelerate the document-based business processes, both inside and outside the organizational boundaries, from simple order processing to complete supply chain management by electronic mail (e-mail), while EDI is primarily interorganizational. In work flow and reengineering applications, technologies such as EDI and e-mail have been widely used for years and are now diffusing into other aspects of commerce. To improve internal business process efficiency, the efforts of the late 1980s and 1990s were focused on moving existing nonelectronic methods to an electronic platform. For reaching and getting close to the customer, today the emphasis has shifted from this narrow focus to the invention of entirely new business applications.

"EDI Concept"

An optimal mix of men, material, and machines.

The effort and expense of an online company can be impacted by EDI in terms of maintaining records. Most of the functions of paper forms are taken over by electronic transactions, and through automation the time is drastically reduced to process them. Because of the amounts, EDI can also reduce postage bills of papers that no longer need to be sent. Then, there is improved customer service and problem resolution. Companies identify and resolve applicable interbusiness problems online using EDI. Somewhere along the way, many such problems come from data entry errors, and EDI can eliminate many of them.

Customer service can be improved by EDI by enabling the quick transfer of business documents and a marked decrease in errors (and so can fill orders faster) and by providing an automatic audit trail that frees accounting staff for more productive activities. Vendor stock replenishment (VSR) is an example of problem resolution and customer service facilitated by EDI and initiated by many retailers such as Walmart. Vendors should maintain appropriate inventory levels in all stores according to this program. Stores do not run out of product with VSR. As soon as the store EDI system reports that it is necessary, suppliers and distributors send stock and automatically bill the client. It cuts days and even weeks from the order fulfillment cycle and ensures that the product is always on the shelf. From not having to copy and fax/mail copies of invoices or purchase orders, saving of time takes place. Suppliers are being ordered by many large manufacturers and retailers to institute an EDI program. *Because they are unable to build bridges to other companies, these are isolated islands of productivity.* The bridge is now available through EDI, e-commerce, online outsourcing, etc. The ability to implement EDI is a big plus today, when evaluating a new product to carry or a new supplier to use, and these same companies tend to stop doing business with suppliers who do not comply.

New ways of doing business and even new types of businesses are being created by information-based business transactions. The applications of e-commerce are quite varied, and in its most common form, e-commerce is also used to denote the paperless exchange of business information using EDI, electronic mail (e-mail), electronic bulletin boards, electronic funds transfer (EFT), and other similar technologies. It appears, at first glance, that the technical foundations for effective e-commerce solutions are the messaging-based technologies such as EDI and mail-enabled applications, combined with database and information management services. However, the full potential of e-commerce cannot be delivered by any single one of these technologies. Integrated architecture, the like of which has never been seen before, is required. We are beginning to see sophisticated applications being developed in the WWW as electronic commerce becomes more mature. The WWW client server model both technically and commercially seems poised to become a dormant technology.

EDI—The Future

> *As rules of the play change to meet the changing*
> *markets, demands, and technologies.*

In the relationship between the retailer and the supplier, perhaps the most dramatic effect of EDI can be seen. *Based on shared information of past sales history, expected unit sales, etc., the material supplier vendors help shorten the order-to-delivery pipeline, commit to efficiency, quality, etc., by improving on-time delivery and shipping accuracy.* It is well worth the risk involved in sharing information more completely between companies and the retailer. This reduces inventory carrying costs and allows greater dependability and availability of material from the supplier on a timely basis. The retailer's commitment is gained by the supplier and has access to greater information for better planning.

It is hard to see how, without a proper framework, EDI can fulfill the role envisioned for it in the future. There is wide recognition of the economic advantages of EDI, but often companies have improved only discrete processes such as automating the accounts payable function or the funds transfer process. Such improvements are limited in their ability to help business transform themselves. To truly improve their productivity, companies need to automate their processes. This is the thrust of the new directions of EDI. For electronic commerce, new EDI services are seen as enabling means that will automate external and internal processes, enabling companies to improve their productivity on a scale as never before. *Information management solutions allow companies to link to their trading community (i.e., suppliers, distributors, customers, banks, and transportation and logistics operations, etc.) electronically in various operations like order entry, purchasing, accounts payable, and funds transfer.* To reduce the cost of setting up an EDI relationship is another goal of new EDI services. Because of the need for a detailed bilateral agreement between the involved partners and for the necessary technical agreement, these costs are still very high. In short-term partnerships, dedicated EDI links are rarely realized because the cost of establishment of such an agreement is too high, and EDI links involving many partners are not advisable because of the negotiation and agreement challenges between multiple partners. Thus dedicated EDI implementations are most successful either in long-term relationships or among a limited number of partners. *Several new types of EDI are emerging with the advent of interorganizational commerce, and they can be broadly categorized as traditional EDI and open EDI.*

EDI Example—Manual Process Using Paper Checks (Limitations)

> *As the rules of play begin to change to meet the changing markets, demands, and technologies.*

Traditional manual methods continue to be used for business-to-business payment. Customers are billed by most firms with paper invoices, and suppliers are mailed paper checks with remittance information. Costly resources, labor, and transportation are consumed in creating and processing these documents. From the invoices, for example, the buyer must manually enter data into its automated accounts payable system, track the receipt of supplies, print remittance documents, and issue and mail checks.

Instruments for debit transfers where the payees collect funds from payers are called checks. To the depositors of checks, funds made available by banks are provisional and may be reversed if the payer does not have sufficient funds in its account to pay the check when it is received by the payer's bank. For two main reasons, businesses use checks to make payments. The first reason is that, despite some uncertainty about receiving final payment, they are familiar and readily accepted form of payment. The second reason is that business benefit from the float created by the delays in the check collection process. *Float is useful to businesses because they can continue to use or invest funds for several days after they have issued the check.* When a delay occurs between the initiation of a payment and availability of funds to the recipient, then float is created. Because checks are delivered through mail, require human handling, and must be transported among banks in the collection chain, delays occur. By drawing checks on banks located in remote locations or by otherwise imposing barriers to the timely collection of checks, some companies improve the float benefit of checks. These practices add to the expenses incurred in collecting checks and delays recipient's access to the funds. More than 96% of all noncash payment in the United States in 1993 was made by paper checks; 55% of these checks were issued by customers, 40% by businesses, and about 5% by the government.

Once the payment has been received, the supplier must manually enter payment data into its automated accounts receivable system and deposit the check with its bank for collection. The supplier's bank (the collecting bank) must transport the financial instrument such as checks to the bank on which the purchaser drew it (the payer bank). Checks are frequently routed by collecting banks through intermediaries, which ultimately deliver the checks to the payer bank. Thus through the collection chain, thus the transportation of checks and the respective handling of them at each bank in the chain contribute significantly to the cost of processing checks. When the payer and the payee bank are in different countries with different regulatory environments, extra steps and paperwork are involved.

Clearing Automation through Truncation and Electronic Check Presentment (TECP)

In Truncation and Electronic Cheque Presentment (TECP) environments, the traditional paper checks will not be exchanged through the clearing system. For exchange purpose, instead, images of checks will be captured electronically and used. At the local processing center serving the branch that received the deposit, the image capture process will generally take place. This separation of physical and electronic information is called truncation. A file of magnetic ink character recognition (MICR) data accompanies the check images, identifying the account number, and other payment details will be transmitted electronically to an exchange network and ultimately to the financial institution that holds the checking account. Images will replace physical checks in the clearing system and assume their official legal status, with the introduction of electronic check presentment. After a relatively short retention period, the original checks will be destroyed. In the clearing system, this shift to electronic image exchange will not only increase efficiency in the settlement and acceptance process, it will also enable service improvements for financial institutions and their customers. End-to-end settlement and acceptance of all clearing items will be completed within 36 hours, with no requirement to move physical checks across the country.

Some payers will seek alternative payment channels, with no paper checks returned to support the payers. From the front desk to the back door, paperless clearing will affect most areas of business and companies with the ability to send clearing-ready images to their financial institutions may be offered improved services or lower clearing costs. It is expected that transmission and clearing images will widen the window during which banks will accept deposits of checks from large enterprises. The daily volume and the value of payments processed will increase, and the availability of funds will improve. In case of seasonal peaks in payment volumes and irregular billing cycles, skilled force and superior processing capability will allow you to benefit from increased throughput of payments. Efficient payment channels facilitate business growth, even if the trading entities are located in disparate geographical locations.

Example—Automated Clearing House (ACH) Transfers

As machines move in to initiate, execute, and close transactions.

Now if EDI through the usage of automated clearing houses (ACH) for domestic and international funds transfer or electronic funds transfer (EFT) were to be used, the process would be highly efficient.

SWIFT (Society for Worldwide Interbank Financial Telecommunications) forms the underlying backbone for such financial EDI. It was initiated In Brussels in 1973 and began operations in 1977. For fund transfer instructions and administrative messages, SWIFT has been a leader in providing standard EDI formats. Credit transfers and debit transfers are the two types of automated clearing house (ACH) transfers used. Funds flow directly from the payer's bank to the payee's in credit transfers which are similar to large dollar funds transfers. Until the morning of the business day following the settlement, the funds received by the payee's bank are provisional. If the sending bank does not have sufficient funds in the account to fund them on the settlement day, the reserve bank may revoke payment. The payee's bank initiates the transfer and receives funds immediately from the payer's when ACH debit transfers are used. Funds made available by banks to collecting businesses are provisional and may be revoked if sufficient funds in the payer's account are not available to cover the transfer on the scheduled settlement day, in the case of checks. For business-to-business payments, the use of ACH is growing rapidly. Businesses typically use ACH credit transfers to pay for goods or services and to make tax payments to state and local governments. ACH debit transfers may be used to transfer funds from the bank accounts of geographically dispersed multiple affiliates and subsidiaries into the company's primary bank account. ACH debit transfers are used by some banks to collect funds from businesses that distribute their products. There is concern on the part of firms to permit other companies to initiate debits on their accounts because this eliminates float. For business-to-business payments, the ACH debit transfers are used less often than credit transfers.

Electronic Funds Transfer (EFT) Process

As machines deliver repeat service with ever reducing costs.

When implementing financial EDI, corporations use various approaches. For a business the most fundamental decision that it must make is whether payment instructions and remittance data should flow together through the banking system, or whether the payment instructions should flow through the banking system while remittance data is transmitted over a direct data communications link with a trading partner or over a dedicated value added network (VAN). By accepting data in a variety of formats, and by converting the incoming data into a format usable by the receiver of the information, the exchange of electronic data is facilitated by VAN. Also transmission schedules are managed and data held by VANs until receivers are ready to accept them. The electronic transmission costs, the extent to which the two trading partners are able to exchange business documents electronically, and the types of electronic payment services offered by their banks, all impact the choices businesses make.

As mentioned earlier, credit transfers between banks where funds flow directly from the payer's bank to the payee's bank are known as electronic funds transfer, and they are almost instantaneous, same-day payments. Although these transactions are carried out on private networks, EFT is one of the earliest examples of payment systems that use online transactions. In the United States, the Federal Reserve's system, Fedwire, and the Clearing House Interbank Payments Systems (CHIPS) of the New York Clearing House are the two biggest funds transfer services. Transfer cannot be revoked after the receiving bank is advised that a reserve bank has credited its account, because the Federal Reserve guarantees Fedwire funds transfers. On the other hand, the members of CHIPS pledge collateral to ensure settlement of CHIPS transfers, and payments become final only at the close of business when all members settle their net positions using Fedwire transfers. Of the total number of noncash payments, funds transfers account for an extremely small portion. When timeliness and certainty of payment are paramount, businesses use EFT, but rarely to pay suppliers for goods and services. They can use ACH transfer for this. Automated clearing house (ACH) transfers are used to process the high volume of relatively small dollar payments for settlement in one or two business days, in contrast to the EFT process. The following services are provided by ACH: preauthorized credits, such as direct deposit of payrolls, preauthorized debits, such as repetitive bill payments and consumer initiated payments (called GIRO in banking circles), and this is primarily a high volume/low dollar, consumer oriented product. Banks not only have set up their own systems but also have shared ACH systems with other banks to provide these and other services. For instance, in over 200 American cities, the pioneer network BANKWIRE is owned and operated by banks. It offers information on such things as loans and account balances in addition to money transfers. The biggest funds transfer system in the United States is Fedwire, the Federal Reserve Board's system. A majority of American domestic transactions by value are handled by it, and banks use it to transfer funds to each other. Of all international dollar transfers made, 90% are processed by CHIPS (Clearing House Interbanks Payments System), which operates out of New York.

Financial Instruments

Instruments changing in form and value over time.

Even after more than three decades of continuous developments in electronic payment systems, cash is still the most prevalent consumer payment instrument. There are some reasons why cash still remains a dominant form of instrument. The banking system's slow, inefficient clearing of noncash transactions and poor interest rates paid on bank deposits are some of the primary causes. Cash can be given or traded with anyone, meaning that it is negotiable. The payee is obliged to take cash because it is a legal tender. Possession of cash is prima facie proof of ownership, meaning cash is a bearer instrument. Cash is a standard medium of exchange and does not have the many risks which exist in other instruments. Additionally cash may be held and used even without having a bank account.

Electronic Token

As money and its exchange turn electronic,
the physical changing of hands takes a leap forward.

For customer-oriented e-commerce environments, most of the current banking and retailing payment methods are not completely adequate in their current form. These assume that the various players will be in personal/physical contact with each other at some point of time. For e-commerce, these assumptions are a significant limitation, and hence such payment mechanisms are being modified and adapted for seamless conduct of business over networks. Financial instruments, which are entirely new in form are being developed. "Electronic token" is one such new financial instrument, similar to other equivalent forms like electronic cash, money, or checks.

There are three categories of electronic tokens—cash or real time, debit or prepaid, and credit or postpaid tokens. In the real-time type of electronic tokens, transactions are settled in cash or by exchange of electronic currency. An example of online currency exchange is electronic cash (e-cash). In case of debit or prepaid electronic tokens type, users pay in advance. Smart cards and electronic purses that store electronic money are examples of prepaid payment mechanisms. In case of credit or postpaid type of electronic tokens, during the purchase transaction, the respective customer's account balance is checked online. Credit/debit cards and electronic checks are examples of postpaid mechanisms. Some tokens are specially customized to handle a certain nature of transactions (e.g., tokens specifically for purchase of small amounts of information commonly known as micropayments), while other tokens are meant for transactions involving traditional products. Some seek more general transactions, while some systems target specific niche transactions. To identify the parties involved, the average amounts, and the purchase interaction is the key. Another dimension is the means of settlement used. To name a few, tokens may be backed by cash, credit, electronic bill payments (prearranged and spontaneous), cashiers checks, IOUs, letters and lines of credit, and wire transfers. Among transaction speed, risk, and cost, each option incurs tradeoffs. Credit cards are used by most transaction settlement methods, while others use other proxies for value, effectively creating currencies of dubious liquidity and with interesting tax, risk, and float implications. The approach to security anonymity and authentication is another dimension. In the protection of privacy and confidentiality of the transactions, electronic tokens vary. Some may be more open to potentially prying eyes or even to the participants themselves. Authentication, non-repudiability, and asset management can be helped by encryption. The next dimension is the question of risk—at what time who assumes what kind of risk. The token might suddenly become worthless, and the customers might have the currency that nobody will accept. Customers may be exposed to risk through usage of smart cards because these are static assets. Discounting or arbitrage of electronic tokens may change their value. If a business transaction has long cycle times between delivery of goods and corresponding payments to merchants, risk may arise, with the merchants exposed to the risk that buyers do not pay after delivery or vice versa that the vendor does not deliver.

E-Cash

E-Cash Basics

On comparing credit and debit cards versus cash, the cards cannot be given away because, technically, they are identification cards owned by the issuer and restricted to one user. Merchants have the right to refuse to accept credit and debit cards because they are not legal tender. The usage of the cards requires an account relationship and authorization system, and so they are not bearer instruments. Similarly, personal knowledge of the payer or a check guarantee system is required for checks. Because credit and debit cards have respective limitations, there is a need to create a novel electronic payment method, and therefore options like e-cash which have some of the properties of cash help. A few common features must be incorporated for implementing an e-cash system. Some of the properties that e-cash must have are monetary value, interoperability, retrievability, and security. E-cash, to have monetary value, must have a suitable supporting mechanism of either cash (currency), corresponding bank-authorized credit, or a bank-certified cashier's check. Reconciliation must occur without any problem when e-cash created by one bank is accepted by others. Without a proper bank support mechanism, e-cash carries the risk of being rejected.

It combines computerized convenience with security and privacy and does not have the usual known limitations of paper cash. A host of new markets and applications are opened up because of its versatility. In customer-oriented electronic payments, e-cash is gradually offsetting cash as the principal payment mechanism and is the only medium for online transactions.

Usage Issues with E-Cash

If the need for anonymity were relaxed, double spending would not be a major problem. When a customer is issued a bank note, in such situations, it is issued to that person's unique license. The old owner adds a tiny bit of information to the bank note, based on the bank note's serial number and his or her license, each time money changes hands. The bank will now be able to use the two bank notes to determine who the cheater is, if someone attempts to spend the money twice. Whoever cheats will get caught, even if the bank notes pass through many different people's hands, and none of the other people will ever have to know.

Since the bank can check the numbers on the e-cash, the downside is that it can tell precisely what a person's buying habits are and the various merchant accounts that are being credited. Letting others know this personal information may make many people feel uncomfortable.

Also the inability of e-cash to get divided into smaller amounts is a drawback of e-cash. Some of the advantages of e-check are that they work in the same way as traditional checks, thus simplifying customer education. E-checks are well suited for clearing micropayments, and their use of convention cryptography makes it much faster than systems based on public cryptography (e-cash).

In business transactions, it is often necessary to get small-denomination change. To deal with the change problem, a number of variations have been developed. In communication and storage, it would be cumbersome for the bank to issue users with enough separate electronic coins of various denominations. So would a method that requires payees to return extra change. Customers are issued a single number called an open check that contains multiple denomination values sufficient for transaction up to a prescribed limit. On the client's computer, at the time of payment, the e-cash software would create a note of the transaction value from the open check.

E-Cash Working Mechanism

For e-cash to be interoperable, it must be exchangeable as payment for other e-cash, paper cash, goods or services, lines of credit, deposits in banking accounts, bank notes or obligations, electronic benefits transfers, and the like. A single bank is used by most e-cash proposals. Because multiple customers are not going to be using the same bank or even be in the same country, therefore in practice, multiple banks are required with an international clearinghouse that handles the exchange ability issues. From home or office or while traveling, remote storage and retrieval (e.g., from a telephone or personal communications device) would allow users to exchange e-cash (e.g., withdraw from and deposit into banking accounts), and therefore e-cash should be storable and retrievable. The cash could be stored on a remote computer's memory, in smart cards, or in other easily transported standard or special purpose devices. It might be preferable to store cash on a dedicated device that cannot be altered, because it might be easy to create counterfeit cash that is stored in a computer. So that the user can view the card's contents, the device should have a suitable interface to facilitate personal authentication using password or other means and a display. Mondex is an example of a device which can store e-cash, thus making it an electronic wallet. While being exchanged, e-cash should be copy-proof and tamperproof, thus preventing duplication and removing the possibility of double spending. The counterfeiter during online shopping over the Internet may be anywhere in the world and consequently may be difficult to physically apprehend even with extensive international arrangements and task forces. In order to audit whether prevention is working, detection is essential. Then double spending poses a tricky issue. For instance, to buy something simultaneously in Japan, India, and the United Kingdom, you could use your e-cash simultaneously. If multiple banks are involved in the transaction, preventing double spending from occurring is extremely difficult. That is why post fact detection and punishment are relied upon by most of the systems. There are two steps involved in purchasing e-cash from an online currency server—setup of an account and having enough money in the account for purchase. To maintain anonymity or because some customers do not have a bank account, they might prefer to purchase e-cash with paper currency. Since customers need access and hence should be able to pay for both foreign services and local services, making the setup of an online account with a bank mandatory for the corresponding e-cash value may be considered overly restrictive for international use and multicurrency transactions. E-cash must be available in multiple currencies backed by several banks, to support access of services to the customer. A service provider in the respective local country could centrally accept tokens of various currencies and redeem them with the issuing banks/bodies. These funds could then be transferred to banks in the local country. A possible approach is to use a set of digital banks (like Visa), which serve as a clearinghouse for the various credit card issuing banks. The e-cash "note" has a random number generated by the e-cash software application. The bank authorizes this note by using its private key as a digital signature in exchange for the money debited from the customer's account and transmits the note to the customer. A "bank note" in effect is being issued by the network currency server, with a serial number and a dollar amount. The bank is committed, once it digitally signs, to back that note with its face value in real dollars. Because neither the payer (customer) nor the merchant (payee) can counterfeit the bank's digital signature (analogous to a watermark on paper currency), this method of generation is very secure. That the payment is valid can be verified by the payer and the payee, because each knows the bank's public key. The user is protected against false accusations and invasion of piracy, the bank against forgery, and the payee against the bank's refusal to honor the legitimate note. In practice the holder (of e-cash) opens an e-cash account at a digital bank (e.g., First Digital Bank) on the Internet. People can withdraw or deposit e-cash, using this account. Digital coins of required denomination are withdrawn from this online account. Random serial numbers are generated for these coins, and the blinding (random number) factor is additionally included. The account of the customer is debited for the respective amount. The bank uses its secret key (digital signature) to encode the blinding numbers. These authenticated coins are sent back to the customer, who finally removes the blinding factor that he or she introduced earlier. The bank has to guarantee their value because the serial numbers plus their signatures are now digital coins. Because there is complete anonymity in e-cash, it allows freedom of usage to buy illegal products such as drugs or pornographic material or to buy legal products or services. Also users can prove unequivocally that they did or did not make a particular payment.

With outsourcing becoming a global phenomenon, colossal cash transactions occur on a regular basis. Digital currency is also used for business transactions. Once the tokens are purchased, the e-cash software on the customer's computer stores digital money undersigned by a bank. At any shop accepting e-cash, the user can spend the digital money, without having to open an account there first or having to transmit credit card numbers. The software collects the necessary amount from the stored tokens, when used by the customer for payments. Typically transactions involving cash are bilateral or two-party (buyer and seller) transactions, whereby the seller checks the veracity of the note's digital signature by using the bank's public key. The merchant stores the digital currency on his machine, if satisfied with the payment, and deposits it later in the bank to redeem the face value of the note. Other than cash the transactions involving financial instruments are usually trilateral or three-party (buyer, seller, and bank) transactions, whereby the notes are sent to the merchant/supplier, who immediately sends them to the digital bank. The validity of these notes is verified by the bank, and that they have not been spent before. The amount of the merchant/supplier is credited, and in this case every note can be used only once.

Because it may be possible to make the copies of the e-cash, double spending becomes possible, forcing banks and merchants/suppliers to take extra precautions. Because of the potential of double spending, in many business situations, the bilateral transaction is not feasible, which is equivalent to bouncing a check. Banks must compare the note passed to it by the merchant against a database of spent notes to uncover double spending. Digital cash can also be protected, just as paper currency is identified by a unique serial number. Some form of registration is involved, so that all notes issued globally can be uniquely identified. In the online world, however, this method of matching notes with the central registry has problems. This method is simply too expensive for most systems which handle high volumes of micropayments. Constant checks and auditing logs and the problem of double spending often load the bank with added overhead activities.

E-Checks Working Mechanism

A way of creating value is through the availability of float, which is an important requirement for commerce, and electronic checks create float. Electronic checks are another form of electronic tokens. Many individuals and entities that might prefer to pay on credit or through some mechanism other than cash can be accommodated through electronic checks. Before they are able to write electronic checks, buyers must register with a third-party account server, and the account server acts as a billing service. To back checks may require a bank account or a credit card, and the registration procedure can vary depending on the particular account server. A buyer can contact sellers of goods and services, once registered. The buyer sends a check to the seller for a certain amount of money to complete a transaction. Using e-mail or other transport methods, these checks can be sent, and when deposited, the check authorizes the transfer of account balances from the account against which the check was drawn to the account to which the check was deposited. Just as a conventional paper check, the e-check method was deliberately created to work in much the same way. An electronic document will be issued by an account holder, and the document contains the name of the payer, the name of the financial institution, the payer's account number, the name of the payee, and the amount of the check. Most information is in uncoded form, like a paper number that authenticates the check as coming from the owner of the account. An e-check will need to be endorsed by the payee, again like a paper check, using another electronic signature before the check can be paid. Through electronic clearinghouses, properly signed and endorsed checks can be electronically exchanged between financial institutions, with the institutions using these endorsed checks as tender to settle accounts. In the case of e-checks, the technology works in the following manner—the seller presents the e-check to the accounting server for verification and payment, after the check has been received. Using the Kerberos authentication scheme, the accounting server verifies the digital signature on the check. An electronic check is a special kind of ticket created by the Kerberos system, and a user's digital signature is used to create one ticket—a check which the seller's digital endorsement transforms into another—an order to a bank computer to fund transfer. Successive layers of information are added by subsequent endorsers onto the tickets, precisely as a large number of banks may wind up stamping the back of the check along its journey through the system.

In order to reap the advantage of float, many companies are resorting to e-check. By charging the buyer or seller a transaction fee or a flat rate fee, the third-party accounting server can make money, or it can act as a bank and provide deposit accounts and make money on the deposit account pool. Easier acceptance can occur, because financial risk is assumed by the accounting server. By using multiple accounting servers, reliability and scalability are provided. To allow buyer and seller to "belong" to different domains, regions, or countries, there can be an interaccount server protocol. Clifford Neumann at the Information Sciences Institute developed a prototype electronic check system called "NetCheque." Independent of other applications, NetCheque will include software for writing and depositing checks and an application programming interface that will allow common functions to be called automatically when integrated with other programs. "Through use of suitable accounting server" software organizations can possibly start online "banks." These would accept paper checks or credit card payments and credit the customer's account for the same. Large organizations will be enabled by such accounting servers to pay bills and settle accounts with NetCheques written with their own banks, in effect integrating their own accounting system with the external financial hierarchy. NetCheque can be used as a resource management tool inside organizations, a form of an internal cash. For example, an account could be given to each user in an organization, and he or she could be allowed to use various resources and be billed for it. Using accounting mechanisms, organizations thus will be able to manage resources more effectively.

Smart Card

Since the early 1980s smart cards have been in existence and hold promise of secure transactions using existing infrastructure. Credit and debit cards and other card products enhanced with microprocessors and capable of holding more information than traditional magnetic stripes are called smart cards. Significantly greater amounts of data can be stored by the chip at its current state of development, and it is estimated to be 80 times more than a magnetic stripe. In countries such as France, Singapore, Japan, and Germany, smart card technology is widely used to pay for public phone calls, transportation, and shopper loyalty programs. In the United State the idea has taken longer to catch up, since a highly reliable and fairly inexpensive telecommunications system has favored the use of credit and debit cards.

Such electronic purses known as debit cards/electronic money replace conventional cash. To maintain and expand their services, financial institutions worldwide are developing new methods to meet the needs of increasingly sophisticated and technically smart customers, as well as to meet the emerging payment needs of electronic commerce. As customers demand payment and financial service products that are user friendly, convenient, and reliable, traditional credit cards are fast evolving into smart cards. An enhancement of the existing card services and/or addition of new services is the relationship-based smart card, which a financial institution delivers to its customers via chip-based card or other device. Included in these new services may be access to multiple financial accounts, value-added marketing programs, or other information cash holders may want to store on their cards.

Smart cards address each individual's specific financial and personal requirements. Cardholder information including name, birth date, personal shopping preferences, and actual purchase records are stored by enhanced credit cards. To increase shopper loyalty, this information will enable merchants to accurately track customer behavior and develop personal programs accordingly. Far greater options will be offered to customers by relationship-based products—access to multiple accounts such as debit, credit, investments, or stored value for e-cash—on one card or an electronic device. Cash access, bill payment, balance inquiry, and funds transfer for selected accounts are some of the other functions. *Multiple interface devices such as automated teller machines (ATMs), screen phones, personal computers, personal digital assistants (PDA), and interactive TVs are compatible with smart cards, thereby allowing usage in various circumstances and locations.* All these services are being incorporated by companies into a personalized banking relationship for each customer.

Smart Cards—Advantages

Despite all their flexibility, the need for a financial instrument to replace cash still remains. Smart cards embedded with programmable microchips can store information about the customer's credit balance and serve as electronic purses. Such are offered by banks, credit card companies, and even government institutions. They may be used for any need including buying food, payment of subway fares, etc. The working of the smart card is fairly simple. It may be topped with a currency amount using an ATM or through an inexpensive special phone. That the card is authentic is verified by the vending machine/card reader, and whether there is enough money available for making the purchase. The value of the purchase is deducted from the balance existing in the smart card and added to the e-cash box in the vending machine. The vending machine displays the remaining balance on the card, or the balance can be checked at an ATM or with a balance-reading machine. Fumbling for change or small bills and waiting for the credit card purchase to be approved will be virtually eliminated by electronic purses in a busy store or a rush hour toll booth. With a prepaid card that "remembers" each transaction, customers can pay for rides and calls. The smart card can be topped up with more money, once the balance on the electronic purse is depleted. The receipts can be collected periodically in person or, more likely in the case of vendor, be telephoned and transferred to a bank account. The cards have been relatively expensive, although the technology has been available for over a decade.

The cards today cost less than $1, and the special telephones that the customers could install at home to recharge the cards are projected to cost as little as $50, and a simple card reader would cost a merchant less than $200.

In the case of smart cards, their benefits will rely on the ubiquity of devices called smart card readers that can communicate with the chip on the smart card. These devices can also support a variety of key management methods, in addition to the reading from and writing to the smart cards. Elements of a personal computer, point-of-sale terminal, and a phone are combined by some smart card readers to allow customers to quickly transact financial transactions without leaving their homes. Color-coded function keys further enhance efficiency of the card reader, which can be programmed to perform the most frequently used operations in a single key stroke. Via an RS 232 serial interface, it can communicate with a full range of transaction automation systems, including computers and electronic cash registers (ECRs). The prominence of card readers in the form of screen phones is increasing. It has been long stated by proponents of screen phone applications that consumer familiarity with phones gives screen phones an entree that computers cannot match. Some screen phones have a four-line screen with a magnetic stripe card reader and a phone keypad to use in complex transactions. Buying users are prompted by phone through transactions using menus patterned after those found on automated teller machines.

For accelerated development, the development system of most smart card readers comes with precoded modules.

Attempts are being made by banks to customize smart cards, offering a menu of services similar to those that come up on the ATM screens. Banks may link up with health care providers, telephone companies, retailers, and airlines to offer frequent shopping and flyer programs and other services, as done in the case of credit cards. Relationship-based cards are credit based, and settlement occurs at the end of the billing cycle.

Example—EDI Usage by Sears Roebuck Organization

Of relative and perceived values of different trading units.

To pay its suppliers, Sears, Roebuck and Company's merchandise group began using automated clearing house (ACH) credit transfers in 1983. To transmit payment instructions and remittance information to its banks, Sears uses EDI format standards. The data is converted by banks to ACH payment formats, which are then processed. If the supplier of Sears requests that remittance data be sent separately, rather than with the payment, Sears transmits the remittance data to the trading partner through the same network used for exchanging other business data with that trading partner. Sears' bank then processes the ACH transfer. Some banks provide VAN-like services with payment service to their corporate customers to facilitate the use of financial EDI.

SLOWDOWN AND OUTSOURCING

Chapter 15

The Slowdown Scenario

The market dynamics of rise and fall, an unending cycle.

Economic Turmoil

As the recession of 2008 deepened, with events like the Wall Street collapse and bankruptcy of gigantic financial institutions, John McCarthy, vice president and principal analyst with the U.S. firm Forrester Research, said that the magnitude of the crisis was so huge that all previous studies, projections, and surveys had become redundant.

The year 2008 witnessed mayhem in financial markets all over the world, with a deep economic recession in the United States. Wall Street, greatly sought after by the investment banking profession, lost its gloss late Sunday, September 21, 2008, with news of Goldman Sachs and Morgan Stanley, two of the street's institutions that had not succumbed to subprime crisis till then, getting changed into commercial banks that would be governed by the U.S. Federal Reserve. The recession caused the most gigantic speed breaker in the Indian IT industry. Corporations started taking all measures, leaving nothing to chance in their drive to trim expense flab. As the looming dark clouds of economic dilemma spread over the horizon, and as sprightly apathy melted, giving rise to despair and gloom, the question arose as to how the Indian IT offshore services industry would contend with the challenging times. The subprime scam and the catastrophe with institutions like Lehman Brothers, Goldman Sachs, and Morgan Stanley had magnified the problem.

The collapse of gigantic firms such as Bear Sterns, Lehman Brothers, Merrill Lynch, and the near tumble of the insurance giant AIG, with exposure to derivatives linked to housing and credit sent the alarm bells ringing across the globe.

The impact of the downturn was quite visible and plummeted almost all world economies into the throes of recession. The outsourcing economy was not spared either. These organizations had large-scale outsourcing business investments worldwide. As they went down, they shook the outsourcing world at its very moorings.

Indices Nosedive Worldwide—Growth Forecasts Downgraded

Money, just a means, not an end.

The global economic mayhem of 2008 dragged China's economic growth down from double digits to single digits for the first time since 2002. "The Chinese economy is slowing. But China will not follow the United States. and much of Europe into the economic abyss," said Andy Rothman, a CLSA economist in Shanghai. Growth forecasts were widely downgraded across the rest of Asia Pacific. According to polls, for 7 out of 12 economies, growth in 2009 was similar to growth in 2008. New Zealand was already in recession, and Singapore was not immune to it. Investment bank Merrill Lynch revised its growth forecast for 2008 in Asia ex-Japan from 8% to 7.7%, and 2009 growth at 7.3%, down from a previous call of 7.8%. Stubborn inflation pressure was to be contended with, although central banks did look like providing support for consumer spending. To support their economies reeling under recession, countries like China, Taiwan, New Zealand, and Australia cut interest rates. India was also struggling with double-digit inflation.

The findings of a Dun and Bradstreet survey stated that business sentiment had plummeted to a six-year low. With the advent of 2009, Indian corporate optimistic level plunged to its lowest in the past six years as consumer spending remained curtailed, bank lending subdued, and companies' expansion plans were put on hold in the wake of the global financial slowdown. Dun and Bradstreet's business optimism index stated that optimism level in the Indian economy for the January–March 2009 quarter had dropped to the lowest in 24 quarters. Composite business optimism index dropped to 95.7 for the first quarter of 2009, the lowest since 2002 when it was introduced. Compared to the previous quarter, the index dropped by a record of 31.1%, and considering a year-to-year basis, the business optimism index fell 43%, the steepest fall ever. For net profits, the optimism index fell to a six and a half year low of 23%, which was almost a 38 percentage point decline compared to Q4 of 2008. New orders index at a seven-year low of 26 % had decreased by 42 percentage points from Q4 of 2008, and the sales volume optimism index dropped 45 percentage points to 23%, the lowest since Q1 of 2002. Selling prices optimism index at 3% was a decrease of 30 percentage points from Q4 of 2008, and for the January–March 2009 quarter, employees' optimism index at 21%, the lowest in four years, was a 12 percentage point decline compared with Q4 2008. Inventory levels optimism index declined by 27 percentage points from Q4 of 2008 and stood at 9%.

The survey of Dun and Bradstreet was based on its sample of companies selected at random across a cross section of industries including basic goods, capital goods, intermediate goods, consumer durables, consumer nondurables, and services sectors. Respondents answered questions regarding six parameters, which included volume of sales, net profit, selling prices, new orders, inventories, and employees. Their expectations regarding the parameters were recorded in the survey; an increase, decrease, or no change in the ensuing quarter compared to the same quarter in the previous year. Calculation of individual indices was then done by subtracting the percentage of respondents expecting decreases from those expecting increases. Compared to previous quarter's levels, all optimism indices decreased. Intermediate goods and basic goods sectors in particular were most pessimistic, while all sectors registered bearish sentiments. The rapid fall in demand for finished goods was likely to hamper the demand for basic and intermediate goods.

Industrial outlook survey (a survey of corporate and businesses on the "quarter ahead" expectations)—business expectations index on outlook for October–December 2008 declined by 2.6% over the corresponding previous quarter. Only 33.7% of respondents were optimistic compared with 50.2% in the previous quarter. The index is derived from net responses, and there was decline in corporate confidence for major indicators such as overall business situation, financial situation, finance availability, production, order books, and profit margins. The survey pointed to negative sentiments and profit margins significantly.

Forecasts Downgraded in India

The sine curve of tide and time.

Although the Indian IT offshore industry had circumvented major financial speed breakers twice in its three-decade history—the first one in 2000 during the Y2K scenario and the second after the dotcom bust in 2002—the last one in 2009 had a severe impact.

Forecasters pointed to further signs of economic downturn as the Reserve Bank of India (RBI) report estimated a 7.7% growth for 2008–2009. In June 2008, the fourth round of the survey was conducted, and in September 2008 the fifth round, and between these two surveys the forecast of real GDP growth for 2008–2009 was downgraded from 7.9% to 7.7%. Industry's sectoral growth rate forecasts were downgraded from 7.5% to 7%. As the slowdown hit, to counter the crisis the RBI introduced cuts in reserve requirement, releasing liquidity to the extent of Rs. INR 1 thousand billion (US$20 billion), to instill more confidence in banks. High priority continued to be accorded to price stability, well-anchored inflation expectations, and orderly conditions in financial markets to promote continuous growth according to the central bank monetary policy stance. *There was a more than 25% crash in stock markets in India, with more severe crashes worldwide, leading to weakening of the Indian rupee and freezing of its global credit markets.*

Keeping in view the gigantic problem, the Indian industry body NASSCOM revised its growth forecast from 30% down to 21% to 24%. "In the near term growth rate is likely to come down. *Many organizations like NASSCOM, Forrester, Gartner, and Tholons, revised their industry growth forecasts as the financial turmoil assumed global proportions.* Software industry growth forecasts have been revised downwards for 2008–2009, yet some analysts felt the industry would meet the $60 billion target by 2010." The financial crisis in the United States certainly impacted the domestic Indian IT industry because a major part of the business comes from the United States. However, by how much was not too clear. The July 2008 growth rate forecast of NASSCOM was between 21% and 24% reaching $50 billion in FY08–09. "*Over the long term the growth potential of the IT–BPO industry remains intact,*" *said Ashok Soota, chairman and managing director of Mindtree, a Bangalore-based IT consultancy.*

With the economic turmoil having taken a heavy toll on most sectors of India's economy, the business and economic outlook indices were at an all-time low, according to a study. Indices nose-dived, with the net business outlook index down 50 index points to stand at an abysmal 6 index points, and the employment figure down 30 points. The employment outlook index for the January–March 2009 quarter stood at 34 index points according to team lease services quarterly report. The employment index is calculated based on the difference between the proportion of respondents who report an increase in hiring needs and those who report a decline in hiring needs over the next three months. Except telecom, there was a decrease in index points of all sectors covered. Telecom and IT enabled services (ITES) had index points of 60 and 53 points, respectively. Maximum decline was seen in the infrastructure sector by 132 points, and telecom sector declined the least by 16 points. The report stated a decrease in hiring across all functions, especially at the entry and the junior level, while an increase in hiring at the middle and the senior levels was indicated. The attrition rate was under 15% for the other sectors, while it remained the highest in the IT and the ITES industry despite job insecurity and not so positive sentiments. The employment outlook index points of all Indian cities has dropped, with Mumbai registering the maximum decrease of index points by 87 points, followed by Kolkata by 69 points.

IT growth rate was cut further by NASSCOM, which seemingly downgraded Indian IT industry's growth projections. NASSCOM president Mr. Som Mittal said, "We had not taken into account the present economic consideration while arriving at the growth projections for the current fiscal. With the global economy taking a new turn, it is possible that the projections may be furthered lowered."

According to a report of the research firm Tholons, the growth and margins of IT firms, though impacted for the first two to three quarters of 2009, expected profits to rise subsequently. Over medium to long term, there will be a strong demand for outsourcing because opportunities and potential are still very much evident in the market, in spite of the prevailing uncertainty. Though clients were cautious as

2008 heaped commotion, the report affirmed that the coming years held a bright future for the outsourcing industry, making it more mature and resilient. Some analysts were of the view that 2009 could prove to be a watershed moment for the global outsourcing industry if a proper approach toward outsourcing was adopted in terms of focus, prudence, and adaptability.

Indian companies registered limited growth in 2009, with some new ventures and businesses in spite of the prevailing uncertainties in the markets that account for most of their revenue. Yet it was widely viewed that that the IT–BPO sector would have to face and surmount the greatest challenge to date in its history. The credit crunch caused companies to renegotiate existing contracts, tap new verticals and geographies, and offer new services. Companies also have to contend with the fluctuating rupee. To rake in cash, companies could offshore to India for top-end skills, although the outlook for 2009 was challenging. Initially it was felt that the recession was more or less virtual for IT firms, and it would not adversely affect India's $50 billion IT–BPO sector.

The economic downturn which commenced in September 2008 in the United States made one analyst say that the events that brought disaster to the Wall Street would also cause the demise of the golden age of offshoring for India.

As the economic slowdown continued, business confidence in India touched an all-time low because of the liquidity crunch and high-interest-rate regime, according to a survey by the Federation of Indian Chambers of Commerce and Industry (FICCI). The survey of 350 companies revealed that the business confidence index fell to the lowest-ever level of 55.9 during the April–June quarter of 2008–2009. Moreover, the survey found that the small and medium enterprises (SMEs) were the hardest hit because of the financial downturn. The survey revealed that interest cost of SMEs stood at 5.5% in the survey period as against 3.5% year over year. "In contrast, the interest cost of large companies has gone up by 1.5% to 2.5% over the last one year," a FICCI release said. The cost of borrowing has gone up due to interest rates rise, thereby denting Indian business confidence. The cash crunch was forcing companies to reconsider or postpone some of their proposed investments in projects. "Amongst those that are going ahead with their scheduled investment plans, a clear discernable trend of dependence on internal accruals to support investments is seen," a FICCI release added. The necessity for government to formulate productivity-linked benefits and incentives for SMEs was felt by more that 80% of the respondents. The Reserve Bank of India's monetary tightening measure for inflation control has lead to banks increasing their prime lending rates from a range of 10% to 10.5% in 2007 to around 13% to 13.5% in 2008.

Indian IT outsourcing businesses continued growing even during the slowdown period and are expected to touch $100 billion by 2012. Electronics and computer software Export Promotion Council (ESC), an autonomous body under the Ministry of Communications and IT, government of India, has been encouraging Indian IT companies, particularly SMEs, to participate in various IT exhibitions.

Economic Situation in the United Kingdom during Slowdown

As euphoria grips the globe.

In Britain, the economic downturn of 2008 took a heavy toll, with a bankruptcy in every five minutes. After recession set in, the slowdown played havoc, with either a British resident or business being declared insolvent every five minutes or so, according to an advocacy group. There was an overwhelming increase in the number of people seeking debt help, and Credit Action claimed that 104 properties were repossessed daily, and average household debt was £9,500. Capital Economics managing director Roger Bootle says that the era of easy credit is actually over. "*The financial landscape will never be the same again.* We have passed through a major event which is on par of much of what occurred in the 1920s and 30s leading up to the Great Depression."

As a pointer, the economic slowdown even delayed funerals in Britain. Payments need to be made in advance for funerals to be carried out, and some poor families were left with no choice but to wait for over two months before receiving government help paying for funerals. Undertakers hit by the financial crisis refused to extend credit for funerals.

Budget Squeeze and IT Spending Declines

As people and organizations play for short positions.

Global firms getting sucked in the economic quicksand took a turn for the worse with the filing of bankruptcy by Lehman Brothers. Hiring, expansion plans, and earning prospects of companies were severely impacted. The $3.41 trillion market was witnessing its first fall since 2001 after the dotcom bubble burst. Underperformance of the IT sector on the bourses and slowdown in U.S. and European markets, which account for almost 80% of the cash inflow of all Indian IT companies, increased financial fears. Also, Indian IT firms draw about 40% of their revenues from the banking, financial services, and insurance (BFSI) vertical, which had been hit the hardest. The financial storm resulted in cost cutting by firms, renegotiation in pricing, and fewer and smaller-sized contracts. Deals to the tune of Rs. 550–700 crores (INR 5.5–7 billion) annually were outsourced by Lehman Brothers to IT firms including major firms like Tata Consultancy Services, Infosys, and Wipro. The adverse effect continued with the buyout of Merrill Lynch by Bank of America, with the consolidation resulting in fewer outsourced deals and further lag in deal making. IT firms had varying revenue exposure to Lehman, ranging from 1% to 3% for some companies and 13% for Eclerx, a knowledge process outsource company, for FY09. With no respite from the financial turmoil at hand and with analysts feeling that the bottom of the economic downturn could still be a couple of quarters away, the problem was further complicated. GDP forecasts had been aggressive, and the high exposure of Indian IT firms to financial services had impacted them significantly. "Furthermore, our U.S. strategists believe that deleveraging of financials could lead to around $5 trillion in assets being sold. Thus we should also brace for the second-level impact, which should come from other parts of the economy slowing down." The weakening of Indian rupee against the U.S. dollar was probably the only favorable factor for Indian IT firms, because they earn in dollars and spend in rupees.

With the deepening of recession there were drastic cuts in IT spending as companies grappled with squeezed budgets and decreasing revenues. A Forrester Research survey mentioned that contracts between outsourcing clients and vendors were being renegotiated at lower rates. The financial services sector slowdown hit technology companies because the sector accounted for a quarter of technology outlays. The surge in interest rates has also been another dampening factor according to Snorek.

As IT budgets got slashed, tech vendors lost billions in revenues. It was estimated that technology companies including Intel and Microsoft that were not impacted in the initial months of recession lost billions of dollars in sales in 2009 as the slowdown caught up with them. IT spending had declined 7% in 2009. "Business kind of stopped dead in the last two weeks," said Snorek, whose firm owns Microsoft and Intel stock among more than $100 billion in assets, speaking of those initial dark days. Consumer spending growth had slowed and corporate budgets squeezed. Software maker SAP AG said orders started dwindling in September 2008. People sentiment was "I have no idea if we are going to have a global meltdown, so I am not going to buy anything right now."

The average deal size almost halved in 2008 compared to 2007 numbers, and it was anticipated that deal sizes would be depressed due to lack of fresh capital coming from the private equity (PE) route. Analysts felt that SME vendors would be preferred by the client sector. "With financial institutions such as Lloyds, TSB/HBOS, and Bank of America/Merrill Lynch merging, service providers will also find themselves bidding against incumbent transnational rivals like IBM, Accenture, and HPEDS for several large-scale integration contracts valued anywhere between $500 million to $1 billion over five years" according to an analyst.

Adding of systems in sectors such as retail banking, consumer banking, cards, and corporate banking had been stopped for the time being. The oscillations that occurred during the economic discord led to greater uncertainty and a cautious decision making cycle by various outsourcing customers that Indian IT vendors served. As the industry went through enormous suffering, it remained to be seen when it finally would emerge rejuvenated, giving rise to uninterrupted growth and value enhancement for stakeholders. For a world surmounting crisis, sustaining cost competitiveness became a dominant driver, and offshore IT services had to offer businesses in the developed world the ability to do more with less. Aggressive corporate cost cutting was resorted to, and India's third-largest IT firm slashed its marketing expenditure and put on hold purchase of any software not considered essential.

With the global economic downturn increasing cost pressure, slicing margins, and heightening credit crunch, many companies were forced to not only take another look at expenses but also redraft the rule compendium of cost cutting. The reality was harsh, as world's prominent economies simultaneously underwent excruciating pain.

Forrester's study released just before the economic crisis set in stated that, while 40% of the large businesses had cut back on IT spending, 90% of the companies in the media and entertainment vertical were not reducing IT spending. Mr. McCarthy said that these sectors could not match the financial services' IT spending. The extensive survey was conducted across North America and Europe.

Various sectors like India's largest carmaker Maruti Suzuki, two-wheeler leader Hero Honda, and top private Telco Bharti Airtel slashed IT budgets. "In this environment the whole focus for every project was on reducing cost and contribute to the bottom line," said Maruti Suzuki India IT head Rajesh Uppal. Compared to the Indian IT sector growth of 25% in 2008, the 2009 growth rate was about 13%. The focus now was on short-term IT projects with significant revenue flow while long-term projects or those requiring new technology were being stalled. "Companies are aiming to reduce their capex by exploring hosted applications, wherein they have to pay as they consume without making any upfront investments in procuring new servers and applications," said Mr. Madanmohan. "On the OpEx (operational expenditure) side, things are stable because running operations is critical; however, new technology investments such as SOA are being held back," Maruti's India IT head Mr. Uppal said, despite the known service-oriented architecture (SOA) advantages like business applications integration, applications delivery as a service to business, and increased IT systems flexibility.

In 2008, around $16 billion revenue was recorded by the Indian market for domestic IT, which included hardware as well as BPO services. Indian and U.S. companies alike were bringing down their operational costs by 10% to 30% in the aftermath of the global downturn. To rein in revenue, companies were exploring IT projects with significant cost savings and reconsidering any new investments in procuring computer hardware. "We are looking at cost saving projects in the area of inventory management," said Mr. Uppal. "Server replacements could be held, and we are looking at handling applications with the current capacity," he added. "We expect the IT budget to be flat in 2009," he said.

Example—Microsoft CEO's View

The impact far and wide.

As the recession deepened, Microsoft also was not immune to the global crisis, according to Steve Microsoft CEO Ballmer, for the global storm hit consumer spending and business spending of companies, and Microsoft was no exception.

According to Ballmer, "Financial issues are going to affect both business spending and consumer spending and particularly spending by the financial services industry. We have a lot of business with the corporate sector as well as with the consumer sector, and whatever happens economically will certainly effect itself on Microsoft." *Ballmer further said, "I think one has to anticipate that no company is immune to these issues," but declined to be more specific.* It was expected that an 8% rise in revenue to a little under $15 billion would be registered by Redmond in its first quarter ending September 2008. "There are parts of our every business which are probably 'safe' in the sense that it is not like our business would go to zero," he said. "On the other hand when businesses have less money—they can borrow less money, they can spend less money—that can't be good. When consumers feel the economic pinch, house prices come down. That can't be good," Ballmer said. As a result of Ballmer's remarks, it was felt by investors that Microsoft's revenues would decrease. "By extension these fears have worked their way over to SAP," a trader said. Despite the $700 billion bank bailout plan rejection, Ballmer was optimistic that the situation could soon be stabilized with the help of Congress. "I have to believe that some of the issues also face the European banks, and I trust that the European central bank will be as intelligent as it needs to be around that," he said. The subprime scam, bad mortgage debts, and deepening recession were causing U.S. banks and insurers to seek bailouts from the government to circumvent a financial system collapse.

Example—Nortel's Bankruptcy

As some go down fighting.

The economic hurricane caused Nortel's bankruptcy, among others. But top Indian IT outsourcing firms like TCS, Wipro Technologies, and Sasken Technologies denied any significant impact on their revenues because of Nortel's bankruptcy, citing low exposure to the business from the beleaguered company. In its report, investment firm JP Morgan said that the impact on Sasken could be the most, because Nortel was one of its top three customers. "Sasken is likely to be impacted most as Nortel is a top three account for Sasken," Ehud Gelblum, analyst with JP Morgan said in his report. "We believe that Norten is a top ten account for Wipro, but contributes only about 1 to 2% of revenues. For Infosys and TCS, Nortel is not a top ten account in our view, and therefore we estimate it contributes less than 1%. Wipro which is India's third biggest software firm and a big regional outsourcing vendor said that Nortel owes around $15 million to the company. Wipro could see business decline from Nortel, but we would expect the overall impact to be small (less than 0.5% on earning per share)," Mr. Gelblum said. Meanwhile, Wipro added that it currently delivers some system integration projects for Nortel, but sees no significant impact. "Wipro is also a partner to Nortel for system integration work in Asia and India, and we expect no impact to our clients. Nortel is a valued client, and we have a longstanding relationship with them. We are in constant dialogue with them to monitor and assess the situation," said Manish Dugar, CFO of Wipro Technologies. Meanwhile the Nortel bankruptcy was not expected to have a significant impact on the financials of TCS, Infosys, and Wipro. "We believe it is a concern of the Indian IT sector as it reflects the weak health of the telecom OEM sector, in our view. Wipro with 10% exposure to telecom OEM, could be hurt more than TCS and Infosys as a result," Mr. Gelblum said. A Sasken official said that Nortel contributed less than 10% of the company's revenues for the quarter ended December 31, 2008. "Nortel currently holds less than 10% of the outstanding shares in our company. Nortel has been in touch with the company and based on the information available to us as of now, we believe that the business will continue as usual for Sasken," Sasken said. Nortel, a Toronto-based company had more than $1 billion in assets and debt, according to the Chapter 11 filing of its U.S. subsidiary.

Example—Satyam Saga—Credibility Loss

And those who do not play by the rules.

The unblemished reputation of the Indian IT industry received a jolt with Satyam's loss of credibility. Cooking of books by Satyam promoters and duping of stakeholders was a blot on the Indian outsourcing industry's credibility. Although quick government action restored stakeholder, client, and employee confidence to an extent, it took some time for the liquidity crisis and business continuity issues to be resolved as Mahindra Group took over Satyam. Root causes of the fraud perpetrated on stakeholders needed to be eliminated and the tarnished reputation repaired. A negative ramification was the denting of client confidence, thereby leading to greater diligence and documentation in outsourcing contract negotiations. Despite the cloud of doubt because of the seriousness of fraud perpetrated on stakeholders, the $50 billion industry would not get derailed by Satyam's credibility loss. Actions of the government and its appointed board to tackle the Satyam crisis was supported by NASSCOM. To restore financial veracity, NASSCOM advised member companies to adopt the highest levels of corporate governance and not have an eye on the clients and employees of Satyam. The Indian IT industry has been built by outstanding entrepreneurs, and of all industries it has done the most to raise India's image at international forums. As a consequence, a majority of Fortune 1000 companies apart from others have reposed confidence in their Indian partners by entrusting data, applications, and processes. Despite the unfortunate Satyam occurrence, the support received from many clients infused confidence in the industry which would prevail over the crisis. Analysts feel the Satyam saga would not have a long-term impact on Indian IT industry. Though the Satyam incident was a shock to the hitherto untarnished credibility of Indian IT industry, corrective government action sent the right signals for restoring investor confidence. The

IT industry reeling under recession felt that fraud by one bad apple should not taint the entire industry, although it should not be construed that everything is above board in the industry. To avoid further occurrence of any such unpalatable situations, key stakeholders should ensure strong additional due diligence. Highest levels of disclosure and an extremely transparent manner of functioning should be adopted by the industry. The Indian government had been proactive in handling the Satyam incident, and one did not see any long-term impact of the unfortunate occurrence on Indian industry's image. The Indian offshore model, with its inherent fundamental strengths, remains unchanged along with the value proposition that global customers have come to rely on. However, it would be naive to just assume that all is well without adequate scrutiny of financial and governance aspects. The Indian offshore model offers a combination of cost advantage and quality value proposition not easily available elsewhere in the world. However, there is need for greater transparency by all service providers offshore, near shore, or on shore. To avoid future disasters, the industry should have nothing to hide and should openly disclose the governance structure, financial management, and internal controls. To leverage the outsourcing model, service providers should ensure that their internal controls and enterprise risk management are in order. For financial and internal controls audit, vendors should consider third-party auditors instead of the regular ones and make results available to clients and prospects.

Satyam BPO CFO Venkatesh Roddam put in his resignation papers. His departure came at a time when the overall IT–BPO industry was impacted by the U.S. economic mayhem. Sources said that his exit had not created a leadership vacuum because a successor had been identified. "Venkatesh Roddam had expressed his desire to pursue other interests outside Satyam BPO. We have accepted his resignation and are in the process of making alternate arrangements," said Satyam computer services chief financial officer V. Srinivas. During the interim period, the company's chief operating officer (COO), Vijay Rangineni, would be in charge. Close on the heels of Venkatesh Roddam's exit, it was learnt that Satyam BPO's CFO M. Satyanarayana was also slated to retire. Satyam BPO was earlier known as Nipuna. It was then a separate legal entity, but Satyam bought out its external shareholders and rechristened it Satyam BPO. Satyam computer services was the fourth-largest IT firm in India before loss of credibility and the resignation of Venkatesh Roddam closely followed Shailesh Shah's exit as chief strategy officer of Satyam. "Roddam was very aggressive in terms of getting the BPO arm's business in line. He was the key reason for the growth of the BPO business of Satyam," said a source close to the development. Insiders were of the view that the conservative top management was not comfortable with Roddam's aggression. Reports of the company reorganizing the composition of its board to streamline management and operations were forthcoming. It intended to tap the sports vertical for revenue. With the multimillion Federation International de Football Association (FIFA)'s world cup deal already in its kitty, the company was making a bid for other sporting events. The company was upbeat on the growing IT opportunities in sports and was eyeing $20 million revenue from the sports vertical according to Sridhar Maturi, head of sports marketing–global marketing and communications at Satyam. Revenue from Satyam BPO for the first quarter ended June 30, 2008, was over Rs. 48.97 crores (INR 489.7 million), and the company registered a loss of Rs. 21.9 crores (INR 219 million) in the same period, after which loss of credibility of Satyam, manipulation of books, and serious fraud perpetrated on stakeholders hit the headlines. To acquire Satyam BPO, outsourcing arm of troubled Satyam Computer Services, ESSAR group's outsourcing arm was set to make a bid. "Satyam BPO's international clients and its presence in telecom, banking, and financial services make it an attractive target," said one person familiar with the matter. A top Aegis executive confirmed the interest of Aegis BPO in acquiring Satyam BPO. The company said, "As a group we constantly keep looking at growth opportunities. We would not like to comment on any specific transaction." The plan to acquire came at time when various companies were sizing up parts of the company which had been in deep trouble after admission of Rs. 7,000 crore fraud by its former chairman, which included cooking of books and inflation of profits for years. Satyam BPO, with an employee strength between 3,500 and 4,000, serviced clients like telecom firms Bellsouth and Verizon, construction equipment firm Caterpillar, and drug maker GlaxoSmithKline. Formerly called Nipuna Services, Satyam BPO, a wholly owned arm of Satyam, was being eyed by Aegis BPO, which had a revenue of about $450 million and had been on an acquisition spree, buying 11 companies in the last four years. Aegis BPO said that it is the largest Indian BPO provider with a significant presence in telecom, banking, and financial services sectors. Some of the acquisitions the company made included Bermuda-based BPO firm Global Vantage, the global BPO of Bharti Teltech, and AOL's BPO arm. To put things in order, the Indian government intervened by getting rid of Satyam's discredited board and replacing them with a new board of directors. Satyam had about 53,000 employees. The new board members said that a merger and an asset sale are some of the options in front of it.

It was being presumed that out of top Indian IT players, Infosys Technologies might benefit the most from Satyam's loss of credibility. Clients were aware of the credibility and reputation of Infosys as a company with high corporate governance standards. The United States listing of Infosys was also a point in its favor. Infosys stock had ended higher despite Ramalinga Raju's confession about manipulating the books. "The senior management of Infosys had come out quite aggressively in the media on maintaining high corporate governance standards," pointed out Ascendia consulting principal analyst Alok Shende. Infosys' pricing was 10% to 15% higher than Satyam's rates, and this could be a hitch according to some analysts who felt that TCS could reap maximum mileage. "It is not going to be as easy as that to say any one vendor will benefit. TCS has probably the largest overlap of clients. General Electric (GE), General Motors, and Citigroup are all clients of TCS as well as Satyam. Citigroup was also a client of Infosys but it is small," said an analyst with foreign brokerage. GE was looking for discounted rates, but Infosys, not willing to compromise on its billing rates, stopped servicing GE, which thereafter moved more work to Satyam. Other than Infosys and TCS, U.S.-headquartered India-based Cognizant Technology could also benefit from the situation. The U.S. domicile status of Cognizant could prove more favorable compared to the Indian domicile status of Infosys according to overseas brokerage Stifel, Nicolaus, and Company Inc. report. "In e-mails to employees, management is already highlighting its U.S. listed status, and compliance with Sarbanes–Oxley laws," according to a report from brokerage firm CLSA. Wipro had asked its salespersons to resort to aggressive messaging to clients, informing them of Wipro's readiness to take on operations running at Satyam, according to CLSA. Some analysts felt that IBM and Accenture would be the greatest gainers because they had a significant offshore presence. IBM has around 75,000 employees in India and Accenture around 35,000. "Best positioned to benefit from such a situation, we believe are the large global, well known MNCs like ACN (Accenture) and IBM. We consider them of tier-1 calibre in terms of offshore capabilities but their size, status, brand, global reputation and high level client relationships (particularly ACN) differentiate them, in our view, and will make them more attractive to worried clients than even the tier-1 offshore firms like Infy and WIT (Wipro)," said an analyst at Stifel Nicolaus. IBM and Accenture could benefit the most because of their large size, established reputation, and brand value, which will put worried clients to rest, according to some analysts. The Indian government appointed a new board of directors at Satyam Computer Services to ensure business continuity and to protect employees, clients, and investors' interests. The board of directors consisted of HDFC chairman Deepak Parekh, former NASSCOM president Kiran Karnik, and former securities appellate tribunal chief C. Achuthan. "By acting in this bold and coordinated manner, the government has sent the right signals to the global community and set an example of what governments can do to protect stakeholder interests while ensuring strict adherence to the rule of law," NASSCOM president Som Mittal said. NASSCOM said that, to prevent Satyam's kind of incidents from happening again, it intended to work with the government and identify new policies that could be instituted. "It is imperative, however, that thorough investigations are completed and all facts ascertained before deciding on what further action is required by all parties concerned," the IT–BPO association said in a statement. The appointment of the new board at Satyam by the Indian government was lauded by analysts who termed it as a step in the right direction.

Examples—Frills Cost Cutting in the IT and BPO Sector

Chips, cheap as potatoes, someday.

IT–BPO and financial services companies, along with other sectors resorted to cost-cutting measures. With fingers crossed, Indian corporations added unprecedented don'ts to their list. Wipro CEO Azim Premji, in an internal letter, asked employees to curtail expenditures.

Deutsche Bank had issued instructions to its employees to seek approvals of respective business unit heads for travels. Across the whole of Asia the decision had been implemented, according to sources. This move was confirmed by an executive, wherein the travel policy required approval from COOs, and at times Asia head, before traveling. Five-star hotel luncheons, off-site meetings abroad, and business-class travel were commonly done away with.

Companies slashed employee cab drops, business-class travel was done away with, and refreshment coupons to employees for guest entertainment was stopped to curtail expenditures. Chocolates, toffees, mints, and topnotch brands of mineral water were no longer served for employees at the office. A leading BPO in Gurgaon, India, stopped providing travel facility to its BPO employees beyond a certain distance from the office during day shifts.

Color printers were no longer used; unnecessary software was not bought any more. Restrictions on the use of printers, air conditioners, and subscriptions of newspapers and magazines were placed.

Executives in a large IT company working overtime, who could earlier get a cab as per their needs, now needed at least three other peers to get dropped back home.

A leading Indian bank had grounded business-class travel for its entire investment banking division within or outside the country, at least for the next one year.

*Switching off the lights when leaving the room, domestic offsites, video conferencing, and black and white printing only if necessary were introduced according to Charul Madan, partner of head-hunting firm Executive Acces*s.

Moody's Estimates on Outsourcing to India

Despite U.S. President Barack Obama coming down heavily against outsourcing, Moody's maintained that India would continue to remain a top outsourcing destination. "India will remain a top outsourcing destination because of its tech-savvy and English-proficient urban workforce whose wages are much lower than their western counterparts," Moody's economy.com economist Sherman Chan said. She added that India's outsourcing industry will definitely be impacted by the financial slowdown, with the weakening in demand for IT support or telemarketing services. After the global economy rebounds, the outsourcing industry will recover well, although gradually, because of caution on the part of businesses regarding investment plans, she said. On being asked whether an increase in developed countries' domestic industry protectionism could impact Indian outsourcing badly, she said, "I don't think businesses leave India mainly because of protectionist sentiment, a more likely reason is that activity is being scaled back in light of a slowing economy." *The $40 billion Indian software and BPO industry, mainly driven by outsourcing, draws 60% of its revenue from the United States.*

India and Other Countries as the Outsourcing Destination

Some are of the view that the U.S. crisis is an opportunity for Indian IT. The worldwide financial turmoil has forced companies to think about how to get their work done in a much more cost-efficient manner without compromising on quality. Although India has all the ingredients to be the best offshore destination for IT service/BPO work, cash crunch has made companies cut budgets and put restructuring work and projects on hold. Analysts feel that after the crisis is over, massive restructuring by companies will bring significant business, and there will be a big role for India's IT sector to play. It is going to be a time of stock taking and putting your house in order. Earlier many world economies were closed and fairly self-contained, and with the start of outsourcing the dynamics of global economy underwent enormous transformation.

India has been one of the most preferred outsourcing destinations for more than a decade now. Outsourcing has contributed immensely to the transformation of global economy by stepping up the pace of integration of national economies. Some analysts felt that India could lose its sheen as the most favored outsourcing destination, with countries such as China, Philippines, and Brazil threatening India's dominant position over the past few years. *A 30-country Gartner survey showed India to be an undisputed leader, with China coming up as the greatest competitor.* China and other low-cost offshore destinations seem to be denting India's outsourcing revenues.

Futures and options and the risks therewith.

Chapter 16

Business Repositioning in Slowdown

Of costs positive, zero, even negative.

Business Repositioning—Slowdown—CEOs Speak at Harvard Meeting on Cause and Measures

Of closing ranks in a contingency.

Harvard sent gloomy signals to the United States, with Bill Gates and other HBS alumni seeing significant depression ahead for America. Those gathered at the school for the meeting in October 2008 were quite disappointed when they heard almost every speaker say that a significant depression was in the cards for the American economy.

Mr. Gates, former CEO, of Microsoft, cited high government taxes and increasing government debt as the main reasons for the recession to set into the American economy. "People are paying the price of leverage. The consumer sentiment has never been so low," Mr. Gates said. "It all depends now on how fast we fix this up, and even if we fix this up, we still have fairly significant depression," he warned. The economic crisis with shrinking growth in successive quarters has taken a heavy toll, with the unemployment level surging alarmingly.

"If we can get liquidity back in the system and we can make sure the productivity capacity continues, it doesn't have to be a long recession," GE CEO and an alumni of the class of 1982, Jeffery Immelt said. Gloom and anger prevailed as one speaker after another spoke about the abysmal economic scenario.

"This is an unprecedented crisis which has set in the last four weeks in the country. There is not a single soul in this room who could have predicted this financial crisis which led to some of the biggest investment banks going bankrupt. We need to do a far better job to find out what caused this," said venture capitalist (VC) firm Kliner Perkins Caufield and Byers partner John Doerr, an alumni of the class of 1979.

"For how long can we borrow money from China and use the money to buy oil from the Middle-East and then just burn up here in America which is leading in climate change?" Despite efforts by Immelt to cheer up the gathering by stating that he was optimistic about the economy because of the steps taken by the American government and the Federal Reserve to bail out beleaguered companies, the alumni were not convinced. "We had created a financial system which did not have transparency. The world is looking for new leadership and fresh ideas," said Mr. Doerr. "With $14 trillion in household debts, the U.S. economy is likely to further worsen as investors pull out from volatile stock markets."

Mahindra and Mahindra vice chairman, Anand Mahindra, who was honored with a top alumni achievement award said, "There is a crisis of confidence. It is frightening. Everyone is either anxious or nervous about their future. But the United States has the resilience, and it would come out of it faster. The good news is that it would be huge booster for countries like India which would benefit out of this crisis."

Business Repositioning—IT Spending and Budget Slash during Slowdown

As institutions moved swiftly to minimize the impact.

In the entire Indian IT industry history the future outlook was the toughest ever seen. There was a top line decline in the Indian software industry for the first time in its history. In the lean period as companies struggled for survival, competitiveness has taken the back seat. According to initial estimates by Phanish Murthy, CEO of U.S.-based iGate, the U.S. financial services industry meltdown and reorganization would result in slashed IT budgets by as much as 25% to 30%. iGate provides combined platform for client's software and business process outsourcing (BPO) needs and has large operations in India. Indian IT vendors get a third of their revenue from the BFSI (banking, financial services, insurance) vertical. One of the worst parts is not knowing when and where the crisis is likely to bottom out.

N.R.N. Murthy of Infosys said that earlier IT budgets were normally fixed annually, but during the slowdown they are being set on a quarterly or even monthly basis across industries. So client CTOs who place the orders themselves do not know where they stand. Srini Rajam, chief of Ittiam, concurred. Ittiam is one of India's leading technology firms which creates intellectual property in the

DSP (digital signal processing) vertical. Global semiconductor companies reaped 20% to 25% less revenue, thereby picturing a bleak outlook for both services and product firms. Apart from IT spending cuts and budgets being fixed for very short periods, the revenue guidance was also sometimes revised on a monthly rather than a quarterly basis. The revenue downturn resulted in increased negative sentiment and firms overreacting. There was an overall fall in consumer sentiment and a rise in unemployment. Dire projections had been issued by companies such as Intel, Samsung, and even Microsoft. Apple seemed to be the only exception. Avinash Vashistha, head of Tholons, says that during the 2001–2002 crisis offshoring revenue growth had slowed, but you should expect almost flat revenue growth in 2009, negative in the first half and positive in the second half.

Business Opportunities during Economic Slowdown

As technologies expand into far frontiers.

War times, recession, and economic slowdown give excellent opportunities to set up new businesses and gain competitive advantage. Capital expenditure and wage costs cannot be any cheaper in these times. Examples of firms born during slowdown are Hyatt, FedEx, GE, Hewlett Packard, and Indian firms like Mindtree and Wipro BPO. New ventures need core marketing and operations talent. Economic slowdown provides such an opportunity to attract such talent cheaply and give them excellent equity rewards and challenging nature of work in return. Top talent is also liable to easily migrate if their growth is not taken care of in terms of salary hikes or promotion, even though in a recession. Capital infrastructure businesses will also find the expenses cheaper than they would in boom times. A product follows the normal PLM (product lifecycle management) graph. It follows five stages: development, introduction, growth, maturity, and decline. The ideal maturity period should end with another phase of boom and beginning of a slowdown.

Though no business can achieve accurate timing, entrepreneurs can time their product launches, gauging the trend of the curve. Raman Roy, founder of three BPO ventures and CEO of Quattro BPO says "that there is no good or bad time to start. If you start selling bullock carts in this age, it won't work even in boom times. Even we started Spectramind in post dotcom bust, and we did very well. If idea is good it will sell. It should satisfy needs of a market." Mr. Roy started Spectramind at the peak of the dotcom bust in 2000, with funding from Chysalis Capital. In two years, the company ramped up to 9,000 employees. It was bought by Wipro for $175 million, after which Roy founded Quattro BPO with his own capital.

Mr. Vinod Dham, a venture capitalist, is quite familiar with the doom and boom periods of the past. He is also considered the father of the Pentium chip, a breakthrough chip for Intel. "After the dotcom bust, everybody said Indian IT growth story was over. But look where they are now. The same thing is likely to repeat itself," he said. *Mr. Dham's Indo–U.S. fund, New Path Ventures, would continue to make investments aggressively.* The first fund was $189 million, and Dham intended to raise a second fund sometime later, notwithstanding the global crisis. The first fund invested in more than 18 ventures, with investments being primarily in tech or tech-enabled sectors like mobile, online services and order process outsourcing. Mr. Dham was very optimistic about the growth of Indian IT firms despite opposite views by some analysts. "We are immediately impacted in India because exits will happen. But damage to India will be much lesser. Banks are well regulated, and there is still growth. There is no inherent weakness, and I am bullish on India in the long term," he said. He further said that, as compared to India, there was much more fear in China, because their exports are manufacturing related. China would be more impacted because of less consumption in the United States of Chinese goods, but Indian exports to the United States are more service based. Mr. Dham reasoned that the crisis would cause U.S. companies to resort to cost-cutting measures by outsourcing to cost-effective locations, and so there would be a growth in Indian revenue. But his view was not subscribed to by many, because in Indian stock markets, IT scrips were among the biggest losers. The fall of the Indian IT scrips was fueled by the cost-cutting and consolidation measures of their financial services clients. Revenues in the future were slated to fall because fewer contracts were being signed by Indian vendors. The financial sector was in turmoil, and there was a wave of panic among the Western banking executives because of the crash of major global investment banks. People were scouting for safer pastures in the wake of job insecurity and layoffs, and many were planning to seek employment in growing economies like India. A spate of resumes and calls were being received by recruitment agencies from executives willing to switch.

Business Repositioning Due to Recession—General Strategies

Resources—budget, men, and machines, perennially in short supply.

As seen in Figure 16.1, it became imperative to have new business approaches in the period of downturn to create new ideas, opportunities, and jobs. Millions of jobs are needed in India itself for the young population. Reliance, Infosys, HCL, and Nirma are some examples of local entrepreneurs which have become large corporate houses providing employment to millions. The government and industry's constant support to local entrepreneurs was needed.

Corporate ethics, good corporate governance practices, data security, strong values, capability, and the ability to adapt became increasingly important factors for companies to survive and grow. John McCarthy, vice president and principal analyst with the U.S. research firm Forrester, said, "It is naive to say an economic

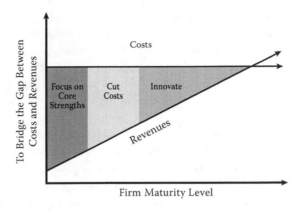

Figure 16.1   What should firms focus on during slowdown?

slowdown is good because cost cutting will lead to higher offshoring. *This is no longer a recession, it is a fundamental restructuring of financial services that is taking place.*"

As flow of revenue dried up from some global markets, Indian outsourcing companies began to tap the domestic market and endeavored to bag large government contracts. Mr. Mohan of Browne and Mohan said a number of firms had to adopt different business models since economic slowdowns existed for a significant period. The slump in U.S. and European markets drove Indian vendors like TCS, Infosys, and Wipro to tap the domestic Indian market. In 2009, according to Browne and Mohan, Indian firms were expected to spend $5.8 to $6 billion on IT services vis à vis $5.6 billion spent on software services by these companies in 2008. To surmount such trying times, many firms were banking on the Indian domestic market. "I can tell you that there are huge, multiyear projects being considered by large Indian corporate and government organizations," said Infosys chairman Narayan Murthy. A study stated that, in 2010, India's internal IT spending grew by 17% to 24%, and Asia Pacific IT spending by 10% to 16%, in spite of the global economic mayhem. In the Asia Pacific region, India and China in particular are large untapped markets, and China grew 10% to 13% compared to 3.3% to 6.5% increase in global IT spending. The IT spending heading includes expenditure on hardware, software, and IT–BPO services. "With shrinking IT budgets of the developed world set to shrink further, IT services companies have been working on realigning growth strategies and looking at opportunities in countries such as India and China," said Mr. Chandremouli. The large presence of small and medium businesses (SMBs) in India and China adds to opportunities in these emerging markets. He said the requirement for building IT infrastructure was greater for companies in their growth phase and located in emerging markets. An overwhelming majority of Indian domestic companies do not have scalable IT systems.

"Service buyers will need to reassess their outsourcing strategies and implement a better mix of multisourcing combining nearshore and offshore models, while service providers will look to growing domestic markets such as China, India, Argentina, and Brazil as a means to hedge against volatility of existing offshore contracts," said Tholons CEO Avinash Vashishtha.

An entrepreneur has to consider various factors, and an entrepreneurship venture which works well in Mexico may not work in China. Entrepreneurship is conditioned by different types of cultural and business environments, realities, and situations on the ground. Economic development of a country is an additional aspect, along with the cultural and social climate.

An outsourcing expert was of the view that, in such trying times when demand for services was low in the United States and Europe, multiyear outsourcing contracts could help Indian firms tide over the crisis and register growth for some time to come. Top Indian software firms like TCS, Infosys, and Wipro got repeat orders resulting in more than 90% of their total revenue over the past couple of years. "Any contract in the range of 3 to 5 years is still very low for the Indian IT service industry and hovers around 20% to 25% of their total contracts currently. In a normal year, companies such as Infosys have around 65% visibility of their future revenues during the course of the fiscal and around 90% visibility on a quarterly basis," said an expert. Long-term contracts would aid in surmounting the financial crisis and increase revenue visibility of Indian IT firms.

Offshoring to reduce costs could accelerate, and the challenge before IT players would be to build new capabilities. Mr. Mittal said that the ability and expertise in offering services at interlinks between IT and business was a critical factor for growth. "Offshoring being one of the established solutions, it could witness an increase in demand," said Rohit Kapoor, president and CEO of EXL services, a Noida-based BPO company.

Business Repositioning—High Exposure to Financial Services Sector Outsourcing

Exposure, risks, and a corrective follow-up approach.

Kaustubh Dhavse, Frost and Sullivan deputy director–ICT practice, said, "Banks in Europe and U.S. will continue to give IT contracts, but the sales cycle will be longer and there will be a lot of scrutiny. Though IT companies in Europe are spread across sectors, the credit crunch means that it will also affect the manufacturing and service sector spends."

Mr. McCarthy of Forrester felt that the financial services sector was overstaffed and conversion of large investment banks and merger and acquisition (M&A) activity would translate into fewer employees and vendors and tighter IT budgets. The impact of these developments would be huge, and the growth from most aggressive technology buyers and financial services would go back to 25% and stay there. Infosys Technologies Limited had shown a revenue growth of 50% in FY07 only from "financial" services clients. Mr. McCarthy felt that such significant exposure of Indian IT companies to financial services clients made them more vulnerable. "The exposure of Indian IT companies to financial services clients is almost double that of their global peers in terms of revenue percentage." There is no denying it will particularly impact Indian companies. In a way they are paying the price for having underinvested in marketing all these years. He further added that the Indian service providers will move closer to their global peers in terms of revenue, and the exceptional growth rates that the Indian providers had experienced in the past were unlikely to be achieved again. "Margins will continue to drift down to 15% and there will be real pressure on the topline," he said.

Tholons felt that in the period of downturn, small U.S. companies would cause BPO revival. To save costs, smaller U.S. companies would outsource, thereby providing a boost to Indian vendors, although the large outsourcers had slashed their IT budgets. "We expect to see a survival in outsourcing, and we are already seeing an uptick in the outsourcing-related activity for engagements that will come to fruition in 9–12 months," Tholons said in its study titled "Top Ten Trends in Services Globalization 2009." According to the study, there would be more outsourcing in the healthcare, education, retail, telecom, and legal services sectors because of consolidation in the financial sector.

Example—Business Strategy of Infosys

Some analysts, however, felt that the Indian IT offshore services industry would inevitably go from strength to strength despite the global meltdown. *Infosys, which had significant exposure to the banking, financial services, and insurance (BFSI) and telecom sectors was working on "software products" that could be introduced into different fields, including media and communication, telecom and retail, more so in emerging markets.* "We are establishing a sound presence in the software product space and launching newer solutions on a regular basis. Apart from our 'Finacle' banking solutions, we are launching solutions addressing other sectors. We have dedicated teams, which are focusing on software product development," said S.D. Shibulal, chief operating officer of Infosys Technologies. According to him, in the recent past, most of the products launched by the company in the emerging or domestic markets were getting good response. "We are putting a lot of focus on emerging markets. Our strategy to address these markets varies from country to country. India is in the forefront of our emerging market strategy," he said. Until mid-2009, software products generated a little less than 4% of the total revenue of Infosys. This primarily consisted of revenues from Finacle, the universal banking solution. A dominant player in the domestic market, Finacle strengthened this position of Infosys, because this core banking application is used by most of the major Indian banks.

Even as uncertainties continued in the global financial market, IT services company Infosys Technologies attempted to increase its revenue share in the software product segment, by making aggressive forays into emerging markets including the Indian domestic outsourcing market.

Business Deals Contracting—Short- and Long-Term

Small moves with far-reaching consequences,
depending on the nature of the game.

IT is becoming vulnerable with short-term deals replacing long-term deals in a turbulent market. The $50 billion IT industry, is faced with decreasing revenues and dwindling orders, a fallout of the global slowdown. The future seemed bleak for this sector given the prevalence of short-duration time and material (T&M) contracts on their order books.

The problem for Indian IT firms is more severe because historically there have been primarily short-duration, T&M contracts coming their way. T&M contracts are those for which fees are based on time taken and manpower used. The duration of T&M contracts typically is between three months and six months, while that of fixed-term contracts is typically longer. T&M contracts are more flexible compared to fixed-price contracts, but are also more risky. Hence, there is some preference for fixed-price contracts by companies. During the good times, with the IT industry growing at a fast pace over the last several years, firms did not pay too much attention to the type of contracts as long as business was coming in. The future for Indian IT firms does not seem to be rosy because most contracts with them are short-term, T&M ones, giving rise to more unpredictability regarding future revenues. "It's a client's call on the kind of contracts, though we are pursuing more fixed-price, long-term deals as part of the de-risk strategy," said the CFO of an IT firm. Currently 70% of contracts currently are short-duration ones (typically, three to six months term) compared to the fixed-price, longer-term contracts. Over 60% of the revenue for large IT firms like HCL Technologies, Infosys Technologies, and Wipro Technologies comes from "T&M" billing. For smaller IT firms this percentage is higher. Earlier, during the boom period, over 90% of the contracts resulted in repeat business. With the financial turmoil and the prevalence of a high percentage of small duration, T&M contracts did somewhat mar the prospects of repeat business for the IT players.

When asked about the dominance of T&M contracts among Indian IT companies, NASSCOM president Som Mittal said during the slowdown period, "It's true that the industry is not doing too many large, fixed-price contracts. But that's because in early years, the IT industry had to prove itself and hence got only the short term contracts.... Now with better domain expertise, the shift to long-term fixed-price contracts will happen." However, with customers cutting costs and slashing IT budgets, it won't be easy to make that shift. The short-term T&M contracts are more sensitive to external business environment changes when compared to fixed-price long-term contracts, which tend to be more stable. "The prevalence of short-term contracts is a big problem, but also a significant opportunity. We are trying to move to more fixed-price contracts as it offers more certainty in contract execution and revenue," says HCL Technologies CEO Vineet Nayar. The long-duration, fixed-price contracts would typically go to large multinational corporation (MNC) service providers such as IBM, Accenture, or HP. "Till now the industry has been focused on quarter-to-quarter targets and has done well as is evident from lot of repeat business. This helped establish a track record and comfort level with clients. But now, companies are keen to shift to fixed-price, long-term contracts as it's more sticky and helps take out the uncertainty in business, particularly during turbulent times," says PricewaterhouseCoopers (PwC) partner and head of consulting practice Ambarish Dasgupta.

Example—Infosys and Wipro Short- and Long-Term Contracts Ratio

This shift to fixed-price contracts is considered by Infosys as an effort to delink revenue growth from manpower growth and move up the value chain. "T&M or fixed-price is a way of billing clients. Lot of contracts that we have are long-term, with over 99% repeat business. We always try to increase the fixed-price contracts, but eventually it depends on the comfort level of the client," says Infosys CFO V. Balakrishanan. Infosys had increased its fixed-price contracts to 34.1% of revenue in Q2, 2008, compared to 27.8% in the same quarter in 2007. Wipro Technologies too had increased it to 31.6% from 26.6% a year back. This shift needs to be accelerated and more stability needs to be built in the pricing models.

Example—Airtel–IBM Long-Term Contract

For example, Bharti Airtel's IT outsourcing arrangement with IBM of over $1 billion is a long-duration contract. The same is true for ABM Amro's $2.2 billion deal shared among IBM, TCS, Infosys, and others.

In the last economic slowdown the offshore presence of global vendors like IBM and Accenture consisted of 2,000 to 3,000 employees, whereas in the current slowdown they have employee strengths of 60,000 to 70,000 in offshore locations.

Business Repositioning through Regional Shifts and Strategy

The geographic upheavals of the financial maelstrom.

Allen Kilgore, principal at Tholons, said, "The U.S. domestic market will see an increase in domestic sourcing to take advantage of the available talent pool at an attractive cost with incentives from local government." Since technology is one of the greatest enablers, providers will implement new technologies to utilize existing resources better and increase margins. With IT budgets being slashed, clients demanded far more stringent service level agreements (SLAs), greater flexibility in contracts, and payment schemes based on output. Vendors had increased focus on large markets like China, India, Brazil, and Argentina, especially with a view to cater to the financial services, telecom and retail verticals by providing customer support and back office services among others.

To bring down the cost of managing IT systems by reducing number of IT systems from around 1,350 to almost 300 by 2010, Telstra proposed to work with one supplier for each domain across product lines. Telstra aimed at consolidating IT needs and bringing down costs through outsourcing. "The company wants to move more than half of this contract to an offshore location such as India, and that is why pure Indian offshore vendors including Infosys and EDS Mphasis are being seriously considered," said a senior executive at one of the top tech firms bidding for the Telstra contract. In 2008, $226 million saving had been realized by Telstra by reducing the number of suppliers by almost 20%.

Citi Technology Services was acquired by Wipro for around $127 million as part of the deal. An over $500 million master service agreement for six years with Wipro was announced by Jagdish Rao for infrastructure services and application development. Citibank proposed to send more IT projects to offshore locations such as India. "As we face these economic challenges, there will be greater demand for moving more work to offshore locations," Mr. Rao, global technology head for Citi, said.

Strategy—Risk Mitigation through Geographical Spread

*As various market practices interact to reach
a mutually acceptable equilibrium.*

The assumption that different countries have different boom and bust periods prompts companies to go to different countries to spread risk. Slowdown in one country could be countered by growth in another country to drive business. *Europe contributes about 20% to 30% of the total revenues of the six top Indian IT outsourcing firms.* To mitigate risk, in the past, Indian firms consciously tried to expand their European business instead of putting all their eggs in the U.S. market. *Forrester Research analyst Sudin Apte said that, "Despite what the percentages say, we still have low penetration in Europe.* It is a smaller market, around $130–$140 billion compared to North America which is a $250 billion market." Shiva Ramani, CEO of Cybernet Slash Support (CSS) during the recession period, said, "The current scenario does not auger well for the Indian service providers who are looking at European market as risk diversification strategy from their large North American exposure, and the rate of growth is likely to be affected," during the slowdown period. CSS gets 5% of its business from Europe.

"We are keenly observing the development in Europe, where we get 20% of our business. There is no information yet from our customers there, so we are in wait and watch mode. But we feel the nationalization of banks means that business will not go down since there will be some recapitalization," Satyam Computer Services CEO Srinivas Vadlamani spoke during the initial recession period.

In September 2008, when three big financial institutions from Europe sought government support, worries of Indian IT firms deepened because they were hoping for Europe to drive growth. However, the financial storm wrecked havoc across the globe, with Belgium Dutch banking and insurance group Fortis and British mortgage lender Bradford and Bingley coming under government control and Germany's commercial property lender Hypo Real Estate Bank getting a rescue package from a consortium of banks, backed with government guarantees. According to an economic and market analysis by Citi on Europe, "As well as the deterioration in credit quality within western Europe, many European banks also have sizeable exposure to probable losses in the U.S. and to potential risks in high credit growth countries in Eastern Europe (including the Baltics)."

The notion that Asia could decouple from the economic meltdown got dispelled, and reliance of the region on its exports for growth was evident. With respect to the U.S. dollar, Asian currencies had been battered, and the turmoil saw flight of capital to safer pastures. Apart from Malaysian ringgit, the Philippine peso, and the Indian rupee, most currencies were severely hit.

The Australian government's budget surplus would enable increased spending or tax cuts, if the economy looks in danger of slipping into recession. "The basic story across the developed world remained disturbing—credit growth, consumption growth, and employment growth all are trending towards weakness," said Rory Robertson, interest rate strategist.

HCL Technologies global head of financial services Prem Kumar S added, "It would be inappropriate to say we are unconcerned. The level of penetration of IT services here is still lesser than the overall market place. Also, it depends on the kind of services offered. If its people centric offering, then it is an issue but not when you are offering transformational or integrate services offering. There is a tentativeness in decision making given the crisis of leadership in buyer organizations but we continue to be bullish. Since the financial services market is interlinked globally we are discovering linkages between European clients and U.S." HCL gets 55% of its revenue from the United States, 30% from Europe, and 15% from Asia Pacific.

Mergers and Acquisitions (M&A)

As organizations continuously adapt to sustain the business continuum.

M&A—Risky Acquisitions

Risk, always part of play.

Notwithstanding the global economic storm, Indian IT firms circles were abuzz with M&A activity at enormous prices, which some analysts felt was very risky. In a bid to counter the effects of recession, many Indian companies resorted to the M&A course. As valuations of overseas firms plunged, Indian IT companies were making bids to acquire them. *The dipping valuations of overseas firms, in some cases by 30%, prompted many Indian IT vendors to tread the M&A path.* Indian IT companies sitting on huge reserves of cash saw this as an ideal opportunity for expansion and portfolio addition. India Inc. went beyond $14 billion in the M&A space by October 2008. "There is a need for growth and growing organically is getting more difficult," said Forrester India head Sudin Apte. "The reasons behind these risky ventures were not entirely unclear." "Growth rates of Indian IT companies are sobering down. You will now see them make multimillion dollar acquisitions," said Kotak Mahindra capital head V. Jayasankar. Earlier cross-border acquisition meant thin margins for Indian IT companies whose revenue inflow then was exceedingly more than their overseas peers, and so business acumen dictated avoiding acquisitions then to prevent denting of margins. This pressure of declining cash inflow during recession was prompting companies to tread the M&A path.

Competition from overseas rivals like IBM, Accenture, and Capgemini was another factor fueling the acquisition trend. With a substantial presence in India these companies were winning transformation deals by offering services at par with their Indian peers. Indian IT firms were realizing the need to go in for large acquisitions rather than small ones in order to compete with their gigantic overseas rivals, despite the fact that large acquisitions are tougher to integrate and conclude apart from being quite time consuming. "They have realized that the scale and experience that comes with an acquisition is also important. Acquiring a small firm in Germany doesn't necessarily put an Indian firm on equal footing with an European service provider with a large local presence," said Ernst and Young transaction advisory leader Ranjan Biswas.

Indian companies such as Infosys, TCS, and Cognizant were bidding for large contracts to the tune of over $100 million in the wake of large global banks like Lloyds TSB and HBOS and Bank of America and Merrill Lynch merging. The merger of banks had given rise to a huge task of integrating their software applications, consolidating their data centers and other trading platforms into a single entity so that customers can perform transactions without being hindered by issues related to the merger. To cut costs and save as much as 30% to 40%, these merged banking entities plan to outsource to providers having significant offshore presence. Banks intend to partner with offshore vendors, because they know the systems better, translating into cost saving for banks. The merged entity comprising Lloyds TSB and HBOS was scouting for partners to help it integrate its retail and whole-sale banking systems through an IT platform. The human resource functions of the company had already been outsourced to Xansa two years ago, in a five-year deal. Meanwhile a consortium of banks including the Royal Bank of Scotland acquired ABN Amro. Both ABN Amro and the Royal Bank of Scotland are Infy customers. "M&A is the silver lining for us in this environment and we are winning transfor-mation deals," Infosys chief executive S. Gopalakrishnan said. "In some of these cases we are fortunate to be incumbents," he said.

"Firms will continue to look for small tuck-in acquisitions to plug gaps in their portfolios and gain client proximity," said Nishant Verma, vice president at Tholons Capital. Due to merger and acquisition activities, it was felt that more business for the legal process outsourcing (LPO) firms would be generated, because analysts were of the view that the financial downturn would lead to consolidations.

Restructuring and Consolidation in Indian Companies—M&A

Making new alignments for enhanced standing.

Due to the reduction in demand for technology services in the United States and Europe during the financial slowdown, small IT companies in India seemed to be in big trouble. According to analysts, there was increased consolidation among small and mid-tier IT service companies in India. In 2007 and early 2008, small and mid-sized IT companies were able to cope with the rapid appreciation of rupee vis-à-vis the U.S. dollar but in the period of deep economic downturn orders shrank. Initially small local firms felt that they would be able to overcome the bad times, but after seeing sustained negative cash flows they realized the stark reality. *It was expected that an overwhelming percentage of Indian outsourcing companies with 1,000 or less employees would either be acquired or run a high risk of closing shop.* Sudin Apte of Forrester Research said that mergers and alliances in the Indian IT industry were under way, but the pace at which consolidations take place may pick up in the next one and half years.

According to estimates, the top 20 players contribute around 60% to 70% of the country's IT services exports, with the remaining coming from small and mid-sized firms. It was a major worry for Indian firms with a revenue of about Rs. 50 million (US$ 1 million) per annum serving the BFSI market in the United States or the United Kingdom, while Indian entities with a top line of around Rs. 500 million (US$ 11 million) were already going for this type of consolidation, analysts said. For instance, just 23% of the approximately 1,550 units registered with STPI Authority Bangalore have gross revenue in excess of Rs. 1 billion (US$ 22 million.

T.R. Madan Mohan of Browne and Mohan, a consultancy firm, was of the view that M&A would occur at a faster pace because private equity (PE) investors and PE firms mounted pressure and encouraged companies to go in for consolidation to mitigate risks. However, there was considerable interest on the part of investors in these companies because of their low valuations and a greater interest in outsourcing, he thought. "I see more M&A activity over the next 12 months to acquire domain skills as more companies look at Indian IT players to cut costs," said Som Mittal, president of NASSCOM during the slowdown period. Mittal said Indian IT firms were exploring new territories in Europe and Asia, thereby decreasing dependence on America. He added that M&A activity had increased because of high scope for embedded designs and manufacturing of hybrid chips. "In third and fourth quarters (of 2008), we will see a large number of acquisitions as the aspirations of the companies are rising and it is cheaper to buy companies as valuations are lower now," Mittal said on the sidelines of the EmergeOut Conclave 2008. The average industry growth is 30% and the small and medium enterprises (SME) growth is faster at about 43%, therefore SME will see more merger and acquisition activity. Analysts agreed with Mittal that the low market sentiment would remain only for the third quarter.

Restructuring of companies could occur, such as HP–EDS, and the supply of talent could exceed demand according to Diptarup Chakroborti, principal research analyst at Gartner, Inc. With the valuation of companies abroad hitting new lows, Indian firms were likely to buy small companies overseas vis-à-vis domestic companies. It was clear that finding a solution to the crisis would take time, and no institution could claim complete insulation from the crisis.

Icall solutions, an Ahmedabad-based company, was investing about $50 million for acquisition, and talks were under way with a few U.S. players with similar businesses and a wide client base. "We are talking to a couple of players for inorganic growth. This is the right time to make acquisitions and leverage our bottom line," said Manish Mathur, senior VP (India operations) at Icall. Evaluation of financial processes, current valuations, and product mix were under way as part of the acquisition activity. Apart from overseas companies, the BPO major also intended to acquire those domestic companies which had presence in multiple cities. Global Tech, another IT company, was also looking for U.S. acquisitions. Recently a majority stake was acquired by the company in Belgium-based Perfectview Belgie at nearly Euro 2 million. "With valuations going down in the U.S. market, we have been scouting for the right company that can give us a firm footing in the U.S.," said managing director Pankaj Shah. In order to sustain, U.S. companies were increasingly resorting to cost cutting, said a senior consultant, and the decline in valuations of U.S. companies by nearly 30% was triggering acquisitions by Indian vendors. "We have been getting queries from small and medium-sized companies on the right valuations. They are actively looking at investing a proportionate amount in acquisitions at this price," he said. To invite business to the Gujarat summit in 2009, a delegation of IT companies based in Gujarat was heading to the United States and Europe, and in an all-cash deal, Polaris Software Lab, a Chennai-based company, acquired SEEC, a U.S.-based company. Polaris Software Lab is a specialty application provider in banking, financial, and insurance sectors and SEEC is a product and component services company. Actual deal size was kept under wraps by the company in an acquisition which included intellectual property rights, business trademarks, trade brands, and infrastructure facilities. By using the SEEC advantage library, customer experience can be delivered across all products, channels, and lines of business by insurance firms. To increase enterprise sales, productivity, and streamline services, SEEC had built hundreds of nonproprietary service-oriented architecture (SOA) software components. These components can be quickly assembled to deliver business solutions.

Amid global financial turmoil, Indian IT companies are cracking deals. India Inc. is treading the M&A street, and despite the financial market meltdown the number of outbound deals are higher than the inbound deals according to Grant Thronton. Until August 2008, just before the global slowdown, the IT sector accounted for more than 10% of the deals in the M&A space, against 3.91% in 2007. Until August 2008, IT and information technology enabled service (ITES) accounted for the maximum number of deals in the M&A space, clocking 81 deals with a combined value of $2.53 billion. Between July and August 2008, there were 16 outbound and one inbound deal in the IT and ITES sector, while there were more than 42 outbound and 12 inbound deals in the sector in the whole year. Two more deals were on the verge of completion, and their outcome would influence the inorganic strategies of other IT companies. Pankaj Karna, head of M&A business at Grant Thronton, feels that, because India is relatively unaffected by the subprime scam, large-value outbound deals could be expected. "IT and ITES sector will remain a hot segment this year too. As valuations have become reasonable following the credit turmoil, many firms are looking at mergers and acquisition as a way to acquire new technology to enter new markets at reasonable rates. Though leveraged high-value deals may not happen in the inbound segment, we are expecting some large deals in the outbound space," he said. "Indian companies which are sitting on cash and are in a position to leverage, but at reasonable cost, would use this opportunity for inorganic growth as valuations oversees are depressed due to the financial turmoil. Primarily these deals will be done by cash in their coffers," said PVD executive director Sanjeev Krishan.

India Inc. was trying to make the most of the ongoing global economic downturn with cash-rich domestic firms treading the M&A path and stepping up outbound acquisition. The ongoing U.S. and European financial mayhem had let down many "big" economies, but Indian firms had outpaced their global counterparts. Outbound acquisition by Indian companies touched $14 billion in the first three quarters of 2008, while their global counterparts made only $8 billion worth of acquisitions in India, a report by M&A consultant Indus View Advisors said.

ONGC Videsh acquired the United Kingdom's Imperial Energy ($2.8 billion) and HDFC bank's buyout of domestic rival Centurion Bank of Punjab ($2.38 billion) were some of the big deals. Cash-rich Indian firms are on an acquisition spree as target companies have become significantly cheaper compared with just before the recession set in. The significance of cash reserves as acquisition currency has gone up as the global financial downturn has driven stock prices worldwide to historic lows. "Significant aspect of the M&A activity has been India Inc. eyes on global opportunities, which have become more prominent in the backdrop of global recession," Indus View Advisor's chairman Bundeep Singh Rangar said. Until September 2008, M&A activity was dominated by infrastructure sector accounting for $11.8 billion. "The traction in the infrastructure M&As is symbolic of the need for world-class facilities, adoption of internationally applicable best practices, experienced global management expertise, and technology applications to accelerate growth in the Indian economy," Rangar said. Of the total M&A deals until September 2008, 25% were in infrastructure-related industries.

The ICICI bank was more focused on domestic opportunities and said that only Japanese banks have the necessary financial standing to acquire U.S. and European banks in this period of financial downturn. Asked about M&A strategy in the face of lower American and European exposure and huge cash and liquidity position, The ICICI bank's managing director and CEO, K, V. Kamath said, "We scan opportunities all the time, but I would think that at this point of time, given the global uncertainties and even with capital, any bank from developing countries has to very carefully look at deployment of capital."

Example—Axon M&A

There was a pitched battle between Indian outsourcing players HCL and Infosys to acquire Axon, a U.K.-based systems applications and products (SAP) consultancy. M&A activity was being witnessed in full sway, and Indian software firm Infosys tried to match and surpass HCL's offer to acquire SAP Consulting from Axon. It was widely speculated that Infosys could make a conditional offer up to 710 to 720 pence to counter HCL's 650 pence offer, although sources said that Infosys could refrain from entering into an extensive bidding war. Notwithstanding the global meltdown, the two companies locked horns, fiercely competing to acquire the London-headquartered SAP Consulting. HCL Technologies took Infosys Technologies head on by making a £441 million counter bid to finally acquire Axon's SAP consulting. Till then HCL had not done any major acquisitions, said a senior investment banker. On the other hand, Infosys had always been acquisition shy and had just one minor acquisition of $23 million to date.

Rumors were rife about TCS's intentions to buy Citigroup's BPO arm. The two deals together were estimated to be worth $1.4 billion. The fruition of these deals led to the total value of IT deals in 2008 to be double the value of deals in 2007, which was $2.9 billion. Analysts were of the opinion that, despite a global economic shakeout, which has impacted IT outsourcing providers, big M&A deals would still continue to happen.

M&A—Example—Impact on Genpact after Wachovia's Assets Sale to Citigroup

Citigroup Corp. acquired Wachovia Corp, a leading commercial bank. Incidentally, Wachovia Corp., until a little while back, was planning to acquire Morgan Stanley, and Citi needed massive bailout during the economic downturn.

The relationship between Genpact and Wachovia was strong, and the U.S. bank had chosen Genpact to set up a dedicated center for back office operations. Genpact is India's largest BPO service provider, and the sale of Wachovia's assets to Citigroup is likely to impact it. Genpact also got an opportunity to diversify its revenue from General Electric. To cut costs, Wachovia moved jobs to the new outsourcing center under a "virtual captive" model. The model was resorted to by banks and insurance providers not wanting to set up their own captive centers. It meant that Genpact could staff and function as back office as though it was Wachovia's own captive. In other words, Wachovia's own captive run by Genpact would service most of Wachovia's outsourced functions. According to the seven-year agreement that hit the headlines, Genpact was expected to get $1 billion of business. The sale of the Wachovia's assets to Citigroup likely hit the BPO provider hard. "No firm that has had relationships with any of the troubled banks will be able to come out unscathed. If you are asking me if Genpact will be affected, the answer is clearly, yes," said an expert with the firm that monitors trends in outsourcing. Typically, most large and long-term contracts are composed of two parts: committed business and expected business. The proportion of committed business is much smaller, but the understanding in these multiyear, multimillion-dollar contracts is that newer business will also flow to the same vendor. "Under these circumstances, the expected business may be in danger," the expert added.

A U.S.-based analyst tracking the outsourcing sector said, "Volumes may decline as Wachovia's back office functions are integrated into Citi's, offset by the potential for business to expand." It seems that Citi's upside is low unless its captive, which has been for sale for sometime, is acquired by Genpact.

M&A Examples

WNS Holdings acquisition of Aviva Global Services for $228 million and Quattro BPO Solutions buying a majority stake in the U.K.-based Babel Media for $110 million were some of the outbound deals between June and August 2008. Also Cbay Systems, an ITES company, bought 69.50% in Medquist Inc. for $287 million.

However, private equity investment in IT and ITES sector remained the lowest with only $302 million which is just a fraction of the PE money that has found its way in sectors like real estate and infrastructure. In 2007 PR firms had invested $744 million in 67 deals with IT companies.

M&A Example—Barclays

The people factor prompted Barclays to move quickly to acquire the North American business of Lehman before employees started leaving the firm. Outsourcing vendors Genpact, Copal Partners, and Wipro were also among those interested in acquiring Lehman's back office operations. Gaurav Gupta country manager Everest Group said, "Such acquisition makes sense for a third-party BPO from a long-term perspective because there are skills, processes, and talent that's difficult to build. In the short term, there may be utilization issues but it could pay off in the long term. It could also make sense for some of large existing captives if they have a ready plan to move some of the work to India." Software firms are optimistic about an early revival.

M&A, Hiring Example by CSC

CSC acquired Covansys in July 2007 and First Consulting (FCG) in January 2008, thereby nearly doubling its India headcount. Notwithstanding the economic downturn, IT services firm CSC announced that an additional 2,000 professionals would be recruited for its India operations in the next six months, due to growing demand for IT services in the manufacturing and financial services verticals. The India operations of CSC accounted for $1 billion worth of revenues in 2007, and the company had around 18,500 professionals in India. "India is CSC's largest world sourcing location outside U.S. and an important part of the company's global success," CSC chairman, president, and CEO Michael W. Laphen said. Rajendra B. Vattikuti, the Indian president of CSC, said that the recruiting plans in India were due to the growth in the manufacturing and financial services and healthcare sectors, which had plans to set up shop in India. In order to tap the market, they would partner with local companies and cater to Indian customers. "The Indian market is very small as of now, but we see opportunities in financial services, telecom, and government verticals," he said. BPO services, infrastructure services, product support, and application development are some of the services provided by the CSC India operations.

Miscellaneous M&A Examples in India

Takeovers, friendly, hostile at times.

Further consolidation and entry of new entrants is inevitable as India is turning into a hub of back office operations. A lot of activity is being witnessed in the merger and acquisition front, with consolidation being the buzzword in the BPO industry with both MNC and India-centric BPO players involved in the acquisition game. In the case of VC-backed companies, the promoters opted for the exit route and in most cases got a decent valuation. The acquisition of Transworks by Indian Rayon, an Aditya Birla group company, and the acquisition of Firstring by ICICI Onesource are notable examples.

IBM stole the limelight by acquiring Daksh on March 31, 2004. Many BPO companies abroad have been acquired by Indian companies like Corpay Solutions by Datamatics, Claims BPO by WNS, C3 in Philippines by Hinduja TMT, Aegis Communications by Essar Group, and Upstream LLC by Godrej. Many niche India-centric companies not necessarily VC-funded have also been acquired, like Vision Healthsource by Perot Systems; iBackoffice was bought by Optimus, and TCS bought out its stake in Swiss Air JV AFS. Apart from acquisitions, firms constantly plan and innovate to augment business. To transform the current clearing processes for checks, a plan has been approved by the board of directors of the Canadian Payment Association (CPA) to move forward with truncation and electronic check presentment (TECP). The Canadian business is presented an opportunity to reap great benefits due to this extensive change to the Canadian check clearing system.

Governments—Support and Control Measures

The underlying framework of policies and support.

Government Mitigation Measures Worldwide

As governments jump in to heave the crash.

New geographic areas were swept by the financial storm that shook the U.S. economy. Apart from U.S. investment banks, European continental banks were also hit hard. The devastating effect of the financial storm continued with no signs of abating, and it caused former President George W. Bush and bipartisan congressional leaders to make urgent pleas in a bid to bailout the staggering Wall Street. But the $700 billion emergency rescue package was defeated by the House of Representatives on September 29, 2008, much to the disappointment of President Bush. This increased the fury of the financial storm, which further brought down old-fashioned European commercial banks. Immediately after the defeat of the vote and rejection of the bill by the House of Representatives, financial markets plunged, with the Dow plummeting over 600 points. Many members of the House of Representatives had felt that the measure was unpopular and did not lend support to the bill. Many European banks were nationalized, and in a bid to save themselves, banks went in for mergers.

There was frenetic activity by various governments, with a troubled mortgage lender being nationalized by the United Kingdom, and with $16.3 billion being coughed up by Belgium, Netherlands, and Luxembourg to save banking major Fortis. A Euro 35 billion loan was granted by the German government to Hypo Real Estate to fend off insolvency, and by buying a 75% stake for Euro 600 million, the Iceland government took control of Glitnir Bank. With the financial industry in the throes of recession, institutions were paring their exposures to banks. Markets were rife with speculation, and some banks and financial institutions had to come out with clarifications time and again about their financial health.

Government Outsourcing Projects

As benevolent governments pumped financial capital
into the markets through various projects.

Various governments have put in place a series of measures and policies for the IT, ITES, and BPO industries to facilitate higher earnings, communication, infrastructure, and quality of manpower leading to sufficient security, quick scaling, and high growth rate. Usage and deployment of new technologies and applications facilitate quick business cash flow, like in the case of digital currency. To provide an impetus to the outsourcing sector, policies during slowdown include offering various direct tax and indirect tax incentives and the introduction of export-oriented promotion schemes such as software technology parks (STP) and special economic zones (SEZ). Development in logistics systems, transportation, and favorable government policies were very much the need of the hour.

Government business outsourcing and alternative energy during slowdown were verticals that registered growth. Mr. Phiroz Vandrevala, executive director, TCS said, "We have historically played a key role in building our national financial infrastructure through projects from the national stock exchange, NSDL, NCDEX, State Bank of India, and the RBI. We have recently bagged a Rs. 1,000 crores (US$ 220 million) Passport Seva Project from the Indian ministry of external affairs to digitise the entire passport delivery services." Indian state governments of Madhya Pradesh, Tamil Nadu, Maharashtra, and Bihar have initiated major e-governance projects; therefore opportunities are immense in this field. Chris Hyman, CEO, Serco Group, thinks that government outsourcing will provide a boost to the IT–BPO sector in India. The $6 billion U.K. services player had acquired local BPO player Infovision, in India.

Challenges Faced by U.S. Administration during Slowdown

As a regional plunge triggered a global meltdown.

The surge in the U.S. jobless rate to the highest level in a quarter century has put tremendous pressure on President Barack Obama. Some analysts say that it is no more a recession but a depression deeper than the Obama administration forecasts, and additional measures may be needed to restart growth. According to the Labor Department, the unemployment rate rose to 8.1% in February 2009 as employers reduced payrolls by 651,000. For the first time since 1939, losses exceeded 600,000 for three straight months, and joblessness had already reached the average rate the White House projected for the whole 2009 year. The administration needs to focus on fixing the banking system and implementing the stimulus instead of getting diverted by other goals such as health care changes, said John Ryding, chief economist at RDQ Economics LLC in New York. "They should be focused on stabilization of financial firms and stimulus and that should not only be job one, that should be the only job right now," Ryding said. "The question is, is it recession or is it something worse than recession?" U.S. stocks nose-dived after a $61.7 billion loss was reported by American International Group Inc., and billionaire investor Warren Buffett said the economy is in "shambles."

U.S. Government Bailout and Regulations

As the financial storm swept all in its path.

While the collapse of investment banks in quick succession caused shivers among the software vendors worldwide, government support and control of institutions like Goldman Sachs and Morgan Stanley gave some reason for solace. When the independent investment status was given up by Goldman Sachs and Morgan Stanley, it translated into more regulations for commercial banks, which meant more business for the software service providers.

Yet some felt that stringent regulations for U.S. banks could mean making adjustments and augmenting their existing technology by adding more software and processes, whereas others were of the view that IT expenditure, like many other spend categories would plummet. Kaustubh Dhavse, deputy director of Frost and Sullivan, felt that it was an opportunity for IT companies, because transformation to traditional banks implied they needed to add quite a few processes, newer functions, and areas. Wait and watch was the main strategy as corporations continued to exercise caution. According to some analysts, it was a little early to determine if tighter bank regulations would have a positive or a negative impact on vendors in India. Eventually, as results due to tighter regulatory policy percolated through the economy, predictions of economic doomsday did the rounds.

Some felt that supply-side trends such as dipping real estate markets, realistic expectation on remuneration, and a dollar-starved Indian economy could prove beneficial for Indian vendors. The existing vendors could have an advantage if the newly regulated banks increased offshoring/contracting activity in India, but others viewed it as just a window that would aid them to borrow credit from the Federal Reserve at a discounted rate.

Example—Legal Requirements When Outsourcing by American Banks

Setting rules to turn the tide.

Requirements mandate that foreign banking organizations should maintain at the U.S. office documentation of the home office's approval of outsourcing arrangements supporting its U.S. operations, whether to a U.S. or a foreign service provider, with the exception of a U.S. branch or agency of a foreign bank that relies on the parent organization for information or transaction processing services. Documentation should be maintained by the organization's U.S. office demonstrating appropriate oversight of the service provider's activities, such as written contracts, audit reports, and other monitoring tools. The Federal Reserve, wherever appropriate, will coordinate with the foreign banking organization's home country supervisor to ensure that it does not object to the outsourcing arrangement. Upon request, documentation relating to outsourcing arrangements of the foreign operations of the U.S. banking organizations with foreign service providers should be made available to examiners. Examiners should determine which information and transaction processing activities critical to the institution's core operations are outsourced, in the development of examination scope and risk profile. The adequacy of the institution's risk management for these critical service providers should be assessed and evaluated during the on-site examination. In the relevant components of the uniform information technology rating system examination rating or the uniform financial institution rating system, the overall assessment should be reflected if an information system rating is not assigned.

It is expected by the Federal Reserve that outsourcing arrangements will be established in a manner that does not diminish the ability of the U.S. supervisors to review effectively the domestic and foreign operations of U.S. banking organizations and U.S. operations of foreign banking organizations. There should be adequate oversight and compliance, and it is expected by the institution to demonstrate adequate oversight of a foreign service provider such as through comprehensive audits conducted by the service provider's internal or external auditors, the institution's own auditors, or foreign banking supervisory authorities. The ability of the institution should not be hindered by the arrangement to comply with all applicable U.S. laws and regulations, including, for example, requirements for accessibility and retention of records under the Bank Secrecy Act. The ability of the U.S. supervisors to reconstruct the U.S. activities of the organization in a timely manner should not be hindered by the outsourcing arrangement. Outsourcing to jurisdictions where full and complete access to information may be impeded by legal or administrative restrictions on information flows will not be acceptable unless copies of records pertaining to U.S. operations are also maintained at the institution's U.S. office. At the institution's U.S. office, copies of the most recent audits of the outsourcing arrangement must be maintained in

English and must be made available to the examiners on request. Provisions must be included in the contingency plan of the institution to ensure timely access to critical information and service resumption in the event of unexpected national or geographical restrictions or disruptions affecting a foreign service provider's ability to provide services.

Investment Wooing by U.S. Government Bodies of Indian Firms

The value of every cent in difficult times.

Indian companies were being wooed by the United States to set up shop in America, and the story had come full circle as states vied to woo IT companies to set up facilities in the United States. Tata Consultancy Services (TCS) was being chased by many U.S. states to set up a facility in their state, while Cincinnati was wooing Infy. A delegation from Cincinnati visited Infosys in India to propose that it set up a campus-like facility in its state. The delegation also wooed other Tata groups to set shop in Cincinnati after its success with TCS. "Yesterday, we met the Tata Group officials, tomorrow we will meet other companies in pharma, consumer, and auto," said Neil Hensley, senior director economic development business attraction and retention, Cincinnati USA partnership. The delegation led by Doug Moormann, vice president, was slated to meet Infosys officials in Bangalore next. "We realize there are opportunities in growing investments in the United States from emerging economies like India and China. The 200-acre facility that TCS took up in Cincinnati represents the largest job creation in our community in a decade," Mr. Hensley said. Aggressive competition broke out among U.S. states and local communities to win investment once the news that TCS would be setting up a facility in the United States became public. The central location of Cincinnati in Eastern United States and its connectivity to all major airports went in its favor, and TCS finally selected it for setting up a campus-like facility. "TCS has committed to employ around 700 U.S. nationals in its facility over a three-year time frame. I don't see India and China as emerging economies but as high growth economies," said Joseph J. Deher, an attorney whose firm Frost Brown Todd advised TCS on setting up its 1,000-seat Cincinnati facility. Other Indian mid-sized firms earlier had also been advised by Mr. Deher and Harvey J. Cohen, an attorney with Dinsmore and Shohl, regarding acquisitions and expansion plans in North America. "It is no longer about outsourcing but round sourcing," quipped Mr. Deher. "No company that wants to be global can afford to be in one location any more," he added, stating that the percentage of TCS workforce was increasing along with the number of non-Indians comprising it. These Indian companies will play a vital role in bringing Americans back to technical fields. "After the dotcom era, there was a feeling that technical jobs would be lost to firms in India, so there were fewer Americans taking them up," said Mr. Moormann. Now, the interest of students in technical fields is getting rekindled because technology companies are connecting to universities. "It is no longer about whether you are an Indian or a Japanese company. What people are interested in is if you are a good company with employee benefits," said Mr. Hensley.

European Government Support during Crisis

For what is the government but an extension of its people?

Europe was completely engulfed by the global financial storm, and the governments pitched in to fight it. After crisis talks, leaders were formulating measures and strategies to overcome the financial mayhem that snowballed out of Wall Street and hit the European banks. German property lender Hypo Real Estate was struggling for survival, with the government coming to its rescue, and Belgium was seeking a buyer for the crisis-ridden bank and insurance group Fortis. "We jointly commit to ensure the soundness and stability of our banking and financial system and will take all the necessary measures to achieve this objective," leaders of France, Germany, Britain, and Italy said in a statement. The emergency meeting stressed the need for governments to work in a coordinated manner. The idea of a pan-European rescue fund for banks was also mooted by a leader. "*We have taken a solemn undertaking as heads of states and government to support the banks and financial institutions in the face of this crisis,*" *the leader said.* During this period of financial turmoil, EU rules which impose limits on national deficits should take into account and allow for exceptional circumstances, a fact that was explicitly referred to in the leader's statement. It meant, any government could plead waiver from the EU deficit limits if it ran up a larger deficit in its bid to rescue banks or maybe just because of the global slowdown. United efforts would infuse confidence in the banking sector and help fend off recession. A leader said that no bank would be allowed to fail for lack of liquidity. "We will continue to do whatever is necessary," he said.

Government of India Support and Policies

*As individuals, organizations, regions, and
governments took up countermeasures.*

The ITES-BPO industry needed the support of the local governments in terms of infrastructure development, intellectual property protection, ease of starting business, tax incentives, and investment incentives and subsidies, especially during tough financial times. Special task teams were set up by governments and strategies devised with a view to boost this industry. Nodal agencies have lobbied with the government to provide benefits and incentives to the ITES-BPO industry. In fact, the growth of outsourcing industry in many countries is attributed to the support provided by the government, nodal agencies, and other associations. India has a highly effective legal system mandating enforcement of contracts and timely resolution of disputes vis-à-vis China, which suffers on account of a lack of a proper intellectual property protection system.

To tackle the pitfalls associated with the outsourcing industry and provide it a boost during the slowdown period the Indian government considered various aspects while framing policies regarding the sector such as IT-related architecture, right social environment, leveraging private sector initiatives, accelerating the development of knowledge hubs, defining thrust areas, creation of infrastructure, and decision making bodies/institutions. The license fee for entering the industry was abolished by the Indian government. Foreign equity participation up to 49% in centers that offer e-business services and 100% foreign participation permission in shared service centers were some of the series of measures taken by the Indian government for attracting domestic and foreign investment in the industry. To improve the quality of life, governance, and economic development, comprehensive packages of incentives and special promotional schemes and policies were announced. Export processing zones (EPZs) and software technology parks (STPs) offer world-class infrastructure and reliable data communication facilities. These technological features immensely aided outsourcing.

A slew of special incentives were offered by the Indian government to leverage outsourcing sector investment which included self-certification under various acts, concession in power tariff for new units, rebate on stamp duty on sale/lease of land, rebate on cost of land, special incentive package for megaprojects which were more than US$10 million (ITCOT report), and tax incentives. "IT industry employment promotion schemes" were introduced at the state level in India. In order to create human resource development programs, IT policies have been announced by the government, so that a trained pool of manpower is available for the ITES industry. Programs to develop skill, aptitude, communicative English, soft skills, accent neutralization, and ITES subdomain training have been given required attention by the government. In India, special thrust on spoken and written English at the school level is being provided by most of the state-level governments, and in the mainstream collegiate education system, special programs have been introduced.

Notifications and orders were promulgated by most of the state governments, permitting all establishments in respective jurisdictions to engage in ITES/BPO services, work on national holidays, allow women to work in night shifts, and allow offices to function for 24 hours a day throughout the year.

Government of India—Taxation Policies during Slowdown

Trying to keep the wheel in motion.

Indian ITES units established under STP/SEZ units were given indirect tax benefits during the slowdown. Import of goods into India was subject to custom duty, but STP/SEZ units could make duty-free imports of specified goods including capital goods required by the units for their activities. Except laptops and desktop computers, second-hand capital goods could also be imported duty free. Networking equipment, video projection systems, office equipment such as facsimiles, copiers, telephone systems, and modular furniture, and storage devices such as tapes, CDs, and floppies could be imported into India by such units without the payment of customs duty, although certain conditions may apply. The conditions envisaged that the eligible equipment is imported on a loan from clients or on lease basis. Excise duty exemption could be availed if the equipment is purchased locally from a manufacturer in India. Supplies received by SEZ/STP units from local manufacturers under certain circumstances were regarded as "deemed export" and were eligible for certain benefits under EXIM policy (Indian foreign trade policy). This should be borne in mind while procuring goods from local manufacturers. Subject to certain conditions, reimbursement of central sales tax (CST) paid on goods procured within India could be claimed. Call centers and medical transcription centers were exempt from service tax, and service tax was not applicable on export of services. Steady growth of contracting/outsourcing had been witnessed in India, and captive service providers such as branches or wholly owned subsidiaries of foreign companies or independent Indian companies carry out outsourcing-related activities in India.

A circular was issued by Central Board of Direct Taxes (CTBT) on January 2, 2004, regarding taxability of income in the hands of foreign entities outsourcing processes to Indian entities.

If the Indian entity which received outsourcing work from the foreign entity was not a permanent establishment of the foreign entity, which means there was no business connection between the foreign and Indian entities, then the Indian unit which was an independent unit is only subject to taxes assessed as a separate entity. The foreign entity would not be liable to tax in India. If the Indian entity carrying out the outsourcing activities of the foreign entity was a permanent establishment of the foreign entity, whereby meaning that a business connection exists between the two, then the Indian entity would be subject to tax according to the Indian IT circular of August 2004.

Special Economic Zones (SEZs) in India during Slowdown

As regions and areas turned into centers of specialized learning.

The special economic zone (SEZ) units got large tax breaks in India and with global recession compounding the problem of joblessness.

Secton 10 AA (7) of the Income Tax Act states that only a proportion of profits based on the proportion of export sales from the SEZ unit to the total to the total turnover of the company will be exempt from taxation. This anomaly in the IT Act needed to be corrected and the Commerce Department had asked the empowered group of ministers (e GOM) to do the same, because in the first five years of operations, SEZ units were entitled to 100% tax holiday.

During the tough recessionary period, a move that significantly benefited India's biggest IT firms was the Indian government's decision to amend the law regarding tax exemption for units operating in special economic zones (SEZs). IT firms like Infosys, Wipro, and Tata Consultancy Services (TCS), which had set up SEZ units under parent companies, were eligible for 100% tax exemption on profits at par with those set up as separate entities. The relevant norms under the Income Tax Act were changed.

As per Indian law, The ITES services that would be eligible for tax holiday according to the Central Board of Direct Taxes (CBDT) consist of call centers; Web site services, content development, and animation; support centers; data processing; revenue accounting; back office operations; remote maintenance, engineering, and design; payroll; geographic information systems services; medical transcription; human resource services; and legal database and insurance claim processing. Thus tax holidays are an incentive and boost to business, especially during slowdown periods.

Examples of Organizations That Managed the Slowdown Successfully

They that managed the downturn, unscathed.

Example—IBM Exception during Slowdown

In the midst of the financial storm that swept the United States and Europe in October 2008, IBM's earnings soothed tech sector's fears. The announcement of a 20% growth in net income at $2.8 billion for the third quarter by global IT major IBM had somewhat calmed tech sector jitters. Because the profit posted by IBM was higher than expected, it calmed some fears about the economic crisis sparking a technology demand meltdown. In the September quarter of 2007 the company had reported a net income of $2.36 billion. The profit news caused a 6% rise in IBM shares, which also provided a boost to other technology shares that had been hammered due to the global slowdown. The net income of International Business Machines Corp. jumped 20% to $2.8 billion. In the year 2007, earnings per share from continuing operations rose to $2.05 compared to $1.68, IBM said. Analyst were looking for earnings of $2.01 per share on revenue of $26.5 billion. Chief executive Samuel J. Palmisano mentioned a confident 2008 outlook for IBM, citing a steady base of recurring revenue and profits and investments for growth in emerging markets. In the technology sector, in 2008, IBM which gets about two-thirds of revenue from outside the United States, has been among the few companies who have been fortunate. Although the hard-pressed financial services sector caters to a quarter of IBM's revenues, about half of its business income is from services and software contracts, which may see the company through a severe financial slowdown. IBM's second quarter profit had surpassed Wall Street expectations, and the company had raised its 2008 profit per share forecast to at least $8.75 or 22% year-on-year growth.

"For companies to be reaffirming their outlook through the end of the year is huge," said Mike Holland, chairman of investment company Holland and Co., which oversees assets in excess of $4 billion, including IBM.

"It is very nice to see some positive news, not just for IBM but for, to a degree, the tech space overall, given the downdraft we have seen in recent weeks," said Chuck Jones, technology analyst for Atlantic Trust Private Wealth Management, which manages $16 billion of assets. But due to the overall market weakness and a sudden drop in sales of companies like European software giant SAP AG SAPG, Jones and other investors were wary of calling a bottom for the battered tech sector. "In this market you are gun shy about everything. It is hard to have a lot of conviction about everything out there," he said, but added, "This also can be a good time to buy stocks. When things look the bleakest, this is a good time to put some money to work."

Example—Outsourcing by JP Morgan Chase

The good news was that, despite the severe global recession, JP Morgan Chase, the second largest U.S. bank, had intentions of increasing outsourcing to India by 25%. After acquiring Washington Mutual and Bear Stearns, JP Morgan wanted to up outsourcing to India to almost $400 million in 2009. With a view to reduce the cost of integrating different information technology (IT) systems, the company will also manage the integration of acquired companies from India. Every year, the company outsources nearly $250 to $300 million worth of IT and back office projects to vendors like Cognizant, TCS, and Accenture, apart from its own captive center in Mumbai. JP Morgan intends to drive several integration projects from India as well as increase outsourcing to India according to Guy Chiarello, CIO of the company. After the U.S. banking meltdown, JP Morgan was one of the first banks to reveal its outsourcing strategy. For many other banks, IT spending was on hold with strategy still undecided. In 2004, JP Morgan had cancelled a $5 billion outsourcing contract with IBM. Some 4,000 IT staff were brought back in-house after a merger, and for the merged entity the then CIO Austin Adams had propounded a "do it yourself" strategy.

Example—M&A—Mergers of Global Banks

Indian companies such as Infosys, TCS, and Cognizant were bidding for large contracts to the tune of over $100 million in the wake of large global banks like Lloyds TSB and HBOS and Bank of America and Merrill Lynch merging. The merger of banks had given rise to a huge task of integrating their software applications and consolidating their data centers and other trading platforms into a single entity so that customers can perform transactions without being hindered by issues related to mergers. *To cut costs and save as much as 30% to 40%, these merged banking entities planned to outsource to providers having significant offshore presence.* Banks intended to partner with offshore vendors, because they knew the systems better, translating into cost savings for banks.

The merged entity comprising Lloyds TSB and HBOS was scouting for partners to help it integrate its retail and wholesale banking systems through an IT platform. The human resource functions of the company had already been outsourced to Xansa two years ago, in a five-year deal. Meanwhile a consortium of banks including the Royal Bank of Scotland acquired ABN Amro. Both ABN Amro and the Royal Bank of Scotland are Infosys customers. "M&A is the silver lining for us in this environment, and we are winning transformation deals," Infosys chief executive Kris Gopalakrishnan said. "In some of these cases we are fortunate to be incumbents," he added.

Example—Omega BPO's Business Strategy

Despite the global financial storm, healthcare BPO firm Omega intended to increase hiring and planned to add 7,000 employees to its India facilities. CEO Gopi Natarajan foresees doubling of the company's client base and revenues growing fourfold by 2012. Omega's staff strength is about 2,000 at its Bangalore and Chennai facilities, and it seeks to invest $50 million in India and grow sales from $15 $20 million to $70–$90 million. Mr. Natarajan said that bulk of the hiring will take place in Bangalore. Omega provides services such as medical coding, billing, claims processing and health care revenue management. "Other countries don't have such a complex healthcare delivery system. Out of 290 million Americans, around 245 million have insurance and around 90% of the revenue cycle management space is untapped," Mr. Natarajan said. The company, whose investors include private equity firm Healthedge and Enam Holdings, operates through intermediaries and through its 65 clients. It caters to some 20 hospitals and 500 physicians. By 2012, it sees itself operating through 125 intermediaries and serving 100 hospitals and 15,000 physicians. *"Medical coding and voice-based process are growing. Only 9% of the work has been outsourced and the rest remains untapped,"* Mr. Natarajan said.

Example—Business Processing Outsourcing by Capita, UK

The importance of India as an outsourcing destination was emphasized when the CEO of Capita, the United Kingdom's largest business process outsourcer, said that Indian was essential to them. The company has expansion plans in the life and pensions business in India. Capita Group Plc. had recently won a £722 million deal from Prudential against Tata Consultancy Services (TCS). The outsourcer is betting big on the life and pensions business and is pursuing opportunities worth over £1 billion in the segment, Capita chief executive Paul Pinder said. Capita's India staff strength has doubled from 1,400 to 3,000 as a result of the Prudential deal, and the company has recently inaugurated another facility at Pune, indicating the importance of India in its growth plans.

Example—Dell Worldwide Launch

In 2008, the importance of India as one of the most favored outsourcing destinations was highlighted once again with the launch of the E series of notebooks by Dell. Three cities were chosen for this important event—London, San Francisco, and New Delhi. Chairman Michael Dell himself did the job in New Delhi to showcase the new line. Dell was actually on a holiday in India, and that he decided to break his holiday and cut the ribbon points to India's importance for the chairman. In the Indian personal computers market, Dell has consolidated its position. The company now ranks third after overtaking Lenovo and is only behind HCL and Hewlett Packard in the global sweepstakes. And what is Dell's sales pitch? "Nobody offers customization like we do in the given lead time," says Dell India country general manager Mr. Sameer Garde, adding, "This is the power customers want." A facility called customer factory integration is offered by Dell to its customers, wherein the company offers to burn images on each customer's computer hard disk before shipment instead of customer's engineers putting images on each machine. Garde said, "I personally met 50 to 60 CIOs in three cities recently and not one of them said IT spends would be cut. The mandate from CEOs is to improve productivity and get more out of the IT spends. They want to buy machines that consume less power and take less space."

Example—Godrej–HP Contract

Braving the global economic storm, a 10-year outsourcing contract was signed between Godrej Industries and Hewlett Packard (HP) in a major domestic outsourcing deal in October 2008. Application development, maintenance, infrastructure management, and transformational initiatives were included in the contract. The agreement envisaged that HP would take over the IT operations staff of both the companies. Ever since the first such outsourcing deal happened between Bharti and IBM, there have been a number of similar deals by Indian business groups. Future and Wipro had signed a similar outsourcing contract for $150 million in February 2008, and as per the arrangement about 265 employees of Pantaloon retail had moved to the IT firm. In the Godrej–HP deal, the staff working in IT management was to be retained by Godrej, while the IT operations staff was to be taken over by Hewlett Packard. These contracts enabled domestic firms to reduce IT costs and induce greater efficiencies.

For multinationals, large, multiyear outsourcing contracts are a new and growing business opportunity in the wake of growing pressures in their home markets. Ernst and Young had been appointed by the Godrej Group to aid them in identifying the most suitable IT partner. For HP, the Godrej win was meaningful, because it was in a segment outside of financial services, which had been its strongest segment traditionally. Some time back, a transformation engagement from Britannia was also won by it.

Example—BPO Operations Execution Example—By Vertex

According to some, despite the economic meltdown in the United States and the crisis in financial markets, contracting/outsourcing is set to grow. BPO firm Vertex was looking at acquisitions of domestic BPO companies in India. The company planned to move 300 jobs in HR and finance among other functions to India. In their home market, employees on these roles would be redeployed in other functions. "We can't be a leading global BPO player without India being a vital part," according to Vertex managing director for private sector Bruce MacLeod. He was recently made accountable for India. According to Mr. MacLeod, the company aimed to do more work for clients in the United Kingdom and North America out of India, as well as expand in India, especially through acquisitions. In order to gain critical mass and a larger presence in India, Vertex was looking to acquire two to three BPO firms. The BPO firm has about 1,200 employees in Indian domestic market and wants to increase it up to 5,000 to 6,000 employees.

Example—Legal Process Outsourcing (LPO)

Some analysts think that the U.S. economic crisis could translate into more business for LPOs (legal process outsourcing) because a lot of credit crisis–related work was being shifted by bankers to India. Therefore this sector could be abuzz with activity in the years to come. Many U.S. corporate houses and investment banks were seeking legal advice because there was a surge in bankruptcy filings in the United States. Thus demand for lawyers increased, and as a cost-cutting measure, U.S. corporate houses were outsourcing work to Indian lawyers, and leading LPOs, such as Pangea 3, Quislex, and Mindcrest, among others, had encountered significant growth in outsourcing activity. "The demand for LPOs is on the rise as legal work related to bankruptcies in the global market has increased," said Pangea 3 VP legal services Antony Alex. The U.S. financial service sector turmoil was causing more outsourcing to India in the LPO sector according to experts. "Since appointing a lawyer is expensive overseas, especially in the United States and the United Kingdom, it is natural for corporations to shift higher-value work to India at this time of crisis," said a source. Currently, the number of LPOs in India is about 200, and the number is expected to increase significantly in the years to come. *The LPO industry has registered a growth of over 60% annually.* In 2007, the industry stood at 630 crores (Rs. 6.3 billion) and is expected to reach Rs. 2,770 crores (Rs. 2.7 billion) in India by the end of 2010, thereby creating jobs for 24,000 people according to a study by Value Notes. The firm provides equity research, financial, and stock market information.

Example—Tesco

Tesco earned considerable revenues through outsourcing initiatives, and it planned to continue outsourcing to its Indian captive center and Indian vendors such as TCS and Wipro. Mike McNamara, director operations and information technology at Tesco, said that by outsourcing to India, $60 million is saved by Tesco every year.

Example—Banking Products

Competition flared up between Indian IT companies as Infosys beat TCS to bag $15 million U.S. bank order. The Union Bank of California, US, chose Infosys banking product Finacle over that of TCS for its core banking solutions (CBS). The bank had shortlisted only these two vendors for the project. Despite the presence of established banking products companies in the United States such as Temenos, Fiserve, and Metavante, among others, only these two Indian vendors were surprisingly invited. Finacle is the banking solution portfolio of Infosys, while BANCS is the banking product of TCS. Both firms with strong focus on providing banking solutions were locked in a close contest. In terms of assets, Union Bank of California is the 25th-largest U.S. bank, with 330 branch offices in California, Washington, and Oregon. The bank headquarters is in San Francisco, with two international offices and facilities in other states. The bank, which has over 10,000 employees, recorded $2.6 billion revenue in 2007. The order bagged by Infosys was significant in the eyes of industry observers because it provided a strong foothold in the U.S. financial market. Oracle Financial Services (the erstwhile i-flex), Infosys, TCS, Nucleus Software, 3 I Infotech, and Infrasoft are some of the leading banking software solutions firms in India. Apart from domestic market, these firms are also focused on Asia Pacific, Africa, Middle East, and European markets.

Examples—Miscellaneous

The many flowers that make up a bouquet.

Decline in global commodity prices and deceleration in growth of raw material costs compared to Q1 2009 brought some relief to Indian companies. There was a dip in the upward pressure on wage costs. *To cope with slashed IT budgets, clients like BT, Citi, GE, and Bank of America outsourced approximately $4 billion worth of new contracts to Indian IT firms like TCS, Infosys, Wipro, and HCL in 2009, notwithstanding the global financial turmoil.* Some top outsourcing deals slated for India in 2009 included a $250 million outsourcing contract by Australian phone firm Telstra and several $50 to $100 million-range contracts from BT, Citi, GE, etc.

Application maintenance contracts would be a part of the new contracts worth almost $4 billion, according to outsourcing expert Sabysachi S. Satyaprasad of

Midplex Consulting, but he added that Indian providers could lose over $300 million because of lower billing rates. "Many large customers reduced their IT budgets by up to 10%, and they plan to seek more cost- and business output-based deliverables from the service providers in these difficult times," he said.

Best Buy, Visa, Nissan, and British Telecom (BT) renewed contracts translating into significant savings. Some time back, BT renegotiated its contracts with Xansa, with a view to save around $123 million over the next six years. However, the deal also resulted in more work for Xansa, estimated to be almost 80% of BT's overall back office projects.

The feel of leaping off a high potential platform.

Chapter 17

Slowdown—Hiring, Layoffs, and Attrition

The web of talking devices, with human interfaces on the fringes.

Attrition

As people come and go.

Attrition is one of the gravest problems that business process outsourcing (BPO) call centers have to contend with. It dents revenue and productivity, and additional cost, time, and effort have to be spent on hiring and training. Here are some tips to reduce attrition.

One interesting effect of recession was that attrition in BPO vertical dropped, and HR managers were more relaxed. *As per statistics, in the BPO sector attrition was down to less than 20%. Before the recession, attrition was high as 50% a year, with smaller BPO companies registering even higher attrition levels.* It had become imperative for companies earlier to recruit hundreds of BPO agents every few months to cope with attrition. With very few jobs in the market during the downturn, employees were forced to keep their existing jobs.

The attrition problem has plagued the industry since its very inception, for more than ten years now. Some factors that prompted recruits to leave BPO industry were night shifts and erratic work timings, higher education, and better job prospects elsewhere. The same was true for the middle- and senior-level management, and it had become quite a challenge to retain them, because one could quickly leapfrog to the senior level elsewhere by working for just about one year at the middle-level management in a major BPO organization. Earlier even incentive schemes could not retain the loyalties of the recruits, but in the recessionary period many were willing to work at lower salaries and incentives due to acute paucity of career options.

WNS had an attrition of 48% during Q4 of 2007, which dropped to 37% for Q1 of fiscal 2008–2009. "Our retention strategy starts from hiring the right candidate by adopting a rigorous recruitment process that includes appropriate profiling techniques. We sensitize new employees to the WNS culture and values. We understand the aspirations and needs of the individual and create enablers for the employee to realize their aspirations," said WNS chief people officer Kartik Sharma. Similarly, Genpact which has a 35,500 workforce globally, reported an attrition of about 25% in the current fiscal conditions. "Let's face it. The BPO industry is just about a decade old. It takes time to mature as a sector and being accepted as a career option. Earlier it was the last resort for losers or a mere time pass. Now a vast range of operations and requisite domain specializations exist," said Genpact HR head Piyush Mehta. In an organization, an overwhelming majority of the positions at the top level are filled through internal promotions.

"In our case only 10% of our operations are voice based, and our value proposition is challenging and intellectually stimulating work for BPO employees. They also offer opportunities to straddle between IT and BPO for employees," said TCS global HR VP and head Ajoy Mukerjee. Its attrition had come down to 20.5%.

Some analysts felt that the ITES/BPO sector had matured, and employees perceived it as a viable long-term career option now. Earlier, the ITES/BPO sector was considered as a means of making quick money by the majority of employees and a stop-gap arrangement till another suitable job was found. "With new business deliverables and verticals being added in their repertoire, the need for specialized skills and trained individuals has become mandatory. The employees have also realized the importance of building a career and know what they are looking for when they enter into the organization," said NASSCOM vice president Sangita Gupta.

As the financial turmoil in the United States and Europe deepened, there was a perceptible fear in BPOs, because many big and small BPO/KPO companies had been impacted. Experts were of the opinion that the sector would be hit severely. The Indian BPO/KPO sector was facing the heat of the U.S. meltdown, particularly due to the financial services markets slowdown. Small and midsized companies' business had taken a further beating because a major part of business comes from banking and financial services firms in the United States. "The slowdown is going to impact the BPO firms in India. This will eventually result in overall slowdown of the BPO industry. But now a large pool of professionals will be able to provide quality services to the Indian BPO/KPO industry at much lower prices," says IDBI capital market services research head Shahina Mukadam. According to a NASSCOM report, Rs. 1,160 crore revenue was generated and employment to 700,000 people was provided in 2007–2008 by the BPO and KPO industry together. In 2007, the United States had the highest share of 61% in the Indian BPO/KPO export market. KPO Azure

Knowledge Center had predicted a slowdown in the financial services by 25% and in the insurance services by 15% by 2008 end. The company is based in Ahmedabad. Azure Knowledge Center director Jay Ruparel said, "The debacle in the U.S. will create a lot of uncertainties regarding the continuity of current financial services contracts and also raise doubts as to how future contracts are signed with the U.S. financial companies." "The employment scenario in the BPO/KPO industry is going through an extremely dull patch and this in turn will have an effect on the growth in this industry," says Karvy Stock Broking, vice president of Ambreesh Baliga. Job insecurity and fear haunts BPOs/KPOs, and companies such as Smart Cube with about 130 employees in 2008 expected the employment rate of the firm to go down by 30% in 2009. Companies were laying off employees en masse, and Smart Cube was exception. Smart Cube managing director Sameer Walia said, "Future hiring rate of BPOs will be far worse off as compared to the KPO firms. The BPO employment rate is projected to decline by 60% within a span of one year." However, Exevo COO Vivek Sharma said, "I see an immediate term negative impact, which will continue for around six to nine months. But in the long term, any other financial institution will fill up the space vacated by Lehman Brothers. We have received around 50 resumes from the ex-employees of Lehman Brothers in the past few days."

As the economic meltdown deepened, attrition in Indian BPO industry reduced, because employees tried to save their jobs. In the BPO industry history, it was the the first time that HR was in relax mode. Before the recession, in the outsourcing industry, the call center agents and HR managers were the two types of people who were very busy. Due to enormous workloads, the call center agents were overworked and had acute paucity of time, while HR was busy trying to hire and retain agents. With no letup in the expansion of contracting/outsourcing industry, the agents continued to be busy, but it was the HR managers who now were more relaxed and had to bother less about agent retention.

Layoffs during Slowdown

As a result of global meltdown, it was not just the ITES–BPO industry that placed employees in the firing line, but hiring had also been put on hold in the aviation and financial services sectors, and there were massive layoffs. Cash crunch, deepening apprehension, and low consumer confidence scuttled hiring and expansion plans of businesses. In just two to three months after the recession began, there was a plunge of 12% to 15% in hiring plans of the hospitality, retail, and automobile sectors. HR managers felt that this could snowball into a much bigger crisis.

This hesitation to spend is causing serious pain for businesses. A BT-CII producers' survey shows just how bad the news is. Demand has shrunk for 90 cent of the respondents in the survey. Nearly 70 per cent rated lack of consumer confidence as the biggest economic problem today—several notches above credit unavailability. There was an internal assessment by all companies of their "head-to-tail" ratio.

A revenue generating source is referred to as a "head," while the "tail" relates to the back end and support functions in HR parlance. "It is primarily the tail functions where recruitment is getting slower," said Mr. Balaji.

Ganesh Shermon of KPMG Human Capital felt that some service sector companies would also resort to layoffs. "Downsizing has already taken place in the IT and aviation sectors. Companies that have hired a lot of retail salesmen and shop floor employees might lay off some people," he warned.

Future Group completed a HR cost optimization exercise and said, "We have recently floated two new companies—Future Learning and Development (for employees training) and Future Knowledge (which is the IT/ITES) arm. A lot of our existing employees have been redeployed there. However, we are yet to feel the impact of the current meltdown," Future Retail HR head Sanjay Jog said.

India director (operations) Cherian Kuruvilla said during the recession period, "Retailers are indeed rationalizing their expansion and recruitment plans." Even the manufacturing sector might slow down on hiring because expansion plans are likely to get affected due to the liquidity crunch. "Sectors like telecom and insurance are unlikely to get impacted since these are already on high growth trajectory," Mr. Kuruvilla said.

In the face of economic downturn, companies were adopting stringent appraisal measures, trimming costs, and improving productivity. Employees were asked to leave across almost all sectors as companies grappled with the global financial storm.

Economic recession was taking its toll and corporations were resorting to layoffs to salvage their positions. *At some top companies, talk of retrenchment of employees was followed by repeated management clarifications on the issue.* There was talk going the rounds of big Indian IT firms laying off thousands of employees. After such reports surfaced in the media, some CEOs mailed all employees, with a view to allay their layoff fears and reassure them. Such mailings were sent to reassure employees against the false reports circulating in the media that the company was handing out pink slips.

Indian Reverse Brain Drain

Back to the roots.

Indian professionals started returning to India as the employment scene worsened in the United States and Europe. Until recently, as a stop-gap arrangement or as a long-term career prospect, such qualified returning Indians including engineers, MBAs, architects, and others could find employment in the booming IT/ITES and financial services businesses' back office sectors, back in India. Such engineers usually opted for the lucrative IT sector and the MNC financial institutions, though other sectors like manufacturing could also have provided employment.

"A lot of CVs have flown in from cities like New York and London," said Korn/Ferry *country head (India) Deepak Gupta.* Delhi-based search firm executive access MD Ronesh Puri agreed, "We are getting quite a few resumes from banking executives in developed nations on a daily basis, and their number has risen by more than 50% in the last two months. Most of them are of Indian origin."

Flagging prospects in the United States and Europe, due to the ongoing slowdown, resulted in reverse brain drain. Burgeoning new economies abroad are causing talented immigrants to be homeward bound. For more than four decades, India and China suffered a major brain drain as many talented professionals left their homes for the United States. The lumbering U.S. immigration rules have caused many with postgraduate and doctorate degrees in management, technology, or science, to move back. Pointing out that America's loss will be the world's gain, Wadhwa, in a study published in the *Washington Post* said, "Immigrants who leave the U.S. will launch companies, file patents, and fill the intellectual coffers of other countries." "Their talent will benefit nations such as India, China, and Canada, not the U.S.," the study said. Foreign nationals account for almost 25% of all international patent applications filed from the United States in 2006, Wadhwa said.

Economy and People's Health

Economic downturn takes a toll on people's health. The financial slowdown has played havoc with America's health, increasing stress and fear regarding personal finances and the economy. As many as 80% of Americans were stressed, with women being the worst sufferers according to a survey by the American Psychological Association. An overwhelming 80% American residents directly blame the declining state of the country's economy for much of the anxiety in their life. "With the deteriorating economy dominating the headlines, it is easy to worry more about your finances than your health, but stress over money and the economy is taking an emotional and physical toll on the United States, especially among women. Many say they are handling their stress well. Yet, people report more physical and emotional symptoms." A survey found that concerns regarding ability to provide for their family's basic needs and fears about job stability were reasons for the increasing stress for more than half of the Americans. Job insecurity, heavy work load, and anxieties about salary resulted in less productivity at work. The increasing level of stress led 60% of poll respondents to report that they were feeling angry as well as irritable, 53% reported fatigue, and 52% said they remain awake at night. Headaches were reported by as many as 47%, 35% had upset stomachs, and 34% experienced muscular tension. Women were likely to suffer more than men, reporting physical symptoms of stress like fatigue (57% compared to 49%), irritability (65% compared to 55%), headaches (56% compared to 36%), and feeling depressed and sad (56% compared to 39%).

An Assocham study says that 68% of CEOs were stressed during the slowdown period. During slowdown in the Indian economy, the study found that 68% of corporate house CEOs with turnover of over 5,000 crores were undergoing restlessness and stress. Of 400 CEOs of public and private-sector companies surveyed, 128 said that they get rid of their stress through activities like yogic exercises, gym, sports such as golf and cycling, music, and morning stroll.

In the wake of the financial downturn, exports crimped tremendously, and despite control on inflation and active government participation to bail out the staggering financial industry, growth rates plummeted across verticals. *A survey poll of 12 Asian economies except Japan projected a health warning, given the global economic turmoil.* Financial markets plunged into utter chaos after U.S. lawmakers rejected a $700 billion plan to bail out Wall Street's. Many Asian economies that have been thriving on exports were hit hard as demand in overseas markets weakened, and sliding stock markets further compound the crisis. Wall Street's collapse increased the pace of global downturn, with the Euro Zone economy shrinking. China, India, and most other Asian economies were impacted by the meltdown, and economists said that Japan was also hit and not insulated.

A fallout of the economic turmoil saw Mumbai, the financial capital of India, register the highest growth in the sale of antidepressant drugs. *Depression and fatigue caused by financial insecurity fears led to soaring antidepression drugs' sales.* Compared to the Indian national average of 8%, Mumbai saw the sale of antidepressant medicines grow by 30%.

HR consultants too vouched for the fear prevailing among executives. "All of a sudden jobs were being cut in hundreds across sectors. There is definitely fear and anxiety due to uncertainties about jobs and loses," said Transsearch International life science partner Tejinder Pal Singh.

Consequences of the global economic recession included massive layoffs by companies and salary ceasing to be attractive anymore. Corridors are abuzz with discussions of employee retrenchment and poor salary hikes, or even no hikes for those lucky enough to save their jobs. Bonuses were out of the question for some time as companies sought to cut costs. The excitement of working had been replaced by fear and job uncertainty. The story held good for professionals across multiple sectors during the slowdown worldwide. Lack of hefty bonuses, increments, and perks led to demotivation of employees and possible fall in productivity, especially in sectors such as banking, financial services, insurance (BFSI), IT, and information technology enabled service (ITES).

Therefore companies should focus on keeping their existing staff in good humor in such times of crisis. Active dialogue could be fruitful, while rumors could compound the crisis. Let people voice their issues and concerns. Provide them with facts and figures regarding the global economy, its impact on India, and its effect on your company. Do not let rumors complicate the issue. "Break it down to the smallest unit possible to explain what the future holds for them.

Prepare them for everything, but give them the true picture," says KPMG India human capital solutions partner and head Ganesh Shermon.

During times of crisis some ways to boost employee morale and keep them in good humor are

A. **Counseling and mentoring:** Counseling can change employee behavior and office environment. Concerns and fears of employees should be treated as your own, because they are the most important asset and therefore should get a sense of belonging.

B. **Inform and clarify:** Inform employees of an alternate plan. You should clarify the difference between a no-go project and a timing delay. In the case of timing delay, explain and elaborate the reasons for it along with an alternate plan.

C. **Avoid a knee jerk reaction or rash action:** Rash actions like huge layoffs to save costs dent an organization's reputation. Decisions should be made after due deliberation to avoid repenting later.

D. **To mitigate attrition and improve staff retention,** mental techniques like suggestion/autosuggestion along with relaxation can be made use of. *This may require the services of a trained psychologist/psychiatrist who may use relaxation techniques to relieve stress and strain and improve productivity.*

E. **Exercise** is a good stress buster which keeps one fit and is a tonic not only for the physical body but also for the mind, for it helps in getting rid of negative emotions and promotes happiness. Providing recreational facilities like a gymnasium, or sports facilities, and free/subsidized meals are small gestures which go a very long way toward retention.

Personnel Retention

Of holding strong through highs and lows.

It makes sense for most firms to hire quality, experienced, technologically tenacious, forward-thinking IT experts with commitment and savvy in technology strategies. But the paradox commences here. Practically it has been seen that the more technically qualified personnel are likely to manage the firm's technology only for a period of time. *Since there are not enough tools or toys to play with, the best IT people will not be with the firm for long, and the more technical the IT persons are, the more difficult they are to retain.* The best IT administrators are busy and happy only with firms with complete network configurations, ample servers, multioffice requirements, and a high user count. The highly technical administrators generally remain on board for less than two years and leave for more challenging and dynamic positions, if firms have 75 or less employees. Minimum working hours and time quotas are foreign to project-minded IT people and can build resentment, while the logic of tracking time is understandable. The time measurement that all other staff adhere to applies to IT people also.

It has been found in accounting firms that they benefit more if they employ people with the following traits: interested in job security, employed late in their career cycle, technical to the extent they are comfortable providing daily administration and troubleshooting, reserved in making change without thorough investigation of the situation, and a strong desire to please end users.

Because India's economy is not limited to just the top few cities but is spread across the whole of India, job seekers spread out all over the country. Indian firms used strategies of diversification and localization to tap new territories for revenue, both domestic and abroad. Hiring started picking up in India, though on a cautious note, 12 to 18 months after the economic meltdown worldwide.

One of the key issues that the human resource department needs to ascertain during interviews is the seriousness of the candidate to stick to the organization for a longer period. Some companies resort to the practice of bonds, wherein new recruits are asked to fill up bonds for 6 months or 1 year or more. It has been found that this does not really act as a strong deterrent, with staff quitting despite the bond being in force. *Companies try to avoid litigation on an employee bond because it means more expenditure, effort, and waste of time.* Usually it is the freshers (those with little or no experience) who are asked to fill up bonds, while the experienced staff that is hired may or may not be asked to do so. Since most freshers have no idea of the kind of work in a call center, a good strategy would be to make them listen in on calls for a couple of hours before offering them employment. Many candidates will surprisingly decide that this is not the kind of work that they would like to do.

The salaries of IT people who are not billable may be lower than other colleagues, and the fact that the IT people are counted as overhead troubles most shareholders. The reality is that the IT salaries are frequently inflated compared to many vocations. Therefore a strategy to increase the firm's revenue consists of using the internal IT staff to provide service to its own clients. The problem of using highly qualified internal IT personnel arises from the notion that, once the system has been implemented, it should run and be left alone until it breaks. Partners are change resistant in the arena of technology, but IT people with a true passion for technology, those with high aptitude, desire and crave change. To stifle their desire for change means to kill their passion, which leads to frustration because they have an intense desire to tinker with programs, install new software, and work on new hardware. Some firms expect their internal IT persons to act as technological visionaries and strategy architects. This may create problems because most network administrators are busy with end user and application issues, and very little time is available to study the market and relevant technology trends. The result may be disappointing if the firm leans on the IT persons for ownership of IT vision and strategy. With the broad range of solutions available in the market today, it may be too much to ask the internal IT administrator to have that kind of knowledge and experience. The technology infrastructure of such firms may be limited, making it difficult to compete with IT consultants that specialize in providing strategic planning, consulting, and system implementations.

People are the most important asset of a company, and various aspects associated with them need to be addressed properly. The lure of better pay packages triggers people to switch companies, and so it is all the more important that issues like stress, strain, job satisfaction, and a congenial office environment be addressed. Staff retention can prove beneficial to the company, leading to less expenditure on hiring and training of new recruits and leveraging from the knowledge of the experienced staff.

Example—Hiring by RBS of Lehman

While suitors were lining up for Lehman's back office operations in India, the Royal Bank of Scotland (RBS) through an innovative hiring move conducted job interviews at a venue in the close vicinity of Lehman BPO to recruit some of the skilled staff for its own back office operations. Though not all operations of Lehman's back office were attractive, a section of its operations were quite high end and involved algorithmic systems in addition to other work commonly referred to as knowledge process outsourcing (KPO). According to an executive working in the capital market's division of Lehman BPO, RBS could also make offers to some of Lehman's employees. The presence of RBS back office in India was already significant because of its acquisition of ABN Amros's captive. In India around 5,000 people were employed by the captive, which did equity research and other related work. In the national capital region of Delhi, India, RBS additionally had an offshore IT firm employing around 1,000 people.

JP Morgan had also sent feelers to hire some of Lehman's employees. But the wages offered by both the firms (RBS and JP Morgan) were lower.

Hiring in India before and during the Financial Slowdown

Initially, during the early stages of the financial slowdown in 2008, India's IT and ITES sector expected hiring to continue in the fourth quarter of 2008, with some companies stating that they intended to increase hiring. An HR consulting firm, Manpower Survey, said that a majority of companies would continue their hiring process in Q4 of 2008. A total of 1,098 companies across the IT, ITES, and BPO space were involved in the survey. India had a net employment outlook of 57%. Of the respondents, about 58% anticipated an increase in employment, while notably only 1% felt a decrease in hiring. About 26% reported no change in their hiring, and the rest did not comment. Analysts said that hiring in the sector could receive a boost due to upcoming IT and ITES special economic zones (SEZ) and parks, and that cost-cutting measures in the developed countries would increase outsourcing to India. In the APAC region, India was leading in creating employment in the services sector, and its employment outlook for the entire sector stood at 47% for Q4 compared to 15% to 21% for countries such as Australia, China, New Zealand, Taiwan, and Singapore. But with the advent of 2009, most of the Indian IT/ITES companies resorted to stringent cost cutting and layoff measures, and as the financial crisis deepened there was a perceptible decrease in hiring.

In India, the recession had a negative hiring impact, despite the fact that the economy was growing at a rate which was among the better growth rates worldwide. The adverse effect of the Indian demographic dividend was also felt by job seekers. In India, every year more than 3 million fresh graduates are ready for employment. They include more than 10,000 engineers just from the top 25 colleges alone, more than 5,000 MBAs from the top 25 business schools, more than 500 textiles, apparel, and accessories designers from the top 10 fashion institutes, more than 2,000 retail professionals from the miscellaneous substreams of specialization, and more than 2,500 aviation sector professionals.

There was decline in hiring across all sectors including some top recruiters like banking, financial services, insurance (BSFI) and IT. Large companies and recruitment agencies alike laid off employees, and for the smaller companies survival was at stake. Earlier when the Indian economy was booming, there was considerable expansion and job opportunity due to the inflow of foreign money. "We were in an employee market so far. *Now it is the employer's market, where companies have the last word in hiring," said ABC Consultants CEO Shiv Aggarwal during the slow-down period.* There was a complete U-turn in the scenario, with hiring either on hold or staff strength being slashed, causing deep trouble for the recruitment agencies. "There are many small consultant companies that were dependent on recruiting people for specific sectors like call centers, and such firms have shut shop," said Mr. Aggarwal. Teamlease chairman Manish Sabherwal agreed, saying that many Bangalore recruitment agencies reduced staff strength by 30% to 40%. "Consultants, especially those offering services in BFSI and IT sectors, have slashed their staff strength," said Mr. Sabherwal. He added, "You either have to be a big player or operate in a niche segment to sustain." With the downturn having just set in, Mr. Aggarwal had not faced any problem, but if the recession did not abate soon, then he would have to take corrective action to increase market share. Analysts felt that freshers would bear the brunt of the recession because higher-level management was necessary to run business. Recruiters for top-level appointments were slow to feel the impact of the recession. "There is still demand for talent at higher and specialized levels in sectors like manufacturing, fast moving consumer goods (FMCGs), financial sector," Mr. Suresh said. Consultants felt that there would be a demand in sectors like pharma, infrastructure, food, and media, in spite of the global meltdown. The investment banking sector, often associated with power and hefty pay packets, received a huge blow.

In the 1990s and early 2000s huge numbers of middle-management jobs running into hundreds of thousands were shed by the United States and the European Union. Many of those jobs were never really filled up even during the boom period of five years before the recession. Creation of jobs actually occurred in different sectors such as financial services, retail, healthcare, and hospitality, to name a few.

There was an acute paucity of jobs, especially as far as the highly educated are concerned. Possibly, it may be a time when it is more difficult for the graduates, postgraduates, and the professionally qualified to find employment compared to the less educated multitudes. Engineers, MBAs, pilots and aviation industry staff, and software professionals, among others were some of the well educated who struggled in the recessionary period to find a decent job. For those in the middle and senior management functions, the problem is more severe. It is very unlikely that prospective employers will resort to aggressive hiring soon even if the overall business scenario improves.

India—Back to Hiring after the Economic Recovery

With the economic recession over in India, hiring is back in a big way. All outsourcing players, Infosys, Wipro, TCS, IBM-India, etc., are aggressively back to hiring. With the Indian economy and job market again becoming very hot propositions, employees are jumping jobs to maximize from this newfound freedom after the recession period. Potential candidates are literally doubling their salaries at all organizational rungs through job switches. Organizations are experiencing large-scale growth at all levels—junior, middle, and senior management levels. The IT and BPO sector is back to its usual attrition levels as employers begin to struggle to retain valued employees and experience. Job placement agents are back in roaring business, and it is again the employee's market.

A sense of belonging over time, to values, systems, and organizations.

OUTSOURCING— MISCELLANEOUS CONCERNS AND THE FUTURE

Chapter 18

Intellectual Property and Data Security

Differentiation in leaps.

Intellectual Property (IP)

Piracy

Values—Enforced, imposed, and self-driven.

It is clear that the speed of technological development has outpaced the legal system. Protecting intellectual property rights and collecting dues from the copyright users promise to be challenging issues. The damage that can be inflicted with a photocopy machine can be vastly surpassed by the degree of potential copyright infringement online. *Countless copies of anything digital, be it a book, a TV or computer program, or a piece of music, can be made by anyone with a computer.* The digital version can be sent to friends or a bulletin board system (BBS) for downloading by anyone with a modem. Stakes have been raised considerably by advances in technology, and virtually any work can readily be "digitized," archived, and used in the digital format. The ease and speed with which work can be reproduced is thus increased, along with the speed with which copies (authorized and unauthorized) can be delivered to the public. Works can be combined with other works into a single medium, such as CD ROM, causing a blurring of traditional lines. High-speed, high-capacity networking makes it possible for an organization to submit perfect copies of digitized works to multiple other organizations and individuals.

315

Similarly, such work may be uploaded to a bulletin board from which large numbers of authorized users may download the same.

IP

That abstract property.

In the absence of appropriate systems to enforce the terms and conditions of copyright, owners may not put their interests at risk by publishing their works. Unless integrity of those works is assured, many related services and the market necessary for the success may not be available. The extracts that form copyright/contractual schemes that attempt to govern the area of the online database world affecting most educational institutions need to be looked at closely. At least, without prior written permission, most terms and conditions prohibit (or appear to prohibit) online searchers from sharing the results with others. *No downloading at all, no electronic storage, no copies or distribution even internally, no copies or distribution to third parties, and specific limitation on various types of use are some of the categories.* If the clauses were strictly enforced, how one would perform searches visually is worth giving a thought. These provisions are often widely ignored by users and are known by the industry to be widely ignored. Copyright violations are being curbed by several new research efforts. To help protect copyrighted works against unauthorized access, reproduction, manipulation, distribution, performance, or display, these efforts aim to use technology. Areas of active research are authentication of copyrighted works and management and licensing of rights. Technology-based protection of digital works can be implemented through hardware, software, or a combination thereof. It can be implemented at the level of copyrighted work or at some distant levels. It can be used to prevent or restrict access to work, as well as reproduction, adaptation, distribution, performance, or display of work. Unauthorized access can be denied in two general ways—by restricting access to the source of work and by restricting manipulation of the electronic file containing the work. Commercial online services, such as America Online and dial-up private bulletin boards and nearly all information providers, not only control access to their system but also vary it depending on the information a user wishes to access (e.g., access to certain data is conditioned to paying a higher fee and having greater access rights). Internet users, on the other hand, can connect to public servers through protocols such as gopher, file transfer protocol (ftp), Telnet, or the WWW. Full unrestricted access to all information contained on their servers is granted by some information providers, so that anyone can access any data stored in their servers, while access is restricted to users with accounts by other information providers or only limited access is granted to unregistered users. A user can always logon as an "anonymous" user using ftp, for instance (a user for whom no account has been created in advance), but access through anonymous ftp is limited to certain data. For this, appropriate security measures need to be implemented. For works found on a server, the control over access to the server may be used as one of the first levels of protection. From completely uncontrolled access (the full contents of the server are accessible without restriction), to partially controlled access (access is given to only a limited data set on server), to completely controlled access (no uncontrolled access whatsoever), server access can thus vary.

IT-related global outsourcing can result in a cost saving of about 15% during the first year, and with the passage of time as improvements are made and experience is gathered the cost savings and quality can improve dramatically. However, a random survey of the global market primarily pertaining to the U.S. market by Snovi Technologies stated that about 51% of the customers abroad were wary of outsourcing security solutions to India, 37% cited lack of adequate protection and intellectual property (IP) rights for their data, 28% cited geo-political reasons, and 11% cited infrastructure inadequacy. To overcome these shortcomings it was suggested that better management skills should be employed. The key drivers need to be identified by the vendors in a market with heightened awareness. In certain companies abroad such as the UK, compliance of DR solutions is mandatory as per certain federal and legal requirements for storing and retrieving data. Thus risk assessment regarding information security should be properly conducted. In the course of business between the buyer and the seller very vital information may be exchanged. Some companies outsource research and development (R&D) work. The security relating to it can be extremely important as it can confer competitive advantage to the company. We are living in the information/knowledge age and specialized knowledge gives an organization cutting edge over its competitors. Huge sums are spent on R&D and the knowledge gained as a result can be extremely vital for the future prospects of the company.

To protect crucial information, some of the basics of copyrights should be reviewed before proceeding further. Copyright is a form of protection provided by U.S. law (Title 17, U.S. Code) to the authors of "original works of authorship" including literary, dramatic, musical, artistic, and certain other intellectual works. *This copyright protection exists for both published and unpublished works.* The owner of the copyright is generally given exclusive right by Section 106 of the Copyright Act to do and to authorize others to do the following—in the case of literary, musical, dramatic, and choreographic works, pantomimes, and pictorial, graphic, or sculptural works, including the individual images of a motion picture or other audiovisual works, the owner can display the copyrighted work publicly. The owner has the right to reproduce the copyrighted work in copies or phonorecords and prepare derivative works based on the copyrighted work. In case of literary, musical, dramatic, and choreographic works, pantomines, and motion pictures and other audiovisual works, the owner can perform the copyrighted work publicly. The owner can distribute copies or phonorecords of the copyrighted work to the public by sale or other transfer of ownership or by rental, lease, or lending. "Original works of authorship" that are fixed in a tangible form of expression are protected by the copyright law. As long as the work can be communicated with the aid of a machine or device, the fixation need not be directly perceptible.

The following categories are included in copyrighted works—literary works, musical works, dramatic works with accompanying music, pantomimes and choreographic work, pictorial graphic, sculptural works, motion pictures and other audiovisual works, sound recordings, and architectural works. These categories are quite broad; for instance, computer programs and most compilations are "literary works," maps are pictorial, graphic, and sculptural works. Digital copyright is not mentioned by Section 106, and to correct this several amendments to the original law have been proposed. For the copyright owner's ability to prevent unauthorized uses of their works, the advent of the information superhighway (Internet) is not the first or the last technological challenge. Among the copyright owners of printed work, for instance, the photocopying machine caused great fear. But on the copyright owner's side were time, cost, and quality. It proved to be more efficient and less expensive to buy a copy of most books than to photocopy them, and the quality of a book from the original publisher is typically higher than that of a photocopy. Problems were posed for copyright owners with the introduction of audio tape recorders, and again the physical attributes of the work made reproductions more expensive and lower in quality, until of course, the introduction of digital audio recorders, which reproduce sound recordings both cheaply and with no degradation of sound quality. With the enactment of the Audio Home Recording Act of 1992, which combined legal and technological safeguards, the threat of sound recordings was answered.

For data security it should be ensured that confidentiality is maintained and copyrighted work not violated. The electronic copyright management system, which was under development, has three distinct components: a registration and recording system, a digital library system with affiliated repositories of copyrighted works, and a rights management system.

Intellectual property is respected in India by most service providers. If intellectual property is not protected, the practical consequences for their business and the country could be severe. National treatment of a member state author is provided for in Berne Convention and UCC, and India is a member country of Berne Convention, Universal Copyright Convention, Paris Convention, Patent Cooperation Treaty (PCT), and World Trade Organization (WTO). Moral rights to an author are provided by the India copyright law.

Intellectual property infrastructure of China is the same as that of India, but practically and legally, enforcement of intellectual property rights is still a significant problem in China, leading to greater risk because processing of customers' personal data will inevitably be done at some level by the supplier. Personal data should be processed according to the data protection principles of U.K. Data Protection Act 1998. Customer and supplier must ensure that the act is complied with, because the customer is the data controller and the supplier is the data processor. In the case of offshore outsourcing, the eighth data protection principle is of particular importance, and the data controller must consider whether there is adequate data protection in the offshore location when personal data is being transferred outside the home country or region (e.g., the European Economic Area (EEA), which comprises the European Union, together with Norway, Iceland and Liechtenstein). The act specifies circumstances in which adequate protection is deemed to exist, although there is a debate over what constitutes "adequate protection." The customer will also want to protect its other confidential information, in addition to the requirements under the act. To improve piracy and crime protection, the Indian government has passed legislation.

Encryption will be used (up to a point) by most digital copyright systems eventually. Of course, protection would be guaranteed by turning computer files into essentially unbreakable codes. But the purpose of online information would be defeated—to make it possible to quickly sift vast storehouses of knowledge. A customer would purchase a cryptographic key to decode the document if he or she wants to buy protected information. From one-time personal rights to an unrestricted license, the price would depend on what the buyer wanted. To identify the owner and the buyer, a cipher could be hidden in the document. Therefore, it would be possible to nail the offending party if the information should leak into a BBS. To prevent unauthorized use, we could also think of embedded ciphers that contain a program. The document would turn into gibberish when transmitted via electronic mail to a third party by a person who has purchased one-time rights. Given that they may have broad usefulness, in sum, protection and management methods must be based on nonproprietary technologies. Moreover, customers may reject works protected under systems that are too cumbersome and complicated. The ultimate judge will be the customer and the marketplace regarding various measures and their usefulness in protecting copyrighted works.

Security

The chain, only as strong as its weakest link.

Security of organization's critical assets, primarily data, are becoming increasing crucial. Through public networks like the Internet, etc., private corporate networks are accessed and sometimes breached. *Such breaches can range from small losses to complete business failure and long-term, large-scale losses.* Organizations must constantly use all means available to counter this ever-present threat.

Malicious Codes and Protection Methods

Common Hacking Examples

Robert Morris, a graduate student in computer science at Cornell University, wrote an experimental, self-replicating, self-propagating program (later dubbed a "worm" by the popular press) and injected it into the Internet. This small piece of code exploited the weakness of "sendmail" and "finger" daemons (holes) and brought the Internet to its knees in 1988. It is among the most infamous examples of this category.

To impersonate users, hackers may use password guessing, password trapping, security holes in programs, or common network access procedures and thereby pose a threat to the business servers.

Unauthorized modification of server data, unauthorized eavesdropping or modification of incoming data packets, and compromise of server systems by exploiting bugs in the server software are some of the threats to servers.

Network servers are much more susceptible to attacks, as compared to stand-alone systems, because legitimate users can be impersonated. A large number of systems, for example, can be accessed by hackers. Therefore, not properly configured computers which are running programs with *security holes* are particularly vulnerable.

To trap user names and unencrypted passwords sent over the network, hackers may use electronic eavesdropping. When the impersonation attack is less likely to be detected, they can monitor the activity on a system continuously and impersonate a user.

To gain unauthorized access to resources or information, hackers can spoof or configure a system to masquerade as another system. By using software that monitors packets sent over the network, hackers can eavesdrop, and many network programs such as telnet and ftp are vulnerable to eavesdroppers who obtain passwords, which are often sent across the network unencrypted.

The client server security problems manifest themselves in three ways.

When individuals gain unauthorized physical access to a computer, physical security holes result. A public workstation room would be a good example, where it would be easy for a wandering hacker to reboot a machine into single-user mode and tamper with the files, if precautions are not taken.

Hackers gain access to network systems by guessing passwords of various users and on the network, this is also a common problem.

When badly written programs or "privileged" software are "compromised" into doing things they should not, software security holes result.

Hackers can try to guess simple passwords using dictionary or more sophisticated password guessing methods after using popular UNIX programs like finger, rsh, or ruser to discover account names. For comparison purposes, hackers could use a password-guessing program in which multiple computer systems are used simultaneously.

The "rlogin" hole in the IBM RS-6000 workstations was a problem, and it enabled a cracker (a malicious hacker) to create a "root" shell (i.e., superuser) access mode. It could result in incalculable damage, because this is the highest level of access possible and could be used to delete the entire file system or create a new account or password file. If a system administrator assembles a combination of hardware and software such that the system is seriously flawed from a security point of view, then the inconsistent usage holes result. The security hole is created by the incompatibility of attempting two unconnected but useful things. Once a system is set up and running, problems like this are difficult to isolate, so it is better to carefully build the system with them in mind.

Operating systems typically offer mechanisms such as access control lists that specify the resources various users and groups are entitled to access. At the file level, by checking user-specific information such as password, protection (also called authorization) access control grants privileges to the system or resource. In the case of e-commerce, the problem is very simple, because if a consumer connects a computer to the Internet, he or she can easily log into it from anywhere that the network reaches. This is the good and bad news, because without proper access control, anyone else can too.

Mobile Code

Mobile code (software agent) is another security threat that is emerging in the e-commerce world, and this mobile code in many ways resembles a more traditional virus threat. *An executable program, the mobile code has the ability to move from machine to machine and also to invoke itself without external influence.* Organizations can install firewalls that filter incoming data packets to circumvent this threat. One can divide these threats into two major categories— first, the threat to the local computing environment from mobile software, and second, access control and threats to servers that include impersonation, eavesdropping, denial of service, packet replay, and packet modification. The Internet is a potential source of potentially harmful virus attacks. The potential exists for this downloaded data to subvert programs running on the systems, in the absence of checks on imported data. When such downloaded data passes through local interpreters on the client system without the user's knowledge, threats to security arise. Malicious data or code, in short, is mostly responsible for client threats. Viruses, worms, Trojan horses, logic bombs, and other deviant software programs are some examples of malicious code, and it is sometimes mistakenly associated only with standalone computers, but can also attack computer networks easily. System outages and staff time for repair are some of the consequences of maliciously written code. In the UNIX mail system, a similar problem existed, whereby a remote user through various escape sequences could invoke the shell program (csh or sh) on the recipient's machine. In most of the new mail systems, this security breach has been plugged.

Virus Examples

Some examples of malicious code are virus, worm, Trojan horse, and logic bombs. Overwriting, resident, stealth, and polymorphic are some of the different types of viruses. A virus is a code segment that replicates by attaching copies of itself to existing executable (.exe) files. When a user executes the host program, the new copy of the virus is executed, and when specific conditions are met, a trigger may occur (e.g., all files are deleted on the hard disk on a particular date). A Trojan horse is a program that, though it performs the desired task, also includes unexpected and undesirable functions. An example is an editing program which has been maliciously modified to randomly delete some of the user's files each time they perform a useful function (editing). These deletions are unexpected and undesirable. In the case of a worm, a host program is not required, and it is a self-replicating program that is self-contained. No user intervention is required, and the program creates a copy of itself and causes it to execute. Worms commonly utilize network services to propagate to other host systems. Malicious data and executable program fragments, such as MIME mail messages and postscript files that are transferred from server to client, should be scanned by clients. It may not be possible to do conclusively, but it is conceivable that the client may need to filter out data and programs known to be dangerous. Determination of program behavior automatically is not computable and is generally referred to in computer science as the "halting program." However, on known dangers, it is possible to perform some heuristics.

Security—Risks in E-Commerce

In their plain text form, for instance, credit card numbers create a risk when transmitted across the Internet, where the possibility of the number falling into the wrong hands is relatively high. Knowing the risk, would you be willing to type in your credit card number, and even worse, would you expose your customers to that risk? Given the possible lawsuits and other liability issues, just the thought of "sniffer" programs that collect credit card numbers en masse is enough to keep merchants away from online shopping. Therefore a major impediment to widespread e-commerce is the lack of business transaction security. Simple password schemes are not sufficient to prevent attacks from sophisticated hackers, with the advent of remote users on the Internet, commercial transactions, mobile computers, and wireless technologies. The problems facing transaction-based e-commerce and the security problems plaguing network administrators resemble one another. In many ways credit card numbers are similar to passwords.

Unauthorized network monitoring is one major threat to data security, and it is called packet sniffing. When the computer is compromised, sniffer attacks begin, and the cracker installs a packet sniffing program that monitors the network to which the machine is attached. Certain kinds of network traffic are watched by the sniffer program, typically the first part of any telnet, ftp, or rlogin sessions—sessions that legitimate users initiate to gain access to another system. The login ID, password, and user name of the person logging into another machine are the first part of the session, all the necessary information a sniffer needs to log into other machines. The sniffer could gather information on local users logging into remote machines in the course of several days. So, on the network, one insecure system can expose to intrusion not only other local machines but also any remote systems to which users connect. It is nothing new, and an acknowledged fact, that someone can extract meaningful information from network traffic. This knowledge is no longer limited to a small set of responsible people, but to a much larger set of potentially malicious folks. Intruders can thus hack into any transit traffic traversing over the entire network of nodes, if the compromised system is on a backbone network. The number of systems that intruders are able to hack into and thus access can rapidly expand through network monitoring. Information like accounts and passwords of users are collected, and they are not aware that their sessions are being monitored, and subsequent intrusions will happen via legitimate accounts on the machines involved.

Network Security

The maze, and people masked by its haze.

For a stream of continuous cash flow, other aspects of the supplier like the supplier's data protection mechanism should be properly considered. Once the initial layer of protection is breached, access control does not preclude copies from being made. Through measures tied to the electronic file containing data, a second level of control can be exerted. Through "rendering" and "viewing" software, one type of restriction can be implemented. A proprietary or unique file format is required by such systems, and the file can be read only be certain software that is developed or is controlled by the information provider, and software is required which incorporates both a control measure to prevent viewing or use of data without authorization from the information provider and manipulation functions to permit the user to view or use the data. If the user enters unauthorized identification or an improper password, rendering or viewing software can be written to deny access. For any unauthorized entry, rendering software can also be written to deny access.

Provision for adequate data protection is mandatory to prevent unauthorized eavesdropping. Data security provides impetus to outsourcing, given that network transmission is a low-cost affair. Safeguarding customer information in outsourcing is imperative, and through user identification access control mechanisms like authentication procedures (login name and password), unauthorized access by users is prevented. A proper security mechanism needs to be in place to protect data of projects/processes, because sensitive information such as passwords, data, and procedures for performing functions may be obtained by hackers by eavesdropping and monitoring the network traffic. Means like wiretapping, radio, and auxiliary ports on computers are used by network programs, and eavesdropping may be resorted to by unethical hackers. Remote file transfer is a common example which is susceptible to eavesdroppers. Network transmission of encrypted images enjoys much greater security, speed, and flexibility, not to mention ease, versus transport of paper items.

The level of security in the network must be realistically reflected in the firewall policies. For instance, a system with secret and confidential data should be isolated from the rest of the corporate network, and a site with top secret or classified data should not be hooked up to the Internet in the first place. The formats of viruses are too varied to monitor them all, and the ways of encoding binary files for transfer over networks too numerous, and therefore firewalls are a poor protection against such threats. Protection against data-driven attacks, in which something is mailed or copied to an internal host and then executed, cannot be provided by a firewall, and this form of attack has occurred in the past against various versions of sendmail. Justifying the expense or effort is not often the hardest part of connecting to the Internet, but it is convincing the management that it is beneficial to do so. The senior management should be convinced that the outsourcing decision will benefit them from the cost, quality, and security angles. Having access to expertise that a company may not have in house is one potential benefit of outsourcing. According to Doug Osborne, self-insured employers should also seek an outsourcing partner that has experienced antifraud investigator, and he calls fraud the Achilles heel of the self-insured market, because the fraudsters have figured out that if you want to get paid, you should go to a self-insured program.

To provide security for exchange of information, proxy gateways may be used, but there are several disadvantages with them. Browser programmers are allowed to ignore the complex networking code necessary to support every firewall protocol and concentrate on important client issues. No protocol functionality is lost by using HTTP between the client and proxy server. This is because ftp, gopher, and other Web protocols are compliant and map with HTTP methods. Thus no changes are needed to ftp, gopher, and WAIS clients to get through a firewall.

On today's public and sometimes even private networks, a growing threat is the theft of passwords and other information that passes over them. An array of tools is available for today's hackers to reach and manipulate information from remote sites as well as to engage in unauthorized eavesdropping. The most vulnerable are the unsuspecting and amateur users logging into remote hosts. There are two types of transaction security issues—data and message security. At a time when people are considering banking and other financial transactions via computers, electronic data is of paramount importance. Also the trend of the computer industry is toward distributed computing, and nomadic or mobile computer users only exacerbate security challenges.

Secure Messaging over Networks

Threats to message security fall into three categories—confidentiality, integrity, and authentication. For uses involving sensitive data such as credit card numbers, confidentiality is important. When other kinds of data, such as employee records, government files, and social security numbers begin traversing the network, the requirement will be amplified. *All message traffic must be protected by the environment.* Messages should be erased from the public environment after their successful delivery to respective destination gateways. The accounting record of entry and delivery is all that remains, including message length, authentication data, and perhaps the audit trail of message transfer agents that processed the message, but no more. *In well-protected systems, all message archiving must be performed. Provision must be made* for the irrevocable emergency *destruction of stored, undelivered messages, where necessary and when needed.* With the use of distributed networks and wireless links, the vulnerability of data communications and message data to interception is exacerbated. Securing communication links between computers via encryption is expected to rise. The requirement of business transactions is that the contents should remain unmodified during transport. The information received, in other words, should have the same content and organization as the information sent. There should be clarity that no one has added, deleted, or modified any part of the message. Unauthorized combination of messages, either by intermixing or concatenating, during submission, validation, processing, or delivery should not be allowed. The capability of reformatting messages if requested by the message originator or the receiving party would be one exception. While passive monitoring of data is prevented by confidentiality, mechanisms of integrity must prevent active attacks involving the modification of data. Some of the methods used to enhance information integrity are error detection codes or checksums, sequence numbers, and encryption techniques. Within a message, error detection codes operate on the entire message or selected fields. Reordering, loss, or replaying of messages by an attacker is prevented by sequence numbers. Modifications of message can be detected by encryption techniques such as digital signatures.

It is important that clients authenticate themselves to servers, and that servers authenticate to clients, that both authenticate to each other for e-commerce. The receiver of a message or a transaction can be confident of the identity of the sender and/or the integrity of the message through the mechanism of authentication. The identity of an entity (a user or a service) is verified by authentication using certain encrypted information transferred from the sender to the receiver.

As confidential information increasingly traverses modern networks, complex issues of security, privacy, authentication, and anonymity have been thrust into the forefront. Secure messaging is a critical business concern. A crucial prerequisite for the functioning of electronic commerce is the confidence, reliability, and protection of this information against security threats. A circumstance, condition, or event with the potential to cause economic hardship to data or network resources in the form of destruction, disclosure, modification of data, denial of service, and/ or fraud, waste, and abuse is a security threat. Two broad types constitute the discussion of security concerns in electronic commerce. To make sure that only valid users and programs have access to information resources such as databases, client server security uses various authorization methods. To ensure that properly authenticated users are allowed access only to those resources that they are entitled to use, access control mechanisms must be set up. Password protection, encrypted smart cards, biometrics, and firewalls are included in such mechanisms. In the second type of security, data and transaction security ensures the privacy and confidentiality in electronic messages and data packets, including the authentication of remote users in network transactions for activities such as online payments. While involved in electronic mail or other form of data communication, the goal is to defeat any attempt to assume another identity. Various cryptographic methods for data encryption are used as preventive measures. One of the biggest headaches system administrators face is client–server network security as they balance the opposing goals of user maneuverability and easy access and site security and confidentiality of local information. Computer security violations cost U.S. businesses half a billion dollars each year, according to the National Center of Computer Crime Data. For commercial organizations, especially the top management, network security on the Internet is a major concern. Many new security concerns have been raised by the Internet recently, and by connecting itself to the Internet, a local network organization may be exposing itself to the entire population on the Internet.

A password scheme is one straightforward security solution that erects a first-level barrier to accidental intrusion. When common words or proper names are selected as passwords, however, password schemes do little against deliberate attack. Many hackers use a simple method which is dictionary comparison, comparing a list of encrypted user passwords against a dictionary of encrypted common words. Because users tend to choose relatively simple or familiar words as passwords, the scheme often works. Experts often recommend using a minimum of eight-character-length mixed-case passwords containing at least one alphanumeric character and changing passwords every 60 to 90 days. Any eavesdropper on the network can simply record the password any time it is used, because passwords in remote login session usually pass over the network in unencrypted form. For distinct devices, having distinct passwords is sometimes a problem, because people will write them down (making them easy for others to find), share them (with people on the same project), or include them in automatic scripts (eliminating the inconvenience of typing them and also eliminating the protection from accidental access). Various approaches have been suggested for creating one-time passwords, including smart cards, randomized tokens, and challenge–response schemes to counter these threats.

It is natural to design security relevant within the proxy, given the firewall design in which the proxy acts as an intermediary. *Security concerns are handled through proxy mediation by eliminating those subsets of the HTTP protocol which might be dangerous*; by imposing client and server access to only specific hosts (an organization should have the capability to specify acceptable Web sites); implementing access control for network services that is lost when the proxy is installed (to restore the security policy enforced by the firewall); and checking various protocols for well-formed commands. Dangerous URLs and malformed commands should be filtered by the proxy. Such filtering has become all the more important with online outsourcing moving up the "knowledge continuum" to tasks that involve expertise and judgment "as opposed to a routine that can be run off a computerized menu," says Ravi Aron, assistant professor of operations and information management at the Wharton School of Business. In a previous version of mosaic browser, a bug existed that permitted servers to download a "Trojan horse" URL to the client that would cause the client to run an arbitrary program.

Protection Mechanisms and Practices against Hacking and Security Risks

Self-defense, a basic instinct.

Several protection methods have existed, and trust-based security was one of them. Trust everyone and do nothing extra for protection was what trust-based security means, quite simply. It assumed that all users were trustworthy and competent in their use of the shared network, and access restrictions of any kind were not needed. That no one would ever make an expensive breach such as getting root access and deleting all files (a common hacker trick), was assumed by this approach. In the past, when the system administrator had to worry about a limited threat, this approach worked, but today this was no longer the case.

In the mainframe era, most organizations practiced a philosophy know as security through obscurity (STO), the notion that any network can be secure as long as nobody outside its management group is allowed to find out anything about its operational details, and users are provided information on a need-to-know basis only. The primary case of STO is hiding account passwords in binary files or scripts with the presumption that "nobody will ever find them." A false sense of security in computing systems by hiding information is provided by STO. This philosophy can mean lifelong trust of a small group of people, although it is sound in theory. The knowledge goes with employees, in reality, due to better pay from competitors, reducing the effectiveness of the method. In the UNIX world, its usefulness is minimal, where users are free to move around the file system, have a great understanding of programming techniques, and have immense computing power at their fingertips. The STO is rendered less effective because widespread networking necessitates greater need for details of how the system works. Through experience, today many users have advanced knowledge of how their operating system works and can guess the bits of knowledge considered confidential. The whole basis of STO is bypassed by this and makes this method of security useless currently.

Make sure that existing system features such as passwords and privileges are in place to ensure security for commercial operations. All access to the network needs to be audited. Managers can be alerted to the need for stronger measures by a system that records all logon attempts, particularly the unsuccessful ones. Additional measures must be taken where secrets are at stake or where important corporate assets must be made available to remote users.

The most secure level of authorization are the "biometric" systems which involve some unique aspect of a person's body. Comparisons of fingerprints, palm prints, retinal patterns, or on signature verification or voice recognition was the basis of past biometric authentication. Implementation costs of biometric systems are falling, and they may be better suited for controlling physical access where one biometric unit can serve for many workers than for network or single-workstation access. In terms of usage, 10 to 30 seconds may be needed to verify an access request by certain architectures and systems. Such systems, moreover, are sometimes seen as intrusive by users who are reluctant to stick a finger or a hand into a slot or sign their name or sit still while the optical system scans their eyeball. Systems that recognize keyboard typing patterns or read infrared facial patterns from passersby using only a simple video camera for image capture are some of the variations of biometric devices that are appearing.

Encryption and Cryptography

The evolving codes over history.

Due to the increasing number of merchants trying to spur commerce on the global network, the lack of data and message security on the Internet has become a high-profile problem.

To ensure protection of copyrighted works/data, security measures must be carefully designed and implemented. Software-based systems are being contemplated for tracking and monitoring uses of copyrighted works. Software-based systems may also be used to implement licensing of rights and metering of use. *To protect, license, and authenticate information, a combination of access controls, encryption technologies, and digital signatures can be used by copyright owners.* Data security measures form a part of the indirect costs.

To inform users about ownership of rights in a work and authorized uses of it, information included in files can also be used. Information regarding authorship, copyright ownership, date of creation, or last modification and terms and conditions of authorized uses can be stored in the header of a file. The information, whether in the header or elsewhere, can be used to limit what can be done with the original or a copy of the file containing the work, in conjunction with the receiving hardware or software. The use of the file can be limited by it to a read, view, or listen only. The number of times the data can be retrieved, opened, duplicated, or printed can also be limited by it.

Cryptographic techniques are used to generate a digital signature, but are not an encryption of work/data; the work/data may remain unencrypted so it can be accessed and used freely. Encryption (like various other methods) restricts unauthorized access to data. To protect work/data, in fact, digital signature and encryption can be used simultaneously. For a copyrighted work/data, generally, a signature is computed first and then it (including the seal) is encrypted. The work is decrypted when it is to be used; the signature (the seal) is verified to be sure the work has not been modified either in its original or encrypted form. The seal need never be removed if the work/data is never changed. A new seal must be computed on the revised information if the work is changed, and generating a digital signature is called "signing" the work/data. Both digital signature and the public key are often appended to the signed copyrighted works/data. For the work/data, the signature serves as a "seal" because the seal enables the information to be independently checked for unauthorized modification. The copyrighted work/data is a bona fide copy of the original work if the seal is verified (independently computed signature matches the original signature) and nothing has been changed either in the header or the work.

The problem of key distribution exists in shared key techniques, since shared keys must be securely distributed to each pair of communicating parties. In large networks, secure key distribution becomes cumbersome. In the secret key cryptography, the constraining factor is having the sender and receiver agree on the secret key without any other person/party finding it out. The reason is that A and B are separate sites, and they must trust not being overheard during face-to-face meetings or over a public messaging system (a phone system, a postal service) when the secret key is being exchanged. If the key is overheard or intercepted by anyone, then he or shecan later read all encrypted messages using that key. Caned key management is the generation, transmission, and storage of keys, and all cryptosystems must deal with key management issues. The secret key method does not scale, although it is quite feasible and practical for one-on-one document interchange. It is impractical to assume that key management will be flawless in a business environment where a company deals with thousands of online customers. Given its difficulty in providing secure key management, it can be safely assumed that secret key cryptography will not be a dominant player in e-commerce.

There exists the problem of eavesdropping, which can be prevented by encryption of data traveling over unsecure networks. Threats of attacks on the server such as denial of service may occur where a user can render the system unusable for legitimate users by "hogging" a resource or by damaging or destroying resources so that they cannot be used. Service overloading and message flooding are the two most common forms of denial-of-service attacks, and servers are especially vulnerable to service overloading. By writing a small loop that sends requests continually for a particular file, for example, the home page, one can easily overload a www server. The server assumes that all requests are legitimate and tries to respond to the request in good faith. Therefore, denial-of-service attacks may be caused, intentionally or unintentionally by runaway software programs such as those caught in an infinite loop. When someone sends a very large file to a message box every few minutes, message overloading occurs. As a result, the message box begins to occupy all the space on the disk, because it is rapidly growing in size, and increases the number of receiving processes on the recipient's machine, tying it up even more and often causing disk crash. Separate areas should be provided to different programs to avoid message overloading and make provision for graceful failure. By restricting access to critical accounts, resources, and files and protecting them from unauthorized users, service attacks can be reduced, although they are hard to prevent.

The provider's capability to protect against denial-of-service threats should be assessed so that legitimate users are not denied access. It is harder to guard against other sophisticated threats like packet replay and modification. The recording and transmission of message packets in the network is packet replay. Because hackers could replay legitimate authentication sequence messages to gain access to secure systems, this is a significant threat for programs that require authentication sequences. Packet replay can be prevented by using methods like packet time stamping and sequence counting, although packet replay is frequently undetectable. An integrity threat is packet modification that involves one computer intercepting and modifying a message packet destined for another system. Packet information may not only be modified in many cases, but its contents may be destroyed before the legitimate users can see them.

By encrypting sensitive information that must travel over public channels such as the Internet, one can protect it. Encryption is the conversion of information (e.g., text, video, graphics, etc.) into a form unreadable by anyone else without the respective decryption key. Broadly speaking, secret key cryptography and public key cryptography are the two types of encryption methods. A shared key is used in secret key cryptography for both encryption by the transmitter and decryption by the receiver.

Encryption amounts to scrambling of data using mathematical principles that can be followed in reverse to unscramble data. To deny access to data in a usable form, encryption technologies are used. From an editable file format, file encryption simply converts a file to a scrambled format. To decrypt the file and restore it to its manipulatable format, authorization in the form of possession of an appropriate password or "key" is required. To control access to data that has been encrypted, encryption techniques use keys, and these keys are actually numbers that are plugged into a mathematical algorithm and used to scramble data. The original sequence of binary digits (1s and 0s that make up a digital file) is transformed using a mathematical algorithm into a new sequence of binary digits in scrambling. The number used to scramble the data according to the specified mathematical algorithm is called the key, and anyone with the key can decrypt the work by plugging the number into a program that applies the mathematical algorithm in reverse to yield the original sequence of digital signals. When someone with the key decrypts the work, there may be no technological protection for the data if it is stored and subsequently distributed in its decrypted or original format. To restrict unauthorized uses of copyrighted works, hardware and/or software can provide protection. Circuitry in digital audio recording devices and digital audio interface devices that controls serial copying is required according to the Audio Home Recording Act. The hardware circuitry will either permit unrestricted copying, based on the information it reads, permit copying but label the copies it makes with codes to restrict further copying, or disallow copying. Unlimited first-generation copying digital reproduction of originals is allowed by the serial copy management system implemented by this circuitry, but prevents further digital copying using those reproductions. Through hardware, software or both, such systems can be implemented using rendering software and encryption technology. For instance, instructions can be included in files containing works to govern or control distribution of work. This information might be placed in the header section of the file or another part of the file.

Based on bibliographic records, search and retrieval can also be supported. In connection with information sold, electronic licenses may be used. For example, users may be informed by providers that a certain action, the entering of a password, to gain access to the service or a particular work, or merely the use of the service will be considered acceptance of the specified terms and conditions of electronic license. The Library of Congress Electronic Copyright Management System may be instrumental in rights management.

For electonic funds transfers, strong cryptography is necessary to provide authentication. Even with strong cryptographic algorithms, it is not clear whether we will ever see EFT on public networks. One needs to carefully consider the balance between risk and return.

Still another aspect is the protection of business information and authentication, such as cryptographically signed certificates, which must not be easily spoofed (falsified). To ascertain that the origination address is valid with respect to the gateway across which the message enters, the client and server must compare the origination address of transactions and messages with information associated with each service gateway.

Digital Signatures

Putting one's hand and seal to the contract.

In ensuring data integrity, digital signatures can play an important role. To create digital signatures, mathematical algorithms can be used that, in effect, place a seal on a digitally represented work. Through hardware or software or both, these algorithms can be implemented. Based on the work being protected, the digital signature algorithm being used, and the key used in digital signature generation, a digital signature, which is a unique sequence of digits, is computed.

To maintain confidentiality of information, various technical uses of digital signatures are being explored by the cryptographic community, so that messages might be time stamped or digitally notarized to establish dates and times at which a recipient might claim to have had access or even read a particular message. If handwritten signatures are to be replaced by digital signatures, they must have equal legal status as handwritten signatures (documents signed by digital signatures must be legally binding). There have been suggestions for an online "notarized time stamping" service that would accept a message and return one showing the date, time, and a digital signature binding the notarized message content and received date and time to the digital public notary. The digital signature provides means to a third party to verify that the notarized object is authentic.

Digital signature standard (DSS) interestingly is to be used to sign the U.S. federal government's purchase orders. Thus the U.S. government lends credence to the legal authority of digital signatures. *Hence digital signatures meet the requirements of legally binding signatures for most purposes, including commercial use as defined in the Uniform Commercial Code (UCC), although there may have been little legal precedence. The Government Accounting Office (GAO) further equates digital signatures to handwritten signatures.* However, the legal status of digital signatures is still to be fully defined. This is possibly because they have not been challenged in court. Such litigations result in issue of suitable court rulings, which hopefully provide a holistic set of methods, key sizes, and security options for digital signatures. The legal authority of digital signatures should be more than handwritten signatures. For instance, on the tenth page, if a ten-page contract is signed by hand, there is a possibility that the initial nine pages may have been altered after the signing. If a digital signature was used to sign a contract, suitable technical means can ensure that not one byte of the contract has been changed. If a series of contracts are wished to be digitally signed by two people, they may first manually sign a paper contract in which they agree to be bound in the future by any contracts digitally signed by them with specified signature methods and key size. The legal consideration of digital notarizing and the binding strength of electronic interchange is a topic well deserving of prompt, qualified, and intense attention.

Public key cryptography can be used for sender authentication, and this is known as digital signature. Implementation of RSA (an online encryption algorithm) dominates in the public key encryption and is considered very secure, but using it for overseas traffic conflicts with the U.S. government's position on export of munitions technology of military importance. (Technical aspects of RSA are further explained in the Appendix.) The Internet and transborder data flow have clearly not been reckoned with by the government.

"Firewall"—Infrastructure Protection

As players spar through the firewall's veil.

Advances in technology have given a gigantic impetus to outsourcing and data protection. A concept in the area of network security on the Internet is called the firewall, which helps to counter some of these server threats. *A firewall is a barrier between the organization's corporate network and the outside world (untrusted network), and this is the most commonly accepted network protection.* A firewall is basically a method of placing a device, a computer, or a router, between the network and the Internet to control and monitor all traffic between the outside world and the local network, although the term firewall can mean many things to many people. While granting access from the outside only selectively based on logon name, password, IP address, or other identifiers, the device allows insiders to have full access to services on the outside. In general, to shield vulnerable areas from some form of danger, we use firewall as a protection device. The firewall is a system, a router, a personal computer, a host, or a collection of hosts set up specifically to shield a site or subnet from protocols and services that can be abused from hosts on the outside of the subnet. Usually, the firewall is located at a gateway point, and the gateway point can be a site's connection to the Internet, but can be located at internal gateways to provide protection for smaller collections of hosts or subnets. Several types of firewalls are available, and they offer various levels of security. The operation of the firewall generally takes place by screening packets and/or the applications that pass through them, to provide controllable filtering of network traffic, allow restricted access to certain applications, and block access to everything else. The firewall can be thought of the as a pair of mechanisms, although the actual mechanism that accomplishes filtering varies widely. One mechanism is used to block incoming traffic, and the other to permit outgoing traffic. Some firewalls emphasize permitting traffic, while others place greater emphasis on blocking traffic. Network security is a function of each host on the network without a firewall, and all hosts must cooperate to achieve a uniformly high level of security. Break-ins can occur as mistakes and lapses in security become more common, and these break-ins are not the result of complex attacks but because of simple errors in configuration and inadequate passwords.

If properly configured, they can plug many security holes. Given the vastly diverse needs of users, screening rules are difficult to specify, and screening rules are fairly inflexible and do not easily extend to deal with functionality different from that preprogrammed by the vendor. The entire network is open to attack if a hacker bypasses the screening router. A special server is the proxy application gateway, which runs on a firewall machine. To access applications such as the World Wide Web from within a secure parameter is their primary use. Each request from the client would be routed to a proxy on the firewall that is defined by the user, instead of talking directly to external WWW servers. The proxy knows how to get through the firewall. For users in an organization, an application-level proxy makes a firewall safety preamble, without creating a potential security hole through which hackers can get into corporate networks. The proxy is a specialized software loaded on the firewall machine. The proxy, on receipt of a request from within the firewall, forwards it to the remote server outside the firewall. All clients within a given subnet use the same proxy, resulting in efficient caching of documents that are requested by a number of clients.

There is a wide range of firewalls, from simple traffic logging systems that record all network traffic flowing through the firewall in a file or database for auditing purposes, to more complex methods such as IP packet screening routers, hardened firewall hosts, and proxy application gateways. The packet filtering gateway or screening router is the simplest firewall. Screening routers also limit the types of services that can pass through them, because they are configured with filters to restrict packet traffic to designated addresses. Application gateways are more complex and secure. To provide proxy services to users on either side, application gateways are essentially computers or UNIX boxes that sit between the Internet and the company's internal network. To FTP in or out through the gateway, a user would connect to FTP software running on the firewall, which then connects to machines on the other side of the gateway. Application gateway firewalls and screening routers are frequently used in combination when security concerns are very high. Subnetworks or hardened firewall machines are set up between the Internet and a company's private network, in cases of heavy traffic. The IP packet screening router is a static traffic routing service placed between the network service provider's router and the internal network. The traffic routing service may be implemented at an IP level, via screening rules in a router, or at an application level, via proxy gateways and services. To permit or deny IP packets based on several screening rules, the firewall route filters incoming packets, and these screening rules implemented into the router are automatically performed.

When considering a service provider for selection for critical information or transaction processing functions, an institution should perform sufficient due diligence to satisfy itself of the service provider's competence technologically and stability, financially and operationally, to provide the expected service and meet any related commitments. The institution and the service provider should have a written contract which clearly specifies, at a level of detail commensurate with the scope and the risks of outsourced activity, all relevant terms and conditions, responsibilities and liabilities of both parties. The institution should assess the terms and conditions to ensure that they are appropriate to the particular service being provided and result in an acceptable level of risk to the institution. The institution's legal counsel should review the contracts for outsourcing of critical functions. Internal control policies and procedures should be implemented by the service provider, including data security and contingency capabilities and other operational controls analogous to those that the institution would utilize if the activity were performed internally.

Financial concerns frequently dictate the technical design—how much will it cost either to buy or to implement? Configuring the router will probably cost staff time, at the low end. It might cost several man months of effort to implement a high-end firewall from scratch, and the system management overhead is also a consideration. Firewalls should not be evaluated only in terms of cost, but also in terms of continuing maintenance costs such as support and upgrades.

Technology is a key enabler for quality and security of work. A stripped-down machine that has been configured for increased security is a hardened firewall host.

Before connecting further, this type of firewall requires inside or outside users to connect to the trusted applications on the firewall machine.

Configuration of firewalls is generally done to protect against unauthenticated interactive logins from the external world. Unauthorized users are thereby prevented from logging into the machines on the network. Greater levels of audit and security can be provided by the hardened firewall host method, in return for increased configuration cost and decreased level of service, because a proxy needs to be developed for each desired service. One must therefore address the old tradeoff between ease of use and security. The protection method in a firewall has related dependencies of ease of use and required security protection. A number of management issues must be addressed by the administrator before putting a firewall into place, and it is his or her responsibility to design, specify, and implement or oversee the installation of the firewall.

Except those services integral to the mission of connecting to the Internet, careful deliberation needs to be done on the purpose of the firewall with respect to the organizational needs. Is the firewall meant to deny all other services, or is the firewall to provide a metered and audited method of regulating access in a nonthreatening manner? Between these two extreme positions, these are varying degrees of paranoia—the final stance may be more the result of political and/or financial reasoning than technical or engineering. To dictate how data must be protected, in short, many corporations and data centers have computing security policies and practices, and a firewall is an embodiment of this security policy. What is the level of monitoring, redundancy, and control is another issue. A checklist is made of what should be monitored, permitted, and denied. Access can be controlled by the firewall computer, for instance, based on the time of the day; organizations may allow employees to run e-mails or FTP at any time, but read a certain news group only between 7 p.m. and 8 p.m. By figuring out the overall objectives, the administrator begins, combines a needs analysis with a risk assessment, then sorts out conflicting requirements into a list to guide the implementation.

The firewall often plays an important role as a security blanket for the management apart from providing real security. For the other users on the Internet, the firewall acts as the corporate "ambassador." Public information about corporate products and services, files to download, bug fixes, and so forth are stored by many corporations by using the firewall as a place to do so. Of the Internet service structure, several of these systems have become important parts and have reflected well on their corporate sponsors.

Building multiple channels for customers, cash flows.

Chapter 19

Reflections about the Future

As the limits begin to stretch, innovation and learning results.

History Revisited

Of days gone by and times to come.

A brief look at the history again. Outsourcing started in the 1980s in the manufacturing sector. It was essentially used to cut costs. Gradually other industries like IT, pharmaceuticals, health care, financial services, etc., embraced it because of its sound business proposition.

Just a few decades ago outsourcing of core engineering jobs faced challenges of nonavailability of suitable technology and computing infrastructure, lack of qualified personnel, etc., a with supplier vendors. There were just a few pockets of technology, resources, and qualified personnel, mostly existing in developed countries like the United States, etc.

The Generations

Shallow whispers that preceded the waves to come by later.

Phase I—1980 to 1990—Tactical Outsourcing— Solve Business-Specific Problems

It was task oriented. Tasks were clearly defined in the outsourcing contract, which the vendor was expected to deliver. Such tasks were not complex and were essentially effort intensive by nature. Tasks were goal based, and very little active monitoring was needed. It did not lead to large-scale organizational restructuring, and core activities were always executed within the organization.

Examples—Logistics and fulfillment, computing services through mainframe computers, low-cost telecom PBX switches. All these basic services primarily leveraged from technology, labor, and facilities.

Phase II—1991 to 2000—Strategic Outsourcing— Build Strategic Relationships

The business relationship between the outsourcing organization and the vendors matured due to the higher quantum of outsourced services and interaction. Relationships became long term, with most of vendor revenues coming from repeat business from existing outsourcing clients.

Business processes were optimized and streamlined. Outsourcing organization and vendors worked closely together with near day-to-day interactions. Vendors brought innovation, subject matter expertise, and valuable experience to the service delivery. Even parts of core organization activities began to get outsourced.

Examples—IT services through software platforms were the mainstay.

Phase III—2001 Onward—Transformational Outsourcing— Create Interdependencies to Bring Innovation

Holistic solutions were delivered by vendors to outsourcing clients. Hence relationships reached new business-to-business highs. Innovation, creation of intellectual property, knowledge process outsourcing (KPO), research and development (R&D), and significant core business activities were part of the outsourcing mix.

Examples—Back office business process outsourcing (BPO) leveraged from offshore labor and global connectivity. Value addition came through holistic solutions and significant additions to intellectual property.

Reflections on the Future of Outsourcing

Population, Labor, and Outsourcing

As people play for positions, real and subtle.

The world population is estimated to be about 7.8 billion people in 2020. Respective world population percent estimates spread across the various continents in 2020 are as follows:

Asia = 56%, China = 19%, India = 17%
Africa = 16%
Americas = 13%, United States = 4%
Former Soviet Union states and Eastern Europe = 7%
Western Europe = 5%
Middle East = 3%

According to U.S. Census Bureau projections, most developed countries have low fertility rates, which are not sufficient to maintain, replace, and sustain their current populations. These include most of Europe, Russia, Japan, Australia, New Zealand, North America, Singapore, Hong Kong, Taiwan, and South Korea. By 2015, the workforce of Japan and most of Europe will decline annually by 1%. The decline is further estimated to grow to 1.5% annually after the 2030s. A minimum fertility level of 2.1 children per woman is necessary to maintain existing population numbers.

In 1950, there were only eight megacities worldwide having populations in excess of 5 million each. By 2015, there will be 59 megacities, with 48 of these being in less developed countries. Currently, about 50% of the world population resides in cities. In the case of developed countries about 75% of the population lives in cities, with 79% in the case of North America. By 2030, about 60% of the world's population will live in cities, with 2.1 billion people being added to cities worldwide.

Currently, about 65% of the population worldwide is linked to the global economy. This presents a scope for its growth into the balance 35%, most of which exists in the developing countries.

The options that exist for the developed countries (largely) are

1. **Higher automation** levels so as to meet required work levels even with a reducing population.
2. **Higher outsourcing** levels. Outsourcing is blurring geographic boundaries and thus bridging this divide.
3. **Higher retirement** ages due to a reducing population.
4. **Higher immigration** levels from the developing countries.

Unionism's Decline in the United States

As customs, trends rise and fall over the sands of time.

Unionism in the United States has seen a gradual decline over the years. Clawson and Clawson (1999) stated five factors largely influencing this decline:

1. Demographic factors
2. State and legal system
3. Globalization and neoliberalism
4. Employer offensive
5. Union-related factors

Additionally, industrial and occupational changes and changing economic environment contributed to the decline. The paradigm shift in global and local business operations further contributed to it. Thus, while outsourcing may have had a significant adverse impact on unionism in the United States, there have been other forces too.

The New Age Worker

As populations begin to shrink, it is estimated that about 5 people will move out of the global economy for every new entrant by 2016. Women's share in the global outsourcing workforce will continue to rise. Regional disparities will continue to fall.

The new age workers have grown up with much more material comforts, systemized education, and technology enablers than any other generation. *The new age outsourcing workers see many more "choices" around than any other past generation of workers.* They thrive on change in the global business environment. They are also exposed to challenges of sudden downsizings, rightsizings, etc. They are much more nomadic, contingent, and opportunity seekers in outlook. Such workers are constantly on the lookout for the vast number of opportunities around. They get bored very soon and hence seek new challenges. Being exposed to the large economic disparities around them, they seek opportunities to get-rich-quick. Thus they have higher risk-taking mentalities. People associations are made with short-term goals and perspectives. Long-term organizational loyalty has little meaning. Since the self overrides the organization, self-employment may be preferred over a long-term job by such. Such workers will be global, itinerant, transactional, project-specific, knowledge workers.

Their beliefs and perspective about work, personal space, and work–life balance are influenced accordingly. Traditional organizations need to relook at their work cultures when venturing into outsourcing so as to successfully manage this young and dynamic workforce.

The India and China Axis

As regions rise and equations change over time.

In the 1500s these two countries together shared half of the world's gross national product (GNP). The whispers are that this is may happen again, soon. The rise of these emerging powers is stated to be a near certainty.

India and China

Innovation and implementation currently dominated by America and Europe will shift significantly to India and China in the future. Technological power play will shift from the West to the East as India and China rise out over the outsourcing horizon. The two countries may play significant roles before time and tide changes again. China and India are well positioned to become technology leaders. The following points reflect the growing influence of India and China on the world stage:

China is one of the largest holders of U.S. Government bonds and thus, has an influence on the U.S. economy.

Sustained high growth rates have historical precedents. China has maintained a steady growth with an annual gross domestic product (GDP) of 7% over the past two decades. India also has a growth rate of 6%, which is expected to rise over the coming years.

China has risen to become the third-largest producer in the manufactured sector. Its share of 12% of the globally manufactured goods has risen from a mere 4% in just one decade. "The China price" is a popular term in manufacturing circles. China will continue to dominate the commercial manufacturing sector.

India and China are witnessing an explosion of outsourcing with related telecom and Internet infrastructures.

China and India, due to rising technological and financial capabilities, will have an increased share of contribution to intellectual property.

India is generally better poised than China to offer outsourcing services to the United States and European countries.

Increasing population trends in countries like India and China will provide higher human resources over the coming years.

India, China, and the United States together make up the majority of engineers, finance/accounting personnel, analysts, and life sciences researchers as per reports from McKinsey Global Institute. Large-scale hiring will continue at outsourcing destinations like India and China.

As China, India, and potential outsourcing countries integrate into the global economy, hundreds of millions of qualified workers will become available for employment. This enormous educated workforce will be an attractive, competitive source of low-cost labor.

India will continue to dominate outsourcing business, back office, IT, BPO, and KPO functions. With the prospective growth in the KPO sector, there will be a high demand for highly qualified professionals like engineers, MBAs, doctors, lawyers, chartered accountants, etc.

Outsourcing will continue to increase in other European countries like Germany, France, and Spain. This will in turn fuel the need for higher learning of German, French, and Spanish in vendor countries.

Internet growth—According to the BCG Report, the Internet penetration of India and China currently is still a very small percent of the total population, so it provides a huge scope for growth. India's current net subscribers growth rate is about 45%. The number of "Internet" subscribers in the Asia-Pacific region was 53 million in 1999, 98 million in 2000, and 245 million in 2004. Internet growth is almost directly linked to the growth of outsourcing.

As India and China emerge, more and more global organizations will become more Asian and less Western in culture.

- India versus China has the following advantages with respect to its future outsourcing potential—India's working-age population will continue to grow even in the 2020s, whereas China's population will reduce due to its one-child policy.
- India has a stable political system of democracy, while China's political system of communism may face challenges which may impact business.
- China will not be able to compete, much less replace India for some time into the future in the outsourcing space because of lack of sufficient English-speaking capabilities, intellectual property protection issues, etc.

The Indian Equation

As means and needs change over the lands.

The ability of countries like India to produce quality outsourcing services acts as a significant driver. Speed, scale, large-scale qualified labor, and low costs have contributed to the outsourcing juggernaut, which has given a significant boost to global business and economy. Its strategies constantly try to improvise on the usage of people, resources, and material.

India will continue to dominate outsourcing segments that need advanced English like knowledge process outsourcing (KPO), data content delivery, medical outsourcing, etc. Its outsourcing players will constantly innovate to strengthen brand, customer base, and process quality at reduced costs. More and more outsourcing businesses will come in. Region-specific abilities and domain knowledge of the outsourcing business will add to its success.

While some argue that jobs losses will occur in the United States, many economists believe that a corresponding number of new jobs are being created concurrently.

The Indian government is constantly alive to global competition and framing of policies to maintain India's leadership position in the outsourcing sector. Various state governments in India are actively propelling setup of IT and BPO industries in smaller cities. Various Indian states are actively setting up government and private IT technology parks. Thus the industry is spreading from tier-1 Indian cities of Delhi-NCR, Bangalore, Mumbai, Chennai, and Pune into tier-2 cities like Chandigarh, Jaipur, and Nagpur. This is because tier-1 cities have higher cost of living, salary inflations, attrition, etc., as compared to tier-2 and tier-3 cities. Outsourcing to tier-2 or tier-3 Indian cities will reap additional reductions in operating costs. Big outsourcing organizations, unlike small players, can choose from any of the cities.

Large-scale financial, accounting, and tax services will be the way of the outsourcing future, with Indian vendors capitalizing on this. This started as a trickle of small services like payroll process outsourcing, basic financial services outsourcing, financial research, etc.

As per industry estimates 70% of KPO industry work will continue to be outsourced to India. *India will continue to dominate the knowledge process outsourcing (KPO) business in the coming future.* Currently India's share is 67%, with other countries having the remaining 33%. India, with its strategic pool of highly qualified and experienced workforce, will be best placed to deliver to KPO's call for complex business ends. According to Tervinderjit Singh, Gartner's research director (Technology and Service Provider Research) "India's KPO market is presently estimated to be $50 to $70 million in size. It is forecast to see a compounded annual growth rate of 25% to 30% through 2013." Other markets and players are also rapidly expanding into this game.

India produces a large number of new IT graduates, about 870,000 annually, as compared to other countries (e.g., the United Kingdom, which produces about 8,000 IT graduates annually). English language fluency and domain knowledge expertise will result in more work being outsourced to India. The United Kingdom continues to remain the foremost outsourcing player in Europe.

India with a large set of qualified lawyers with English language proficiency will benefit from legal process outsourcing (LPO). Speaking of LPO delivery costs in India, Kamlani says, "Law firms in the U.S. charge an average of $400 to $450 per hour, and we do the same work for $75 to $100 an hour."

Indian vendors are also repositioning to tap the domestic Indian outsourcing market. In 2009, according to Browne and Mohan, domestic Indian firms spent approximately $5.8 to $6 billion on IT services vis-à-vis $5.6 billion in 2008. Such business is used to tide over economic slowdowns in the West. Many Indian vendor firms are actively chasing outsourcing deals in the domestic Indian market. "I can tell you that there are huge, multiyear projects being considered by large Indian corporate and government organizations," said Infosys chairman Mr. Narayan Murthy.

Challenges for India

1. Higher costs of living, market conditions, and inflated salaries may cause outsourcing to spread to more affordable tier-2 cities. Outsourcing hubs in India like NCR and Bangalore will need to transform business strategically to retain their viability.
2. Infrastructure facilities available in the city will need to be constantly upgraded to meet the best in class.
3. Workers will need to continuously upgrade their work-related skills to manage the fast pace of technology and business change.

4. Sustained profitable turnover will continue to be one of the biggest concerns of BPO industry.
5. China is aggressively building its outsourcing capabilities with sufficient drive from its government. Cheaper alternatives like Latin America, Eastern Europe, and South Africa may continue to push outsourcing costs downward.

Miscellaneous Outsourcing Countries

Countries like India, China, Philippines, and Brazil have a significant percentage of their total population involved in agriculture. Similar to the past years, over the coming years too, there will be a shift of population from the agriculture into the services and manufacturing fields. Aspirant countries will try to emulate India and China by following their approaches and framing suitable guidelines, etc. Countries will have specific skill sets which set them apart from others.

Trends

As the slowly rising wave becomes a trend, engulfing the masses.

Foreseeing new trends and leveraging technology to change business value will be the hallmark of the new outsourcing leaders.

Idea versus Size

Large diverse organizations will face real competition from small niche players because the future will be driven by value and competing ideas, not so much by competing organizational sizes. While large and medium-sized organizations may temporarily dominate the outsourcing space, small players will jump in, in increasing numbers. As new players crowd the outsourcing space, global competition and costing will become ever fiercer. Small players existing in remote regions will compete with big multinational businesses by creating a need for little-known services and products in the global marketplace. Brands can plunge from hero to zero in a matter of minutes.

Outsourcing Promiscuity

Until recently, the traditional mind-set was that, once organizations having business relationships formed an emotional bond, such would be a long-term relationship. That may have been the case when there were a limited number of brands, suppliers, channels, target audience, etc., but now the choices are huge, and hence competition is fierce.

Organizations will no longer be loyal to vendor suppliers and partners on a long term. Outsourcing would be done to whoever is offering the best deal at that point in time. Hence organizations must learn to play the game with ever-changing rules and market circumstances. Scale business relationships or perish will be the new mantra. As the outsourcing horizons expand, borders, old alignments, and equations will become meaningless to be replaced by a global network of telecommunications, finance, business, education, medicine, and almost every field of industry.

Causes of relationship promiscuity include

- *Products and services are being commoditized* and becoming increasing transactional. Hence a long-term perspective may be a defective approach.
- *Costs* continue to play a role as the world becomes more closely knit with better interconnectivity.
- *Innovation* is in. Technology is constantly pushing mass production costs lower; hence the agility to read the market and react to the competition is imperative.
- Outsourcing relationships are becoming more and more *holistic*, driving deep into new, previously untouched areas.

Business models will move to transaction and outcome based so that ownership, responsibility, rewards, and risks are more equitably shared by both outsourcing organization and the vendor. Long-term partnerships though existent will give way to transaction-specific, deal-to-deal relationships. Predetermined pricing will give way to alternative approaches like auction-based bidding, holistic request for proposal (RFP), etc. The new-generation contracts will be risk reward and equity based. Such outsourcing contracts will be partner based in spirit. Co-ownership and win–win business approaches will be the future of most business contracts, with rewards and risks being shared. Pricing models will become utility based, leading to flexible pricing based on respective customer usage. Time and materials (T&M), fixed-price contracts of today will see their gradual decline. Service level agreements (SLAs) may gradually give way to holistic outsourcing solutions in more business areas. Though businesses are overwhelmed by choice, research has shown that *businesses usually use a limited set of evaluation options toward decision making*, which is influenced by factors like nature of business, organizational culture, etc.

Outsourcing Highlights

Present	Future
Cost reduction	Business transformation, value, efficiency
Vendor management	Partnership approach, strategic relationship
Limited access to internal knowledge pool	Niche consulting and shared intellectual property
SLA driven	Transactional, outcome driven
Applications-driven approach	Solution- and tools-driven approach
Low risks, low gains	High risks, high gains

Transformational Outsourcing

Outsourcing will strive for business transformation so as to enable exponential technology-driven gains by effective integration of infrastructure solutions and services into streamlined processes. Outsourcing organizations will have business-transformational value when partnering with vendor experts. A word of caution, though—value perceptions change over time. The best practices of delivery today will become an expected basic norm of the future as the rules of the game continue to mutate so fast. Vendors will need to provide integration services to disparate business components through ever-innovative technology-driven approaches. Vendors will constantly raise the bar by delivering on time, under budget, meeting high quality standards through innovative automation and high-end computing. A 2009 survey of a set of global CIOs and CFOs showed that access to niche skills not available in house is the most important driver of outsourcing, followed by cost reduction. The outsourcing evolution rolls from tactical cost cutting into a strategy-driven business advantage. As organizations begin to use outsourcing strategically for transformational ends, the limits of business process excellence, speed to market, quality, and standards will continue to be stretched. Says Daniel Marovitz, technology managing director for Deutsche Bank's global businesses on outsourcing, "This isn't about labor cost. The issue is that if you don't do it, you won't survive."

End-to-End Solutions

The fusion of IT and BPO as a joint offering has given such vendors a significant edge. Abid Ali, vice president of Tata Consultancy Services (TCS), refers to this as *"IT–BPO synergy."* Value gains from the twin offering under one umbrella will add significant benefits.

The previous view, "If you can't control it, then don't outsource it" is giving way. Complete outsourcing of logical parts of the business cycle is the forthcoming trend. Doing this brings about greater responsibility on the supplier vendor. Firms will increasingly resort to outsourcing complete units of process life cycles to achieve desired results. Organizations thus do not need to micromanage, leading to the practice, "The more control you relinquish, greater the value." *Peter Drucker says, "Do what you do best and outsource the rest."*

Need for Speed

Outsourcing businesses of the future can "not" afford to overplan. Speed, agility, and flexibility in a world of accelerated changes will become critical. Outsourcing businesses of the future will need to constantly reinvent their game plan in a very fast-changing business landscape.

Intermediary Dissipation

"Anything that has involved an intermediary will be changed. New kinds of intermediaries will emerge, but the old ones—especially in businesses that have created high margins by being in the middle of transactions—will find their very existences at risk," says Dan Gillmor, longtime technology journalist.

The Education Alignment

Education system will align and upgrade suitably so as to produce more "employable" candidates for the outsourcing business. The gap between the two has long been a bone of contention.

Government Support

Favorable government laws will boost the outsourcing climate as countries jostle for space in the outsourcing world.

The Governing Systems

High proliferation of technology, connectivity, and a more integrated economy will add its own challenges to governments. World communities and global businesses will have an increasing influence on government policy. Government will be forced to become increasingly transparent and accessible over matters of outsourcing, and protectionism may not be sustainable. Of the top 100 economic players, one half are sovereign states, with the remaining half being multinational organizations.

Global Integration

Global sourcing and procurement will become commonly prevalent. Outsourcing phenomenon will go from strength to strength as more and more countries jump onto the outsourcing bandwagon. The United States, United Kingdom, India, and China (emerging) will dominate the outsourcing future. As the outsourcing game grows bigger and bigger, so will the interplay of money, resources, people, products, and services.

End User Say

Power will continue to migrate downward in the supply chain channel toward the end user. End user benefit, gains, and perspective will play an increasingly important role in shaping outsourcing deals. End customer focus will have a growing influence in new business propositions.

Business Metamorphosis

The nature of outsourcing business will move up the value chain into intellectual, knowledge-ended, holistic business cycles.

Rise of Global Players

As the world economy becomes more and more free due to liberalitation, technology advancements, and so forth, an increasing number of outsourcing organizations will ride this wave to become global. Large multinational companies will continue to invest in captive BPO units in multiple vendor countries. Big vendor organizations will continue to increase their global footprint so as to include delivery of all types of outsourcing (i.e., onshoring, nearshoring, and offshoring) into their business portfolio. Outsourcing will thus blur the lines between in-house execution, onshoring, nearshoring, and offshoring. Old global organizations will face higher competition and challenges from these new players.

Outsourcing at all times needs to be transparent, be on time, have suitable reporting mechanisms, and be in line with the organization's criteria for success.

Outsourcing Functions

Traditional outsourcing in the fields of customer care, financial services, manufacturing, IT, ITES, and BPO will continue to grow. Outsourcing will continue to grow in various industry verticals. Only large outsourcing organizations may consider outsourcing certain human resources (HR) functions like hiring, employee management, etc. Small outsourcing firms will continue to in-house HR as specific complimentary domains' skill sets are needed from the relatively small employee pool.

Economy Impact

The outsourcing economy itself will generate both structural and efficiency gains. Outsourcing will add to the prosperity and economy of developing nations, allowing people in various continents a better standard of living.

Outsourcing: Private and Government Deals

Outsourcing organizations, including large multinationals, will be largely private enterprises, though governments will also become large outsourcing players. Government sectors globally will resort to ever-increasing outsourcing levels. Even now, government sectors lead in terms of total outsourced deals' value. Small, big, and megadeals worth billions will be signed in outsourcing in the future. Such outsourcing projects and sizes will be increasingly customized, venturing into ever-growing vistas. The U.K. government has outsourced business megadeals of billions of pounds to British Telecom (BT).

Temporary Demand Spikes

Organizations through outsourcing will meet sudden surges and spikes in business demand by exponentially scaling up or down resources, manpower, etc., without needing to hire and fire additional employees and invest in additional infrastructure. Outsourcing is inherently designed to handle and benefit from such demand spikes.

Currency Interchange

Appreciation and depreciation of currencies as economies rise and fall will continue to impact the outsourcing business favorability and potential. Outsourcing firms geographically located and operating from developed, mature markets will continue to leverage from outsourcing as long as their currencies are stronger than that of the vendor countries.

Internet Growth and Outsourcing

The Internet will be more deeply integrated in our physical environments, and high-speed connections will proliferate. The "always-on" Internet, combined with networked computers, will continue to give a boost to outsourcing.

New Quality Definitions

Companies will produce better quality of products while sharing revenues for value-added contributions, leading to a win–win synergy.

Synergy between Outsourcing Players

In the words of Raymond A. Kulweic (editor, vice president, *Modern Materials Handling*) in his July 1998 editorial, "No longer can your vision be limited to the four walls of your plant or warehouse. Instead, you must expand your borders to include your supplier's supplier and your customers' customer, in an ongoing quest to efficiently convert standing inventory to products on the move."

Growth of New Business Avenues

As outsourcing, Internet, and other mediums become increasingly integrated, personal entertainment (e.g., chat, online games, audio, videos, etc.) will spawn new sets of services and products. Connections across commerce, outsourcing, media, entertainment, and advertising will become stronger, with future margins going to a new breed of digital media titans.

Useless Data Volumes

The challenge for both future businesses and consumers is this: As the world continues to get more complex, how do we find the stuff of value, ignore the unwanted stuff, and avoid the overload of large data volumes in this search process? The challenge for outsourcing businesses is in making sense of highly dynamic, interactive, and large data volumes. The smart strategy is to enable the user (the outsourcing organization, supplier, or end customer, whichever the case) to access and use the data as per their respective need by mastering the complexity. Sufficiently flexible and easy-to-use options should allow the user to get customized/personalized results from the underlying maze of data volumes. The dissemination of information will increasingly become the dissemination of drivel in the outsourcing explosion. As more and more "data" is posted and processed, there will be increasingly less "information."

Education and Certifications

Enabled by information technologies, the pace of learning will increase, bringing newer pressures on outsourcing professionals to either learn quickly and survive or fail and exit.

In ten years, most students will spend at least part of their "school days" in virtual classes, grouped online with others who share their interests, mastery, and skills.

Inventory

Inventory systems will continue to shift from "push" to "pull" in the outsourcing business as organizations give access to providers of their resource needs. Outsourcing operations will leverage from best practices in inventory management using "just in time" or any other suitable techniques as needed. Outsourcing will foster a high degree of reuse of components, reduce overproduction, reduce wastage, minimize error rates, minimize standing inventories, save capital for suitable redeployment, reduce paper transactions, and also save on energy.

Agriculture Outsourcing

To meet human food needs of the next 40 years worldwide, agriculture will need to produce as much food as has been produced during all of recorded human history. This may create niche segments in agriculture outsourcing in areas of designer genetically engineered crops.

As demands soar to feed an ever hungry globe.

Tourism Outsourcing

Politically stable countries with weaker currencies will also attract more tourists from relatively stronger-currency nations, leading to increased outsourcing in the tourism sector.

Oil Impact

Oil price fluctuations will put pressure on economies, further driving the outsourcing curve up. Oil-consuming countries like the United States will be pushed to innovate or run out eventually.

Contingency Planning

Contingency moves to de-risk natural disasters, war, etc., will form part of the outsourcing business scope.

Job Loss

While technology eliminates, it also creates wholly new sectors, fields, industries, and thrust areas. The higher the complexity and skill set of the outsourcing work, the lower the job loss in the outsourcing country. Some examples of nature of outsourcing work which do not lead to job loss in the outsourcing country are R&D, product design and engineering, marketing, and sales. On the other hand, outsourcing low-end back office jobs may result in some job losses. Loss of jobs perception and political antagonism will decline as people come to accept the outsourcing reality as economies and business practices mature.

Startup Cost

McKinsey consultant Lowell Bryan estimated that "today, U.S. companies require 20% less in the way of tangible assets to produce a dollar's worth of sales than they did a generation ago."

World Security

Interdependencies in the business of outsourcing will make the world a more networked, mutually responsible, and a safer place to live in, not including the usually occupational risks that come with the nature of business outsourced. The interplay of heterogeneous supply chains, resources, and interdependent businesses across multiple countries in the outsourcing pie will bring about pressure on governments to promote an era of peace and economic well-being. Outsourcing, however, is froth with the usual "occupational" risks as large volumes of information fly back and forth over the global networks day and night.

Individual Privacy

Privacy, a defining right by law in most countries, seems to be falling steeply. Corporate databases are collecting large volumes of data on individual creditworthiness, incomes, spending patterns, brand choices, medical conditions, lifestyles, etc. Video cameras continue to proliferate into many aspects of living in large and medium-sized cities worldwide.

What Will Not Be Outsourced

The future may see organizations retaining control only of organization brand, key customers' management, business stakeholders, and the overseeing network of the business life cycle, while increasingly outsourcing core processes, value creation, and specific aspects of business strategy planning (e.g., to strategy consultants like McKinsey).

Growth of Outsourcing in Information Technology and BPO Domains

As per McKinsey Global Institute reports, the outsourcing business in IT and BPO will show sustained growth in the coming five to ten years.

Supply factors will have a significant influence on offshore IT and BPO growth in the countries mentioned in Figure 19.1 and Figure 19.2. Globally, the rate of BPO growth is expected to be faster than IT outsourcing growth.

As the phenomenon explodes, impacting all in its path.

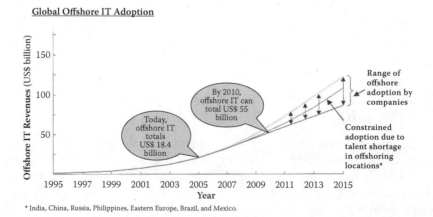

Global Offshore IT Adoption

* India, China, Russia, Philippines, Eastern Europe, Brazil, and Mexico.

Figure 19.1 Predicted annual growth of global offshore IT adoption. (With permission of the McKinsey Global Institute.).

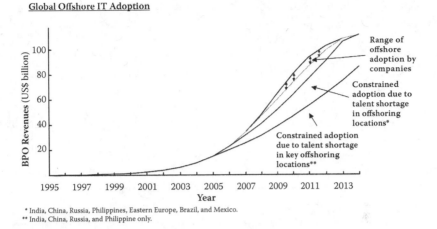

Global Offshore IT Adoption

Figure 19.2   Predicted annual growth of global offshore BPO adoption. (With permission of the McKinsey Global Institute.)

Automation, Technology, and Outsourcing

Plug and play, by night and day, so they say.

Technological progress over the past decade has been tremendous, but the next ten years are going to be simply astounding. *Historically, growth in computing power has followed Moore's Law, which states that computing capability roughly doubles every two years.*

Automation and outsourcing, while continuing to impact the manufacturing sector including manual operations, will also have a deep penetration into automating niche, skilled, and experiential knowledge. Six-figures knowledge workers may be rendered obsolete as technology automates their skills. Such knowledge workers will need to have the learnability to mutate their existing knowledge into a new sought-after profession. Because workforce salaries usually constitute the most significant portion of an organization's costs, automation of human resource work will always be a very welcome proposition.

The Technology Curve

Innovation, experiential knowledge, subject matter expertise, business process excellence, products and services life-cycle shortening, integrated holistic solutions offering, speed of closure, and cost reduction will be the highlights of the future world of outsourcing. Vendors will compete globally, and competition will be fierce due to rapid innovations in technology, lower-cost outsourcing destinations, etc. Vast strides in wide area networks, Internet, telecom, power, infrastructure, and suitable government policies will continue to boost the outsourcing growth.

Technology and innovation will continue to push the limits of quality, deliverables, etc. Technology and innovations will continue to add ever-increasing value to outsourcing deliveries. On-demand business will drive certain industries like the exploding telecom sector. Through strategic outsourcing, organizations seek to deliver products and solutions to the marketplace faster, thereby maintaining business dominance. Outsourcing through automation will continue to drive the cost of services and products, allowing a reduction in prices without any fall in profits. Mass production through innovation and outsourcing has seen the prices of goods like electronics products fall steeply. Outsourcing through automation will lead to a sustainable and entrenched economic interdependence in society. Technology and innovation will lead to creation of new outsourcing business models and also result in disruption of existing ones. Innovative outsourcing driven by technology will cause a force-multiplying convergence of information, resources, people, products, and services.

Example—Compare McDonalds with Google: In 2008 McDonalds employed 400,000 people with an average revenue of $59,000 per head. Google, with just 20,000 employees, had an average of over a million dollars per head.

E-Materialization

Dematerialization from paper to computerized e-files is a great saver. Dematerialization is a core outcome of the outsourcing process. Paper and its related products are getting e-materialized through the outsourcing phenomenon. Paper based photographs, documents, etc., no longer manually transport, but simply stream through the electronic networks at dizzying speeds. The Internet and dedicated wide area networks links will continue to drive this growth by providing requisite supporting infrastructure framework.

Example—From 1995 onward, Cisco moved its technical support system onto the Internet. This was so well received by customers, resellers, partners, etc., for their needs like placing orders, products inquiry, technical support, downloading software, etc., that by 1997 the site started logging about one million hits per month. Even today about 80% of all customer service inquiries are met by this Web portal. Such an approach has led to low error rates of 2%. In the words of CFO Larry Carter to the *Economist*, "We just collect the money." This operational practice will continue to be embraced by small and big businesses.

Example—Publishing houses like newspapers, etc., will increasingly outsource preproduction work to India. MediaNews papers of California, by outsourcing preproduction work to India, reduced their costs by about 65%. Other aspects like copy editing, designing, advertisement production, etc., will also see increased outsourcing.

It thus has large-scale energy saving and environmental protection impacts.

Example—Organizations like Royal Dutch/Shell Group, the world's largest oil company largely use "dematerialization" through a sustained focus on outsourcing.

Workplaces Metamorphosis

Outsourcing organizations existing in multiple geographies all over the globe will work in close coordination on a day-to-day basis. While there will be a need for physical proximity in specific cases, advanced communications systems will continue to change the nature of the workplace.

As outsourcing grows, both business-to-consumer and business-to-business will follow suit. Hence, such jobs that have limited in-person dependence may increasing get executed from home instead traditional office workplaces. Higher numbers of people working from home using suitable communication networks will result in time, travel, resources, energy, etc., savings. Thus, office space costs will continue to be driven downward. Outsourcing has the potential to minimize office spaces, turn warehouses into efficient computerized supply chain systems, dematerialize paper, etc.

Example—IBM U.S. from 1992 onward, through the use of laptop computers, secure networks, processes, and enabling systems, allows a significant fraction of its sales and service organizations to work from outside its office spaces (i.e., telework). In five years, from 1992 to 1997, savings of $1 billion were achieved. Space occupancy expenses previously $5.7 billion fell to $3.3 billion, a staggering reduction of 40+%. This enables most of IBM's sales force to operate outside an office workplace. About 12,500 personnel operate as such. Worldwide, almost 17% of IBM's total employees have the equipment, training, and support systems to work from alternative work places.

Lee Dayton, IBM's vice president for corporate development and real estate, stated, "If they're not going to work in IBM office, we want to eliminate the dedicated space with all of its overhead and services."

This has additionally led to savings in office space, travel, resources, systems, time, and also annual energy savings of 4%.

The Swedish telecommunications company, Ericsson, also emulated this model, allowing about 25% of its workforce to telework out of the office.

Impact on Transportation

- People commuting giving way to higher *telecommuting*. Video-teleconferencing has less than 1% energy consumption and greenhouse gas emissions versus respective airline travel.
- In-person shopping giving way to higher *teleshopping*.
- Air travel will give way to higher *teleconferencing*. This has led to significant budget and cost reductions.
- The digital age will *transport voluminous amounts of data*, significantly reducing human transportation.

As humans and devices roam the globe, across spaces real and virtual.

Examples of Future Business Forays of Outsourcing

As the phenomenon explodes, impacting all in its path.

Microcommerce Business Opportunities

Not just big outsourcing deals but also microservices and products priced less than $5 will become very popular. Over the next years, outsourcing will increasingly lead to a traditional spinoff of errands; some of them will be fairly low priced (a few dollars).

Highlights of these are

- Purchase decision of small numbers need low trigger given the low cost. End user impulse buying is also applicable. Higher order numbers could call for suitable negotiations between outsourcing organization and supplier vendor.
- Needs a mass delivery mechanism for achieving threshold revenue levels. Hence automated servicing mechanisms like the Internet, mobile networks, ATM networks, and automated dispensers are needed with human intervention at its requisite minimal.
- Making available at the right time and place of need adds to value and revenues.

Steps of microcommerce:

1. Services and products business proposition
2. Micropayment by outsourcing customer and/or end user
3. Delivery mechanism of services and products
4. Postsale interactions (e.g., reviews, support, replacement, etc.) if applicable.

Examples

Microservices and Microproducts

Microservices—article reviews, content search, subject matter consulting, parking reservations, dispatching, e-ticketing, e-couponing, mobile auctions, mobile taxi reservations, retail purchases using mobile phone, automated dispensers of fast-moving consumer goods

Microproducts—specialized weather updates, music tracks, news, ringtones, white papers, iTunes music downloads, eBay auction of small items, smart cards sale, PayPal for payments

Person-to-Person Outsourcing (P2P Offshoring)

Offshoring is normally associated with big and middle-size businesses. The new trend in outsourcing, person-to-person outsourcing, will evolve as communication-enabling mechanisms explode in reach and implode inwards reducing costs.

People-to-people services will usually be transaction based with clear expected outcomes of delivery of service and/or product. This will create a new class of freelance providers who work in multiple time zones and mostly deliver from home. Such services do not require team engagement and can be done by a single professional. Some examples are given below. (For more examples refer to Chapter 11.)

- Coding work
- Design of application and/or respective reviews
- Technical consulting for problem resolution
- Inviting experts for training
- Simple documentation work
- Research and development, product development
- Consultancy services
- Project planning and management services
- Back office services (transaction processing, e.g., data entry, processing)
- Web catalog and content management services
- Technology services—software verification and validation

Knowledge Process Outsourcing (KPO)

The capital of future outsourcing will no longer be money, but knowledge. Information economy and knowledge economy will bring about another era of the industrial revolution. Firms will climb the knowledge spectrum. Knowledge and skills will take on an acquisition velocity over ever-decreasing timelines till the very limits of human learning and assimilation start getting pushed.

The KPO market is growing at 34% compound annual growth rate (CAGR). Outsourcing will combine a dynamic mix of fast-paced markets, flexible business model changes, and domain specializations, in varying proportions depending on the (so to say) need of the hour. The law of supply and demand will add its portion of challenges toward such point-in-time availability. New value chains will be created as altogether new industries spring up around the delivery of the KPO business.

While intellectual property rights (IPR) filings will leapfrog, there will also be a corresponding growth in the humanitarian perspective of releasing such intellectual property as would benefit mankind. International intellectual property rights enforcement will improve as the outsourcing business integrates organizations and countries.

KPO will encompass IT and BPO sectors, verticals like R&D, legal process outsourcing (LPO), publishing, etc. Knowledge process outsourcing (KPO) requires domain expertise because the respective business deliverables are knowledge dependent and of high business complexity. KPO provides niche business expertise instead of mere process expertise done by BPOs. Intellectual property creation is a usual outcome of such engagements.

Hence KPO vendors are highly trusted and usually empowered to make decisions on behalf of their outsourcing clients.

Outsourcing of R&D

Not just basic R&D, organizations are outsourcing R&D toward breaking into never seen virgin areas through need creation in end users, products innovation, etc. Outsourcing of R&D will become popular in specific outsourcing domains. Companies with R&D outsourcing to India are Cisco Systems, Motorola, Hewlett-Packard, Google., General Motors Corp., and Boeing Co., among others.

In pharmaceuticals outsourcing, Indian vendors will continue to contribute significantly in codevelopment and co-ownership through production, R&D, clinical trials, etc., for new drugs.

This will lead to new industries and fields leveraging from outsourcing.

Legal Outsourcing (LPO)

Indian lawyers with experience in the American, British, etc., legal systems can offer paralegal support, legal support, and patent services. This currently exists only in a small measure and has great potential for exponential growth.

Energy Outsourcing

Outsourcing vendors have moved into energy cogeneration/production on-site, financing, setting up, managing, and owning the entire energy system of their clients. Such forward-looking, long-term contracts lead to large-scale savings of cost and energy over a period of five to ten years. Energy savings up to 40% are achievable through such strategic outsourcing. Energy outsourcing has tremendous future potential.

Example—Sempra Energy Solutions, in an energy outsourcing tie-up with DreamWorks SKG, took over setup and maintenance of the entire energy system of its new animation campus. Significant investments are made by both parties toward achieving their long-term energy goals.

Pacific Gas and Electric (PG&E) Energy Services, through an energy outsourcing deal with Ultramar Diamond Shamrock, aimed to cut its oil refinery's energy costs by $440 million over a period of seven years. This parent approach envisaged using energy efficiency approaches and production through cogeneration.

Miscellaneous Examples of the Near Future of Outsourcing

- Unconstrained natural language recognition as people from different geographies interact
- Intelligent agents, robots' widespread usage for automated execution of tasks
- Remote virtual meetings between organizations, vendors, customers, etc.

The Bow and Final Words

The bird's-eye view.

As outsourcing continues to make inroads into new unexplored vistas, realms, and industries, aspiring organizations should deliberate holistically by breaking down their overall activities and functions. The decision to retain an activity in-house (say by integrating it vertically) or outsource it is a strategic one and often has far-reaching results.

Core projects/processes which give the company strategic advantage when using outsourcing are the "need of the hour." Niche suppliers with vast reserves of experience and knowledge provide exponential gains by leapfrogging over the competition, sometimes impacting the very approach to doing business. *Critical, noncore projects which are important but not competitive differentiators for the company are also potential candidates for outsourcing. Noncore, noncritical, repetitive processes which are required to make the business, systems, and environment work are potential candidates too. Cost reduction is a well-known reason for outsourcing.*

Holistic, comprehensive vendors are the way of the future. They handle whole transactional, administrative, and technological aspects of projects and processes by introducing best practices, technology enablers, and skilled workforce. *Customization and innovation are their characteristics.* Being experts in their respective fields, they can comprehend buyers' requirements and predict performance and results through past experience. *To ensure that the vendor supplier remains "on their toes," periodic benchmarking against existing best practices should be carried out by the outsourcing client.*

The outcome and gain-sharing models are becoming increasingly popular. This brings in a shared responsibility between the outsourcing organization and the vendor. *It is advantageous because the vendor benefits if the outsourcing client benefits. It is a form of incentive for continuous improvement.* Transactional pricing models will also continue to be popular.

The advent of the Internet is almost as significant as electricity, the assembly line, the telephone, or the steam engine. *The Internet, a large network of computers (analyst firm Forrester forecasts that worldwide computer numbers will rise to 2 billion by 2015) located around the world, provides a powerful infrastructure for outsourcing.*

Web outsourcing models and frameworks suggest innovative and largely unexplored ideas, concepts, designs, and frameworks. These new approaches can mostly be deployed with relatively small investments.

Some *examples of Web-based outsourcing* are consulting, training, animation, business writing, music composition, illustrations, photography, instructional design, editing, textbook manuscript layout, screenwriting, video editing, photo editing, storyboarding, creative writing, graphic design, proofreading, technical writing, cover design, art, white paper development, etc.

Web Outsourcing—Criteria for Success and Challenges include "nature" of business proposition, online; market readiness; reuse of related past works, knowledge, experience, etc.; sifting of valuable information from vast online information volumes; transparency and interoperability between networked systems; quality; delivery time and speed; convenience and self-service; personalization and customization for end user; confidentiality online; training; online vendor/providers specialized domain, business, and technology skills; online outsourcing organization's specialized business skills; risk management; employee retention; risks of access to critical and sensitive data by partners, online vendors, and unauthorized users; different language nuances used online; presentation and readability challenges online for enabling quick decision taking in Web-based applications; online payment systems and electronic data interface (EDI) challenges; and recession and low market economic conditions.

Web Outsourcing—Advantages include reaping exponential advantages from pioneering into unexplored fields; usage of highly skilled people and resources in a borderless world with 24/7 × 365 operations; accentuating speed; strategic focus; de-risking from vendors' geographical spread; delivering personalized and customized services; low budgets for setup and working; reaping from the information superhighway; dematerialization by migrating manual/paper records to electronic media; financial and cross-currency conversion benefits; higher organizational integration; reduced learning curve; enhanced brand building; interoperable communications; quality and continuous benchmarking; long-term career paths for employees; reduced liability and risk mitigation; knowledge-driven business practices; lowering of linguistic barriers; manual tasks automation through software agents; online payments through e-commerce, operational efficiency; and substantial saving impact on the society and environment.

War times, recession, and economic slowdown offer excellent opportunities to set up new businesses and gain competitive advantages. Corporate ethics, good corporate governance practices, data security, strong values, capability, and the ability to adapt became increasingly important factors for companies to survive and grow during a slowdown. *The dipping valuations of overseas firms, in some cases by 30%, prompted many Indian IT vendors to tread the M&A path. Competition from overseas rivals like IBM, Accenture, and Capgemini was another factor fueling the acquisition trend. Top Indian software firms like TCS, Infosys, and Wipro got repeat orders resulting in more than 90% of their total revenue over the past couple of years. Focus on "software products" (instead of the previous services delivery) in different fields like media, communication, telecom, and retail grew.* Governments worldwide put in place series of measures and policies for various industries to facilitate recovery including financial bailout, large projects outsourcing, etc.

For both published and unpublished works, copyright protection exists. The following categories are included in copyrighted works: literary works, musical works, dramatic works with accompanying music, pantomimes and choreographic work, pictorial, graphic, and sculptural works, motion pictures and other audiovisual works, sound recordings, and architectural works. These categories are quite broad; for instance, computer programs and most compilations are "literary works," maps are "pictorial, graphic, and sculptural works."

Security of organizations' critical assets, primarily data, are becoming increasingly crucial. *Such breaches can range from small losses to complete business failure and long-term, large-scale losses.* Through public networks like the Internet, private corporate networks are accessed and sometimes breached. Organizations must constantly use all means available to counter this ever-present threat.

India continues to be the favored outsourcing destination due to its highly skilled workforce, fluency in English, cheaper costs, efficient services, dedicated workforce aiming at making a long-term career in outsourcing, lower attrition rates compared to the West, and compatible time zone difference with the West.

In time hopefully we may learn to transcend time.

Appendix: Enabling Infrastructure and Components

Each playing their part in an interdependent maze.

The following may be some of the *infrastructure needs* of outsourcing organizations and providers.

Hardware Deployment

The traditional models of information management do not lend themselves to the new paradigm, the challenges facing server selection, design, and deployment. We are no longer dealing with only structured, alphanumeric (ASCII) data; instead, the data is radically different. When trying to deliver large pieces of complex data to users through new interactive applications, the computing platforms that we are familiar with pose potential bottlenecks. New data types, for example, cannot be handled by so-called mainframe platforms which are costly and slow. Standalone computers lack the scalability and ability to manage a large number of transactions, and hence the gap is expected to be filled with multimedia servers. A key element of the solution, clearly, is the choice of platform. Platform choices include multi-processing, multitasking, and multithreaded systems for true information management. The ability to support the concurrent execution of several tasks on multiple processors is called multiprocessing. For executing programs, this implies the ability of using more than one CPU, and the processors can be tightly or loosely coupled. Each processor has its own local memory in loosely coupled systems. The processors share common memory in tightly coupled systems, which is a more popular architecture. Using a special memory bus, processors interact with memory, but each processor has its own RAM cache, which reduces the traffic on the memory bus. To ensure that data in these RAM caches are consistent across the different processors requires synchronization procedures. For some time, the hardware world has been toying with multiple processor architecture designs. Software, as always, has lagged behind hardware, and this is a part of the problem. Attempts to add multiprocessing capabilities to UNIX are some of the more successful early efforts involved. Multimedia servers are being implemented by vendors on multiple processors to increase multimedia processing speed and performance. Servers are permitted by multimedia processors to do either symmetric or functional multiprocessing. All processors are treated as equal by symmetric multiprocessing, which means any processor can do the work of any other processor. To be run concurrently on any available processor, applications are broken down into tasks, processes, and threads. The goal of this approach is to minimize processor usage or total throughput, and if there is work to be done, the processor does not sit idle. A task can be dynamically assigned to any processor that might be free through symmetric multiprocessing. The network operating system or the server operating system usually performs this task assignment. Windows NT and OS/2 are capable of symmetric multiprocessing. In contrast, asymmetric multiprocessing assigns each task to a specialized processor. For example, network services are assigned to one processor, disk I/O is assigned to another, and data storage and manipulation is assigned to a third. Work is not evenly distributed across the separate CPUs, and this is a problem with asymmetric multiprocessing (ASMP). What is expected by users is that a six-processor machine could run six programs as well as a three-processor machine could run three. The operating system, unfortunately, could be the bottleneck, because it can run only on a specific CPU on the machine. Although the scalability of the multiprocessor architecture is limited by this restriction, it relieves the operating system architect of a great many synchronization problems, because the operating system only does one thing at a time.

The ability of the modern operating system to run multiple programs is called multitasking. Because of large numbers of CPUs available in a server, the user feels that they are running simultaneously, even though there may be an internal extremely fast switching control happening between the CPUs processing the respective tasks. Preemptive and non-preemptive are the two types of multitasking used. Preemptive multitasking is offered by advanced server operating systems such as Windows XP, which means that it can distribute CPU time among programs with or without their consent. A sophisticated form of multitasking is multithreading, which refers to the ability to support separate paths of execution within a single address space (process). By creating multiple processes, older operating systems achieve multitasking, which creates a great deal of overhead. A process is broken into independent executable tasks called threads, in a multithreaded environment. A process is the smallest unit of execution that a system can allocate resources to or schedule a run in multitasking. A process consists of several threads or paths of execution. A thread is the smallest unit of execution that a system can schedule to run in multithreading. A stack, an instruction pointer, a priority queue, a CPU state, and an entry in the system scheduler about its state constitute a thread. For input the state of a thread can be blocked or scheduled for execution or executing.

Office Equipment Products

Devices such as joysticks, trackballs, light pens, and voice recognition systems are widely available, and the computer has a full function keyboard and a mouse for pointing, clicking, and highlighting. To permit selection from menus, the set top will use a handheld remote control, possibly a joystick, trackball, or other handheld cursor control borrowed from video games as compared to a TV. There are far more flexible and powerful ways to interact with a computer.

Common platform enumeration (CPE) products like voice over Internet protocol (VoIP), private branch exchanges (PBXs), telephones, facsimile products, modems, voice processing equipment, and video communication equipment additionally support the Web-based outsourcing of business. Such products have low unit prices because the respective product industries are mature. Product groups such as telephones, telephone answering machines, shipments of modems, and voice processing and video communication equipment are booming. Users through these devices can send, store, and receive information over either wire line or wireless networks, and these devices combine voice, data, and video functions. They have led to huge reductions in travel and corresponding expenses for the various players.

The Client–Server Model and E-Commerce

The client–server model is followed commonly by applications. Information is requested from servers through devices plus software called clients. The traditional mainframe-based models have been replaced by client–server model. Computers are linked to the storage; in contrast, in the client–server architecture, most of the computing is done on the client. Reengineering has to be done to accommodate new data types even on existing client–server models based on servers which are providing back end technology for scalable and flexible database management. Message passing is the paradigm which allows the client to interact with the server in the client–server model through request reply sequence. The client devices (from personal digital assistants to computers) handle the user interface, while the server manages application tasks, handles storage and security, and provides scalability ability to add more clients as needed for serving more customers. Critical elements such as distribution, connectivity, security, and accounting are handled by the multimedia server, and this is expected to simplify and make scale more cost effective. It will take several more years for the full impact of the fundamental shift in the computing paradigm from a host–terminal architecture to a networked client–server architecture to be realized. Before the installed base of mainframes and minicomputers is networked or replaced by workstations and standalone Computers, there is still a long way to go. A trend that e-commerce will accelerate is that commercial users have begun downsizing their applications to run on client–server networks. Integral to e-commerce applications are the internal processes involved in the storage, retrieval, and management of multimedia data objects. Raw data are converted into usable information and then dished out to users who need it by a multimedia server which is a combination of hardware and software. Text, images, audio, and video are captured, processed, managed, and delivered by it. To display, create, and manipulate multimedia documents, most multimedia servers provide a core set of functions, so that multimedia documents can be transmitted and received over computer networks, and multimedia documents can be stored and retrieved. A server must handle thousands of simultaneous users, manage the transactions of these users like purchase, specific information requests, and customer billing, and deliver information streams to customers at affordable costs in order to make interactive multimedia a reality. The traditional models of information management do not lend themselves to the new paradigm, and that is a technical challenge.

Consider video on demand as an example. A single 90-minute video consuming over 100 gigabytes of storage space must be distributed to a large number of consumers. Therefore, high-end symmetric multiprocessors, clustered architecture, and massive parallel systems are required. The power of cheap processors is harnessed by massive parallel systems and intricately chained to create a web that behaves as one single unit, although each processor has its own communications pathway to the outside world.

Middleware

Middleware, like so many other inventions, came into being out of necessity and is a relatively new concept. Middleware was not needed by users in the 1970s, when vendors delivered homogenous systems that worked. The organizations could not cope when the conditions changed along with the hardware and the software—the tools were inadequate, the backlog was enormous, and the pressure was overwhelming. All the interface, translation, transformation, and interpretation problems were driving application developers crazy, and something needed to be done, and the users were dissatisfied. The problems of getting all the pieces to work together grew from formidable to horrendous, with the growth of networks, client–server technology, and the need for communicating between heterogeneous platforms. Users demanded interaction between dissimilar systems, networks that permitted shared resources, and applications that could be accessed by multiple software programs, as the cry for distributed computing spread. Middleware, in simple terms, is the ultimate mediator between software programs that enables them to talk to one another. The computing shift from application-centric to data-centric is another reason for middleware. Instead of applications controlling data, remote data control all the applications in the network. Middleware services primarily handle three aspects to achieve data-centric computing. These three are transparency, transaction security and management, and distributed object management and services. The network of servers should provide a holistic resource, and users need not know where individual resources are located in this collection of servers.

Network

For transfer, whenever a message enters a public Internet, it must bear some unambiguous identification of the source system from which it originated. This identification is usually in the IP address of the system. The delivery program will insert the identification, if it is lacking. At the time a sender submits a message, sender authentication will be performed by the gateway system when a message is delivered to it. An unambiguous origin identification is generated by the computer systems attached to the Internet. An important responsibility is the assignment of identifiers and their management. For each requested service, authentication in e-commerce basically requires the user to prove his or her identity. In the e-commerce today, the race among various vendors is to provide an authentication method that is easy to use, secure, reliable, and scalable. Within a distributed network environment, third party authentication services must exist where a sender cannot be trusted to identify itself correctly to a receiver. In the implementation of business transaction security, in short, authentication plays an important role.

The technology of the Internet must be selected to best match future business needs by using today's tools, taking into consideration the myriad transactions among businesses. Little return will be yielded on investment if the highway is too narrow to handle the traffic. Transportation costs must be paid and routing issues must be addressed after building the highway and having suitable transport vehicles. The nature of vehicular traffic is extremely important on the Internet. The type of vehicle needed is determined by the information and media content. Much the way an eighteen-wheeler may be restricted from traveling roads that cannot accommodate it, similarly a breakdown of potential everyday e-commerce vehicles into their technological components shows that they vary widely in complexity and may even travel different routes on the Internet. For example, movies consist of video and audio, digital games consist of music, video, and software, while electronic books consist of text, data, graphics, music, photographs, and video. Where will the multimedia content vehicles be housed once they are created? To store and deliver the multimedia cargo, what type of distribution warehouses are needed? Multimedia content is stored in the form of electronic documents in the electronic "highway system." The digital storages store digitized, compressed, computerized libraries. They are accessed through various servers over networks using suitable intermediate applications. Traditional goods move in a similar manner between distribution warehouses. The messaging software fulfills this role on the Internet, in a number of forms like e-mail, electronic data interchange (EDI), or point-to-point file transfers. Other key components of commercial transactions need to be examined, in addition to the development of new vehicles and systems. Safe delivery needs to be assured to the customer by businesses, and means need to be devised so that the customer can pay for using the Internet. To ensure the security of the contents while traveling the Internet and at their destination, various encryption and authentication methods have been developed, and to handle highly complex transactions with high reliability, numerous electronic payment schemes are being developed. In long-established transportation systems, these logical issues are difficult to address.

Network infrastructure capable of supporting multimedia types of information have come into being because of the emergence of integrated electronic commerce applications in health care, manufacturing, education, and other industries. A high-capacity (broadband) interactive (two-way) electronic pipeline, basically, is described by the term, and this pipeline to the home or office is capable of simultaneously supporting a large number of electronic commerce applications and also providing interactive phone-like connectivity between users and services and between users and other users. Long distance and local telephone operators are laying new high-speed fiber optic links to the home, for example. Either coaxial cable is being upgraded, or fiber optic links are being installed by cable television operators.

Proxy

Network functions can be managed by proxies and audit trails of client transactions including client IP address, date and time, byte count, and success code can be created thorough proxying. Candidates for logging are any regular fields and metainformation fields in a transaction. Access to services for individual methods, host, and domain and the like can also be controlled by the proxy. It is natural to design security relevant media within the proxy, given this firewall design in which the proxy acts as an intermediary. Security concerns are handled through proxy mediation by eliminating those subsets of HTTP protocol which might be dangerous, by imposing client and server access to only specific hosts (an organization should have the capability to specify acceptable Web sites), by implementing access control for network services that are lost when the proxy is installed (to restore the security policy enforced by the firewall), and by checking various protocols for well-formed commands.

Routers

The Internet has been impacted by the digital switch industry in a major way. The switching industry underwent major technological development in the 1990s. Let us have an insight into how the switch works. Whether digital bits represent a movie, an opera, an electronic newspaper, or a phone call, all digital bits are essentially alike. Data moves from one point to its destination in a computer network, because it is tagged on the front with a small bundle of identifying digits known as the header. There is no difference in video programming. The digital data pass through switches that route them to their intended destination, either one or multiple recipients, just like any other data (CD-quality music, video games, or video conferencing). This routing technique is known as fast packet switching, because the bundles of data are known as packets and the packets move through a network at very high speeds. Different switching techniques, including asynchronous transfer mode (ATM), are being evaluated and tested by cable companies, and ATM is quickly gaining acceptance as an international standard. So that more content can be sent to everyone in a "broadcast" or "point-to-multipoint" style of communication, the pipeline has been enlarged, and there have been capacity expansions through fiber optic upgrades and digital compression. The growing ability to switch or route content from a sender to a single receiver (known in telecommunications as "point-to-point" communication) is the longer-term benefit of digitization of program content. If 400 to 1,000 channels can be sent to a neighborhood of 300 homes, channel capacity will become so great that individual channels can be sent to individual homes or even individual viewers within that home, a true video-on-demand capability. Routers play a major role for building internetworks. Internet devices that intelligently connect to local area networks (LANs) and backbone wide area networks (WANs) of various providers are routers. Communication between separate networks and access to computing resources distributed throughout an organization are the major benefits of internetworks. Multiprotocol routers are required currently to process LAN and WAN traffic by businesses with many disparate protocols running in their computing environment. So that the problem of one segment does not bring down another department, routers allow companies to departmentalize and segment their networks. Hubs act as the wiring centers for large LANs in contrast to routers, and hubs can diagnose line failure, measure and manage traffic flow, and greatly simplify reconfiguring large LANs. Both the efficiency and predictability problems with the Ethernet LAN topology are solved by adding switching technology to hubs. Each user essentially is given by the switching hub his own private line on the network, a feature that can eliminate collisions (two stations trying to talk at once) and allow traffic to flow more evenly. By more than an order of magnitude, switching hubs can improve network efficiency. The hub and the router will likely become one box, as technology develops and the fine line between the two technologies blurs.

Telecom Networks

Fiber optic long distance networks and satellites are the two major technologies underpinning high global information distribution networks. Cable (coaxial or fiber) owned by long distance or interexchange carriers (IXCs) provide long distance connectivity. The importance of fiber optic cable for international transmission is likely to grow, and for selected routes where the growth in demand for communications capacity is high, submarine cables provide an attractive economic advantage. For interactive applications, cables provide better quality service. By teaming with firms in the wireless and cable TV business, the IXCs also play a significant role in the local access market. Alternative arrangements are being explored by IXCs that would lower cost of using the local network, an expense that exceeded $30 billion in 1993.

AT&T owned nearly 90% of the long distance business at the time of divestiture in 1984, but in the months and years that followed, its chief competitors, MCI and Sprint, invested in new technology to chip away at that market share. In 1984, MCI first started deploying fiber optic cable, when it had revenues close to $2 billion and nearly 5% of the long distance market. Nearly 17% of the long distance business was owned by MCI in 1993, and it was an $11 billion company. Sprint owns nearly 10% of the total U.S. market and has tripled in size since 1984, and Sprint was growing so fast in 1984 that it stopped accepting orders in the 35 markets in which it operated because its network had reached capacity. Telecom lines in Europe until October 1, 1994, had been state monopolies, and prices varied considerably from country to country. Fierce competition came with liberalization and the perception that competition is the key to homogenize services, lower costs, improve levels of technology, and increase efficiency levels.

The telecommunication companies use long distance telephone lines and local telephone lines for information delivery. Cable TV coaxial, fiber optics, and satellite lines are used by cable television companies. The computer-based online servers use Internet, commercial online service providers for delivering information, while the wireless communications use cellular and radio networks and paging systems as the method for information delivery.

Satellites

During the last 15 years, the role of satellites in the communications industry has changed substantially. Initially, satellites were used for long distance telecommunications and one-way video broadcast. In the global communications industry, the advent of fiber optics in the early 1980s changed the role of satellites. Fiber optics are capable of providing higher bandwidth than satellites and are also immune to electromagnetic interference, so fiber optics has emerged as the technology of choice. To carry international traffic, long distance infrastructure is now being deployed undersea, and fiber has been extensively deployed in the United States. Some of the advantages that satellites have over terrestrial networks is that they are accessible from any spot on the globe, can provide broadband digital services, including voice, data, and video, to many points without the cost of acquiring right of way and wire installation, and can add receiving and transmitting sites without significant additional costs. Satellites are a crucial part of the global communications infrastructure and have been commercially available since 1965. A wide range of services are being provided by more than 150 communications satellites in geosynchronous orbit (GEO). Some of the services include broadcast of audio, video content, and overseas telephone links, etc. GEO satellites are placed in an orbit approximately 22,300 miles above the equator. Since GEO satellites rotate with the earth, they appear to be stationary. GEO ensures wide area coverage; in general, geosynchronous satellites are designed to broadcast a wide beam. To provide nearly global coverage, only three GEO satellites are required for such a large broadcast "footprint," and the network's receiving stations require large antennas to capture the relatively weak signal. Areas that cannot be reached by fiber are accessed by another class of satellites. These focus the transmitted energy on a small geographic area and were developed around the 1980s. This class uses small ground antennas to provide low-data-rate point-to-point network services and came to be known as very small aperture terminal (VSAT) satellites. Large corporations are increasingly using VSAT networks to link hundreds of retail sites.

Data Compression

Animation and full motion video become difficult to achieve because of tremendous data requirements from the linked storage box. The time to transfer data from storage to display is the most obvious problem. Nearly 30 MB per second is enough to choke almost any I/O port or data bus. Storage and processing are other problems. Compression of data is the solution. Compression is very important for both data storage and data transmission. Because text compression applies to saving of space on disks, most computer users are familiar with it. Because an enormous quantity of data (several terabytes) will be sent and received as a result of the various commerce activities on the superhighway, understanding various compression approaches is vital.

Lossless and lossy are the two major categories into which compression techniques can be divided, and these terms refer to the state of giving a block of data after it has undergone a complete cycle of compression and decompression. Under certain circumstances, each is appropriate. In the case of lossy, after a cycle of compression and decompression, a given set of data will undergo a loss of accuracy or resolution. On voice, graphics, and video data, this kind of compression is usually performed. Tremendous reduction in space is sometimes yielded by lossy compression, to the order of 1000:1. Generally a loss of resolution and clarity is the tradeoff for more compression. In the case of lossless compression, the compressed output produced is exactly the same as the input. On text and numeric data, lossless compression is used. Because a perfect reconstruction of the original text is required, text always requires lossless compression.

The management of the enormous storage capacity required for the new forms of data, in particular digital video, is one of the most compelling technical challenges. Several magnitudes of compression are accomplished by using video compression standards such as Motion Pictures Expert Group (MPEG); nevertheless new types of video servers need to be developed to address these technical challenges.

Relatively expensive infrastructure should be used to store content which is required to be accessed more frequently, and content requested less often will be housed on less expensive media such as backup optical disks and magnetic tape.

Data Encryption

It is the technological breakthroughs that lead to more proficiency and information security. As discussed earlier, cryptography can be used to protect sensitive information. Data encryption standard (DES) is a widely adopted implementation of secret key cryptography. To anyone who has access to the Internet, the actual software to perform DES is readily available at no cost. In 1975, DES was introduced by IBM, the National Security Agency (NSA), and the National Bureau of Standards (NBS), now known as the National Institute of Standards and Technology (NIST). Over the last couple of decades, extensive research on DES has been carried out, and thus it is definitely the most well-known and widely used cryptosystem in the world. In communication, both the sender and the receiver encrypt and decrypt the message through the same secret key, because DES is a secret key "symmetric" cryptosystem.

For single-user encryption, DES can also be used, for instance, to store files on a hard disk in encrypted form. It operates on 64-bit blocks with a 56-bit secret key and is designed for hardware implementation. DES defines a whole set of encryption algorithms, instead of defining just one encryption algorithm, and for each secret key, a different algorithm is generated, with a few exceptions. Thus knowing one decryption algorithm will be of little help, and it is nearly impossible to break the cipher even through extensively large amounts of computing power, though the algorithm is well known. Thus DES has withstood the test of time. Triple encryption (triple DES) is a new technique for improving the security of DES. Different message blocks are encrypted using three different keys in succession. Decryption by unauthorized parties using single-key exhaustive search will fail, because triple DES is thought to be equivalent to doubling the key size of DES to 112 bits. It is virtually impossible to break it using existing algorithms if one uses DES three times on the same message with different secret keys. DES remains the most frequently used, although several new faster symmetrical algorithms have been developed over the past few years. The use of public key is a more powerful form of cryptography. A pair of keys are involved in the public key techniques, a private key and a public key associated with each user. Only by using the corresponding public key, can information encrypted by private key be decrypted. To encrypt the transmitted information by the user, the private key used is kept secret. A successful decryption using the respective public key verifies the identity of the author, since only the bona fide author of an encrypted message has knowledge of the private key. Public keys can be maintained in some central repository and retrieved to decode or encode information. The problem of key distribution is alleviated in public key techniques, and attempting to find out the private key from the corresponding public key is not possible, and this is an advantage of public key cryptography. Hence only the management of private keys needs to be done. Sharing of public information between the sender and the receiver over public channels is completely eliminated—all transactions involve only public keys, and no private key is ever transmitted or shared. Hence confidential messages can be sent by using a public key, and that message can be decrypted only with a private key in the sole possession of the intended recipient because the secret key never leaves the user's computer.

Encryption—RSA

In 1977, Ron Rivest, Adi Shamir, and Leonard Adleman jointly developed RSA, a public key cryptosystem. It is used for both encryption and authentication. A matched pair of encryption and decryption keys are used by RSA's system, each performing a one-way transformation of the data. Digital signatures are also being developed by RSA, which are mathematical algorithms that encrypt an entire document. In the case of RSA, security is predicated on the fact that it is extremely difficult even for the fastest computers to factor large numbers that are the products of two prime numbers (keys), each greater than 2 raised to the power 512. Digital signatures are enabled by RSA, and they authenticate electronic documents as handwritten signatures do for paper documents. RSA may become ubiquitous, because its use is undergoing a period of rapid expansion. RSA is currently used worldwide in a vast range of products, platforms, and industries. It is being incorporated in worldwide browsers such as Netscape, giving it a wider audience. As far as hardware is concerned, RSA can be found in secure telephones, on Ethernet cards, and on smart cards. For authentication (digital signatures), adoption of RSA seems to be proceeding more quickly, compared to privacy (encryption), perhaps in part because products for authentication are easier to export than those for privacy. Two important functions exist in RSA which do not exist in DES (i.e., digital signature and secure key exchange without prior exchange of keys). RSA and DES are usually used together for encrypting messages. First encryption of the message is done using a random DES key. This DES key is further encrypted using RSA and thereafter transmitted over an insecure communications channel. This protocol, which combines the RSA-encrypted DES with the DES encrypted message is known as the RSA digital envelope.

Video Conferencing

As a communication tool, desktop video conferencing is gaining momentum, thanks to the increasing digital video capabilities of computers. Face-to-face video conferences are already a common practice for many business users, allowing distant colleagues to communicate without the expense and inconvenience of traveling. Costly video equipment was utilized earlier to provide room-based conferencing in which participants at a location gathered in a specially equipped conference room and a view monitor displayed similar rooms at remote sites. Due to desktop video conferencing, the old room paradigm is fast becoming obsolete, and participants now sit on their own desks and call others using their computers, much like a telephone. Internetworking and compression enable business users to replicate the meeting environment from the desktop. On the computer screen, three to four credit card–size windows may appear. Everyone can interact to either edit a commercial in real time or revise a spreadsheet, and one of these is a shared space equivalent to a meeting table. For writing notes, analyzing data, reading electronic or video mail, or even doodling during the meeting, each participant also has a private workspace window. Similar to stepping out of the meeting room into the corridor for private conversation, each participant has a feature for mute control. For business and personal communications, three factors have made desktop video conferencing a viable solution—price, standards, and compression. Video conferencing systems have become very economical, and their costs have fallen dramatically. Digital video capture and playback boards enable good quality capture and processing of desktop video at economical prices.

To allow interoperable communication between machines from different vendors, a worldwide standard for video conferencing is emerging. The limiting factor or the bottleneck has traditionally been the bandwidth. A lot of bandwidth is required to send video through a communication channel. The overheads associated with video conferencing are getting reduced due to better and faster compression methods. Video conferencing is quickly leaping from corporate systems to desktops. Vendors have introduced packages that turn computers into videophones at very affordable prices, by leveraging the power of faster processors along with new advancements in video, sound, and data compression techniques. Users can place long- distance video calls over regular POTS lines for the price of a regular phone call, once the computer is equipped. Significant investment is required for video conferencing, along with technical skill and the use of dedicated facilities with special communications lines, so its applicability and appeal to business have been limited, and viability does not mean widespread usage.

Multimedia—Evolution Challenges

Changes have been phenomenal in the computer market. A 15 frame per second (fps) video at quarter-screen resolution was state of the art in early 1994, and video editing tools were immature and incomplete. Advances in capture boards, processors, and graphics technologies made 30 fps, full-screen video playback achievable by the end of 1994. From audio cassettes and LPs to digital CDs, this conversion in the 1980s is an example of how technological advances and cost reduction in digital technology can change an industry. A similar change which surmounted an extremely significant barrier was the switching over from analog to digital video and the vast amount of data that digital video requires. About 100 CDs were required to store an hour-long video in digital form and an impractical amount of bandwidth was required for transmitting an uncompressed digital video program. While a critical starting point is overcoming technological barriers, it is not enough to solidify digital video's role in corporate or consumer markets. To use it appropriately, several lessons were learned. For instance, video clips from 3 to 5 seconds had a positive impact, but anything longer resulted in users loosing interest. A lot of consumer behavior research regarding video will be needed.

With breathtaking technological growth taking place, the desktop video has changed in a very short time from an advent grade technology to a practical communication tool. Digital video is binary data that represents a sequence of frames, each representing one image, and at about 30 updates per second the frames must be shown to fool the eye into perceiving that they are continuous or smooth motion. A synchronized sound track may be contained in a digital video. An audio file can be a digital movie with just a sound track with no video track, whereas a still image can be a digital movie of just a single frame.

In various electronic commerce applications, digital video is a core component. Corporate developers will face ever-increasing demands from end users to store and manipulate digital video as the developers become accustomed to working with text documents as a data type. Finally the point has been reached where with desktop computing power you can display images with photographic resolution and color fidelity, play stereo sound to rival a CD, and display a video on any monitor. In the early 1980s, digital video first appeared in teleconferencing applications. It was centered on high definition television (HDTV) in the initial stages. In that decade, the business use of video expanded when compression technology improved and video transmission over high speed data lines became economically viable. Phillips CD-I interactive CD player and a few Japanese karaoke players powered by C cube chips were the only digital video systems on the consumer market in 1993. The attractiveness of the digital video changed drastically just one year later as hundreds and thousands of computer add-on cards for video-CD playback, along with the 400,000 direcTV systems appeared. Virtually all top computer system vendors started actively exploring the market for digital video–based set top boxes.

For electronic commerce, one type of media that is becoming a key technology is digital video. Video conferencing, video on demand, and distance education are some of the typical applications of digital video. A multimedia entity (e.g., video image), regardless of its type or transport means, must pass through a series of stages from inception to display. In case of image capture/generation, the image can be captured by a sensor such as a television camera and is generated by an electronic device such as a computer. In the raw image, the volume of information may be too large to be able to send it through an affordable information channel. To reduce its volume, the data must be compressed in such a way that the picture can be reconstructed without degradation at the receiving end. The compressed data can be stored on a CD-ROM or network storage servers. For transmission, the data representing the image is prepared. The picture, sound, and associated data (i.e., each component of the video program) are separately organized into packets of data. In each packet, address and descriptive information are included. For transmission, packets are aggregated into a single bit stream and this bit stream is then transmitted through a data communications network. The characteristics of the medium determine the speed of transmission. By adding extra bits to the data stream, protection against loss or corruption of the signal is provided. The earlier steps are reversed, once the image is received, and the bits that were added to aid in transmission are removed, and the video, audio, and data streams for each program are separated. Thus the data stream containing the images may be stored, ready for display, and the images are then compressed or formatted or displayed on a television, computer monitor, or other appliances.

Advances in technology help to create business value. Imagine the following in the future world of electronic commerce in which a 21-inch monitor displays a rotating 3D graphic of a car that you want to purchase in one window, a video of a news anchorman reporting on an impending hurricane, an open window with a real-time video conferencing with your client in a third, and information about stock portfolio is flashed into a fourth window as the stock market goes through its daily volatility.

In the case of digital video, ISO (International Standard Organization) is the moving pictures experts group whose purpose is to generate high-quality video (sequences of images in time) with sound. To develop a standard for digital video for compression, when MPEG began its work, its goal was to develop an algorithm that could compress a video signal and then be able to play it off a CD-ROM or over telephone lines at a low bit rate (less than 1.5 Mbps). The goal was to achieve quality level in order to match that of a VHS video tape. The committee identified two standards: MPEG-1 and MPEG-2. A bit stream of compressed video and audio optimized to fit into a bandwidth (data rate) of 1.5 Mbps is defined by MPEG-1. Because this is the data rate of uncompressed audio CDs and DATs, this rate is special. The standard consists of video, audio, and systems, and in the last part integration of audio and video streams occurs, with the proper time stamping to allow synchronization of audio and video. In commercial chips in which MPEG-1 is implemented, users can compress and play back MPEG-1 video. To process video at SIF (source input format) resolution (352×240 pixels) at 30 frames per second is the primary use of MPEG-1 standard, and this is one-fourth the resolution of the broadcast television resolution standard (CCIR 601) which calls for 720×480 pixels.

MPEG is compatible with PAL, the European television format. By interpolating additional pixels, SIF resolution video display at CCIR standard levels is possible, but such interpolation cannot restore the details already lost in original downsampling. The audio CD data rate is about 1.5 Mbps, as mentioned earlier, and with no loss in discernible quality, one can compress the same stereo program down to 256 kbps and that is about 6:1 compression. For video, therefore a MPEG stream would have about 1.115 Mbps left, with the rest of the system data for synchronization. The video compression ratio from the numbers here is about 26:1. It is a little short of a miracle, if you step back and think about that. When comparing the original to the decompressed video, it is hard to see the loss, although it is lossy compression. The quality of decompressed video is measured by the number of displayable colors, the number of pixels per frame (resolution), and number of frames per second. Each of these elements can be traded off for the benefit of another, and all can be traded off for better transmission rates, but it is impossible to combine all of them and the television broadcast quality at low transmission speeds.

MPEG-2 is the second MPEG specification, and it compresses signals for broadcast-quality video. Many companies with proprietary schemes are now becoming deeply involved in bringing their technology in line with the rest of the industry, because the work of MPEG-2 is complete and the interest in broadcast digital video is apparent. A compression algorithm incorporated by MPEG-2 processes video at full resolution, and even at low data transmission rates. For the needs of the broadcasters, the second phase of MPEG work concentrated on optimizing the specifications by providing better performance, fully supporting interlaced video sources (which were not supported in the first algorithm) driven by semiconductor advances and lower manufacturing costs to meet the price range of consumer set top decoders. For high-quality "entertainment level" digital video, MPEG-2 technically specifies the coded bit stream, is downward compatible with MPEG-1 standard, and supports interlaced video formats with additional advanced functionality, including support for HDTV. For digital video transmission requiring a bandwidth of 2 to 15 Mbps over cable, satellite, or broadcast channels including digital storage media and other communication applications, MPEG-2 main profile is the standard. At 60 fps this specification calls for 720×480 resolution and data rates of 4 to 8 megabits per second, which puts it well out of reach of ordinary desktop computer applications. In the rapid evolution of cable TV's new set top boxes, MPEG-2 is useful, and for proposed 500-channel cable networks MPEG-2 decoder chips appear to provide hardware support. MPEG-2 is expected to play a crucial role in interactive video and video-on-demand services. The advanced applications may have a trickle down effect on the cost of MPEG in the desktop computer market because MPEG-2 devices are downward compatible with MPEG-1. There are two more standards—MPEG-3 and MPEG-4, but MPEG-3 has been dropped and incorporated with MPEG-2 high level 1440 specification. It focused on HDTV with sampling division of 1920×1080 at 30 frames per second. Bit rates between 20 and 40 Mbps were addressed by the standard. MPEG-2 can work very well at HDTV rates with a little tweaking.

Defined by joint photographic experts group, JPEG is a still image compression algorithm and serves as the foundation for digital video. In the digital video world, JPEG is used in two ways—as part of MPEG or as motion JPEG. Each image frame is compressed in both these methods as though it were a still image. For video sequences, the JPEG standard has been widely adopted because its compression chips are relatively inexpensive, and motion JPEG allows easy access to any frame in a digitized sequence.

The potential payback for those who hold the winning numbers is a powerful driving force behind the development of the infrastructure and the convergence of numerous industries, although no one knows what applications of electronic commerce will be successful in the long run. For e-commerce applications, multimedia content can be considered both fuel and traffic. The use of digital data in more than one format such as a combination of text, audio, video, and graphics in a computer file/document is the technical definition of multimedia. The natural way people communicate is mimicked by multimedia. To combine the interactivity of a user-friendly interface with multiple forms of content is the purpose of multimedia. Multimedia is associated with hardware convergence taking place in the telecommunications, computers, and cable industries according to the popular press. The combination of computers, television, and telephone capabilities in a single device is multimedia from this perspective. Conventional database systems are oriented toward numeric processing or number crunching, whereas multimedia systems do much more than them. More than 90% of the information that firms use for business operations and decision making lives outside the "traditional" database systems. For smooth organizational functioning this external information is crucial, and it is in the form of technical manuals, memos, e-mail, problem reports, sales brochures, and product design. The goal of multimedia is to increase the utility of all information through the processing and distribution of new forms such as images, audio, and video, because most business systems support only a fraction of the information and communications found in the workplace. Which multimedia applications will have the greatest impact on their particular business operations is a question many managers charting strategic directions ask. Because computing and networking have advanced to the point where the distribution of multimedia is not only possible but also inexpensive, the above question is being more frequently asked. Few have a clear idea of what multimedia is all about, although everyone agrees that multimedia represents the next generation of computing. The problem is compounded because telecommunications, cable/broadcasters, and computer software and hardware providers each have different views of what multimedia means. Whatever multimedia proves to be, everyone agrees that business must be involved in it one way or another. In the world of multimedia, the traditional separate divisions no longer hold true. For instance, apart from only text, an electronic book includes photographs, voice, video clips, animation, and a host of other things.

The technical definition of multimedia is the use of digital data in more than one format, such as the combination of text, audio, and image data in a computer file. Digitizing traditional media words, pictures, sounds, and motion and mixing them together with elements of database technology that provide data storage, management, and control enables the creation of a new generation of applications. The size of new data types and the synchronization required for video and audio is one of the problems and challenges for multimedia developers. The storage, network bandwidth, compression/decompression schemes, data content manipulation techniques, and even processing power are affected by the size of multimedia data types. Into a given amount of storage space, data compression attempts to pack as much information as possible and ranges from as little as 2:1 to as much as 200:1, depending on the compression/decompression scheme and level of quality required. Data compression works by eliminating redundancy, and each block of data has underlying information content, usually expressed as a number of bits. The underlying information content may be 100 bits in a block of text data containing 1000 bits, with the rest being white space. In data compression, the goal is to make the size of the 1000-bit message as close as possible to the 100 bits of underlying information. Users are often amazed at how rapidly digitized video and sound fill up a disk, and the need for compression is apparent. For a 1-minute recording, an 8-bit digitized sound track sampled at 11 kHz requires just 660 KB, and a 16-bit stereo track sampled at 44 kHz (CD quality) requires nearly 11 MB of disk space for a full minute. It may appear that sound files are a little hungry for disk space, but the video images are positively ravenous.

But a solid understanding of technology behind various multimedia types is necessary. The information pertaining to multimedia is more than plain text and includes graphics, animation, sound, and video. Multimedia means different things in different circles, like many other technology terms. The horizon is clouded by many vendors, by using terms in association with products whose claim to multimedia status is tenuous.

Sophisticated multimedia can be supported by some networks and systems, but much of today's installed base of desktop computers and networks cannot support it, and the challenge is to build the kind of networking and systems infrastructure that will support multimedia-based electronic commerce applications. Many common features are shared by these information types—all are digital data, flow through the same networks, and display on the same workstations. Multimedia information has the power to inform, persuade, and enlighten once it is combined and shaped by a competent information surgeon, but the tools and training needed for information surgery are not very clear.

Video Server

Video servers are designed to deliver information to hundreds of consumers simultaneously via public telecommunications and cable networks, and this is one important difference between video servers and the current client–server computer systems which are used extensively for data processing. When providing on-demand services to large numbers of homes, video servers overcome the "simultaneous overlapping" supply problem. Either simultaneously or at overlapping times, numerous households will want to watch a film. This problem can be approached either from the software or the hardware end, and by using thousands of inexpensive microprocessors that are interlinked to create the illusion of one large computer, servers can harness the power of massive parallel architecture, and this is a hardware solution. To enable a single film to be viewed by numerous households on demand, each processor acts as a "video pump" and distributes a portion of the film. The 512 processors, each equivalent to an Intel Pentium chip, are contained in a cube, which is one example of a video server. Microsoft has approached the problem as a customizable software issue, rather than looking at the delivery of continuous media on demand (e.g., audio and video as a hardware problem solved with massive parallel machines). Based on Windows NT operating system, the software architecture was being developed under the code name Tiger because all video servers need not be hardware based. The implementation of Tiger is expected on personal computers for individual or work group use, on corporate servers for small or midsized private networks, and on large servers for large-scale consumer use. To give users split-second access to thousands of media files, and to allow laser disc–type functions such as pause, reverse, fast forward, and jump ahead to user-specific locations, increasing the power of functionality and scalability are the goals. Which approach will eventually dominate, only time, economics, and consumer preferences will decide.

Telecommunication, video conferencing, and geographical information systems require resources of storage, maps, multimedia applications, production studios, shopping kiosks, etc. A range of interactive services such as shopping, video navigation (e.g., interactive TV guides), and directories (e.g., interactive telephone yellow pages), and video on demand are included in consumer applications. In interactive TV trials, the need for large-scale video storage has led to a unique business partnership between technology/transport and media companies and has resulted in the development of new video servers. An important link between the content providers (entertainment/media) and transport providers (telecos/wireless/ cable operators) is the video server.

Huge amounts of information can be rapidly delivered one way to the home through existing cable television systems, but must be modified to allow a significant return flow. Compared with cable, computers traditionally talk to each other over phone lines, which have sharply limited capacity, but new modems and networks let them communicate over high-capacity cable lines. To deliver the vast volume of data needed for digitized video-like movies on demand, the ultimately dominant system will need high-capacity lines. The set top box is really a special-purpose computer with powerful graphics and communications features but limited versatility. It can be said that the set top box is largely the slave to the central computers of the interactive systems. Interactive applications are only a small part of what computers can do, and personal computers are very versatile. Single-use hardware has usually lost out to more versatile hardware in the history of new technologies, and centralized control has usually given way to autonomy for users. Nearly everyone is familiar and comfortable using a TV, because it is in nearly every household. More than half the households receive cable service, and video games, the closest analog to the set top box's interface with the user, are commonplace. Those computers that are easiest and most comfortable to use are rapidly gaining acceptance in the home and are selling especially briskly. The people most attracted to computers are most likely to use interactive systems. Universality of TV is less advantageous than it appears, and the leap to interactive use is greater from passive television watching than from active computer use.

Pictures

Compression algorithms for JPEG pictures and data leverage from known limitations of human sight, and they discard small color details and small details of light and dark from the original source file, hence reducing its size. Thus no visual difference is perceptible between the original source file and the uncompressed file copy. Although the image degrades noticeably if the compression exceeds 20:1, JPEG compression is fast and can capture full-screen, full-rate video. For compressing full-color (24 bit) grey-scale digital images of natural real-world scenes, JPEG is usually used. Black and white (one bit/pixel) images are not handled by JPEG, and it also does not handle motion picture compression. Its compressed image is not quite identical with the input, meaning that JPEG is lossy. Analysis of such compression, though invisible to human sight, will show up errors (introduced by JPEG) if a machine analysis is done. Three steps are used in JPEG, which is a highly sophisticated technique. 8×8 pixel matrices are carefully analyzed by the first technique known as discrete cosine transformation (DCT). By using run length encoding (RLE) techniques, a process called quantization manipulates the data and compresses the strings of identical pixels next. The image is compressed even further, finally, using a variant of Huffman encoding that replaces redundant series of bits with shorter token values from a token table that is dynamically repeated during the decoding process. The degree of lossiness can be manually adjusted by adjusting the compression parameters. This is a useful feature of JPEG. Thus a decision can be consciously taken regarding trade-off between file size and picture quality. If poor picture quality is acceptable, extremely small files are possible, which may be useful for indexing image archives, making thumbnail views or icons, etc. Conversely, the quality of the picture can be raised to satisfaction with lesser compression if required.

For what is life mostly, but a sum total of actions.

Some Definitions

Captive onshore activity: Company distributing its work operations across its own offices located in different regions of the same country.

Captive offshore activity: Company distributing its work operations across its own offices located in different countries.

Outsourced onshore activity: Company distributing its work operations to another company located in the same country.

Outsourced offshore activity: Company distributing its work operations to another company located in another country.

Other Books on the Outsourcing Subject That Include Model II

Offshore Software Development—Outsourcing for SMEs and Individuals, by John King.
IT, Software and Services: Outsourcing and Offshoring, by Robin Sood.

Bibliography

http://articles.economictimes.indiatimes.com/2008-09-23/news/27708823_1_rbs-third-party-bpo-firms-bpo-acquisition

http://articles.economictimes.indiatimes.com/2008-09-29/news/28397374_1_acquisition-indian-companies-indian-firm

http://articles.economictimes.indiatimes.com/2008-09-29/news/28397374_1_acquisition-indian-companies-indian-firm

http://articles.economictimes.indiatimes.com/2008-09-29/news/28397374_1_acquisition-indian-companies-indian-firm

http://articles.economictimes.indiatimes.com/2008-10-01/news/28410496_1_genpact-wachovia-bpo-provider

http://articles.economictimes.indiatimes.com/2008-10-01/news/28410496_1_genpact-wachovia-bpo-provider

http://articles.economictimes.indiatimes.com/2008-10-01/news/28482987_1_european-business-europe-business-satyam-s-europe

http://articles.economictimes.indiatimes.com/2008-10-03/news/27731424_1_pearl-group-pension-businesses-life-and-pension

http://articles.economictimes.indiatimes.com/2008-10-14/news/27731432_1_credit-crisis-microsoft-survival

http://articles.economictimes.indiatimes.com/2008-10-15/news/28397444_1_financial-crisis-alumni-anand-mahindra

http://articles.economictimes.indiatimes.com/2008-10-15/news/28397444_1_financial-crisis-alumni-anand-mahindra

http://articles.economictimes.indiatimes.com/2008-10-15/news/28397444_1_financial-crisis-alumni-anand-mahindra

http://articles.economictimes.indiatimes.com/2008-10-17/news/27703607_1_pe-firms-mid-tier-consolidation

http://articles.economictimes.indiatimes.com/2008-10-20/news/28467309_1_finacle-banking-nucleus-software

http://articles.economictimes.indiatimes.com/2008-10-24/news/28493598_1_depressant-mumbai-tops-segment

http://articles.economictimes.indiatimes.com/2008-10-30/news/27710802_1_short-term-contracts-short-term-deals-infosys-technologies/2

http://articles.economictimes.indiatimes.com/2008-10-30/news/27710802_1_short-term-contracts-short-term-deals-infosys-technologies

http://articles.economictimes.indiatimes.com/2008-10-30/news/27710802_1_short-term-contracts-short-term-deals-infosys-technologies/2

http://articles.economictimes.indiatimes.com/2009-01-05/news/28413737_1_offshoring-som-mittal-global-companies

http://articles.economictimes.indiatimes.com/2009-01-05/news/28413737_1_offshoring-som-mittal-global-companies

http://articles.economictimes.indiatimes.com/2009-01-12/news/28418244_1_australian-phone-firm-telstra-telstra-contract-new-outsourcing-contracts

http://articles.economictimes.indiatimes.com/2009-01-12/news/28418244_1_australian-phone-firm-telstra-telstra-contract-new-outsourcing-contracts

http://articles.economictimes.indiatimes.com/2009-01-12/news/28418244_1_australian-phone-firm-telstra-telstra-contract-new-outsourcing-contracts

http://articles.economictimes.indiatimes.com/2009-01-13/news/27646290_1_infosys-technologies-satyam-scam-accenture

http://articles.economictimes.indiatimes.com/2009-01-13/news/27646290_1_infosys-technologies-satyam-scam-accenture

http://articles.economictimes.indiatimes.com/2009-01-16/news/27651949_1_satyam-bpo-aegis-bpo-outsourcing-arm

http://articles.economictimes.indiatimes.com/2009-01-16/news/28459846_1_servers-soa-indian-market

http://articles.economictimes.indiatimes.com/2009-01-16/news/28459846_1_servers-soa-indian-market

http://articles.economictimes.indiatimes.com/2009-01-16/news/28459846_1_servers-soa-indian-market

http://articles.economictimes.indiatimes.com/2009-01-16/news/28473700_1_nortel-bankruptcy-infosys-and-wipro-wipro-technologies

http://articles.economictimes.indiatimes.com/2009-01-21/news/28400267_1_m-a-and-pe-inbound-deals-outbound-deals

http://articles.economictimes.indiatimes.com/2009-01-27/news/27643360_1_lpos-unitedlex-legal-outsourcing

http://articles.economictimes.indiatimes.com/2009-03-08/news/27648623_1_brain-drain-immigrants-economies

http://articles.economictimes.indiatimes.com/2009-03-09/news/27655671_1_top-outsourcing-outsourcing-industry-software-and-bpo-export

http://articles.economictimes.indiatimes.com/2009-03-09/news/28420029_1_offshore-outsourcing-hbos-bank-one

http://articles.economictimes.indiatimes.com/2009-03-19/news/27655451_1_infosys-technologies-s-d-shibulal-nandan-nilekani/2

http://articles.economictimes.indiatimes.com/keyword/vinod-dham/featured/2

http://articles.economictimes.indiatimes.com/keyword/vinod-dham/featured/2

http://articles.timesofindia.indiatimes.com/2008-10-01/india-business/27913051_1_bpo-firms-kpo-firms-sameer-walia

http://articles.timesofindia.indiatimes.com/2008-10-01/india-business/27913051_1_bpo-firms-kpo-firms-sameer-walia

http://articles.timesofindia.indiatimes.com/2008-10-01/india-business/27913051_1_bpo-firms-kpo-firms-sameer-walia

http://articles.timesofindia.indiatimes.com/2008-10-01/india-business/27913051_1_bpo-firms-kpo-firms-sameer-walia

http://articles.timesofindia.indiatimes.com/2008-10-01/india-business/27913051_1_bpo-firms-kpo-firms-sameer-walia

http://articles.timesofindia.indiatimes.com/2008-10-03/strategy/27927564_1_inbound-deals-citigroup-total-value

http://b2b.statefarm.com/b2b/guides/edi.asp

http://beeindia.blogspot.com/2009/01/satyam-scam-infosys-ibm-accenture-may.html

http://bhaveshthaker.blogspot.com/2008/10/it-companies-worried-over-european.html

http://blog.onestopview.com/uk-bankruptcy-now-every-five-minutes.html

http://blog.onestopview.com/uk-bankruptcy-now-every-five-minutes.html

http://books.google.co.in/books?id=6t8r1UY0yIMC&printsec=frontcover#v=onepage&q&f=false

http://books.google.co.in/books?id=pkkPSQL9UlIC&pg=PA15&lpg=PA15&dq=oliver+-williamson+ideal+machine&source=bl&ots=k9b-cAuWn1&sig=gQZxH-boO6QgtbC_kap4FgsDW8o&hl=en#v=onepage&q=oliver%20williamson%20ideal%20machine&f=false

http://books.google.co.in/books?id=PsE_fv16bEUC&pg=PA45&lpg=PA45&dq=robert+eaton+salute+smartly&source=bl&ots=qQ1LtygZro&sig=MsDXn9T8UxaIW9U4msdOcPe4DMk&hl=en&ei=y0pGTtDaNJG3rAfdlanjAw&sa=X&oi=book_result&ct=result&resnum=1&ved=0CBgQ6AEwAA#v=onepage&q=robert%20eaton%20salute%20smartly&f=false

http://books.google.co.in/books?id=vFi0kJY9kGcC&pg=PA1928&lpg=PA1928&dq=Computer+security+violations+cost+U.S.+businesses+half+a+billion+dollars+each+year,+according+to+the+National+Center+of+Computer+Crime+Data&source=bl&ots=Ytx8BAyYii&sig=ym7ouSae80-qINIY3MHUs-b5ibI&hl=en&ei=s_xMTobpNcHHrQfn8fy9Aw&sa=X&oi=book_result&ct=result&resnum=1&ved=0CBgQ6AEwAA#v=onepage&q=Computer%20security%20violations%20cost%20U.S.%20businesses%20half%20a%20billion%20dollars%20each%20year%2C%20according%20to%20the%20National%20Center%20of%20Computer%20Crime%20Data&f=false

http://books.google.co.in/books?id=vFi0kJY9kGcC&pg=PA349&lpg=PA349&dq=edi+handbook+agreed+standard&source=bl&ots=Ytx8xxq2dd&sig=6d-RzbaMQ0l3O83mdz6KLrd5c8Q&hl=en&ei=5U9GTvquKMTorQfxkfj0Aw&sa=X&oi=book_result&ct=result&resnum=1&ved=0CBgQ6AEwAA#v=onepage&q=edi%20handbook%20agreed%20standard&f=false

http://books.google.co.in/books?id=vFi0kJY9kGcC&pg=PA35&lpg=PA35&dq=bell+atlantic+within+four+clicks+decision&source=bl&ots=Ytx8xwyZgi&sig=WalXyS6tAhachu2nHSNuWzQdSe0&hl=en&ei=REZGTp65AcXmrAfO3qHvAw&sa=X&oi=book_result&ct=result&resnum=6&ved=0CD4Q6AEwBQ#v=onepage&q=bell%20atlantic%20within%20four%20clicks%20decision&f=false

http://books.google.co.in/books?id=vFi0kJY9kGcC&pg=PA36&lpg=PA36&dq=disney+65%25++++remember++video+rented+week&source=bl&ots=Ytx8xwy1ki&sig=SLNrpb1jQGmqintAt_uOHhsufGQ&hl=en&ei=_EdGTryKJ4jsrAfV1NCIBA&sa=X&oi=book_result&ct=result&resnum=6&ved=0CD4Q6AEwBQ#v=onepage&q=disney%2065%25%20%20%20%20remember%20%20video%20rented%20week&f=false

http://bpoawards2008.indiatimes.com/BPO%20Awards%202008%20-%20Winners%20
    List.PDF
http://bpoindia.blog.com/tag/bpo-services/
http://businesstoday.intoday.in/story/time-to-talk/1/3846.html
http://buyerbehaviour.blogspot.com/2008_10_01_archive.html
http://coreadvisor.com/globalwise/category/uncategorized/page/48/
http://discuss.itacumens.com/index.php?topic=29758.75
http://economictimes.indiatimes.com/articleshow/3658654.cms
http://en.wikipedia.org/wiki/History_of_the_Internet
http://en.wikipedia.org/wiki/National_Institute_of_Standards_and_Technology
http://en.wikipedia.org/wiki/RSA
http://en.wikipedia.org/wiki/World_population
http://ericadewolf.wordpress.com/2008/07/18/inhouse-email-results/
http://esciencenews.com/sources/physorg/2008/10/02/outsourcing.aids.many.data.thefts.
    verizon.says
http://hightea.timesjobs.com/candidate/chatTranscript.html?chatId=1
http://hrlink.in/news/it-spending-to-increase-in-india-china-2
http://hsc.csu.edu.au/economics/policies_mgt/2614/Topic4Tutorial2.html
http://hyd-news.blogspot.com/2009_03_09_archive.html
http://ibnlive.in.com/news/india-inc-not-worried-by-obamas-antioutsourcing-
    tirade/91863-7.html
http://in.reuters.com/article/2008/10/15/idINIndia-35975220081015
http://iteslatest.blogspot.com/2008_04_01_archive.html
http://iteslatest.blogspot.com/2009_01_01_archive.html
http://iteslatest.blogspot.com/2009_01_01_archive.html
http://itinformation-india.blogspot.com/2008_09_28_archive.html
http://itoutsourcing.blogsome.com/2008/10/04/
http://itoutsourcing.blogsome.com/2009/01/05/
http://itoutsourcing.blogsome.com/2009/01/05/
http://joomla-outsourcing.com/news/outsourcing-news_7.php
http://knowledge.wharton.upenn.edu/india/article.cfm?articleid=4330
http://knowledge.wharton.upenn.edu/papers/1071.pdf
http://knowledge.wharton.upenn.edu/papers/1071.pdf
http://knowledge.wpcarey.asu.edu/article.cfm?articleid=1071
http://m.economictimes.com/PDAET/articleshow/3519863.cms
http://m.economictimes.com/PDAET/articleshow/3625524.cms
http://m.economictimes.com/PDAET/articleshow/msid-3546451,curpg-2.cms
http://m.economictimes.com/PDAET/articleshow/msid-3546451,curpg-2.cms
http://mmadan.wordpress.com/2010/02/04/idcs-predicts-mild-increase-in-global-it-spend-
    for-2010/
http://money.cnn.com/magazines/business2/business2_archive/2006/04/01/8372814/
http://mpcrm.manpower.co.in/survey/MEOS/MEOSQ12011_release.pdf
http://news.cnet.com/8301-1001_3-10062066-92.html
http://news.cnet.com/8301-1001_3-10062066-92.html
http://outsourceportfolio.com/legal-process-outsourcing-lpo-sunshine-outsourcing-sector/
http://paperboardgroup.blogspot.com/2006/02/jumping-into-outsourcing.html
http://pragmaticinvestments.wordpress.com/page/155/
http://rajesshcherian.wordpress.com/tag/pink-slip/

http://searchcio.techtarget.com/news/950602/Top-10-risks-of-offshore-outsourcing

http://secfilings.nyse.com/filing.php?doc=1&attach=ON&ipage=5791294&rid=23

http://swarnmriga.wordpress.com/

http://thisbluemarble.com/showthread.php?t=5552

http://toms1m.wordpress.com/

http://books.google.co.in/books?id=vFi0kJY9kGcC&pg=PA358&lpg=PA358&dq=unctad
+10%25+paperwork+complex+formalities&source=bl&ots=Ytx8wAs0ej&sig=E6bcx
cfL9KWidFduJKgIShibw24&hl=en&ei=jEVFTuz2OYaIrAfI87iPBA&sa=X&oi=bo
ok_result&ct=result&resnum=1&ved=0CBgQ6AEwAA#v=onepage&q=unctad%20
10%25%20paperwork%20complex%20formalities&f=false

http://www.3a-strategy.com/about-us-career-resources/offshoring/knowhow/outsourcing-
hiddencosts

http://www.alsbridge.com/news-events/archives/39/Three-Tips-for-Renegotiating-
Outsourcing-Contracts.html

http://www.ananthapuri.com/article.asp?title=High-Quality-in-the-Indian-Outsourcing-
Industry&id=62

http://www.bcg.com/documents/file58645.pdf

http://www.bloomberg.com/apps/news?pid=newsarchive&sid=a2sWlnEIj58U

http://www.bloomberg.com/apps/news?pid=newsarchive&sid=aF20xiBJxvXc

http://www.bobsguide.com/guide/news/2004/Mar/12/study-uncovers-need-for-digital-
mailroom-within-global-organizations.html

http://www.bpowatchindia.com/bpo_features/hiring_india/january-29-2009/job_biz_out-
look_at_all_time_low.html

http://www.bpowatchindia.com/bpo_news/attrition_recruitment/september-23-2008/attri-
tion_bpo_recruitment.html

http://www.bpowatchindia.com/bpo_news/bpo_industry/september-27-2008/infosys_
bpo_company_of_the_year_at_bpo_industry_awards_2008.html

http://www.bpowatchindia.com/bpo_news/nasscom_growth/september-30-2008/nasscom_
growth_fiscal_2008.html

http://www.bpowatchindia.com/bpo_news/outsourcing_aids/october-06-2008/outsourc-
ing_aids_data_thefts.html

http://www.bpowatchindia.com/bpo_news/vertex_global/september-24-2008/vertex_
acquisition_hub.html

http://www.business-standard.com/india/news/2009-will-bebleakest-ever-for-
it/02/57/347406/

http://www.business-standard.com/india/news/2009-will-bebleakest-ever-for-
it/02/57/347406/

http://www.business-standard.com/india/news/balancing-act-growth-inflation-financial-
stability/338347/

http://www.business-standard.com/india/storypage.php?autono=336027

http://www.business-standard.com/india/storypage.php?autono=336503

http://www.businessweek.com/globalbiz/content/sep2008/gb20080926_444664.htm

http://www.chnsourcing.com/research-center/industry-studies/content/312.html

http://www.ciol.com/Enterprise/Outsourcing/Feature/Trends-for-global-outsourcing-in-09-
Tholons/7109114505/0/

http://www.ciol.com/News/News-Reports/Indian-IT-BPO-industry-grows-28-pc-
Nasscom/9708107804/0/

http://www.csc.com/in/press_releases/5948-csc_chairman_to_visit_csc_operations_in_india

http://www.cybermedia.co.in/press/pressrelease104.html

http://www.dnaindia.com/money/interview_infosys-to-focus-on-winning-deals-to-meet-fy-
guidance_1565129

http://www.dnaindia.com/money/report_no-global-m-and-a-plans-better-opportunities-in-
india-icici_1196717

http://www.dnb.co.in/BOIq12009_1.html

http://www.docstoc.com/docs/2970588/SEZ-units-may-not-get-100-tax-break-for-now29-
Sep-2008-0027-hrs-

http://www.economist.com/node/215691

http://www.elcina.com/fortnightlynewsletter/15-10-08.htm

http://www.elcina.com/fortnightlynewsletter/31-01-2009.htm

http://www.elon.edu/predictions/q7.aspx

http://www.fas.org/sgp/crs/misc/RL32701.pdf

http://www.financialexpress.com/news/a-bankruptcy-in-uk-every-5-mins/372510/

http://www.financialexpress.com/news/high-interest-rates-strict-credit-may-hit-
bottomlines-ficci/369763/

http://www.financialexpress.com/news/india-inc-set-to-cash-in-on-global-financial-
crisis/371354/2

http://www.forrester.com/ER/Press/Release/0,1769,1225,00.html

http://www.forrester.com/rb/research

http://www.ft.com/cms/s/0/30594642-9213-11dd-98b5-0000779fd18c.
html#axzz1VYxGeiqV

http://www.gartner.com

http://www.gartner.com/it/page.jsp?id=1500514

http://www.gbsonline.co.in/news-updates.php

http://www.gbsonline.co.in/news-updates.php

http://www.google.co.in/url?sa=t&source=web&cd=1&ved=0CBwQFjAA&url=http%3A
%2F%2Fciteseerx.ist.psu.edu%2Fviewdoc%2Fdownload%3Fdoi%3D10.1.1.170.1
730%26rep%3Drep1%26type%3Dpdf&rct=j&q=A%20survey%20poll%20of%20
12%20Asian%20economies%20projected%20a%20health%20warning%2C%20
given%20the%20global%20economic%20turmoil%20recession&ei=ez5OTsXTG8vi
rAf4jd20Aw&usg=AFQjCNGVACNk6cTVI6ZWEOaxV8a3v9s4xw&cad=rja

http://www.gtnews.com/article/6215.cfm

http://www.helium.com/items/1348631-what-is-the-impact-of-economic-slowdown-and-
recession-on-offshore-outsourcing/print

http://www.immagic.com/eLibrary/ARCHIVES/GENERAL/FORR_US/F080409S.pdf

http://www.indianexpress.com/news/nortel-impact-it-stocks-down-sasken-plunge/411337/

http://www.intelassist.net/visitors/News.php

http://www.ischool.utexas.edu/~ssoy/pubs/l389c5a.htm

http://www.itexaminer.com/satyam-bpo-ceo-walks-away.aspx

http://www.kpoexperts.com/kpo-india/what-is-kpo.htm

http://www.leadershipnow.com/leadershop/8381-3excerpt.html

http://www.livemint.com/2008/10/03001257/Layoffs-on-the-rise-as-Indian.html

http://www.livemint.com/2008/10/24001548/RBI-sees-growth-at-77-wants.html

http://www.mbaclubindia.com/news/print_this_page.asp?news_item_id=2031

http://www.mckinsey.com/mgi/

http://www.mckinsey.com/mgi/reports/pdfs/emerginggloballabormarket/part1/MGI_demand_fullreport.pdf

http://www.mhia.org/downloads/news/onthemove/ON_THE_MOVE_Spring2000.pdf

http://www.moneycontrol.com/news/cnbc-tv18-comments/2010-hiring-forecast-an-analysis_432672.html

http://www.msnbc.msn.com/id/26990313/ns/technology_and_science-security/t/outsourcing-aids-data-thefts-verizon-says/

http://www.mydigitalfc.com/companies/nortel-has-15-share-wipro-848

http://www.mydigitalfc.com/economy/asia-economic-slowdown-becoming-more-severe

http://www.mydigitalfc.com/economy/asia-economic-slowdown-becoming-more-severe

http://www.myjobs-india.com/page/14/

http://www.nasscom.in/Nasscom/templates/NormalPage.aspx?id=55556

http://www.nasscom.in/Nasscom/templates/NormalPage.aspx?id=55556

http://www.nasscom.in/strategic2005.asp

http://www.nytimes.com/2008/09/29/business/worldbusiness/29iht-asiabank.1.16550895.html

http://www.oup.com/uk/orc/bin/9780199288304/henry_ch05.pdf

http://www.pcpro.co.uk/news/227646/ballmer-credit-crunch-will-hit-microsoft-too

http://www.pewinternet.org/

http://www.popehat.com/page/122/

http://www.proguidemc.com/ArtNot.php?interior=8&seccion=2

http://www.prolaunchmanager.com/productlaunchmarketing/do-what-you-do-best-and-outsource-the-rest

http://www.prweb.com/releases/2011/8/prweb8705811.htm

http://www.rediff.com/money/2008/jul/09bpo.htm

http://www.rediff.com/money/2009/jan/06bpo-strong-long-term-demand-seen-for-outsourcing-tholons.htm

http://www.sans.org/reading_room/whitepapers/threats/vulnerabilities-vulnerability-scanning_1195

http://www.scribd.com/doc/32323943/Infosys-Technologies-International-Strategy-and-Global-Meltdown

http://www.scribd.com/doc/44543014/Day-2-1110-Dhiraj-Dolwani

http://www.siliconindia.com/shownews/Indian_IT_vendors_cheer_on_status_conversion_of_Goldman_Morgan_-nid-47020.html

http://www.siliconindia.com/shownews/US_financial_crisis_brings_more_business_for_Indian_LPOs-nid-46943.html

http://www.skyscrapercity.com/archive/index.php/t-368794-p-5.html

http://www.skyscrapercity.com/showthread.php?t=368794&page=51

http://www.spi-bpo.com/images/upload/Briefings/PDF/Presentation_to_PSP_Books_Committee.pdf

http://www.tata.com/media/reports/inside.aspx?artid=iMrynXURcrs=

http://www.telegraphindia.com/1090511/jsp/business/story_10946858.jsp

http://www.telegraphindia.com/1090511/jsp/business/story_10946858.jsp

http://www.thefreelibrary.com/IBM+profits+up,+%27confident%27+for+year-a01611673870

http://www.thehindubusinessline.com/todays-paper/article1039070.ece

http://www.thehindubusinessline.in/bline/2008/10/07/stories/2008100750050700.htm
http://www.tholons.com/pages/news.aspx?Y=2010&M=September
http://www.vereon.ch/upload/whitepaper/Engel-Flechsig_Anhang_2_20_26.pdf
http://www.wipro.com/resource-center/wipro-council-for-industry-research/pdf/outsourc-
    ing_trends_future.pdf
http://www.yourmindyourbody.org/american-stories-of-recession-despair-and-resilience/
http://www3.imperial.ac.uk/pls/portallive/docs/1/50135697.PDF
https://microsite.accenture.com/foundations/oursolutions/salesmarketingsolution/commer-
    cialbusinessintelligence/Documents/Accenture_CGS_Commercial_Intelligence.pdf
https://www.pubservice.com/MSStore/ProductDetails.aspx?ID=75198

Index

Author Biographies

Vivek Sharma is a post-graduate in management, with a bachelor's degree in engineering in computer science. He has 18 years of I.T. consulting experience, primarily with Infosys Technologies Ltd., where he has anchored various corporate and in-house training sessions, as well as received various corporate awards. He is well traveled, having managed consulting assignments across the U.S., the U.K., and Singapore. He is the founder of Value Adders, and has filed two patents jointly, in India and the U.S., with co-author Varun Sharma. (These are discussed as business models in the chapter "Web Outsourcing Models, Frameworks.") He has authored an International Technical paper on  Dataguard, published in 2006 in the *International IUOG Journal*, and has additionally authored various thought papers for in-house use at Infosys. He lives in India and is passionate about poetry, yoga, microlight aviation, and dancing (Salsa, Indian classical, and folk).

Varun Sharma is a post-graduate in management, with a bachelor's degree in engineering in computer science. He has over 17 years of I.T./I.T.E.S. consulting experience, is the founder of Infinity Services, and has filed two patents jointly, in India and the U.S., with co-author Vivek Sharma. An expert in deploying cross-domain knowledge, he has applied various innovative solutions and methods to drive down attrition in call centers, including hypnosis and autosuggestion/suggestion techniques for stress management. He has analyzed I.T./B.P.O. share trends on the stock market using various financial

tools and also from an astrological perspective. He has anchored various corporate and in-house training sessions in IT/BPO processes, soft skills, and personality development, and has the taken the I.E.L.T.S. exam to augment workshop programs. He lives in India and is passionate about Vaastu (the Indian science of architecture), yoga, dancing, and alternate systems of healing.